AMERICAN SUTRA

AMERICAN SUTRA

A STORY OF FAITH AND FREEDOM
IN THE SECOND WORLD WAR

DUNCAN RYŪKEN WILLIAMS

THE BELKNAP PRESS OF HARVARD UNIVERSITY PRESS

Cambridge, Massachusetts   London, England

2019

Third printing

LIBRARY OF CONGRESS CATALOGING-IN-PUBLICATION DATA

Names: Williams, Duncan Ryūken, 1969– author.
Title: American sutra : a story of faith and freedom in the Second World
    War / Duncan Ryuken Williams.
Description: Cambridge, Massachusetts : The Belknap Press of Harvard
    University Press, 2019. | Includes bibliographical references and index.
Identifiers: LCCN 2018036377 | ISBN 9780674986534 (alk. paper)
Subjects: LCSH: Japanese Americans—Evacuation and relocation,
    1942–1945. | Buddhists—United States—History—20th century. |
    Buddhism and state—United States—History—20th century. |
    Buddhism and politics—United States—History—20th century. |
    World War, 1939–1945—Japanese Americans. | United States—Race
    relations—History—20th century.
Classification: LCC D769.8.A6 W55 2019 | DDC 940.53/1773089956—
dc23 LC record available at https://lccn.loc.gov/2018036377

To the memory of Professor Masatoshi Nagatomi
and Masumi (Kimura) Nagatomi

CONTENTS

AMERICAN SUTRA

PROLOGUE

Thus Have I Heard: An American Sutra

Thus have I heard:
The army ordered
All Japanese faces to be evacuated
From the city of Los Angeles.
This homeless monk has nothing but a Japanese face.
He stayed here thirteen springs
Meditating with all faces
From all parts of the world,
And studied the teaching of Buddha with them.
Wherever he goes, he may form other groups
Inviting friends of all faces,
Beckoning them with the empty hands of Zen.

—Nyogen Senzaki, "Parting," May 7, 1942

THE STORY OF AMERICA has long been cast as one of westward exploration and expansion, beginning with settlers from Europe who crossed the Atlantic Ocean to the New World, and radiating out from initial outposts on the Atlantic coast across the plains of the Midwest to the Pacific coast and beyond. As the nineteenth-century doctrines of manifest destiny and American expansionism make clear, claiming territories to accommodate the ever-increasing populations of immigrants from Europe was justified in terms of both culture and religion; the United

States was described as uniquely destined and divinely ordained to take on the role of a "civilizing influence" that would spread Anglo-Protestant values into lands supposedly empty of civilization. Implicit in this view of history has been the idea that America is, at its base, a Christian nation.

But what happens when we flip the map? For the hundreds of thousands of Asian immigrants who crossed the Pacific to reach America in the nineteenth and early twentieth centuries, the American West was the Pacific East.[1] Their American story has an eastward trajectory—one that begins in the mid-1800s on the sugar plantations of Hawai'i and moves through California and the Pacific Northwest and eventually towards the Atlantic coast. Just as settlers from Europe saw themselves as pioneers, working their way westward as they spread their values and mores, these immigrants from Asia brought their own cultures and religions as they moved further eastward.

American Buddhism thus begins with the migration of Asians who brought the teachings, practices, and institutions of a 2,500-year-old religion across the Pacific. These immigrants saw in America the promise of a country that could provide not only a source of livelihood, but also the right to freely practice their own religious beliefs. In this, they were putting their faith in one of the central tenets of the United States Constitution: the First Amendment, which, agreed upon and ratified by the Founding Fathers, guarantees religious freedom.

So which is it? Is America best defined as a fundamentally white and Christian nation? Or is it a land of multiple races and ethnicities and a haven for religious freedom? More pointedly, does the fact of being nonwhite and non-Christian make one less American?

Never has this question been asked with more urgency and consequence than it was in the time of the mass incarceration of Japanese Americans during World War II. War, with its reflexive interrogation of who can be trusted and who cannot, who belongs and who is the enemy, often brings to the surface the deepest questioning of a nation's identity. In the wake of the Pearl Harbor attack, the question of whether persons of Japanese ancestry would remain loyal to the United States became the subject of considerable debate among government and military officials, the media, and the general public. At stake were issues of both morality and law—two-thirds of the Japanese American popula-

tion were American citizens and thus presumed to have constitution-
ally guaranteed rights of equal protection, due process, and religious
freedom. But could they be trusted? Within months, debate was brought
to a swift and irrevocable conclusion when, on February 19, 1942, President Franklin D. Roosevelt signed into law Executive Order 9066. This
gave the military discretion to do whatever it deemed necessary to secure the safety and security of the United States. Pursuant to it, the Army
removed all persons of Japanese ancestry—more than 110,000 men,
women, and children—from the west coast and put them in camps surrounded by barbed wire and guard towers. Anyone with even a drop of
Japanese blood was rounded up and incarcerated.

Marked as they are by ethnic, racial, and cultural differences from
the majority European-origin population of the United States, Asian
immigrants have long faced such nativist prejudices. Starting with the
1882 Chinese Exclusion Act, which erected a symbolic wall on the
Pacific to keep out the "heathen Chinee," and continuing on through
various laws that banned Asian immigrants from naturalizing as citizens, owning land, or marrying white Americans, decades of legal and
social structures of exclusion anticipated what happened to the Japanese
Americans after Pearl Harbor.

But while it has become commonplace to view their wartime incarceration through the prism of race, the role that religion played in the
evaluation of whether or not they could be considered fully American—
and, indeed, the rationale for the legal exclusion of Asian immigrants
before that—is no less significant. Their racial designation and national
origin made it impossible for Japanese Americans to elide into whiteness.
But the vast majority of them were also Buddhists; in fact, Japanese
Americans constituted the largest group of Buddhists in the United States
at the time. The Asian origins of their religious faith meant that their
place in America could not be easily captured by the notion of a Judeo-
Christian nation, which, in addition to the predominant Anglo-Protestant
religious traditions, encompassed Catholicism and Judaism—or by the
more expansive grouping of the so-called Abrahamic faiths, incorpo-
rating Islam.[2] Religious difference acted as a multiplier of suspiciousness,
making it even more difficult for Japanese Americans to be perceived
as anything other than perpetually foreign and potentially dangerous.

People of Japanese ancestry were thus deemed to be a threat to national security and incarcerated indiscriminately and en masse, something that did not happen to Americans of German and Italian heritage, despite the fact that the United States was also at war with Germany and Italy.

Yet, even though there are many insightful works on the experiences of Japanese Americans during World War II, Buddhism remains a neglected aspect of that history.[3] Why has this aspect of the Japanese American incarceration been so hard to see? The reasons are many and varied, but two of the most significant are the invisibility of communities that do not share religious heritage with the monotheisms of the West; and the postwar political imperatives of foregrounding a story about Japanese Americans that conformed to prevailing narratives about what makes a person American. In short, Buddhism disappears from view, paradoxically, due to the same underlying presumption of America as a white and Christian nation that contributed to the wartime incarceration of Japanese Americans in the first place.

By recentering Buddhism—not only as a corrective to the way the wartime incarceration story is narrated, but also as a means of shifting our presumptions about whose stories matter in American history— *American Sutra* brings into focus those who, even as their loyalty was being questioned, insisted on the right to be Buddhist and American at the same time.

American Sutra is thus, on the one hand, a story about America. Doubly excluded from whiteness and Christendom, Japanese American Buddhists during World War II represent a particularly poignant object lesson about the perceived boundaries of who can claim the rights of being American. Their insistence on maintaining their Buddhist practices and beliefs despite imprisonment—using the searchlights from guard towers to focus their meditation practice, building Buddhist altars for their barracks rooms out of wood scavenged from the desert, or insisting that space be made available for them to congregate and worship as Buddhists—constitutes one of the most inspiring assertions of religious freedom and civil liberties in American history.

But *American Sutra* is also, on the other hand, a story about Buddhism in America: how a new form of Buddhism was forged in the crucible of war—in incarceration camps, under martial law on the Hawaiian islands, and on the battlefields of Europe and the Pacific theater. Looking more closely at the wartime experiences of Japanese Americans not only takes us to the heart of this nation's history of conflating race, religion, and American belonging, it also shows how the roots of what is now a much more popularly accepted religion were cultivated. American Buddhism was nourished by the experiences of a community that strove to remain grounded in tradition while also adapting to the multisectarian, multigenerational, and multiethnic realities of Buddhist life in the United States.

Given how thoroughly Japanese American Buddhists have been excluded from the narrative of American belonging, it is perhaps not surprising that their stories are not readily found in most histories of that time. Thus, in addition to looking at government documents, articles in the print media, or other reports, I have sought to bring to light accounts by Japanese American Buddhists themselves, drawing from sources such as previously untranslated diaries and letters written in Japanese, dozens of new oral histories, and the ephemera of camp newsletters and religious service programs. These allow a telling of the story from the inside out, and make it possible for us to understand how the faith of these Buddhists gave them purpose and meaning at a time of loss, uncertainty, dislocation, and deep questioning of their place in the world. Their religious faith might have contributed to their loss of freedom, but it was also indispensable to their attempts to endure that loss.

A sutra is a Buddhist scripture, a text that contains Buddhism's most essential teachings. But these insights cannot be transmitted without people to actualize them. To understand how something called American Buddhism came to exist and persist, we must look to the people who embodied the teachings of the Buddha even during the crucible of wartime exclusion. Among those who exemplified this struggle to find a place for themselves and their religion in America is the Zen Buddhist priest Nyogen Senzaki.

By the time Senzaki penned the poem "Parting," which opens this book, in May of 1942, he had already been in the United States for close to four decades.[4] But six months earlier, everything had changed when Japanese naval planes attacked Pearl Harbor on December 7, 1941. A day later, his adopted country had declared war on his native country, and most of his fellow Buddhist priests had been rounded up and imprisoned, some of them before the smoke had cleared at Pearl Harbor.

Senzaki stands out because although he had trained in the traditional Buddhist monasteries of Japan, he had made it his life's work to translate Buddhism into teachings that would be meaningful to his fellow Japanese immigrants and their English-speaking, American-born children, as well as to non-Japanese American converts.

Born in 1876 on the Kamchatka Peninsula in northeastern Siberia to an unknown father and a Japanese mother, Senzaki was rescued by a Japanese Buddhist priest from the edge of a frozen riverbank where his mother had died giving birth. From there he was taken to Japan's northern Aomori Prefecture, where he was adopted into a Buddhist temple family, and eventually ordained as a novice priest.[5] His Zen teacher became the first Japanese Zen priest to visit the United States, invited in 1893 to represent Buddhism at the World Parliament of Religions in Chicago. A dozen years later, with barely any English, the twenty-nine-year old Senzaki followed his teacher's example and arrived in America. Frustrated by the rigidity of Buddhism in Japan, he had decided to cross the Pacific in the hopes of finding a new path forward for the religion in the land he had read about as a teenager in Benjamin Franklin's autobiography. "See whether it conquers you or you conquer it," his Zen master had told the young priest as he began his new life in California.[6]

After landing in San Francisco, Senzaki studied the works of Ralph Waldo Emerson and William James in the public library while working at menial jobs. He then moved to Los Angeles where, over the course of "thirteen springs," he succeeded in building up a vibrant Buddhist community consisting of Japanese immigrants and converts from a variety of ethnic backgrounds—"Meditating with all faces / From all parts of the world," as he writes in the poem. He saw in the American outlook an openness that might potentially welcome the teachings of Buddhism. William James's "philosophy of practicality," for example, struck him as a new name for the older philosophy of Zen. In one of his essays, Senzaki writes: "Americans in general are lovers of freedom and equality . . . they make natural Zen students."[7]

This optimism was tested but not broken by the US Army's order for "all persons of Japanese ancestry" to assemble for immediate removal from the Pacific coast. "Parting," written on the eve of his departure from the community he had worked so hard to build, is not only a Buddhist commentary upon the US government's incarceration process, it is also a Buddhist teaching he was leaving behind for those in a home to which he might not be able to return. Addressing the Los Angeles Zen community, he begins the poem with the classic opening words for a sutra or Buddhist teaching: "Thus have I heard." This phrase is attributed by legend to one of the Buddha's chief attendants and disciples, Ānanda.[8] In a rainy-season assembly held three months after the death of the Buddha, Ānanda is said to have recited from memory an extensive collection of the master's discourses, qualifying his recollections with these words.[9] For the community that continued after the death of the historical Buddha, the retelling of these sermons represented a transmission of religious guidance that could enable the Buddha to be ever present.[10]

"Parting" employs this classic preamble at another traumatic moment for Buddhists, but the Buddhist lesson Senzaki shares is not culled from stories from an Indic past, but rather inspired by an American present. "The army ordered / All Japanese faces to be evacuated," his poem recounts. "This homeless monk has nothing but a Japanese face." As someone who had experienced dislocation a number of times before finding a home in Los Angeles, Senzaki calmly accepted this new forcible migration. But while the poem serves as a chronicle of his experiences, it is also deeply imbued with Buddhist resonances and his identity as a Zen priest. Upon ordination, Senzaki had dedicated himself to the Buddhist path; a journey that is traditionally termed "leaving home."[11] As a "homeless monk," Senzaki is guided not by the comforts of social convention, but by an understanding that nowhere and everywhere can be a home in which to practice Buddhism. Yet, despite the exigencies of war and facing an unknown period of incarceration, he asserts the possibility of a place for Buddhism in the United States, noting that "Wherever he goes, he may / form other groups / Inviting friends of all faces, / Beckoning them with the empty hands of Zen."[12] For Senzaki, the act of continuing the practice of Buddhism, even under incarceration, was to serve as witness to the realities of the present moment and make the teachings of the historical Buddha come alive in it.

According to certain commentarial traditions, the Buddha's sermons were delivered in his native tongue of Old Māgadhī, but heard by each disciple in his or her native language.[13] An act of sacred utterance was simultaneously an act of translation, making the teachings comprehensible and relevant to all listeners. Senzaki believed that the powers of ultimate truths, spiritual practices, and ethical acts could only be activated when religious teachings were able to escape their hermetically sealed texts and engage with the existential struggles of life. In this view, the reinscription of scripture in a contemporary idiom is a potent act of religious imagination that gave life purpose and meaning. It is by reflecting on his forcible relocation that Senzaki is thus given the chance to write a Buddhist scripture—an American sutra—inspired by the terrible circumstances of his times.

After being deported from Los Angeles, Senzaki initially spent several months in temporary quarters just east of Los Angeles. The War Relocation Authority (WRA) had not yet finished construction of the ten incarceration camps that were to be used for the duration of the war. While those were being built, Senzaki, along with roughly eighteen thousand other people of Japanese ancestry, had been sent to the Santa Anita Racetrack, where they were forced to live in hastily converted horse stalls. Upon hearing that he would be moving again—this time to the now-completed WRA camp in Wyoming called Heart Mountain—Senzaki wrote another poem, entitled "Leaving Santa Anita":

> This morning, the winding train, like a big black snake
> Takes us as far as Wyoming.
> The current of Buddhist thought always runs eastward.
> This policy may support the tendency of the teaching.
> Who knows?[14]

By writing that the "current of Buddhist thought always runs eastward," Senzaki is evoking ideas found as early as the late eighth and early ninth century in Japanese texts such as the popular collection of Buddhist tales called the *Nihon ryōiki*.[15] This belief has its origin in a prophesy by the historical Buddha that, after he died, his teachings—the Dharma—would inevitably be transmitted eastward.[16] In the traditional formulation of Buddhism's eastward advance (*bukkyō tōzen*), at least as it is described in Japan, the spread of the religion begins in India, then moves to China and Korea before finding an endpoint in the islands of Japan. But by the late nineteenth century and early twentieth century, some Buddhists who were migrating to the Americas had begun to think of their journey as a further extension of this eastward trajectory.

It is this tradition of thought that Senzaki invokes when suggesting another, more hopeful interpretation of the forced migration that was being enacted through the US government's discriminatory policy: as unexpected and devastating as it might seem, perhaps it could be understood as yet another opportunity to fulfill the Buddha's prophecy of an eastward migration of his teachings. Indeed, once Senzaki arrived at the Wyoming camp, he went so far as to call his makeshift barracks the Tōzen Zenkutsu—The Meditation Hall of the Eastbound Teaching.[17] Far from giving up on his faith, Senzaki designates his new home surrounded by guard towers as a Zen meditation hall; a new locus for American Buddhism. Confronted with unthinkable hardships, Senzaki and other Buddhists found that they would have to draw upon the deepest currents of Buddhist thought in order to persist and endure. In this, they were laying claim to the belief that, regardless of circumstance, Buddhism could not only survive but indeed flourish in the United States.

These poems by Senzaki could easily have vanished as ephemera of the war. Were it not for Senzaki's Buddhist teachings, which inspired efforts by postwar Zen adherents to preserve the sermons, letters, and miscellany of their teacher whose perspective they valued so highly, it is likely that this contemporaneous record of a Buddhist perspective on the wartime incarceration would simply have disappeared. Likewise, the diaries, letters, and other fragments of memories about the wartime experience on which I have drawn to write this book could easily have been relegated to the ash heap of history. But, like the Buddhism they describe, they have endured. They were preserved by individuals and families in acts large and small, who somehow sensed that there was something inherently valuable—and indelible—in the Buddhism that they had been born into or had brought with them.

BURIED TEXTS, BURIED MEMORIES

The text that initially inspired the writing of this book was an almost sixty-year-old manuscript that had been written behind barbed wire in the War Relocation Authority (WRA) camp at Manzanar in eastern California. In 2000, shortly after the death of my graduate school advisor, Professor Masatoshi Nagatomi, his widow asked me to help sort out his papers. Mrs. Nagatomi especially wanted me to examine materials written in Japanese so as to set aside any materials of a personal nature. For over forty years, starting in 1958 when he joined the faculty as an instructor in Sanskrit and later as the university's first professor of Buddhist studies, Nagatomi had mentored students of Buddhism at Harvard University.[18] A generation of scholars of Indo-Tibetan and Sino-Japanese Buddhism had studied under Nagatomi before me, many of whom ended up teaching at leading American universities. I was one of his last students. At the time, I was focused on turning my just-completed dissertation into a book and thought a quick report to my late professor's wife would be the end of it.[19] Little did I know that I would discover a story so compelling that it would propel me into seventeen years of research into the experiences of Japanese American Buddhists during World War II.

His files were, needless to say, voluminous. But buried in his great mass of papers—mixed with dissertation chapter drafts and letters from journals—was a handwritten Japanese document with the name Nagatomi written on it, though not in my professor's familiar script. After a few days, I realized I had come across personal notes penned by Professor Nagatomi's father, Shinjō Nagatomi. Though Professor Nagatomi rarely spoke about it, his father had done pioneering work as a Buddhist priest, first in Canada and then in the United States. The notes I found included amongst my professor's papers included a journal and drafts of sermons Shinjō Nagatomi had delivered in the tarpaper barrack that had served as his Buddhist temple in the Manzanar camp.

Curious, I arranged to meet with Masumi Nagatomi in the beautiful garden of her home in Cambridge, Massachusetts to ask about them. At the time of her husband's passing, Mrs. Nagatomi was still in good health and exuded the elegance and composure of many Japanese American

women of her generation. She requested that I spot-translate several se-
lections of the notes, and I did. One of them urged the elderly to perse-
vere, despite the loss of their homes, livelihoods, and everything they
had worked for as immigrants to the United States. Another exhorted
young Japanese Americans to be law-abiding Buddhists and loyal to
their country, despite the war with their ancestral homeland.

That day, as I translated from her father-in-law's notes, she took a deep
breath and said with a sigh, "You know—Mas [my professor's nickname]
was separated from his family during the camp days." Over the next several weeks, in her garden, Mrs. Nagatomi told me of her husband's
experiences and hardships during the war. At the time of the attack on
Pearl Harbor, Masatoshi Nagatomi, the future Harvard professor, was
fifteen years old and living with relatives in rural Yamaguchi Prefecture,
having traveled there without his mother, father, and siblings, who remained home in San Francisco. With the outbreak of hostilities, he found
himself unable to return to the United States, and spent the remainder
of the war stuck in Japan, where his only news of his parents and sisters
would come from the rare International Red Cross letters his father sent
him from behind barbed wire. In one short telegram in 1943, he learned
of the birth in a camp called Manzanar of another sister—Shinobu.[20]

Conscripted to the shipyards of the port city of Kobe, Masatoshi Nagatomi struggled with others there to survive horrific working conditions and ever-diminishing food rations. Granted a brief leave to visit
his relatives, he found himself on a train packed with weary and wounded
soldiers that passed through the city of Hiroshima on August 6, 1945,
the day it was bombed. Ordered to close the window blinds, Nagatomi
could only peek at the devastation. Amid the chaos of the final days of
the war, he resolved to rejoin his family in America as soon as he could.

As Mrs. Nagatomi told me her husband's story, she would also occasionally reflect on her own wartime experiences as a child and, in dribs
and drabs, her own wartime story began to emerge. Masumi Kimura
(her maiden name) was ten years old and living with her parents in
Madera, California, when the Japanese planes attacked Pearl Harbor.
More than sixty years later, she still vividly recalled the tension and fear
that gripped her family and hometown that December day. Word had
quickly spread that all the Buddhist priests at the nearby Fresno Buddhist

Temple had been arrested, and white teenagers had shot up the temple's front door.[21] The Madera Temple's board president had also been apprehended by the FBI, a matter of great concern for Masumi's father, who was a prominent board member of the rural temple. Like many residents of the small farming community in California's Central Valley, her parents were issei—first-generation Japanese Americans—and Buddhists.

Three weeks after Pearl Harbor, FBI agents showed up at the Kimura family's farmhouse to question her father. Nobuichi Kimura, Masumi's father, was carrying a shotgun when he answered the door and, seeing the gun, the agents wrestled him to the floor. Minutes later, Masumi arrived home from school, only to find her father pinned down by one agent and another pointing a gun at her mother's head. Her parents, who had immigrated from Wakayama Prefecture in Japan some years earlier, were trying in their broken English to explain the gun to the agents. Though terrified, Masumi's English was better than that of her parents. She translated the agent's questions to her father, who explained he had been preparing to shoot rabbits in the garden when they had arrived. Temporarily satisfied, the agents left. But in subsequent weeks they returned to the Kimura home to conduct further interrogations concerning Mr. Kimura's leadership at the Buddhist temple, which was seen as aligned too closely with Japan and potentially a threat to national security.

It was in this climate of growing suspicion and hostility that Masumi's father decided to take steps to prove the family's loyalty to America. One day shortly after that first FBI visit, Masumi was performing her daily chore of lighting the furnace next to their Japanese-style bathtub when her father entered the room. He was carrying items he had found throughout the house that had Japanese language inscriptions or "Made in Japan" written on them. Among them were Masumi's precious Hina-matsuri dolls, which had been given to her on Girl's Day. As tears rolled down her cheeks, she watched him throw the dolls and all the other Japanese artifacts into the fire.[22]

Her father did not burn everything, however. He could not bring himself to destroy the bound edition of Buddhist sutras that had been handed down through generations of the family. Instead, he asked his

wife to find boxes and some Japanese kimono cloth while he went outside and dug a hole behind their garage with a backhoe. After wrapping
the Buddhist scriptures and the minutes of board meetings from the
Madera Buddhist Temple in the kimono cloth, he placed them in tin
rice-cracker boxes, carefully lowered them into the hole, and covered
them with dirt. By burying them next to the garage, he hoped to be able
to find and recover them at some later date.

Shortly thereafter, in April 1942, the Kimuras were ordered to report
to the Fresno Assembly Center, which had been set up at the local county
fairgrounds. They ended up having to sell their farm to their neighbors
for less than one-twentieth of its market value, and, after depositing a
single suitcase of their most valued remaining possessions at the Fresno
Buddhist Temple for safekeeping, they arrived at the center, where they
were quartered in a horse stable designated Barrack E-17-2. They were
however more fortunate than the majority of Japanese Americans. Instead of being transferred to one of the more permanent WRA incarceration camps, the Kimuras were among the handful of families
approved to join work programs east of the military zone, so they ended
up in Utah, where they worked as cheap farm labor for the duration of
the war.

After the war ended, the Kimura family returned to Madera in the
hopes that they would be able to buy their farm back and recover their
home. But the new owners demanded a sum ten times greater than what
the Kimuras had accepted for the farm three years earlier. They had also
torn down the garage, making it impossible for the Kimuras to find the
precious belongings they had buried near it. Their single suitcase of valu-
ables, which had been stored away for safekeeping, had been lost as well
when vandals ransacked the Fresno Buddhist Temple during the war.
Unable to raise the money to buy back the farm, the Kimuras went to
live with relatives in Los Angeles.

This story, told to me in the gardens of my advisor's widow, has stayed
with me over the years. Though just one among tens of thousands of stories of Japanese American Buddhist families during World War II, it
encapsulates both the loss and the hope that made possible the birth of
an American form of Buddhism. Though the Kimuras were willing to
let go of their Japanese national identity by burning objects symbolically

linked to Japan, the one thing they refused to erase was their Buddhist faith. Indeed, they ended up quite literally placing Buddhism into the soil of America for safekeeping. Like Senzaki and many others, their actions demonstrated their firm conviction that their adopted homeland would one day be a place where their faith could grow and flourish.[23]

The Buddha taught that identity is neither permanent nor disconnected from the realities of other identities. From this vantage point, America is a nation that is always dynamically evolving—a nation of becoming, its composition and character constantly transformed by migrations from many corners of the world, its promise made manifest not by an assertion of a singular or supremacist racial and religious identity, but by the recognition of the interconnected realities of a complex of peoples, cultures, and religions that enrich everyone.

By uncovering buried texts and buried memories, *American Sutra* aspires to open up a discourse about how faith in both Buddhism and America can contribute to a vision of the nation that values multiplicity over singularity, hybridity over purity, and inclusivity over exclusivity.

The long-ignored stories of Japanese American Buddhists attempting to build a free America—not a Christian nation, but one of religious freedom—do not contain final answers, but they do teach us something about the dynamics of becoming: what it means to become American—and Buddhist—as part of an interconnected and dynamically shifting world.

These stories, like Senzaki's poem, constitute an American sutra.

Thus have I heard.

1

AMERICA:

A NATION OF RELIGIOUS FREEDOM?

LIKE MOST AMERICANS IN 1941, Japanese Americans reserved Sundays for religious, family, and sports gatherings. The vast majority were Buddhist, and from around 8 AM on the morning of December 7, many on the Hawaiian island of Oahu were arriving at their temples.[1] At a Sunday school hosted by the Zen Buddhist-affiliated Nana Gakuen in Honolulu, eleven-year-old Chiye Sumiya was singing a popular Japanese children's song, "Ame-Ame, Fure-Fure" (Rain-Rain, Fall-Fall), when the cheerful chorus was interrupted by a loud noise. Unbeknownst to the children, the Imperial Japanese Navy's planes had commenced their devastating attack on Pearl Harbor. The next day, President Franklin D. Roosevelt would declare it "a date which will live in infamy."[2]

"Our teacher in charge told us it wasn't anything to worry about and to continue singing," recalled Chiye many years after the attack. "A few minutes later a second 'boom' sounded, and soon after that, the third 'boom' struck our building. The auditorium shook, debris was flying all over, and children were screaming. We all frantically trampled down the wide stairway like a herd of cattle. Going down, I witnessed children who were badly hurt. I later found out that the girl sitting close to me had died from shrapnel wounds."[3] At least four Japanese American children under the age of eight died that day.[4]

By 9 AM, American anti-aircraft defenses were firing at the second wave of Japanese planes attacking the US Navy base at Pearl Harbor and the US Army Air Corps bases at Hickam Field and Wheeler Field. The initial Japanese wave had already hit these and other military installations in a surprise operation aimed at crippling the capital ships of the Navy's Pacific Fleet and grounding any air capabilities that could challenge the attack. In the chaotic response, some of the anti-aircraft rounds went awry and landed in civilian areas of Pearl Harbor and Honolulu, killing an estimated seventy civilians.[5] One of those misfired shells landed without exploding in the driveway of Territorial Governor Joseph Poindexter's home.[6] Another killed Private Torao Migita of Company D, 298th Infantry Regiment, who had enlisted in the US Army to serve his country six months earlier and was returning from a weekend pass when the shell struck.[7] He was the only Japanese American member of the US armed services among the 2,335 American servicemen who perished in the attack.[8] Later that day, when Private Migita's sixty-five-year-old mother learned of her son's death, she searched for a Buddhist priest to officiate at the young US Army soldier's wake and funeral.[9] But Buddhist priests were suddenly unavailable.

DECEMBER 7, 1941

Even as bombs were still dropping on Pearl Harbor, US Attorney General Francis Biddle orally issued a blanket warrant to arrest all those on a government custodial detention list, including the Buddhist priest of the temple where the Migita family were members.[10] The disappearance of Buddhist priests, the majority of whom were classified to be detained, was linked to a long-standing belief among many Americans that such community leaders—being neither white nor Christian—were not only a threat to national identity, but a threat to national security.[11] In anticipation of war, the government had created secret registries of "dangerous" individuals, and they were used by the FBI to round up hundreds of Buddhist priests and lay leaders in Hawai'i and the continental US by the end of that fateful Sunday.[12]

December 7, 1941 forever changed the lives of everyone in the Japanese American community, regardless of whether they were among those arrested. In the days that followed, many work colleagues, schoolmates, and neighbors looked upon them with suspicion or shunned them. But especially affected by the FBI's arrests were Japanese American Buddhist families.

The first person to be picked up on December 7 was Bishop Gikyō Kuchiba, the head of the Nishi Hongwanji Buddhist sect in Hawai'i. He was arrested at 3 PM, only hours after the attack. Thirty minutes later, authorities declared martial law and installed Army Lieutenant General Walter Short as the new military governor of the islands, replacing Poindexter, the territorial governor.[13] Shortly thereafter, soldiers apprehended the head priest of the Taiheiji Temple near Pearl Harbor. During the attack, the priest had led his members to higher ground to take cover. When it seemed safe to move again, he returned to the Zen temple, where a group of US Army soldiers had surrounded the main hall. They demanded to know who he was and what he was doing. "In my rush to evacuate I forgot to feed the birds in their cage," he told them.[14] The soldiers escorted him into the building housing the main Buddha image, where he fed the birds and, fearing they might starve after he left, released them out of the temple windows. As the birds went free, the soldiers took the Zen priest into custody.

Elsewhere in Honolulu, at the Nichiren Buddhist Mission, FBI agents shoved the head priest into a car with others who had been detained. Agents ordered the passengers not to speak, and the car passed in silence by columns of heavy smoke from the fires still raging at Pearl Harbor and Hickham Air Force Base. When it stopped at the gates of the Honolulu Immigration Station Building, two MPs pointed guns with bayonets affixed at the passengers. The agents announced them as "prisoners," and escorted them to the detention barracks in the Immigration and Naturalization Service (INS) building.[15]

Inside the barracks, an owner of a local Japanese bookstore softly recited the *Lotus Sutra* as the station filled.[16] A prominent newspaper editor noted that the room on the upper floor was filled with a "rank and sultry air" with "164 of us, all Japanese, packed like sushi into a space for about half as many. . . . A washroom and toilets were next door, but they were always crowded and soon became dirty and foul-smelling beyond description."[17] Several Buddhist priests, brought in wearing handcuffs, appeared "badly shaken."[18]

FIGURE 1.1 Rev. Hōryū Asaeda of the Liliha Shingonji Mission being fingerprinted by MPs at the Honolulu immigration station, soon after his arrest.   JIR Files, Folder 272, University Archives & Manuscripts Department, University of Hawai'i at Manoa Library.

Among the most prominent of the priests was the Bishop of the Jōdo Buddhist sect.[19] FBI agents had arrested him at his temple while he was still in his Buddhist robes and refused to allow him to pick up any clothes or other belongings, or to tell him what he was being charged with.[20] As a Japanese national, when he learned about the full extent of the surprise attack by his homeland's military on his adopted home, he quietly recited the Buddha's name over and over.[21]

The arrests began in the vicinity of Pearl Harbor, but the dragnet quickly spread to the neighboring islands and the continental US. Only a few hours after news broke about the Japanese attack on Oahu, the authorities arrested the head priest of the Naalehu Hongwanji Mission on the Big Island. He was told to wear and pack warm clothes, since he was to be taken to the Kilauea Military Camp, which was prone to colder temperatures in the evenings. As he changed clothes, the priest slipped a copy of his sect's Buddhist sacred scriptures, the *Shinshū Seiten,* into his jacket pocket.[22]

In the continental US, especially in areas considered militarily sensitive, the arrests were also swift. Terminal Island in southern California—home to a thriving Japanese fishing community—hosted a naval air base and was close to the Long Beach Naval Station. The *Los Angeles Times* reported that the military on December 7 "halted all motorists and required identification and particularly questioned all Orientals attempting to enter or leave the area."[23] The priest serving the island's Zen Buddhists was taken immediately. Rev. Seytsū Takahashi of the Kōyasan Buddhist Temple in Los Angeles—who by chance had made a trip to Terminal Island to meet with temple supporters that Sunday—was blocked from crossing the suspension bridge back to Los Angeles. Guards with bayonets were checking anyone trying to leave the island.[24]

The priest was unaware of how thoroughly the Pearl Harbor attack was disrupting the Japanese American community. He realized that something was amiss when he noted the heavy military presence on the bridge and was then rebuffed at the island's post office as he tried to mail a donor registry back to his temple. A clerk told him that no letters with Japanese writing could be mailed off the island. After staying overnight at a temple member's residence, he was allowed by the guards to cross the bridge the following day. They "thought I was Mexican because I didn't shave myself that day and I was tall," he said.[25] Upon returning to the Little Tokyo district of Los Angeles, where his temple was located, he was immediately arrested by the FBI.

In the continental US, those arrested on December 7 and 8 were generally taken to local city or county jails, where they were fingerprinted and photographed before being transferred to "enemy alien" detention facilities.[26] Rev. Takahashi was initially taken from Little Tokyo to a police station near the University of Southern California and then transferred to the Los Angeles County Jail.[27] During his ten-day stay there, many other prominent temple members arrived. Indeed, the small room on the top floor of the jail soon became so crowded that even the bathroom floor had to be used.

Conditions quickly deteriorated at the County Jail. Two people committed suicide.[28] In the midst of this upheaval, the thirty-five-year-old Takahashi preached to his fellow Japanese about the medieval Zen Master Takuan, exhorting listeners to draw from his example. He related a classic tale about the Shogun Tokugawa Iemitsu who had received a large tiger from Korea as a gift and challenged the master swordsman Yagyū Munemori to enter its cage. With his sword at the ready, he stared down the tiger and came out of the cage alive and relieved, but sweating profusely. Then the shogun challenged the priest Takuan to enter the same cage. He walked calmly into the cage without any weapons, but with a gentle mind of meditation. The Zen master sat still, and the tiger nestled up to him and fell asleep. Rev. Takahashi encouraged his fellow prisoners to draw from the same quiet strength of Buddhist meditation and to act in a dignified manner despite the difficult conditions.[29]

Ultimately, nearly two hundred Buddhist priests were rounded up, targeted in a way that the handful of Christian ministers arrested had not been.[30] Both military and civilian governmental agencies considered Buddhist and Shinto priests greater threats to national security.[31] Other groups of particular interest were Japanese consular officials and those acting as unpaid liaisons (*toritsuginin*) between the community and the consulates, who were arrested because of their assumed connections to the Japanese government.[32] The roundup also targeted martial arts instructors (for their possible connection to Japanese militarism), fishermen (presumably because they might assist Japanese naval advances), language school instructors (for their potential to indoctrinate students with pro-Japan ideologies), and business leaders such as bank presidents and wealthy agriculturalists (thought to have the means to fund and organize subversive groups).[33]

Religion, not just race, mattered in the unfolding process of interning enemy aliens. Fearing the large and influential network of Buddhists on the Hawaiian Islands, authorities were particularly anxious to remove leaders of the religious community. One report, issued by the Armed Service Forces' Office of the Provost Marshal General, noted that while religion was "a strong centralizing factor on the Pacific coast," it was probably "secondary to the Japanese consulate domination of social, political, and semi-military organizations." By contrast, the report claimed: "In Hawaii the Buddhist Church is a much stronger controlling element."[34]

Indeed, two weeks before the Pearl Harbor attack, Lt. Colonel George W. Bicknell prepared a memorandum to the Army contact office in Honolulu titled "Seizure and Detention Plan (Japanese)" highlighting those to be prioritized for a roundup in case "war may develop with Japan":

> The first group to be seized and detained will include all consular agents of Japan, certain known dangerous Buddhist and Shinto priests as well as certain known dangerous Japanese aliens among the language school principals, merchants, bankers, and other civilians.[35]

Just four days prior to the attack, the FBI further compiled a list of names for custodial detention that included 347 Japanese individuals residing on the Hawaiian Islands. They were divided into three groups: consular agents for Japan (the majority on the list), "priests" (here meaning Buddhist and Shinto-related clerics and not Christian ministers), and "other" (business leaders and Japanese-language school principals).[36]

The arrests of the majority of Buddhist leaders in the initial roundup were not simply a panicked reaction to a sudden military emergency, but the enactment of an already considered contingency plan. Years of surveillance of temples, investigations of particular priests and organizations, and intelligence reports had informed analyses of the potential loyalty or disloyalty of Buddhists to America in the event of a war with Japan. Decades of fearmongering by nativist politicians and the press about the "yellow peril" posed by a growing presence of inscrutable and uncivilized "heathens" and "pagans"—as Asian American Buddhists were frequently labeled—had paved the way for the immigration restrictions that targeted Asians and built an invisible wall on the Pacific. Japanese Americans were not targets just because of their race or national origin. The supposed incompatibility of their religious faith also played into their treatment by America.

Far from threatening the fabric of American life, Japanese American Buddhists during World War II strengthened it. Their story stands as powerful testimony to America's foundational claim to be a nation of

religious freedom. Buddhists not only endured in their faith, but maintained their faith in America as a land of religious liberty despite their
hardships. Indeed, that fateful Sunday was a harbinger of the various
trials they would endure during the war. The Japanese American community in Hawai'i faced a martial law regime which, unconstrained by
normal Constitutional protections, prohibited Buddhist temples and
Shinto shrines from operating and encouraged Japanese Americans to
attend Christian churches as a way to demonstrate loyalty to America.
In the continental US, President Roosevelt's issuance of Executive Order
9066 led to the forcible removal of the entire west coast Japanese American community, and incarcerated its members in hastily constructed
camps surrounded by barbed wire. In those camps, the Buddhist majority again experienced the suspicions and derision of those who believed Americanism required abandoning anything linked to Japan and
its religions or culture. Even the US Army gave preferential treatment
to Christians, despite the tens of thousands of Japanese American Buddhists who served in the armed services during World War II in both
the Pacific and European theaters. The long history of prejudice and discrimination suffered by this religious community helps explain how its
story unfolded.

AMERICAN BUDDHISM: MIGRATIONS TO FREEDOM

Japanese Buddhism first came to the Americas with migrant laborers
seeking new opportunities across the Pacific. The first Japanese community to settle in what is now an American territory consisted of 153 contract laborers who emigrated to Hawai'i, then a sovereign nation ruled
by King Kamehameha V, to work on the island's sugar plantations. The
group was later dubbed the "Gannenmono" because they were people
(mono) who had left in the first year (gannen) of the Meiji government,
which was established in 1868.[37] The twelve-hour workdays on the
American-owned sugar plantations, the wretched housing conditions,
the language barriers with the overseers, and the mistreatment of the
laborers proved too much for many in the group to endure.[38] But those
who remained in Hawai'i represented the beginnings of a major migra-

tion during the next four decades of nearly half a million Japanese, over 99 percent of them Buddhists, to the Americas.[39]

Whether working on the sugar cane plantations of Hawai'i or the sugar beet farms or railroads of the American West, these immigrants encountered a racially stratified wage and social structure. On the continental US, as the notion of a yellow peril in the late nineteenth and early twentieth centuries led to hostile receptions for Asians, they were vilified in the press and subjected to laws that codified racial discrimination. To these forces of exclusion was added the hostility of a great many Christians who viewed Buddhism as a heathen religion to be eradicated by the civilizing force of Christianity. An editorial in the *San Francisco Call* expressed shock at the arrival of the first Buddhist priests, Shūe (Shuye) Sonoda and Kakuryō Nishijima, to North America from Japan in 1899: "We have sent missionaries abroad to convert the heathen, and now the heathen send missionaries to convert us."[40]

Nonetheless, once a critical mass of Japanese Buddhists had migrated to the Americas, sanghas—Buddhist communities of ordained clerics and laypeople—began gathering to share the teachings. In Hawai'i they met initially in buildings on sugar plantations; on the west coast, they rented hotel spaces or met in private residences. Later, they established formal temple structures after securing permits from local American officials and support from the headquarters of Japanese Buddhist sects.[41] These temples served as community and cultural centers for Buddhist families, including the nisei (the American-born second-generation Japanese Americans) who organized themselves in Young Buddhist Associations (YBAs).

While the construction of these spaces was often greeted with hostility, the growing sanghas also attracted a small number of sympathizers and converts to Buddhism, most of them white. These new students of the Dharma confirmed the universality of the religion and assisted the predominantly Japanese American temples in navigating the legal and other obstacles to the development of an American Buddhism.[42]

The increasing presence and visibility of these sanghas provoked a variety of reactions from the broader American public. For most white Christian missionaries in Hawai'i, the rise of Buddhism was cause for consternation. One publication from the early twentieth century fretfully

FIGURE 1.2 Sunday Dharma School group photo at the Tacoma Hongwanji Buddhist Church (Tacoma, Washington, 1930s).   Courtesy of the Fujii and Mori Families Collection, Densho Digital Repository, ddr-densho-321–810.

queried: "Which shall Hawaii be, Buddhist or Christian? The Lord's work had suffered its most critical setback by the influence of Buddhism and the Asiatic standards of life."[43] The mere arrival in their midst of immigrants who happened to be Buddhists felt like a threat to some Christians, who therefore advocated stemming the tide of migration.

On the other hand, E. A. Sturge, who led the Presbyterians' Japanese Mission on the Pacific coast, saw the eastward flow of Asians as an opportunity to fulfill a mandate to Christianize and civilize the nation and the world. "Our cry should not be 'Exclude the Japanese,'" he wrote, "but rather Americanize and Christianize them and all foreigners who find their way to our shores, for in this we may best help to save America and our world."[44] From this viewpoint, Asian immigration was a part of God's plan and simply proof that God had ordained America as a missionary nation unto the so-called heathen.[45] In an interesting turn of logic, liberal Protestant missionaries like Sidney Gulick, who had served his mission in Kyoto and taught at Dōshisha University, believed that

Buddhism had come to America through migration to have the possibility to assimilate into Christianity:

> Buddhists as a rule do not acknowledge their debt to Jesus—probably because they do not realize it—yet as a mere matter of fact, it is His spirit of active love and His positive social program, His optimism, His attitude toward nature and God that are increasingly accepted by Buddhist teachers and believers.[46]

In either view—whether to fear or welcome the Japanese immigrants—the assumption was the same: America was a Christian nation. This view animated more racially motivated calls to ban all Asian immigration to the United States and its territories. As early as 1882, the Chinese Exclusion Act halted labor migration from China. Nativists argued that the "heathen Chinee"—a popular slur for Chinese immigrants in California during the 1870s—represented an unassimilable religion and race.[47] In the 1876 congressional hearings on Chinese immigration, California state senator Frank McCoppin testified that the west coast was "in danger of being overrun by this pagan horde, unless their coming be checked by legislation."[48]

A 1907 "Gentlemen's Agreement" between Japan and the United States, by which the Japanese government voluntarily proscribed emigration, was eventually supplanted by an outright US ban on labor migration from all Asian nations. The Immigration Act of 1924, commonly known as the Oriental Exclusion Act, did not specifically identify races or religions to be banned, but used a quota system to manipulate which national origins would be privileged and welcomed to America.[49] In addition to the Japanese on the west coast, the quota system targeted the growing number of Italians, eastern European Jews, Slavs, and Greeks on the east coast. Further, the law excluded "aliens ineligible for citizenship"—code for Asians—from coming to the United States. This legislation almost completely shut down immigration from Asia.

Especially after mass migration from Japan had been halted, Christian leaders on the Hawaiian Islands concentrated on stemming what they called the "repaganization of Hawai'i"—that is, the growth of Buddhism among the second-generation American citizens of Japanese ancestry. In the eyes of many Christians, the existence of young, American-born Buddhists was undoing the good done by the missionaries' destruction of the original "pagan" native Hawaiian religions.[50]

During the 1920s, newspapers continued to sound the alarm. The *Honolulu Advertiser* editorialized that "paganism is increasing and heretics are infesting the community."[51] The Rev. Henry P. Judd noted that a third of the islands' people were "worshippers of Buddha or Shinto" and that every time Christian residents heard "the booming of temple bells" they should be "reminded of the process of repaganization."[52] He warned: "We cannot be complacent and say it is none of our business for it is our business, this matter of a pagan religion encroaching upon our Christian civilization. The only way to Americanize Hawaii is to Christianize her."[53]

The notion of Christianization as Americanization was widespread. Even within the Japanese American community, the especially zealous among the small number who had converted to Christianity—such as Rev. Takie Okumura—promulgated this idea. Okumura tried to persuade his fellow Japanese Americans that they could never consider themselves "true Americans" unless they could say to white Christian Americans, "Your country is my country; your God is my God."[54]

Most Buddhists did not accept this view, instead asserting their right to exist in a country that had been founded on a robust vision of religious freedom. Yemyō Imamura, the bishop of the largest of the Japanese Buddhist sects in Hawaiʻi, argued against Okumura, whom he refers to here as "a polemist":

> As we live in America, we must have political allegiance to it and observe its laws. However, a polemist argues that Americanization means spiritual servility and that true Americanization is to forsake Japanese religion and thoughts and adopt those of America. This contradicts the Founding Spirit of America. America esteems freedom, equality, and independence, spiritual independence to the utmost. It never asks for spiritual servility.[55]

Undeterred by their various detractors, the sanghas persisted and grew. By the time of the Pearl Harbor attack, the Hawaiian Buddhist community had a seventy-year history behind it and included the majority of Japanese Americans. During these decades prior to the outbreak of war, however, intelligence agencies had been taking note. They began forming opinions that Buddhism was not just antithetical to national identity, but also a threat to national security.

BUDDHISM AS A NATIONAL SECURITY THREAT

Years prior to Pearl Harbor, the US Army's G-2 intelligence section, the Office of Naval Intelligence (ONI), and the FBI had all commissioned investigations of Buddhism as a potential threat to US national security. Kilsoo Haan of the Sino-Korean People's League—writing dispatches under the pen name of W. K. Lyhan—became an informant for the G-2 section in Hawai'i as early as 1931. In his various reports, he routinely identified Buddhist and Shinto organizations as a hindrance to Americanization. In the same vein as the white Christian missionaries who had worried about the "repaganization" of the islands, he wrote in his 1933 report, *The Japanese Problem in Hawaii*:

> The hard working and God fearing American missionary pioneers have founded the Republic of Hawaii in the crossroads of the Pacific. . . . However, little did these builders of Hawaii ever dream of facing a racial problem so distinct and so peculiar in character and spirit as the Japanese racial problem. [The Japanese] pound into the minds of the younger generation . . . religious faith in Buddhism and Shintoism as a necessary condition to emancipate their souls. . . . Buddhism serves as an indirect agency in keeping the spirit of Mikadoism alive in Hawaii and as one of the best mediums of pro-Japanese propaganda. [The Young Men's Buddhist Association's] chief aim is to bring American citizens of Japanese ancestry closer to Japanized Buddhism, Japanese culture, ideals of religio-patriotism . . . we doubt whether the American citizens of alien-Japanese parentage can be truly loyal to America. It would be like asking a tadpole to change himself to a frog within an hour of his birth.[56]

Lyhan identified the Japanese-language schools along with "Buddhists in Hawaii, "The Young Men's Buddhist Association," and the "Japanese press in Hawaii" as the four groups most detrimental to Americanization.[57] He believed that Buddhist organizations were dangerous to the social order and pointed to temples and youth groups as hotbeds of potential indoctrination, likely to steer even full-fledged citizens of Japanese American descent into disloyal and unpatriotic behavior.

The idea that Japan, and by extension the Japanese community in America, posed a military threat to the national security of the US became widespread after Japan defeated Russia in the Russo-Japanese War (1904–1905).[58] On December 20, 1906, for example, the *San Francisco Examiner* suggested in an article that the Japanese had sent their soldiers from that war to Hawai'i in the "guise of coolies [but] secretly preparing for hostilities."[59]

Between the Russo-Japanese War and the end of World War I, anti-Asian animus increasingly focused on Japan and those of Japanese heritage because of Japan's demonstration of its military power. Franklin D. Roosevelt—assistant secretary of the Navy in this period and later president of the United States—especially worried about a future war with Japan at sea.[60] That a supposedly inferior race was militarily capable of threatening the United States led to discussions about the mysterious nature of these "heathen" peoples.

By World War I, US postal censors decided to screen letters written by members of the Japanese community for signs of potential subversion, despite the fact that Japan was an ally of the United States during that war. Historian Gary Okihiro, in a close analysis of a 1919 report by Captain Philip Spalding, an Assistant Military Censor, explains how potential disloyalty to the United States was discerned:

> [Spalding] divided the Japanese into two groups, Christians and non-Christians, that cut across generations and citizenship. [According to Spalding] Christians showed "an independence of thought" and were imbued with "more of the ideals of American democracy"; non-Christians, who constituted "a very large majority," worshipped the Emperor.[61]

Among the letters that Spalding highlighted were two written by Buddhist priests that did indeed challenge the existing racial hierarchies and social norms of the islands. In one, a Buddhist priest described a new effort by a Japanese businessman to develop a Japanese-owned sugar plantation on the Kona coast. The priest praised this effort, complaining of a subservient mentality among many Japanese who had hitherto accepted a racially stratified wage and social structure that meant lower wages for the same work done by Portuguese and native Hawaiian plantation workers. "Japanese children are too submissive to white men," he wrote. "They are taught to look upon white men as supermen." In the second letter, Spalding condemned what he believed was the anti-Americanism of another priest, Rev. Nishiyama of Kohala Mills, who called Japanese Christians "traitors" to the Japanese American community for aligning themselves with the territorial government's effort to shut down Japanese-language schools, many of them run by Buddhist temples. Okihiro concludes that, for Spalding, "Americanization was a matter of national defense for the army," and that Christianity and English-language education "were essential to the fulfillment of the military's mission in Hawaii."[62]

After World War I, the US military focused on both Japan's military capabilities and what it considered anti-American elements in the Japanese immigrant community. During the 1920s and 1930s, the Military Intelligence Department and the Army G-2 issued half a dozen reports stressing how Buddhist temples and Shinto shrines in Hawai'i "retarded" Americanization and should be considered "military liabilities" in the event of a war with Japan.[63]

These conclusions were reached despite internal evidence that Buddhists would likely be loyal to the United States if it went to war with Japan. Captain Charles C. Cavender, stationed at Fort Shafter in the ONI's Hawaiian Department, for example, produced a confidential intelligence report in 1939 titled "Loyalty of Immigrants in the Event of War." It explicitly assessed "citizen Buddhists versus Christians" and "alien Buddhists versus Christians" on their relative "adherence" to Japan or the United States, to "totalitarianism" or "democracy," and to "Japanese authoritarianism" or "American liberal education." Cavender concluded that "except for a few who stated they would be neutral, the majority of the citizen group stated they would adhere to the United States," and that even the aliens, "while stating they would adhere, for the most part, to Japan, were unanimous in stating that they would encourage their children to adhere to the United States."[64]

Other Honolulu-based assessments were similarly guarded about broad claims of disloyalty or fifth-column potential in the Japanese American community. FBI special agent Robert L. Shivers, who headed the Honolulu field office, filed a report to FBI Director J. Edgar Hoover that attested to the general loyalty of the community.[65] Captain John A. Burns was the head of the Honolulu Police Department and leader of the Police Espionage Unit (and a three-term Governor after the war).[66] Having grown up in a mixed neighborhood in Honolulu with many local Japanese, including some who would become members of his own police department, he was willing to put his own reputation on the line with public statements attesting to their loyalty. Just weeks before Pearl Harbor, he published a guest editorial titled "Why Attack the People of Hawaii?" for the *Honolulu Star Bulletin*, writing:

> Regarding the loyalty of our citizens and aliens, there is a lot of loose talk. It is said that the Japanese maintain their own schools . . . traditions and respect for those traditions. . . . They are not alone in this. . . . those units which have been investigating [them] have not found facts which would prove disloyalty but rather the reverse. . . . Let's be Americans. Basically that means equal justice. . . . [We should] not allow our people to be condemned without proper reason.[67]

Despite these voices from respected law enforcement officials who knew the Japanese American community well, the prevailing attitude lumped together individuals through guilt by association, whether by race or religion, with the potential enemy of Japan. The minority reports, which suggested that the religious affiliation of Christian or Buddhist would not determine loyalty to the United States, were mainly ignored.

The US government and military ultimately took the view that Buddhists, Shintoists, and Japanese-language school affiliates were part of an anti-American majority within the Japanese American community. From this perspective, only a minority of individuals were considered trustworthy—mostly Christian converts, especially those who spied on the Japanese American community on behalf of US governmental agencies. In the months before Pearl Harbor, the Honolulu field office of the FBI had seventy-three such confidential informants and other "loyal and reliable" Japanese who acted as "listening posts" in the community and gathered information on targeted groups such as the Buddhist and Shinto leadership.[68]

Indeed, military reports emphasized that Buddhism was an alien religion whose entire leadership collectively posed a threat to national security. Just three days before Pearl Harbor, in December 1941, the Counter Subversion Section of the ONI shared its *Japanese Intelligence and Propaganda in the United States During 1941* report with the FBI, Army Intelligence, and the State Department. It concluded:

> The Buddhist and Shinto priests in the US and Territory of Hawaii number over 350. . . . To fully appreciate the potentialities of these organizations as media for subversive activity, it should be noted first, that there are well over 100,000 Buddhists in the continental US alone, and secondly, that <u>every</u> Japanese, no matter what his professed faith, is a Shintoist. . . . Affiliated with Buddhist and Shinto temples are Japanese Language Schools, welfare societies, young people's Buddhist societies, and Buddhist women's associations. They provide excellent resources for intelligence operations, have proved to be very receptive to Japanese propaganda, and in many cases have contributed considerable sums to the Japanese war effort. Japanese Christian Churches are much less closely affiliated with the Japanese Government, and there is considerable evidence to indicate that their major concern outside of religious matters centers on improving Japanese-American relations and the restoration of peace in Eastern Asia. At the same time, it is true that some individuals and groups among Japanese Christians are working against the interests of this country.[69]

The last line in that excerpt is important to note, as it shows the distinct way in which Japanese Christians were treated by the document and many others like it. Within their community, the US government focused on specific individuals and groups as potentially dangerous to the nation's interests. Buddhists and Shintoists, by contrast, were perceived as an entire group to be un-American, or even anti-American, and a threat to national security. This threat assessment strategy would have a measurable impact on both the initial dragnet after Pearl Harbor and on the mass incarceration following President Roosevelt's issuance of Executive Order 9066, which gave the War Department broad powers to forcibly remove people from their communities. Although that executive order did not mention nationalities, it was used only against Japanese Americans.

SURVEILLING BUDDHISM

On the US continent, both the FBI and the ONI believed that "various Buddhist and Shinto shrines, particularly around Los Angeles, were . . . either already integrated or in the process of being integrated into the Japanese espionage machinery in Southern California."[70] In Los Angeles, the Kōyasan Buddhist Temple in particular came under scrutiny because of its connection to Itaru Tachibana, a Japanese naval officer. In 1941, the ONI's Lt. Commander Kenneth Ringle oversaw a break-in at the Japanese Consulate in Los Angeles, where his unit discovered lists of Japanese sympathizers and agents, including Tachibana. The Japanese naval officer was arrested in June 1941, along with Toraichi Kōno—Charlie Chaplin's valet for a time—in a joint FBI-ONI sting.[71] Tachibana was charged with paying an informant money to obtain classified information on US naval affairs. Those charges were eventually dropped but he was deported to Japan. His case was one of only a handful of espionage cases prosecuted against anyone of Japanese heritage by the US government.[72]

Tachibana was connected to the Kōyasan Buddhist Temple through its devout members Dr. Takashi Furusawa and his wife Sachiko, who were also arrested.[73] Dr. Furusawa's private hospital was suspected to be the Los Angeles hub for Japanese spies. American intelligence agencies were concerned with the comings and goings not only of Japanese consular officials there, but also of certain university students whom the intelligence agencies identified as Japanese naval officers, members of the Japanese underworld in Los Angeles (presumed to be the primary actors for a potential fifth column), and German operatives.[74]

Further questions were raised concerning Sachiko Furusawa, who had been dubbed the "mother of the Japanese Navy" by fellow issei because of the attention she showered on Japanese naval officers visiting Los Angeles. Historian Yuji Ichioka notes that in 1938, Mrs. Furusawa (accompanied by Ms. Akiko Murase, the president of the Kōyasan Buddhist Temple Women's Association) went to Japan as a "special emissary representing the women's societies of Southern California to console Japanese military personnel who had been injured in the Sino-Japanese War."[75] Aware of that visit, the FBI put the temple under constant surveillance.

The same temple was also investigated for a purported plot to store drums of chemicals developed by a German-Japanese team in Mexico to be used against the steel plates of American battleships. A nearby Shinto shrine was placed under surveillance, too, on the suspicion that it was training carrier pigeons equipped with German cameras to fly over militarily sensitive areas and return with photos.[76]

Suspicions of potential spy rings and plots (all later shown to be unfounded) were the exception. Most of the government's suspicions fell on relatively innocuous activities. American Buddhist support for Japan's military prior to the outbreak of war in the Pacific ranged from offering prayers for Japanese war dead to extending hospitality to members of the Japanese military on shore leave. Most common was the preparation of care packages, particularly by Buddhist women's associations (Fujinkai), for those in the Japanese military on the front lines in Asia.[77]

In Hawai'i, the Waianae Buddhist Temple Women's Association sent care packages through the Japanese Navy Department. The Honolulu Buddhist women approached Japanese people on Fort and King Streets asking them to contribute stitches to "thousand-stitch" amulets (senninbari) for Japanese soldiers, and the Kona Hongwanji Women's Association used local household cooperative groups to collect money for its care packages.[78] It was no different on the US continent. In 1939, the Buddhist Mission of North America sent cash donations directly to the Japanese

Imperial Army through the Yokohama Species Bank. Individual temples and women's associations, such as those at Fresno and San Jose, also held campaigns to raise funds for the Imperial Army.[79] These activities also took place at many Japanese American Christian churches.[80] Most issei—both Buddhist and Christian—naturally desired to support their homeland, which they believed was taking its rightful place as an imperial power, equal to the Europeans and Americans. By contrast, most nisei did not feel the same emotional connection to the land of their parents. Having been born in America, many nisei Buddhists and Christians were more skeptical of Japan's militaristic intentions, and a significant number vocally expressed their concerns.[81]

Historically, many ethnic groups in the United States had practiced similar forms of support to their homelands without becoming suspected or incarcerated en masse as national security threats. For example, in 1935, after Mussolini's invasion of Ethiopia led to the United States' ordering embargoes on oil and raw materials to Italy, fascist sympathizers in America responded, with women donating gold wedding rings for the Italian war effort and men voluntarily paying the "bachelor tax" Mussolini had imposed on Italy. To make up for a copper shortage, Italians in America sent eight hundred tons of the metal to Italy in the form of copper postcards.[82] Similar activities within the Japanese American community, however, heightened suspicions that it was a breeding ground of Japanese militarism and anti-Americanism.

Nine months prior to the Pearl Harbor attack, the only Buddhist spy to have been identified by the US military was actually a loyal American agent (and citizen) recruited by the US Army Counter Intelligence Corps to spy on Japan. Born in a sugar plantation community in Puunene, Maui, Richard Sakakida was the first and only US citizen of Japanese descent to have been offered full scholarships to both West Point and Ryukoku, the Nishi Hongwanji sect's prestigious Buddhist university in Japan. Turning both down, he ended up serving the US armed forces as an undercover agent in the Philippines during the war, providing critical military intelligence to General Douglas MacArthur even after being captured and tortured by the Japanese military.

Richard Sakakida stands as one of the many individuals this book will name who were adamant that one could be Buddhist and American at the same time. Yet, in the preparation for a possible war with Japan, the recruitment of individuals like Sakakida was overshadowed by a systematic program of animus against Buddhists. The generalized suspicion of the "heathen" religion as a threat to national identity and security and the surveillance of specific temples went hand in hand with the compilation of lists of "dangerous" individuals. These lists would guide the dragnet that swept up Buddhist leaders in the days and weeks following the attack on Pearl Harbor.

COMPILING REGISTRIES

As early as 1922, intelligence agencies began compiling registries of potentially subversive Japanese. In March of that year, the FBI issued a report by agent A. A. Hopkins titled *Japanese Espionage—Hawaii* that listed 157 potentially subversive Japanese individuals, most of whom were Buddhist priests, Japanese-language school principals, and prominent businessmen.[83]

In 1936, five years prior to the Pearl Harbor attack, in a confidential memorandum to the military's chief of operations, President Roosevelt endorsed the plan to maintain a secret list of Japanese to be detained. Having formerly served as assistant secretary of the Navy, he articulated his concerns about Japanese naval ships visiting Hawai'i, recommending that "every Japanese citizen or non-citizen on the Island of Oahu who meets these Japanese ships or has any connection with their officers or men should be secretly but definitely identified and his or her name placed on a special list of those who would be the first to be placed in a concentration camp" if trouble arose.[84]

George S. Patton, Jr., whose command of troops in the European theater during World War II would make him one of America's most famous generals, compiled one such list of supposedly dangerous individuals. Patton's *A General Staff Study: Plan: Initial Seizure of Orange Nationals,* written during his tenure as assistant chief of staff and intelligence officer of the Hawaiian Department from 1935 to 1937, called for the roundup of prominent issei and nisei "as hostages to guarantee the quiescence of Hawai'i's 151,000-member Japanese community in the event of war with Japan."[85] Patton's report detailed how to proclaim martial law and shut down certain businesses and amateur radio stations in conjunction with a roundup. The report's appendix listed people to be taken into custody. Notable among the 128 potential hostages, which included ninety-five issei and thirty-three American citizens, was a sizable contingent of Buddhist and Shinto leaders. Most such lists exempted Christian ministers, but Patton's registry included one Christian leader, Umetarō Okumura, as well as the white Buddhist priest Rev. Ernest Hunt, an American convert. The use of the word "hostage" instead of "prisoner" suggests that Patton intended to use the lives of those taken into custody as a bargaining chip in case Japan seriously encroached on the American territory.[86] These early lists of potential national security threats developed by the Army's G-2 section, the ONI, and units within the Justice Department such as the FBI and the Special Defense Unit, served as precursors for the ones later used to arrest large numbers of Buddhist and Shinto priests and lay leaders in the aftermath of Pearl Harbor.

Despite some efforts at interdepartmental cooperation, the FBI and ONI independently compiled their own registries on potentially dangerous Japanese nationals.[87] The minutes of a weekly intelligence conference held on July 29, 1940 between representatives of the FBI, ONI, MID, and the Treasury Department show considerable interest in consular agents in Hawai'i and report that "many of [the persons of interest] are non-quota aliens engaged as Buddhist priests and principals or teachers in the Japanese Language Schools." An entire section of the meeting was devoted to investigating Buddhists and Shintoists because they were seen to be well positioned "to disseminate Japanese propaganda." Officials were especially concerned about the largest of the Buddhist sects in America—the Hongwanji sect—because it had once been the case that its head was related to the Japanese imperial family.[88]

Additionally, a memo from FBI Director J. Edgar Hoover to military intelligence, dated November 15, 1940, claimed that the vast majority of the issei would be loyal to America in case of war, but that a dangerous, small minority might include "Buddhist and Shintoist priests, the Japanese-language schoolteachers, the consular agents, and a small percentage of prominent alien Japanese businessmen."[89] Hoover's memo recommended the internment of this "inner circle" and followed his initial orders on November 9, 1939, for the compilation of a custodial detention list of persons of Japanese, German, and Italian ancestry to be rounded up if the United States entered the war.[90]

Under the DOJ's Special Defense Unit, established in spring 1940 to coordinate the department's interests in espionage and national security, Director Lawrence M.C. 'Sam" Smith began sorting the lists of individuals, and their membership and associations with potentially anti-American organizations, into degrees of risk to national security. To facilitate a custodial detention program, he classified the names into three levels of risk (A, B, and C) signifying the level of confidence in the assessment.[91]

Group A, considered the most dangerous of subversive suspects, were to be arrested in the event of war. This group included those affiliated with the Japanese consulate, many Buddhist and Shinto priests, Japanese language instructors, fishermen, martial arts teachers, those thought to be members of associations such as the paramilitary organization Kokuryūkai (Black Dragon Society), and various Japanese veterans' groups.[92] The "potentially dangerous" Group B individuals, which included leaders of various *nihonjinkai* (Japanese associations), were those who were perhaps not considered imminent threats to national security, but who had standing in the community to potentially become dangerous, should they choose to act.[93] Group C included those who were "least dangerous," but were "guilty by association." As members of Japanese organizations with ties to the homeland, they were thought to harbor pro-Japanese sentiments and might be brought into possible activity against US interests.[94]

The compilation of detention lists and secret registries was coupled with overt measures to reassure an increasingly concerned American public that the government was fully cognizant of foreign espionage and prepared for foreign threats. By the spring of 1940, Congress passed the Alien Registration Act, popularly called the Smith Act (after Howard W. Smith, the Virginia Democrat who introduced the bill in the House of Representatives), which was signed into law by President Roosevelt in June. It mandated the registration and fingerprinting of over four million "resident aliens," ostensibly to make it easier to track them in a time

FIGURE 1.3 Consecration ceremony of new Seattle Buddhist temple building (October 1941).   Courtesy of the Frank Kubo Collection, Densho Digital Repository, ddr-densho-128-121.

of war. The law required them to report any changes of residence or address within five days of a move.[95] For a time, all aliens without permanent residence in the United States were compelled to report to authorities every three months.[96]

The US government was thus poised to execute a roundup of listed individuals within hours of any national emergency. Triggered by the outbreak of war, a program long in the making was about to sweep up the leaders of the Japanese American community, disproportionately targeting those affiliated with Shinto and Buddhism.

2

MARTIAL LAW

A MEMORABLE SCENE in Martin Scorsese's 2016 Academy Award-nominated film, *Silence*, set in 1670 near Nagasaki, depicts the interrogation of four prisoners by Japanese officials determined to stamp out Christianity in their country. The scene, witnessed by a Portuguese Catholic missionary named Rodrigues, unfolds with one of the officials telling the prisoners that their interrogations and tortures will end if they simply step on an image of Christ—a practice called *fumi-e* (literally, stepping on an image)—placed on the ground in front of them. "This is just a formality, really. Just one step, that's all," the official reassures him. "We're not asking you to do it sincerely. It's only for appearances, just putting your foot on the thing won't betray your faith, whatever it is."[1]

In Honolulu in December 1941, when an Army interrogator asked twenty-one-year-old David Kobata, an American citizen, to step on an image of the Japanese Emperor to prove his loyalty to the United States, the parallel to the ancient Japanese practice of *fumi-e* was not lost on Kobata. After the Japanese attack, the US Army had declared martial law on the islands of Hawai'i, and rounded up not only enemy aliens or Japanese nationals, but also American citizens of Japanese descent. Kobata had been working as a truck driver at Pearl Harbor and other waterfront areas, but authorities had deemed him a security risk and swiftly confiscated his truck-operator license. Though American-born and raised, he had spent some years in Hiroshima Prefecture during his youth, living with his devout Buddhist grandmother. Three of his brothers were living in Japan when war broke out, and his mother was stranded there, having recently traveled with his deceased father's ashes to perform Buddhist rites in her husband's hometown temple. As a so-called kibei (an American-born citizen of Japanese descent, educated to some extent in Japan), Kobata was a target of the animus and suspicion directed toward anyone assumed to have dubious or split loyalties.

"You, David Kobata, say you pledge your loyalty to the United States. Can you prove it to me by stepping on the Emperor's picture?" the Army interrogator asked.

"Oh, yes, I will, but under one condition," Kobata said.

"What is the condition?"

"You lay down President Roosevelt's picture on the floor and you step on that, too. If you do, I will step on the Emperor's picture."

"Why do you want that?"

"Even though it is President Roosevelt's picture, I don't believe that you are going to be disloyal to the President," Kobata told the interrogator. "How can you take it as proof that if I step on the Emperor's picture I am proving my loyalty to the country America?"[2]

Kobata later recalled, "They let me go, but when I came out of the office I had cold sweat, because I thought that if this was in Japan and I had said that, I think I would be dead by now. But, I said to myself, this is America. They respect the freedom of speech."[3]

Nonetheless, like other American Buddhists at the time who persisted in believing both in their religion and in their American constitutional rights, Kobata was subjected to numerous interrogations by the Army, the Office of Naval Intelligence, and the FBI. He maintained his loyalty to the United States despite his ethnic, cultural, and religious connections to Japan.

BUDDHIST LIFE UNDER MARTIAL LAW

Young Japanese American adults like Kobata who had spent time living in Japan—the kibei—were deemed particularly suspect by the military authorities.[4] In the first year and a half of the war, the Army's Counter Intelligence Corps focused on the "approximately 5,000" kibei living in

Hawai'i as well as the "large and active Japanese fishing fleet," while simultaneously launching "projects involving Buddhist and Shinto priests, consular agents, and language school officials."[5] Ultimately, a select group of individuals, composed of roughly two-thirds issei and one-third nisei (almost all kibei), were rounded up in Hawai'i, many of them influential members of the community.[6] In a military intelligence memorandum "prepared to assist agents investigating Japanese to evaluate properly the loyalties of the individuals investigated," the fourteen key factors identified for determining whether to intern kibei included their religious affiliation.[7] Being Buddhist—while being American—was a red flag for investigators.[8]

Kobata managed to escape arrest, but other American citizens on the Hawaiian Islands were not as fortunate. A number of American citizen Shinto and Buddhist priests—but no Christian ministers—were taken into custody and interned as if they were enemy aliens.[9] Since habeas corpus was suspended, any civilian, including American citizens, could be confined indefinitely without charge as long as they resided on the islands.[10]

Among them, the Buddhist nun Ryūto Tsuda (also known as Shinsho Hirai), a charismatic female leader with a reputation for healing abilities, stands out. She was born in Kona, Hawai'i, but trained as a nun at Tōdaiji Temple in Nara, Japan (leading her to become the first official "missionary" of that temple's sect to America).[11] Despite her US citizenship, government officials considered her a national security threat because she had studied for four years in Japan and was suspected by the authorities of praying for Japan's success at war while at the temple. At one of her hearings later during the war, the parole board led by Lt. Col. Edward Massee, found her to be "bright, sharp, and shrewd . . . a religious woman of the fanatical type. . . . In conclusion, the Board believes that she is dangerous to the public peace, safety, and internal security of the United States."[12] The Buddhist nun was one of nine ordained American Buddhist or Shinto clerics, including a number of other females, thought to be of such a danger to national security that they were arrested in the weeks and months following the Pearl Harbor attack.[13]

The early roundup of the Buddhist leadership, whether citizen or not, was a harbinger of a broader persecution of non-Christian religions on the Hawaiian Islands. Under martial law, the misguided presumption that Japanese American Christians were necessarily more loyal to the United States became increasingly apparent, and the historical animus against Buddhism and Shinto intensified.

Although the military authorities in Hawai'i would ultimately forgo a mass incarceration of the Japanese like the one carried out in the continental United States, this outcome was not assured in the initial days and weeks after the attack.[14] On December 18, Navy Secretary Frank Knox went so far as to recommend that all Japanese aliens be removed from the island of Oahu, where Pearl Harbor was located, and detained on another island. The Army's chief of staff, General George Marshall, similarly recommended the eventual incarceration of the entirety of the Japanese American population, and the immediate removal of the most dangerous twenty thousand people to either the island of Molokai or "*a concentration camp* located on the US mainland."[15] However, the new commander of Hawai'i's martial law government, Lieutenant General Delos C. Emmons, cited the logistical difficulty of removing such a large number of people, and his view prevailed when Secretary of War Stimson agreed that such a massive relocation would be impractical.[16] Still, fears of another attack by the Japanese military and of fifth column activity by Japanese Americans, one of the largest ethnic groups on the islands, led officials to take measures beyond the initial arrests to restrict, constrain, and surveille the community.

For much of the war, the Hawaiian Islands were under strict blackout orders from 6 PM to 7 AM.[17] Under martial law, this nighttime curfew, as well as the requirements to carry new government-issued ID cards and to submit to mail censorship and long-distance telephone call monitoring, were shared by everyone on the islands.[18] Gas masks were issued to all civilians, including children, with instructions to carry them everywhere. The son of Rev. Tadao Kouchi, of the Lanai Hongwanji Mission on Maui, recalled: "Living in Lanai changed. We had to be fitted for gas masks, and sleep with no lights on. . . . [Bulbs were] painted black, with the exception of the bottom. I guess they didn't want to show the Japanese bombers where we lived."[19]

Strict observance of blackouts was required. At the Puna Hongwanji temple, American soldiers shot their rifles at a flashing light in the tower after one insisted it was a spy sending coded light signals to the Japanese in violation of the blackout regulations. Explaining that the tower was a columbarium where the deceased members' ashes were kept, a lay Buddhist member of the temple led the soldiers up the stairs, where they found a large mirror, reflecting the moonlight.[20]

In addition to these general regulations, military authorities applied restrictions specific to Japanese nationals residing on the islands. They were forbidden to travel beyond a ten-mile radius of their homes, or to change residences or occupations without registering the change and securing the approval of the Provost Marshal General's office. Members of the US Army Signal Corps conducted house-to-house searches for contraband in Japanese neighborhoods.[21] In their confusion, some Japanese families voluntarily turned in precious family heirlooms, such as samurai swords and kimonos, to their local police stations.[22]

Because the Japanese were prohibited from owning boats and made to surrender their crafts, seven hundred fishermen lost their livelihoods.[23] Authorities on the islands also banned issei, and a number of nisei, from other types of jobs, such as photography and teaching.[24] And despite their American citizenship, nisei were compelled to wear so-called black badges issued by the military government. Actually ringed in black, these badges prominently featured the word RESTRICTED, and in many cases prevented Japanese Americans from returning to jobs located in sensitive areas.[25] Ignoring the constitutional protection of religious freedom, the Office of the Military Governor's official policy was to "discourage Japanese religious activities other than Christian."[26] This policy would continue until April 1944.

Thus, during the first several years of the war, Buddhists and Shintoists were restricted from practicing their religion, and had to petition the Army's G-2 intelligence division for permission, most often denied, to meet at their temples and shrines. Several Shinto shrines, such as the Izumo Taisha shrine in Honolulu, were simply confiscated and declared "gifts" to the city and county of Honolulu.[27] On the island of Kauai, the Military Governor's Office coordinated the closure of the island's Japanese-language schools with the dissolution of Buddhist temples. Ultimately, thirteen of the island's nineteen Buddhist temples were eliminated.[28]

In the midst of the general suppression of Buddhism, the white priest Rev. Ernest Hunt was the one of a handful of Buddhist leaders who managed to obtain an exemption from General Emmons to hold public services. On one occasion at a Buddhist temple in Olaa, on the Big Island, a military official barged into the temple during the middle of a service Hunt was officiating. The officer grabbed Rev. Hunt's priestly robes and questioned what he was doing there, especially as a "Caucasian," and backed down only when Hunt showed him Emmons's letter.[29] With a portable Buddhist altar *(butsudan)* on his back, Hunt trekked to remote plantations and even "ministered to the forgotten patients of a tuberculosis sanitarium" as the rare individual given permission to serve tens of thousands of Buddhists on the islands.[30]

While serving the US government as a staffer in military intelligence, the nisei Buddhist priest Rev. Egan Yoshikami also managed to receive permission to conduct occasional funerals at his sect's head temple in Honolulu.[31] And the female issei Buddhist priest Yoshiko Tatsuguchi took care of the Shinshū Kyōkai Mission in Honolulu, substituting for her interned husband.[32] With the quiet consent of the congregation, she hid her priestly status during the war so that she could avoid internment and care for her six children.[33]

The remnants of the Buddhist leadership who were not arrested operated in an anti-Buddhist environment engineered by the military government and aided by social pressure from nongovernmental groups. On December 18, 1941, the Hawaii Territorial Office of Civilian Defense started up a civilian group called the Morale Section, made up of representatives of various ethnic groups. The Morale Section, in turn, formed many subcommittees, including ones on each of the main islands to function as intermediaries between the Japanese American community and the Army. At first, these "Emergency Service Committees" seemed reasonable to the majority-Buddhist Japanese American community, but when Committee members criticized anything that might appear culturally un-American, many felt under attack. One of the main Morale Section leaders, school principal Shigeo Yoshida, urged the elimination of "all vestiges of alien influences and practices which are inconsistent with American ideals and practices and which retard the full Americanization, in a cultural sense, of our group and obstruct our full integration with the rest of the community."[34]

Anything deemed too Japanese was a target. The most obvious symbol, the Japanese flag, was banned under martial law in Hawai'i. At the Shinto shrine in Hilo, the Daijingū, the Japanese flag was painted black for the duration of the war.[35] Also in Honolulu, city and county workers tore down the Japanese Hō-ō (celestial bird of good tidings) at the Waikiki Natatorium, and the tokonoma (Japanese alcove) at the Honolulu Academy of Arts was dismantled.[36]

Like the military authorities, these civilian groups encouraged Japanese Americans to demonstrate their loyalty by attending Christian churches. The Morale Committee conducted a "Speak American" campaign, advocated for the dissolution of Japanese-language schools, and proposed to the authorities that Buddhist temples and Shinto shrines, which they regarded as hubs of a "foreign" religion, be shut down until after the war.

Buddhists were forced to contend with these echoes of the prewar tensions with Japanese American Christians. Indeed, the leaders of the prewar anti-Buddhist campaigns, such as Christian pastor Takie Okumura and his son Umetarō, worked closely with authorities and plantation owners to close Buddhist temples during the war. According to Rev. Hunt, the Okumuras even threatened individual Buddhists by putting "pressure on the Buddhist youth with implied threats of the concentration camps unless the children attend [Christian] church."[37]

The threats were not just verbal. In the first months after Pearl Harbor, Buddhist statuary and temples on the islands suffered a rash of attacks. White American soldiers vandalized the stone bodhisattva Jizō statues in Wahiawa and Kawailoa. Another Jizō statue, installed outside of Ryūsenji Temple, was thrown into the river. Soldiers also used the Buddhist statue at Kaahapai for target practice.[38]

Anti-Buddhist violence also came in the form of arson, which struck the Papaikou Hongwanji Mission on the Big Island and Ewa Hongwanji Mission on Oahu.[39] In another suspected arson case, the Pahala Hongwanji on the Big Island burned down.[40] Temple members managed to run into the main hall just in time to save the Buddha statue and altar accessories. The wife of that temple's priest recalled installing the rescued Buddha statue at a nearby temple of a different sect: "Upon seeing the figure of Amida Buddha safely housed in the Shingon-shu temple Taishi-do next door, I folded my hands in *gassho*, tears rolling down my cheek."[41] After the temple burned, local Buddhist families asked the plantation manager if a plantation building could be used to house a Buddhist Sunday School for the children. He told them, "There is no need to have two Sunday Schools. The Christian Sunday School should be enough."[42]

Before it burned, the Pahala temple had been forcibly taken over by the military, as were dozens of other temples.[43] Among them was Kona's Zen temple Daifukuji. One of its members, who also owned a popular restaurant in Kona, recalled:

> The temple was filled with soldiers. At night, there were black-outs so the soldiers had to use candles and were afraid of ghosts. They came over to my family's store to buy cokes. When my restaurant was opened in 1942, some soldiers were still around so we served them chicken *hekka* two or three times in the hall . . . My mother used to say to me, "*Kannonsama* [the bodhisattva Kannon] is crying" because there were only soldiers in the temple.[44]

Many of the temples seized by the military were vandalized.[45] The Jōdo Buddhist temple on Makiki Street in Honolulu, which was converted into an infantry battalion headquarters, was ransacked, and the Hilo Hongwanji Temple was desecrated and looted by soldiers.[46] Although the theft of the temple's equipment was reported to the authorities, no compensation was made.[47] And when a white soldier tried to steal the Kishimonjin statue at the Nichiren Mission of Hawaii, a devout laywoman "frantically shouted" at the soldier and chased him away, and then began guarding the temple at night to protect it.[48]

It would fall to these people—ordinary laypeople, the wives of interned priests, the handful of elderly or infirm issei priests, and nisei and white convert priests—to protect and maintain a semblance of Buddhist life under martial law. With its leadership arrested and imprisoned, new segments of the community kept Buddhism alive in the face of violent attacks on temples, official military suppression of their religion, and pervasive social pressure to avoid displaying any symbol or engaging in any activity associated with Buddhist or Japanese culture.

CAMPS IN THE LAND OF ALOHA

To house those swept up as dangerous enemy aliens, the military established the Sand Island Detention Center, a former public health quarantine station, on a small island in Honolulu Harbor on December 8, the day after the attack. Contravening Geneva Convention rules, the Buddhist priests and other internees were forced to build their own prison, living in tents for the first six months of their detention until the compounds were completed.[49] Almost everyone detained on the islands spent time there before it closed in March 1943.

The first couple hundred Japanese imprisoned at Sand Island had to build their own prison fences the day after their arrival, according to a memoir by the Zen priest of Waiahole's Tōmonji Temple: "The men who dug the holes for the fence posts and pulled wheelbarrows filled with mixed cement, felt humiliated to be prodded along by guards bearing guns."[50]

About ten feet before the barbed wire fence was a white line that demarcated the zone beyond which anyone who crossed would be "considered a fugitive and could be shot dead."[51] Three close calls occurred within the first few weeks, when a Buddhist priest, a Shinto priest, and a Japanese-language school principal each disregarded the line and were nearly shot.

The detainees lived eight men to a tent, with cots simply placed on the ground. They were not allowed to keep their trunks with them; luggage was kept in a separate storage area. In the six months before barracks were built, they slept on wet ground as rain poured into their tents. This particularly affected any elderly detainees who suffered from arthritis, pulmonary problems, or other common ailments of age.

The food served presented another difficulty for this primarily issei group. Accustomed to Japanese cuisine with its reliance on rice, vegetables, and fish, they (especially those Buddhist priests who were religiously

FIGURE 2.1 The internment camp at Sand Island, Hawai'i (February 13, 1942).   Courtesy of the US Army Collection, Japanese Cultural Center of Hawai'i, JCCH 2129.

vegetarian), did not relish the daily meals of pork, beans, and bread served up to them by a German detainee cook. Sand Island's camp director, Captain Carl Eifler, was irritated when the priests and others did not finish all the food given to them. He announced that the Japanese who failed to finish the food on their plates would be served their leftovers at the next meal. When one elderly internee, who had been picked up without his dentures, attempted to throw away a tough piece of meat, full of gristle, Eifler ordered him to clean his plate.[52]

As a solution, a Nichiren Buddhist priest proposed growing vegetables on site. He pulled together a group of priests of different sects, and they secured permission to plant lettuce and other greens.[53] The Bishop of the Jōdo Buddhist mission tended the garden in the only clothes he had, the priestly robes he had been wearing when he was arrested.[54] Although most of these men were transferred to the continental United States before they could enjoy the fruits of their labor, some of the vegetables were harvested the following February by other detained Japanese leaders arriving at Sand Island.[55]

Since Eifler generally regarded the detainees as highly subversive individuals, the Buddhist priests were under constant surveillance. On one occasion, Eifler forced them to strip naked and stand in the burning sun to extract a confession after a spoon had gone missing from the mess hall. Eifler believed that a stolen spoon could be used as a weapon.[56] It was later found lying on top of the mess hall cupboard.

During a routine inspection on December 14, 1941, Rev. Ryōshin Okano, a Nishi Hongwanji Buddhist priest from Pearl City, was found to have made a crude and flimsy knife from a metal strapping tie, so that he could cut up food into smaller bites. What happened next would later be referred to by the detainees as the "Okano Incident." According to a later account, "everyone in the group was gathered into an open field and forced to strip, have their anuses probed, and stand in the cold until the guards were satisfied that no one else had anything dangerous hidden in their clothes or tents."[57] As another detainee recalled, "It was a most unusual sight, both pathetic and comical [of] a group of men, young and old," including "elderly men, such as Bishop Kubokawa, Bishop Kuchiba. . . . Everyone was angry at the commander, not at Reverend Okano."[58]

Masaji Marumoto, a well-known attorney and a devout Buddhist who would serve as the chief justice of Hawai'i's supreme court after the war, was permitted to visit his friends interned at Sand Island thanks to his connection with the Honolulu FBI office's special agent in charge, Robert Shivers.[59] Marumoto found the conditions "appalling," he wrote. "The internees were shabby and unshaven. When I saw them, I knew why [Lt. General] Emmons did not have any committee visit them. They were being treated like POWs instead of civilian internees."[60]

Authorities prohibited detainees from congregating in groups of three or more, and from leaving their tents after 8 PM except to go to the latrine (in which case, if encountered by a guard, the protocol was to immediately call out "Prisoner!").[61] On one occasion when Bishop Kuchiba was observed in conversation with two other men, guards took them out of the camp to a spot on the island where an artillery shell from an American anti-aircraft gun had landed but failed to explode. They were handed picks and shovels and ordered to dig it out.[62] Despite the official prohibition on meetings, after several months, some of the detainees quietly formed a group to "pass the time" in the evenings and learn from each other. The group conducted their activities in the pitch dark with "neither the speaker nor the audience [able to see] faces clearly," recalled one detainee. "The Reverend Kuchiba talked about his visits to South China and the South Pacific islands in the company of [Hongwanji Buddhist leader] Abbot Kozui Otani and about his experience being shipwrecked off Taiwan, where he narrowly escaped death. His stories were very entertaining."[63] These activities became more problematic after June 1942, when the administration opened new barracks installed with a radio and speaker system that enabled office staff to listen in on conversations.[64]

While the detainees were allowed by Geneva Prisoner of War (POW) Convention rules to communicate with others outside of camp, their letters and postcards were heavily censored. Nonetheless, one letter written by the priest who arrived at Sand Island in his Buddhist robes, Kyokujō Kubokawa, sent in 1942 to his headquarters in Japan, describes his experience at the detention center:

[We] have been living in tents on a small island. It was as if I was exiled like Hōnen [the Jōdo sect's founder, who had been banished by the authorities for his teachings in medieval Japan]. On January 15, we held a Memorial Service for Hōnen despite not having a scroll with the sacred words. Being locked up in a remote place where we couldn't prepare any incense, flowers, or candles, we gathered all members and gave gratitude to the teachings simply by placing our palms together and reciting Buddhist scriptures. The Jōdo Mission of Hawai'i Betsuin in Honolulu was occupied by the US Army. . . . There are a total of [redacted] Jōdo Mission priests from the various islands of Hawai'i who have already been captured and sent to the US continent. The priests have been dispersed to various internment camps, but I do not know who has been taken where. I don't know the whereabouts of the five [Hawaiian] priests or of Revs. Nozaki and Mukushina of Los Angeles.[65]

US military censors crossed out the number of detainees, which they determined should be hidden for national security reasons, and Rev.

Kubokawa's ignorance of "who has been taken where," was caused by the deliberate decision by the FBI and DOJ to split up internees, move them from camp to camp, and deny them information. Geneva Convention rules permitted authorities to view detainee correspondence and subject it to censorship if national security might be compromised. Although the Convention was originally focused only on POWs, Buddhist priests in these camps received its coverage after US Secretary of State Cordell Hull communicated to the Japanese through Swiss diplomatic channels that the United States would apply and adapt the rules to cover enemy alien civilians as well.[66]

These Geneva Convention regulations guaranteed freedom of religious expression and barred forced labor beyond what was needed for basic camp upkeep and internee health and welfare.[67] They were often disregarded, however, by US officials.[68] At Sand Island, detainees were forced to work unless they were sick.[69] Amidst this regimen of hard labor and continuous surveillance, the first large-scale Buddhist gathering was held at Sand Island in May 1942, to memorialize an inmate who had died. Initially, authorities refused to permit a funeral for Hisahiko Kokubo, who was taken by a heart attack that March. "Without benefit of a wake service or the reading of the Sutra, it is a lonely send off," one detainee lamented.[70] But after repeated requests, the community was allowed to hold Mr. Kokubo's seventh-day memorial service. The mourners each withdrew ten cents from accounts they had been allowed to set up at the main office and sent condolence money to the grieving family. Once Mr. Kokubo's body was sent back to the island of Kauai, a Buddhist priest held at the Kalaheo Stockade there was granted special temporary leave to officiate at the funeral.[71]

Most of the Sand Island Buddhist priests were ultimately transferred to internment camps on the US continent. By July 1942, the Immigration and Naturalization Service branch of the US Department of Justice was operating forty-nine detention stations, nineteen of which held Japanese nationals. Many of these were later closed as the more permanent, Army-run camps began taking over the responsibility of housing those not released or paroled.[72] The first ship departed from Hawai'i to the continent on February 17, 1942 carrying 172 Japanese Americans, and the tenth and last ship left on December 2, 1943 with thirty Japanese Americans.[73] In total, eight women and 694 men were transported. Many ended up at locations like the Lordsburg Internment Camp (in New Mexico, the largest camp on the continental United States run by the Army), the Santa Fe Detention Center (run by the DOJ in New Mexico), and the Crystal City Alien Enemy Detention Facility (in Texas).

A smaller group spent the rest of the war on the Hawaiian Islands at the Honouliuli Internment Camp. Opened in Honouliuli Gulch on March 2, 1943, the day after the closure of Sand Island, it was nicknamed by the internees *Jigoku Dani* (Hell Valley) because of how the gulch trapped heat.[74] Later that hot summer, a ritual drum brought in from the Nichiren Buddhist temple was used to celebrate Obon, the Buddhist festival honoring ancestors. Maintaining a Buddhist ritual calendar despite the inhospitable conditions, Zenkyō Komagata, the Sōtō Zen Buddhist Bishop of Hawai'i, officiated at the Obon ceremony at Honouliuli.[75]

Komagata was one of the few Japanese nationals held at Honouliuli rather than shipped to continental US camps.[76] Those housed at Honouliuli were primarily American citizens, most of them kibei. Authorities deemed it legally risky to transfer any American citizens arrested without due process to the continental United States, where the Constitution was still in effect.

All told, most issei Buddhist priests and a significant number of nisei Buddhist priests were detained in this initial selective incarceration process.[77] The small group not initially arrested included six nuns (or ordained wives of interned male Buddhist priests), three retired or elderly priests, and several priests (such as Rev. Shinjō Nagatomi and Rev. Nyogen Senzaki) who accompanied other east coast Japanese and Japanese Americans to the WRA camps as part of the mass incarceration.[78]

In the weeks and months that followed Pearl Harbor, nearly three-quarters of the American Buddhist leadership and all Shinto priests were detained as threats to national security, as compared to just 17 percent of Japanese Christian ministers.[79] Only a handful of Christian leaders were arrested in Hawai'i—most of them in their capacity as *toritsuginin* (or volunteer liaisons with the Japanese Consulate)—while a couple of hundred Buddhist and Shinto priests were rounded up.[80] Many of the Japanese Christian ministers initially detained, in Hawai'i and the continent, were soon released and allowed to rejoin their families, but this

FIGURE 2.2 Honouliuli headquarters prisoner of war processing station. Courtesy of the R. H. Lodge Collection, Japanese Cultural Center of Hawaiʻi.

FIGURE 2.3 Barracks at Honouliuli internment camp. Courtesy of the R. H. Lodge Collection, Japanese Cultural Center of Hawaiʻi / Hawaiʻi Plantation Village.

privilege was not afforded to Buddhist and Shinto priests until much later in the war, if at all.[81]

It was not the official policy of the government to overtly discriminate against Buddhists and Shintoists or to favor Christians in the initial dragnet after Pearl Harbor. Nor did President Roosevelt's order, which caused the mass incarceration of over 110,000 persons of Japanese ancestry on the west coast—include any overt reference to Japan, the Japanese, or Japanese Americans. Executive Order 9066, on its face, did not constitute an official directive to target one ethnic community. Yet, the result of the order was clear. Despite also being at war with Italy and Germany, the United States would subject only its Japanese American community to detention and mass incarceration.

The pressure for harsher measures was slowly building across the Pacific. Local politicians and newspapers in California, Oregon, and Washington began calling for the forcible removal of all persons of Japanese ancestry from their homes. The ethnic cleansing of anyone with "even a drop of Japanese blood," as one of the main architects of the mass removal from the west coast put it, represented a different kind of constitutional crisis that, like martial law in Hawai'i, devastated the Japanese American community.

3

JAPANESE AMERICA UNDER SIEGE

IN A MEMOIR WRITTEN later in his life, Rev. Bunyū Fujimura recalled the hysteria that swept through Salinas, California, in the aftermath of the news about Pearl Harbor. On December 8, 1941, he remembered, the "Salinas Chief of Police came and ordered me to take down our temple gong." The police chief gave the reason:

> He said that the people of Salinas were frightened that if the Japanese Imperial Navy sailed into Monterey Bay, our gong could be used to signal them. He said if we did not take our gong down, he would burn the tower containing it. The sound of our temple gong could hardly be heard upwind in the city, and only a few miles downwind. How ridiculous to even think that its sound could be heard in Monterey, 19 miles away. And how much more ridiculous to think that sounding it would be any help to an invading army. But this is an indication of the hysteria among some people in Salinas about the Japanese Imperial Navy. I was not sure how to comply with the Police Chief's order, because most Japanese were so frightened they did not dare step outside their homes. Fortunately, the Osugi Garage was located just in front of our temple. I asked Mr. Osugi if he would bring a chain hoist used to raise cars. With the help of Mr. Kihei Yamashita, a member of our temple, I cut a hole in the platform of the tower, and used the hoist to lower the gong to the ground.[1]

Several weeks later, Fujimura was arrested; he would go on to be incarcerated in a series of camps run by the US Army (Fort Lincoln, Camp McCoy, and Camp Livingston) and the DOJ camp in Santa Fe, New Mexico.[2] As the FBI agents took Rev. Fujimura away, he gazed back at the temple and saw ten policemen surrounding the main temple building, arresting several other Buddhist priests affiliated with the temple.[3] He later joked that the authorities may have sent ten policemen because one of the priests, Rev. Kōyo Tamanaha, had "a fifth-degree black belt in judo."[4]

Unlike in Hawai'i, many of the continental US arrests came weeks or months after the December attack and, in the intervening period, many Buddhists faced harassment and increased scrutiny. The hysteria was fanned by the media before and during the arrests of the priests. The *Salinas Index-Journal* featured the news of the roundup on its front page and the *New York Times* reported that raids by federal agents and police in the Monterey Bay region had resulted in the arrest of thirty-eight people, including (according to the FBI agents quoted) their "best catch," the black-belted Buddhist priest "Tamanaka" [sic] who was thought to have been a "police official in Tokyo."[5] The *Times* also noted the seizure of "large quantities of contraband material such as fifth columnists might find useful." *Life Magazine*'s article entitled "US Uproots Jap Aliens" featured a photo of the Salinas Buddhist Temple's bell platform, minus the gong.[6]

On the evening of his arrest, Rev. Fujimura was interrogated by an FBI special agent, who accused him of being a Japanese naval officer and spy taking his orders from the Emperor. To this absurd line of questioning, the priest replied: "How can a skinny person like myself be a Japanese Naval Officer? This should be apparent even to you."[7] Since the police chief and the FBI agent knew little about Japanese religion and culture, Rev. Fujimura spent much of the interrogation providing information about himself and his faith. As one of the first priests of his sect to be interrogated, he was aware that the "activity of the two or three inches of my tongue would influence the treatment of all other ministers." Even though he believed he might be taken away and executed, he wanted to "repay my debt to the dharma" and "answer all questions truthfully, but courageously."[8]

WAR HYSTERIA

At the same time that the Buddhist leadership in Salinas was being arrested and featured in the media as the face of a subversive enemy, Rev. Kiyoshi Noji of the local Presbyterian Church was having a different experience. "FBI men from San Francisco came to Salinas every day," he recalled later, and "most of the issei men had a couple of small suitcases packed and ready."[9] But unlike the Buddhist priests, the Christian pastor was never arrested or even restricted in his movements. "The Salinas Chief of Police gave me permission to go wherever I wanted," he said.[10] This differential treatment between issei Buddhist and Christian leaders was repeated in multiple towns and cities on the west coast.[11] In Kent, Washington, the prominent Japanese Episcopalian minister and recent arrival to the United States Rev. Daisuke Kitagawa, rather than being arrested, worked with the mayor, chief of police, and the chairman of the town's Civilian Defense Committee, serving as a liaison between the local government and the Japanese American community.[12]

Because the roundup usually required local law enforcement officials to coordinate with the FBI, the arrests varied considerably by region and by religion.[13] Some families learned that the authorities dropped investigations of their family members because they were Christian. Midori Kimura was relieved that, despite the arrest of many community leaders in San Jose, California, her husband, who was the president of the Japanese Association, was not picked up. "We had helpful members of the Council of Churches in San Jose," she explained.[14] The white pastor of their Christian church had given them church membership cards, and she was told that "if we had those cards, the American government would have no reason to expel us. . . . I remember thinking, 'Is it right for me to have this card and expect different treatment?' It seemed to me that it should not matter whether we were Buddhists or Christians. We were all Japanese."[15]

A handful of Christian Japanese-language schoolteachers were targeted, but others were shielded from the roundup by their Christian affiliation.[16] In Los Angeles, the daughter of one Christian Japanese-language school teacher recalled:

these two FBI men came to pick up my mother because she was a Japanese schoolteacher and we were so scared. My gosh, they were just going to take her that day. And they were looking around, I know we had already buried things like the radio and knives and things like that . . . Then one of them looked up at the wall and said—there was a picture of Jesus sitting there—and they said, "Whose picture is that?" And my mother said, "That's my Lord and savior," and they says, "Oh, you're Christian?" And my mother said, "Yes." So the one fellow says, "We can't take her, she's a Christian."[17]

Among those picked up, many were released quickly because of their Christian affiliation. Natsu Saitō was detained in Seattle on December 9, 1941 because of the hospitality she had shown to Japanese naval officers when they had visited the region. Her husband had served in the Japanese military, and a report claimed that her son, Lincoln, was in the Japanese military. But Rev. Rudy Anderson, pastor of the First Methodist Church in Aberdeen, Washington, intervened on the family's behalf, submitting twelve notarized letters of support from white businesspeople in town. The hearing board panelists were persuaded of her loyalty to America when it was emphasized that Lincoln was actually in Japan as a student in a Presbyterian seminary and that her other son, Perry, had been the President of the Aberdeen Methodist Youth Fellowship.[18]

This differential treatment led some in the Japanese American community to shift their religious allegiances. They believed that, by aligning religiously with the Christian majority, even if they could not transform their racially minority status, their precarious place in America would be strengthened. One of the few white Christians who stood up for both Christians and Buddhists in the Japanese American community, Herbert V. Nicholson (a Quaker who also served a Japanese Baptist Church congregation in Los Angeles), later recalled: "As war clouds gathered, a great many Buddhists had begun to attend services at the Japanese Baptist Church, thinking that as Christians they would be better treated in a national emergency. This turned out to be true. The Japanese Christians had more Caucasian friends."[19]

In one remarkable show of Christian fellowship and cross-racial solidarity in Salem, Oregon, on the evening of December 7, 1941, a group of five white Christians confronted a large mob that had converged on the Lake Labish Japanese Church. Glenn A. Olds, a student at Willamette University in Oregon and a Christian student pastor at the time, recalled:

> The [mob] had guns, clubs, the works; and their intent was to "burn those Japs out!" [Dr.] Purdy [the Christian pastor] reminded them that they [the Japanese Americans] were Americans as we all were . . . we were also soldiers, of the army of Jesus Christ, who had fought such bigotry for 2000 years, and said, "We are only five that stand here against you, but everything you know in your hearts, and we represent, gives lie to what you are about to do. Men, you'll have to go over us first, and tomorrow, you'll be the sorriest men in Salem."[20]

This impassioned speech prevented the burning of the Japanese Christian church. In contrast, Buddhists had fewer allies in the white community and Buddhist symbols were often believed to represent the new Japanese "enemy." In Vacaville, California, the local newspaper reported that "some impetuous youth" had shot up the town's Buddhist temple in the evening of December 8, but that the Buddhist priest and his wife, who resided on the premises, were uninjured.[21] Local white youth also took their shotguns to the Fresno Buddhist Temple and used the front entrance of the building for target practice. Their potshots were particularly aimed at the ancient Buddhist symbol called the *manji*, which represents an aerial view of a *stūpa* (a structure housing the Buddha's relics). Coincidentally and unfortunately, the *manji* resembles a swastika, though it predates the Nazi use of the symbol by thousands of years.[22]

But the weeks and months after Pearl Harbor proved a poor time to educate non-Buddhists on the difference between a *manji* and a swastika. In Seattle on December 8, dozens of Japanese American members of the Young Buddhist Association (YBA) who were wearing what authorities called "swastika lapel pins" were arrested and spent the night in jail. Though the young Buddhists had regularly donned the *manji* before the war, the authorities were certain they were "fifth columnists" bearing secret signs.[23] In response to these incidents, the Nisei Buddhist leadership urged temples to take down the ancient symbol.[24] The Seattle YBA removed all "swastika inscriptions" from their church. Similarly, in Oakland, California, YBA members climbed their main temple building's roof to take down roof tiles engraved with the *manji*.[25]

The Seattle YBA was particularly sensitive to how they were perceived by the authorities and the general public. Twenty members of the Seattle Buddhist Temple's Lotus Association drama club had learned of the Pearl Harbor attack just as they were about to go onstage at Harmony Hall in Portland. The performance was a fundraiser to help rebuild the Seattle temple's Social Hall. Hearing the news, the group hastily put away a large Japanese flag that had been unfurled backstage, which was normally featured in their Japanese-style *shibai* performance, and cancelled the show. On their bus ride home, as they passed through Chehalis, Washington, soldiers from nearby Fort Lewis stopped the bus and put the group in the local jail overnight. They were released the following morning.[26]

Days after their return, the young Buddhists held a massive Americanization Rally, sponsored by the Japanese American Citizens League (JACL) and the Emergency Defense Council (EDC), in the Social Hall. With 1,500 attendees, it marked the largest political gathering by Japanese Americans in the city's history.[27] One of the Buddhist organizers of the rally, Takeo Nagaki, told the press, "Citizenship and loyalty are not matters of skin. We may look like Japanese but our hearts are American." The JACL organizers launched a petition drive at the rally that read in part:

> We Americans of Japanese ancestry and the members of our parent generation here assembled and elsewhere reaffirm allegiance and loyalty to the United States of America and pledge our efforts toward a victorious prosecution of the war by extending unstinting co-operation to the President of the United States and the duly constituted authorities.[28]

Public presentations of loyalty were frequent during this period. While the vast majority of the issei Buddhist leadership was incarcerated in the DOJ and Army-run internment camps, the remaining Buddhist priests and lay leaders issued statements affirming Buddhist support for the United States. Nisei Buddhist priests, who were American citizens, began to take more prominent leadership positions at the temples and Buddhist organizations, both as a practical necessity after the roundup of the issei priests and as a clear demonstration of the "American" character of Buddhism. For example, a young, American-born minister was appointed to be the Kōyasan Buddhist Temple's new head priest, replacing Rev. Seytsū Takahashi, the priest who had happened to be on Terminal Island on December 8 and was arrested after crossing the bridge back to Los Angeles.[29]

Other nisei priests acted behind the scenes, calling the San Francisco FBI and Naval Intelligence Bureau frequently to explain Buddhist organizations' activities.[30] Indeed, the Buddhist Mission of North America (BMNA) headquarters in San Francisco was under orders from the Office of Naval Intelligence to submit all communications and bulletins between that organization and its affiliated temples to both the ONI and the FBI.[31]

Many of these communications from headquarters to affiliate temples were written by the American-born priest Rev. Kenryō Kumata. In one letter, Kumata urged all the sect's temples and members to ignore scaremongers who spread rumors that "Buddhist organizations have disbanded and Buddhists have destroyed or hidden family altars while others have withdrawn from church membership."[32] The priest reassured Buddhists that officials from the federal government had promised him "that unreasonable persecution shall never be brought against Buddhism or Buddhists." He exhorted fellow Buddhists "to face the ordeals and sacrifices to the end that these United States of America shall be defended from her enemies. Buddhists! With true faith in the Buddha, let us serve our country, the United States of America, in silence."[33]

As the new BMNA spokesperson, Rev. Kumata signed numerous "bulletins" with titles like "Cooperate in the Defense of the United States of America" and "A United America in Action," which urged fellow Buddhists to publically demonstrate loyalty to the United States. He encouraged everyone to register for civilian defense and to buy US Defense bonds and stamps, arguing that such purchases "give you the highest return on the guarantee of democracy."[34] In response, a letter from the Oakland Buddhist Church described the temple's campaign to encourage members to volunteer at the Red Cross and buy Defense bonds using a portion of the member's regular offerings. They also offered the temple building for any defense-related activity.[35]

A document entitled the "American Buddhist Pledge," urging Buddhists to volunteer for civil defense or the American Red Cross and purchase war bonds, was widely circulated. It cautioned Buddhists to "keep our eyes and ears open AND OUR MOUTHS SHUT," and advocated "reporting anything suspicious or un-American to the nearest FBI or police headquarters."[36]

At an emergency meeting on February 15, 1942, the BMNA voted to change its name to the Buddhist Churches of America (BCA).[37] A "more American" organizational structure was accompanied by a curious alliance with the JACL. Under normal circumstances, the Buddhist headquarters would not have allied itself with the JACL, an emerging and still small organization. The JACL aimed to replace issei community leadership with nisei, and its members tended toward Christianity as a demonstration of Americanism. Given the arrests of many of the issei Buddhist priests and the freeze on its assets as a "Japanese" entity, BMNA wanted to install American-born citizens into the organization's legal structure, and reached out to attorney and JACL president Saburo Kido to ask for advice.[38] The California Young Buddhist League's President Carl Sato further declared that the times demanded an effort to "Americanize Buddhism for its lasting preservation" and that "real, American Buddhism must be born, not necessarily for immediate effect, but on a long-range program."[39]

The numerous expressions of loyalty to America would do little to take the heat off the Japanese American community. For the majority of Americans who presumed national identity to be essentially white and Christian, such public demonstrations were often ignored or dismissed as the duplicitous pronouncements of disloyal aliens.

TIGHTENING THE NOOSE

Voices of support for Japanese Americans were extremely rare. Certain individuals and organizations associated with liberal Christianity spoke up for the need for "fair play," especially toward the American-born nisei. On December 8, 1941, the Seattle Council of Churches and Christian Education issued a remarkable press release urging Christians to distance themselves from discrimination—in particular, employment discrimination—against those of Japanese descent.[40] The First Presbyterian Church in Long Beach extended a welcoming hand to Japanese American Christians from neighboring churches by inviting them to join its Sunday evening service processional march.[41] On December 12, the *Northwest Enterprise,* the widely circulated African American newspaper based in Seattle, advised its readers to avoid a "mob spirit which would have you single them out for slaughter or reprisal" because that mentality "has tracked you through the forest to string you up at some crossroad. The Japanese [in America] are not responsible for this war."[42]

But most white and black Americans favored the public crackdown on the Japanese American community in the name of national security. The stigmatization and marginalization of the Japanese American community was further exacerbated by campaigns by fearful members of other Asian American communities to distance themselves from Japanese Americans. Buttons appeared that read "I am Chinese American." Magazines made awkward attempts to distinguish the two communities with articles such as "How to Tell Japs from the Chinese," published in the December 22, 1941 edition of *Life* magazine. Using stock stereotypes of facial features to "distinguish friendly Chinese from enemy alien Japs," this article purported to protect Chinese Americans from becoming victims of hostility. But of course, these articles encouraged widespread prejudice toward Japanese Americans and rarely condemned violence against them.[43]

Koreans in Los Angeles developed a "certified identification" system, issuing cards and buttons to those presenting proof that they were Korean. In Montana, the C. S. Hahn family, in an interview with a local paper in Target Range, pleaded with the community to understand that the two groups were not of the same "stock" and asserted that the Koreans' hatred for the Japanese "could be traced back for centuries."[44] Indeed, because of anti-Japanese antipathy, dozens of Koreans volunteered to work as interpreters and translators for the INS, Military Intelligence, the War Censorship Office, the Office of Strategic Services, and the Office of War Information. (Many had been forced to learn Japanese during Japan's colonial rule of Korea, which began in 1910.)[45]

Given that Japan had attacked the Philippines at the same time as Pearl Harbor, the Japanese American community faced immense hostility from Filipinos on the west coast and in Hawai'i.[46] As one Japanese American recalled, "The Filipinos sometimes tried to attack us. I always carried a screwdriver with me in case they pulled a knife."[47] On December 23, two Filipinos purportedly stabbed to death a nisei who had just been discharged due to the military's new policy of removing Japanese Americans from US Army units. Two days later, a fifty-five-year-old Japanese garage attendant was killed in Stockton, California, and local Japanese businesses were looted by Filipino gangs. The violence continued through January with shootings of Japanese by Filipinos in California cities including Sacramento, Costa Mesa, and San Jose.[48]

In Salinas, California, where sizable Japanese and Filipino agricultural communities lived side by side, the tensions were palpable. Rev. Fujimura of the Salinas Buddhist Temple recalled the uneasiness on the evening of December 10:

> A Philippine congregation held a meeting at a Christian Church located just in front of our temple. They passed resolutions to not work for Japanese farmers, and to boycott all Japanese stores. The dreary rain added to the eeriness of that night. We continued hearing rumors that in retaliation for the Japanese attack on Manila, a group of Filipinos would set fire to the homes of us Japanese. I carefully made plans for all three of us Buddhist ministers in case a fire started.[49]

Like the Chinese and Koreans, Filipinos were sometimes mistaken for Japanese and so they also began distributing identification buttons.[50] When Rev. Fujimura was arrested and taken to the local jail in Salinas, he observed that everyone in the jail's basement was a prominent leader in the Japanese community, and all were members of the Buddhist temple—with one exception. That was a Filipino who had been picked up from a "cheap boarding house managed by a Japanese named Sensho. He was undoubtedly mistaken for a Japanese because to the police 'they all look alike.'"[51]

The antipathy against the Japanese American community from many quarters, especially against elements that seemed to express religious and cultural difference, such as Buddhism, was widespread and gaining steam. In such an environment, it was not surprising that government officials began placing further restrictions on the entirety of Japanese America. Rev. Daishō Tana, the resident priest of the Nishi Hongwanji Buddhist temple in Lompoc, California, kept a diary of his wartime experiences in the high-security camps run by the Army and the Department of Justice (DOJ), including the DOJ-run camp located in Santa Fe, New Mexico.[52] In it, he wrote about what happened just prior to his arrest:

> At 3 PM, the FBI and three city policemen came to the door to investigate me. I asked them if they intended to arrest me and they said yes. I had to sign off on their search warrant after which they searched the house from the basement to the attic and into the inner recesses of the Buddhist altar room. They asked if I had firearms, radios, or any other items prohibited to enemy aliens to which I replied that I didn't. They went to every extreme to try to locate these items, but having come up with nothing, they ended their search at 5 PM.[53]

Japanese homes were increasingly raided for items that governmental authorities had deemed illegal or "contraband," with or without search warrants. Symbols of belonging to a "foreign" or potentially subversive religion became a liability that could spark hostility from white agents during the raids. Even Buddhist families living far from Hawai'i or the west coast were not spared. Historian Thomas Walls provides an account of a 1942 raid on the farm and home of Torata Akagi and his wife, Beatrice, near Sheldon, Texas:

> While one [FBI] man herded the family and hired help into the living room, four others searched the house—the term "ransacked" would be more accurate, since the contents of drawers and closets were strewn around. In one corner of the house stood a small wooden Buddhist altar called a *butsudan*. . . . During the search one of the men strode towards the corner, and, in obvious contempt, swept the *butsudan* from its pedestal, smashing it on the floor. Later one of the official intruders sneeringly asked Beatrice, the only non-Japanese in the family and the wife of Torata Akagi, whether she wasn't now sorry she had married a "Jap." "No, of course not" was her icy reply.[54]

The FBI took away the family's elderly grandfather, Fukutarō, for internment, although he was returned to the family three months later, after Beatrice and sympathetic white neighbors vigorously campaigned for his release. Officials provided no evidence of any anti-American activity during his hearing.

The searches were accompanied by campaigns to voluntarily hand in "contraband" to local authorities. In Vacaville, California, soon after news of the Pearl Harbor attack, the police chief urged enemy aliens to register and turn in any cameras and guns "to avoid any trouble in the future that might be stirred up by hotheads of either nationality." He reported that fifty guns and twenty cameras were immediately turned in.[55] On December 27, the US Attorney General made registration of cameras, guns, and radios mandatory, requiring all aliens in the seven Western states to turn them in.[56]

Japanese living in rural areas, where guns were commonly used for household protection, lost their means to defend themselves and their property. In Vacaville, California, Japanese had "chickens stolen, gasoline taken, and cars stripped of parts. White men tied up George Nishioka and ransacked his store."[57] While the police chief was unsympathetic, the local newspaper editor voiced support for the Japanese: "The numerous robberies and attacks being committed upon Japanese residents of this and other localities are crimes of the lowest caliber," the paper editorialized. "When tornadoes or earthquakes strike, looters are shot on sight, and in our present encounter with those who are taking advantage of the disarmed Japanese, similar punishment for the perpetrators would be a just reward."[58]

On a daily basis, "enemy aliens" were subject to a nighttime curfew, initiated by a proclamation by US Attorney General Francis Biddle on February 4, 1942, and extended by General John L. DeWitt to include Japanese American citizens on March 24.[59] An active YBA member in Los Angeles, and later ordained priest, Arthur Takemoto, recalled how on the very first day of the 8 PM to 6 AM curfew, he got back home from working the fruit stands a little late: "Two men come to the door, and I was interrogated for two hours for being, 5, 10 minutes late."[60]

The new regulations had negative ripple effects in local economies. When the Treasury Department canceled the licenses of Japanese-owned business such as banks or shipping companies, for example, all their employees lost their jobs. In situations where landlords were noncitizens, the Trading with the Enemy Act meant that tenants could not legally pay rent, and household help could not collect wages. Thus the restrictions devastated many families. When the Treasury Department ordered all issei bank accounts to be frozen, families lost access to savings as well as income.[61] In his memoir, Rev. Fujimura of Salinas recalled the reactions of issei parents. Unable to hide their distress, their "faces turned ashen."[62]

Though the banking restriction was later relaxed to allow issei families to withdraw $100 per month, the financial consequences of frozen accounts, combined with other federal and local restrictions, ruined many. In Oregon, just ten days after Pearl Harbor, the Multnomah County sheriff ordered all persons of Japanese ancestry who lived in Portland and the surrounding area to pay the next year's property tax without delay or face immediate foreclosure.[63] As American citizens, the nisei should have had greater legal protections, but they, too, were targeted by government-sanctioned employment discrimination. In February 1942, the California State Personnel Board barred descendants of enemy aliens from civil service positions. Nisei state employees were forced to take unpaid leave or were dismissed.

For many families, the FBI's targeted arrests of primary bread winners had already produced major hardships. With the addition of the bank assets freeze and employment discrimination, Japanese Americans were plunged seriously into crisis. Little did they know that worse was yet to come.

EXECUTIVE ORDER 9066

In a speech on January 2, 1942, President Roosevelt urged Americans to "Remember the Nazi technique: 'Pit race against race, religion against religion, prejudice against prejudice. Divide and conquer.' We must not let that happen here."[64]

The next month, on February 19, 1942, Roosevelt issued Executive Order 9066, authorizing the mass incarceration of Japanese Americans on the US continent. Under that order, the Army initiated a series of wholesale removals of people on the west coast from their homes. During the spring and summer of that year, it targeted American citizens of Japanese heritage as well as Japanese nationals. This mass incarceration dispensed with the justifications previously proffered by the government for the targeted internment of Buddhist priests, Japanese consular agents, martial arts instructors, and fishermen. There were to be no exceptions.

Prior to Pearl Harbor, there had been discussion of a mass incarceration. In August 1941, as tensions between Japan and the United States rose, Rep. John D. Dingell (D-MI) wrote to President Roosevelt urging him to "cause the forceful detention or imprisonment in a concentration camp of ten thousand alien Japanese in Hawaii . . . It would be well to remind Japan that there are perhaps one hundred fifty thousand additional alien Japanese in the United States who [can] be held in a reprisal reserve."[65] Dingell focused on "alien Japanese" as hostages and potential targets of reprisal to discourage Japan from mistreating Americans in Japan.[66]

The potential for a segment of the Japanese population on the west coast to sabotage critical national security assets was also noted in the "Munson Report," issued in November 1941. Curtis B. Munson, a Chicago businessman working freelance for the White House spy team headed by John Franklin Carter, wrote the twenty-five-page report. Munson's sabotage argument was ultimately used as a justification for the mass removal despite his primary finding that he did not believe the

Japanese "would be any more disloyal than any other group in the United States with whom we went to war."[67]

After the Pearl Harbor attack, plans for a possible mass removal and incarceration were hatched during the latter half of December 1941 within the US Fourth Army and Western Defense Command (WDC), both headquartered in San Francisco and headed by Lt. General John L. DeWitt. The Army's Provost Marshal General, Allen W. Gullion, who for some time had been interested in testing the legal limits of military control over civilians, argued to DeWitt that even though the west coast was outside any zone of actual combat, it could be declared a "theater of operations." This, he proposed, offered a legal pathway for a mass roundup of all Japanese aliens and Japanese American citizens without a declaration of martial law.[68]

At first, DeWitt balked at rounding up citizens. "An American citizen, after all, is an American citizen," he told Gullion on December 26. "And while they all may not be loyal, I think we can weed the disloyal out of the loyal and lock them up if necessary."[69] This view changed in the first weeks of January 1942 after Captain (later Colonel) Karl R. Bendetsen, Guillon's chief of the Alien Division, arrived in San Francisco. Under the influence of Bendetsen, DeWitt became a major advocate for the mass removal of both Japanese aliens and Japanese American citizens from the Pacific coast.[70]

Scholars have extensively chronicled the administrative, legal, and political machinations within the military and civilian government agencies that ultimately led to the US President's issuance of Executive Order 9066.[71] Prior to this order, a series of events in January established the conditions for wholesale removal of "dangerous" persons from areas identified by the military as "sensitive."

First was the January 24 release, just in time for the Sunday papers, of the "Roberts Report" by a committee, chaired by Supreme Court Justice Owen J. Roberts, charged with ascertaining the responsibility for the surprise attack on Pearl Harbor. The media emphasized a small portion of the report that claimed the attack was aided by Japanese residents in Hawai'i.[72] Such anti-Japanese sentiments in the media and pressure from various special interest groups inflamed public opinion and ratcheted up the rhetoric of politicians. Rep. Martin Dies (D-TX), head of the House Committee on Un-American Activities, who had warned of Japanese attacks before the war, contended that within the Japanese American community was a potential fifth column that could aid the Japanese military.[73] The political pressure to do something dramatic grew.

The first official announcement of a group exclusion in the west coast came from the Justice Department on January 29, 1942, and specified a first phase to be enacted between February 15 and February 24. It ordered the total exclusion of enemy aliens from highly sensitive areas around military and defense-related locations (listed in the announcement as Category A zones), and the close monitoring of them in eight other sectors of the Pacific coast (designated Category B zones).[74] This program targeted citizens of enemy countries, not American citizens, and included German and Italian aliens as well as the Japanese who lived in these zones. But while, in the United States as a whole, the German and Italian population was much larger than the Japanese population, this was not the case in these designated areas. Only tiny numbers of Germans and Italians were affected by this measure.[75]

For Gullion, Bendetsen, and eventually DeWitt, this first exclusion effort was far from sufficient. They pressed for a mass removal of all Japanese "native-born or foreign born"—that is, both American citizens and aliens. They pointedly did not advocate the mass removal of German Americans or Italian Americans.[76] To drum up support for the proposed escalation, DeWitt pointed to absurd threats to military and defense installations by saboteurs, and used racial language to conflate Japanese nationals and Japanese American citizens. "The Japanese race is an enemy race," he flatly concluded in his final recommendations, on February 14, 1942, and "potential enemies, of Japanese extraction, are at large today."[77] Just over a year later, he would tell a congressional committee: "It makes no difference whether he is an American citizen, he is still a Japanese. American citizenship does not necessarily determine loyalty."[78]

Numerous politicians, including Mayor Fletcher Bowron of Los Angeles, also urged wholesale action against citizens of Japanese descent. Bowron questioned the loyalty of the nisei and urged mass incarceration to prevent "another Pearl Harbor episode in Southern California."[79]

By February 13, the entire Pacific coast congressional delegation had petitioned the president to effect an "immediate evacuation of all persons of Japanese lineage and all others, aliens and citizens alike, whose presence shall be deemed dangerous or inimical to the defense of the United States" from the west coast states of California, Oregon, Washington, and Alaska.[80]

The press piled on. In early February, the *Los Angeles Times* editorialized, "A viper is nonetheless a viper wherever the egg is hatched—so a Japanese-American, born of Japanese parents—grows up to be a Japanese, not an American."[81] Letters to the White House from private citizens echoed these prejudices. A Seattle woman wrote to the President on January 24, 1942: "Kindly give some thought to ridding our beloved Country of these Japs who hold no love or loyalty to our God, our ideals or traditions, or our Government. They should *never* have been allowed here."[82]

The growing pressure for dramatic action in the first two weeks of February 1942 would overwhelm not only the legal resistance from the attorney general's office, but also resistance on practical grounds from the headquarters of General Mark Clark. An official memorandum from this office argued against a "mass exodus," calculating that the risks for sabotage were not high enough to justify the costs of manpower and diversion of resources from the front.[83] But by February 11, 1942, President Roosevelt had secretly given the go-ahead, based on the framework of "military necessity" that Bendetsen and DeWitt created. He advised the army to do what it deemed necessary with respect to citizens, and indicated that he would issue an executive order to that effect, appending the afterthought: "Be as reasonable as you can."[84] Misinformation, political pressure, and bad counsel, combined with a predisposition to believe and expect the worst of the Japanese, convinced Roosevelt to sign the executive order. Ultimately, the president's long-time view of the Japanese as a racialized group and potential threat caused him to regard them differently from Germans and Italians, for whom he explicitly denied the need for mass incarceration.[85]

Executive Order 9066, signed by Roosevelt on February 19, gave the Secretary of War and his military subordinates authority to designate "military areas" from which they could exclude "any or all persons." The order did not mention Japanese or Japanese Americans specifically, but it was understood that this group, and not German Americans and Italian Americans, would suffer mass incarceration. There also had been no official wording or policy to specifically target Buddhists and Shintoists in the selective incarceration program. But in practice, these groups were seen by intelligence agencies as more dangerous than Christians and were targeted disproportionately after Pearl Harbor. Through legalistic and euphemistic wording of official documents, the government carefully avoided direct targeting of a specific religious group for selective internment, which would be a constitutional violation of freedom of religion.

Similarly, in the case of Executive Order 9066 and mass incarceration, the documents also avoided explicitly targeting a group based on race or national origin. But such legalistic maneuvering failed to disguise a long-held American prejudice that "heathens" like Buddhists and Shintoists, and indeed all "Orientals" of Japanese heritage, including American citizens and Christians, were thought to be un-American, if not anti-American.

Since the executive order did *not* specifically name the Japanese American community, and since even the most ardent advocates for the mass removal had not fully thought through the logistics of such a massive undertaking, the period in late February and early March 1942 was one of great uncertainty for both the government planners and the Japanese American community. For the latter, which had already seen many of its leaders arrested and detained, new shocks arrived. Entire communities were now uprooted, owing to the January 29 order to exclude enemy aliens from the original eighty-six prohibited and restricted zones in California, and similar zones in Oregon and Washington.[86] These included areas next to oil fields, airplane manufacturing plants, munitions factories, and hydroelectric facilities. The wholesale removal of such individuals began immediately and concluded on February 15, while all others who lived in those zones were vacated by February 24.

Japanese and Italian fishermen near militarily sensitive zones in coastal areas were especially hard hit. Not only were they prohibited from fishing, but the US Army and Navy requisitioned their boats and ordered them to leave their homes by the deadline.[87] The order was first enacted on Terminal Island, California, by the US Navy on February 14 when signs were posted declaring that the over three thousand persons of Japanese heritage living on the island, a part of the strategically significant port of Los Angeles, would be evicted from their homes.[88] The February 14 notice stated that all persons of Japanese heritage had to remove themselves from the island by March 14. That order was abruptly shifted on February 25, when new notices went up ordering all Japanese and Japanese American residents to get their affairs in order and remove themselves by midnight two days later. As they prepared their belongings for life away from their homes, and surrendered their hard-won possessions or sold them for pennies on the dollar to predatory merchants, these families experienced a sense of sudden upheaval soon shared by others up and down the coast.

To assist the suddenly homeless community members, Buddhists in Los Angeles sprang into action. The Kōyasan Buddhist Temple assisted the forty members of the Shingon sect living on the island to find shelter.[89] The Nichiren Buddhist Minobusan Betsuin opened up its dining hall for several families belonging to its sect.[90] One of the few white Buddhist priests, Rev. Julius Goldwater, assisted the even larger number of families belonging to the Nishi Hongwanji sect to provide housing for the Terminal Islanders.[91] Every available classroom on the second and third floors of the Los Angeles headquarters temple, and also its basement and hallways, were used to house the dislocated Buddhists and to store their luggage.[92]

The Terminal Island refugees were perhaps most aided by the extraordinary work of the couple who staffed the Terminal Island Baptist Church: Rev. Kichitarō Yamamoto and his white wife, Virginia Swanson, who had served as a missionary in Japan prior to the war.[93] Because of this dynamic couple, Terminal Island, unlike most regions, had a sizeable contingent of both issei and nisei Christians. The Baptist Church Sunday school served as many as four hundred children. During the initial dislocation, the couple focused on the need to quickly store furnishings that could not be sold, and to distribute blankets and other bare essentials to assist those suddenly made homeless.[94]

As a white Christian missionary, Swanson had gained access to government authorities—including the navy office in Los Angeles—and the liberal white church organizations willing to help. She coordinated not only with her own American Baptist denomination for external assistance, but also with the Quakers—formally, the American Friends Service Committee (AFSC)—and with the Presbyterian Mission Board that owned the Forsythe Memorial School in Boyle Heights, where some of the evicted Japanese families were offered shelter. The Baptist Moody Institute approached Rev. Goldwater at the Nishi Hongwanji Buddhist Temple to offer mattresses, pillows, and blankets to cover the temple's third floor, which he received with gratitude.[95] Swanson also surveyed 561 Japanese households on the island to create a detailed chart of each family's situation. She passed this chart on to the AFSC and persuaded Quaker leaders to help find temporary housing for the families. In just forty-eight hours, the three hundred or so families who could not be placed with sympathetic Buddhist and Christian families found shelter at various Nishi Hongwanji Buddhist temples, two Japanese-language schools run by the Baptists that had been closed down because of the war, and rural Japanese-language schools the AFSC had acquired at El Monte, Norwalk, and East Whittier.[96] Once all were housed, Swanson arranged for the Terminal Island issei women and nisei children to meet with their husbands and fathers who had been picked up by the FBI.[97]

As the first group eviction of the Japanese American community was underway, special interest groups ramped up their public pronouncements demanding a mass removal of all Japanese from the west coast.[98] Perhaps more importantly, a series of Congressional hearings in the cities of Los Angeles, San Francisco, Portland, and Seattle were held to ascertain west coast opinions about a forcible mass removal, euphemistically termed a "national defense migration."[99] At these hearings, chaired by Rep. John H. Tolan (D-CA), many witnesses spoke favorably about German and Italian aliens and citizens, but unfavorably about aliens and citizens of Japanese heritage.[100]

An Oregon state senator, Ronald E. Jones, told the committee that "the Buddhist religion is looked on as a national Japanese custom" and "even among the children, there isn't much social mixing between the Buddhist and the Christian children."[101] Still, arguments about religious differences were less common than purely racial ones. One of the most influential people questioned in the Tolan hearings was California's

Attorney General, Earl Warren, on his way to being elected California governor and ultimately to become US Supreme Court chief justice.[102] He testified:

> I am afraid many of our people in other parts of the country are of the opinion that because we have had no sabotage and no fifth column activities in this State since the beginning of the war, that means that none have been planned for us. But I take the view that that is the most ominous sign in our whole situation. It convinces me . . . the fifth column activities that we are to get, are timed just like Pearl Harbor was timed. . . .
>
> We believe that when we are dealing with the Caucasian race we have methods that will test the loyalty of them. . . . But when we deal with the Japanese we are in an entirely different field.[103]

The notion of inscrutable Japanese whose unknowable loyalty threatened national security was repeated so often that the few public officials who opposed the mass removal stood out. Notable among these was Harry P. Cain, the mayor of Tacoma, Washington, who insisted that loyalty should be determined on an individual, not collective, basis. But even Cain cited religion and citizenship as criteria for loyalty: "I think that a man's background . . . has much to do with what he is going to do. If born in this country; if a Christian; if employed side by side with others who fill that same classification, for years; if educated in our schools . . . I should think that person could be construed to be a loyal American citizen."[104]

In the Portland hearings, Azalia Emma Peet, a former Methodist missionary to Japan, was the lone voice of caution. She pointed out to the Tolan Committee that there was no evidence of acts of sabotage or any observable disloyal actions.[105] Progressive Christians like Peet were among the few dissenting voices. Floyd Schmoe of the Quaker-affiliated AFSC offered a pragmatic dissent, warning that any mass removal of Japanese Americans would only play into the propaganda of imperial Japan: "There is no better way in which we could help the Japanese Government," he told the committee, "than to give them cause to make this a 'holy war' of race."[106] Rev. Harold Jensen of Seattle's First Baptist

Church, representing the Seattle Council of Churches, stated that to single out the Japanese was "definite race prejudice."[107] Three Christian leaders who would later become central to the Protestant Commission for Japanese Service—Galen Fisher, Frank Herron Smith, and Gordon Chapman—testified to the loyalty and character of Japanese Americans at the hearings in San Francisco.[108] Smith, a Methodist leader who had been a missionary in Japan, stated: "fully 90 percent of the first-generation Christian aliens are loyal to America." As for the second generation, he continued, "these young Christians are loyal to America almost to a man. I regret I do not know the young Buddhists very well but I am quite confident that in spite of their un-American practices and leadership the great majority of them too are loyal to America."[109]

The Socialist Party, led by Norman Thomas, was a rare organizational voice opposing the mass exclusion in every aspect.[110] Despite these sympathetic voices, the presumption was that America was essentially a Christian nation. Indeed, the voices of dissent were so marginal that even the national American Civil Liberties Union (ACLU), an organization founded solely to fight against exactly this sort of violation of civil rights, chose not to condemn the mass removal on the grounds of military necessity.

DeWitt's broad interpretation led to a number of German and Italian nationals being forced to remove themselves from the Pacific coast. But the Japanese American community became the primary target of the exclusion.[111] Despite DeWitt's threat to put several thousand German and Italian aliens in "relocation centers in a manner similar to that employed in the case of persons of Japanese ancestry," they were not ensnared in a mass incarceration.[112]

A May 4, 1942 Army report from Lt. Col. William A. Boekel to Col. Karl Bendetsen made the Western Defense Command's reasoning explicit:

> In the case of the Japanese, their oriental habits of life, their and our inability to assimilate biologically, and, what is more important, our inability to distinguish the subverters and saboteurs from the rest of the mass made necessary their class evacuation on a horizontal basis. In the case of the Germans and Italians, such mass evacuation is neither necessary nor desirable.[113]

This "class evacuation" included women, children, and even orphans of mixed-race Japanese heritage, all of whom were rounded up as national security threats. The decades-long prejudice against Japanese Americans, combined with the war hysteria whipped up in public hearings and the media, led to a methodical ethnic cleansing of the west coast targeting all persons of Japanese ancestry in the spring of 1942.

THE FORCED "RELOCATION"

The mass removal of persons of Japanese ancestry from Military Area No. 1, declared in early March, was locked in with Congress's passage of Public Law No. 503, which made it a crime to disobey military orders based on Executive Order 9066, and with DeWitt's issuance of Public Proclamation No. 4 on March 27 (effective March 29), which banned citizens or aliens of Japanese heritage from leaving the west coast. The brief window for voluntarily moving east of the restricted zone along the west coast—open from the time of the President's executive order announcement in February until DeWitt's March 27 proclamation—rapidly closed, and the massive project of forced removal was set in motion.

Even those who had successfully made a voluntary move to eastern parts of California were again put in danger a few weeks later when DeWitt extended the ban to eastern portions of the state. In February 1942 the large family of Rev. Taigan Hata, who had been renting an apartment in Oakland, California and heading the Kyūdōkai Mission, voluntarily moved eastward. The family, with all eight children, relocated to a fruit farm run by a Buddhist family in Vacaville, California. But a few months later they, too, became subject to the evacuation order, and were sent first to the Turlock Assembly Center operated by the Wartime Civil Control Administration (WCCA) and later to the Gila River camp in Arizona, run by the War Relocation Authority (WRA).[114]

Some fled farther east. Ultimately, 1,963 were able to escape to Colorado, another 1,519 to Utah, 305 to Idaho, 208 to eastern Washington, and 115 to eastern Oregon. Of those who made the attempt, a number had difficulty buying gasoline along the way. Many were thrown in jail overnight by overzealous sheriffs and, at the Nevada state line, families encountered armed posses determined to turn back anyone of Japanese heritage.[115]

Most went to Colorado. Gov. Ralph L. Carr was one of the few politicians sympathetic to the Japanese American community and welcomed them. Mrs. Hisa Aoki, the wife of Rev. Tokumon Aoki, who had been arrested by the FBI, hoped that she and her children might join a group of seventeen families a lay temple member was organizing to move from Los Angeles to a Colorado farm. She quickly packed her household belongings and sold her Frigidaire refrigerator and recently purchased Maytag washing machine, but couldn't arrange her family's affairs in the few days before the window of opportunity closed. Her March 26 diary entry states, "After Sunday, going to another state will not be allowed. I had no connection with Colorado after all. . . . I am exhausted with remorse and sadness, and my body may soon be reduced to skin and bones."[116] She knew that her husband, who had been taken to the nearby Tuna Canyon Detention Center, was likely going to be transferred to the Santa Fe Internment Camp in New Mexico that day. She wrote: "Tears flowed as I thought of not meeting again until the war was over."[117]

Other religious-based efforts to escape the impending forced removal of the community from the Pacific coast included an idea floated by two Protestant pastors, Methodist Hideo Hashimoto and Presbyterian Keiichi Imai, of developing a large-scale farming cooperative in a deserted eastern part of Fresno County in California. The idea of the project, called the Cooperative Farms, Inc., was that college-educated nisei Christian leaders would lead it; its Christian character would assuage local residents' concerns about a mass influx of Japanese Americans. With its plan to build three farms, a church, school, post office, and co-op stores, the proposal gained the support of some governmental agencies and sympathetic white Christian leaders, including Galen Fisher, who mentioned it during his Tolan Committee testimony. The project, however, was ultimately shelved as impractical.[118]

Father Hugh Lavery and James Caffry of the Maryknoll Japanese Catholic Church of Los Angeles led another experiment in moving to locations east of the restricted zone. This program encouraged Japanese Americans to voluntarily migrate two hundred miles east, to the Owens

Valley Reception Center in the California desert.[119] The Maryknoll order was eager to keep Japanese Catholic families together, and they encouraged them to participate in this voluntary program before being compelled by the Army to leave.[120] The Maryknoll headquarters encouraged Lavery to also "include as many pagans as possible for evacuation plans." Catholics represented a very small segment of the Japanese American community, and including Buddhists would enable the church to scale up the project.[121]

Under the auspices of the WCCA, a newly-formed Army unit, Owens Valley—later transformed into the WRA Manzanar camp—became the first "reception center." Fourteen additional "assembly centers" were hastily set up at racetracks and fairgrounds requisitioned by the US Army. The program in Owens Valley began with eighty-three individuals, including a doctor, cooks, and carpenters, who set out for the center in March.[122] A short film about the Manzanar volunteers, credited to a group called the Nisei Writers and Artists Mobilization for Democracy, was first shown in Los Angeles on April 6, 1942, to an estimated audience of 2,500 at the Kōyasan Buddhist temple hall.[123] Despite such promotion of early voluntary relocation, Father Lavery's project found few volunteers among Buddhists. According to the Catholic priest, "due to the vicious tides of evil rumors, only 816 volunteers responded."[124] Among them was the Catholic convert and World War I veteran Joseph Kurihara, who helped clear brush, dig ditches, and lay foundations for the barracks. But despite a promise from Father Lavery that volunteers would be able to bring their families and relatives to Manzanar, Kurihara's relatives were sent to the WRA camps Poston (in southwestern Arizona) and Rohwer (in southeastern Arkansas). "The Army made fools of us volunteers," he later recalled, "and a liar out of a Catholic priest."[125]

It was not that Buddhist organizations were opposed to cooperating with government and military officials—indeed, the national spokesperson for the largest Buddhist group assured the government that the "Buddhist Churches shall offer its fullest cooperation to the evacuation of enemy-aliens from Prohibited areas."[126] It was unlikely, however, that a large portion of the community could be motivated to cooperation by a white Catholic priest.

Once it became clear that private entities could not possibly move 110,000 persons to regions east of the exclusion zone, the forcible Army roundup began. Data that the Census Bureau had collected on race ("Japanese") in 1940 was used to plan the geographic boundaries for mass removal.[127]

On March 24, 1942, DeWitt issued Civilian Exclusion Order No. 1, ordering all Japanese Americans on Bainbridge Island near Seattle to prepare for removal on March 30. It was the first of 108 exclusion orders he would issue. The 257 Japanese-American residents on Bainbridge had six days to sell or lease their farms, store belongings, organize finances, and pack personal belongings before being shipped to the Owens Valley Reception Center run by the WCCA—with exceptions being made for the severely physically and mentally ill in hospitals and sanatoriums, and criminals in prisons.[128] Starting with the Bainbridge Islanders on March 30 and continuing through June 5, WCCA officials removed all others of Japanese ancestry from Military Area No. 1, which covered the western coastal portions of Washington, Oregon, and California and a southern section of Arizona.[129] Notices to alert the populace, often tacked to telephone poles, directed them to initial registration at one of sixty-four WCCA stations: "All persons of Japanese ancestry, both alien and nonalien, will be evacuated from the above designated area by 12:00 o'clock noon . . ."[130]

Registration and processing stations included both Buddhist temples and Christian churches. In Los Angeles, the Nishi Hongwanji Buddhist Betsuin temple (the current location of the Japanese American National Museum) was designated one such gathering spot. In Berkeley, California, the First Congregational Church served as a place to rest before the uncertain journey ahead. Many were grateful for the friendliness of white church staff, who prepared tea and sandwiches for the displaced people. The church's secretary recalled a day when "a Japanese man came to the office and said, 'Would you mind if I left the church a small donation?' 'Goodness,' I said, 'what we are doing is only a small thing—we'd like to do lots more. But we'd be happier if you would save your donation for some play equipment for the children when you get to camp.' The man smiled and bowed, 'We do appreciate what your church has done,' he said again, adding as an afterthought, 'I'm a Buddhist.'"[131]

FIGURE 3.1 Use of Nishi Hongwanji Temple (Los Angeles, California) as a processing station for those being forcibly transported to assembly centers. Courtesy of
photographer Tōyō Miyatake, M 0001A.

Mrs. Hisa Aoki reported in May 1942 to the processing station at the
Nishi Hongwanji Betsuin, the Los Angeles temple where her husband
Rev. Tokumon Aoki had served. She had to figure out what to do with
her family's possessions once it became clear that the government would
not be protecting them from bargain hunters. The US government had a
program for storing items, but many people lacked confidence their belongings would be protected, a fear that proved well-founded. Most personal effects placed in warehouses by the government—by some accounts,
80 percent of them—were lost or damaged by vandalism or looting.

Mrs. Aoki was able to collect only $75 for their family's piano, auto-
matic gas range, and many furniture items worth hundreds of dollars.
Like many others in her situation, she put other items in storage at the
Buddhist temple.[132] Her March 27, 1942 diary entry described the temple's
preparations:

> Putting bars on windows, making double doors, having a night
> guard, they say they will guard the goods until the war's end. . . .
> The storage fee was calculated based on the war lasting two years
> and totaled $19. If these items worth $1,700–$1,800 are returned
> safely to me at the end of the war, it's cheap. About 70 percent
> of Japantown is shut down, and it is painful, and one feels a lone-
> liness with a sunken feeling.[133]

Ultimately, Mrs. Aoki and her two daughters were not forcibly evacuated until early May, giving her time to store more items at the Higashi
Honganji temple.

The Buddhist temple storage project was broadly advertised in the
Japanese American press. The *Kashu Mainichi*'s March 21, 1942 edition—
the last issue to appear before the newspaper was shut down—featured
a front-page announcement about a Buddhist service that would be held
that day at the Honpa Hongwanji Temple, and added that the temple
was opening its entire building as a "storage-warehouse" for an estimated 2,500 "evacuee trunks." The article touted the safety of the
Buddhist temple, which had arranged for bars on all the windows, theft
insurance, and a night watchman. It noted that the temple "with the aid
of Jane Cleveland, former buying executive at Bullock's Department
Store, [would] sponsor an evacuation auction at which Japanese may dispose of their goods at the least possible overhead expense."[134] To make
room for the massive storage project, the YBA took the lead in removing
the pews from the temple's Hondō (main hall) and cataloguing and providing receipts for all the items that came to be stored at this temple in
Los Angeles.[135]

After missing the opportunity to move to Colorado, Mrs. Aoki sought
to band together with other wives of Buddhist priests who had been
taken away by the FBI. Three families of Buddhist wives without their
husbands registered and relocated together to the horse stables at Santa
Anita Assembly Center, hoping to make the experience less difficult for
their children.[136]

Another group of families from Southern California was disturbed
by news that Manzanar, with its windy and harsh conditions, was not

FIGURE 3.2 Forcible removal from San Pedro, California (April 5, 1942). Photograph by Clem Albers, courtesy National Archives and Records Administration.

ready to receive families with younger children. They contacted one of the few nisei Buddhist priests not yet in custody, Rev. Newton Ishiura, to try to secure an arrangement with the US government to allow these families to remain together and avoid Manzanar. With his help, they persuaded the government to register the entire forty-one-person Buddhist group as the "Hongwanji Family #18390."[137] As they dutifully complied with the government order to register themselves and head to the Santa Anita Assembly Center, this large Buddhist family became part of the nearly 110,000 people (109,427 from the west coast and 151 from the territory of Alaska) who ultimately ended up in the WCCA-run Assembly Centers and WRA-run camps during the spring of 1942.[138]

The authorities permitted only luggage that could be carried. Families debated what would be packed into their suitcases for a destination unknown. Some brought Buddhist scriptures, bells and incense, or their ancestors' memorial tablets, but most families hurriedly packed the essentials of bedding, eating utensils, clothes, irreplaceable photos and memorabilia, and food for the journey. Their Buddhism would need to be moved as faith and memories in their hearts. As with their original dislocation in migrating from Japan, during and after their forced removal to the various incarceration camps, Buddhists drew on their tradition's teachings to re-orient themselves behind barbed wire and write a new chapter in American Buddhist history.

4

CAMP DHARMA

DESPITE BEING TARGETED by government authorities, most Buddhists did not allow fear to diminish their faith behind barbed-wire fences.[1] In the high-security camps run by the US Army and the DOJ, the incarcerated Buddhist priests were predominantly issei men who had migrated from Japan for the explicit purpose of bringing the Buddhist religion to the Americas. These priests' outlook, values, and practices were unlikely to waver. They believed that Buddhism had something to offer the American religious landscape.

Stripped of their freedom and of the outward symbols of their faith, Buddhists drew on whatever was available to sustain their faith and freely practice their religion. Imprisonment became an opportunity to discover freedom—a liberation that the Buddha himself attained only after embarking on a spiritual journey filled with many obstacles and hardships. That journey began when he let go of his comfortable life as a prince in the royal palace of the Shakya clan into which he was born, an acknowledgment that unease and suffering were not only part of being alive, but essential to discovering one's own nature and the world's.

In Buddhism, the practice of delving into the depths of this world so as to transcend it is sometimes symbolized by the image of a beautiful lotus flower emerging out of muddy waters. The lotus flower represents enlightenment and in sculptural traditions is the seat upon which the Buddha is centered. Muddy water represents delusion and greed, or anything that hinders enlightenment and causes suffering. While some traditions of Buddhism center on the need to transcend the muddy water to attain a state of enlightenment, most Japanese Buddhist traditions emphasize that for the lotus flower to exist, the nutrients from the muddy waters are essential. It is a metaphor that emphasizes how the karmic obstacles of this world are interconnected with liberation and enlightenment.

For the interned Buddhist priests, incarceration often served as muddy water. Their American sutra was written not in a realm of purity and formality but in the swamps of Louisiana and deserts of New Mexico. The internment camps became new arenas for deepening religious practice for those whose mission it was to offer valuable Buddhist teachings to America.

At Camp McCoy in Wisconsin, Bishop Kyokujō Kubokawa of the Jōdo sect—the priest who had been arrested in Hawai'i in his Buddhist robes—officiated at the first Buddha birthday ceremony. With these robes, he had arrived in the internment camp as the only priest with the appropriate attire to officiate at such an auspicious occasion. One priest wrote that he had only a single pair of underwear, a pair of pants he'd been unable to wash, and a belt made of rope.[2] To the disheveled men, Bishop Kubokawa delivered his sermon. "Your participation in those filthy clothes can be likened to the Buddha's teaching of the lotus blooming in the mud," he said.[3] In these muddiest of waters, the men found ways to embrace all manner of karmic hindrances to realize the lotus mind of freedom, wisdom, and compassion.[4]

At another Buddha's birthday celebration in Fort Lincoln Internment Camp (North Dakota), Rev. Bunyū Fujimura from the Salinas Buddhist Temple noted how the group managed to improvise without the normal items typically employed on the auspicious day:

> We did not, of course, have a single religious implement to use for Buddhist services. We did not have a *tanjobutsu* [Baby Buddha statue], *butsu-gu* [Buddhist ritual tools], flowers, incense, or any of the implements used in Hanamatsuri [Buddha's birthday] celebration. Fortunately, we were with many people who were clever with their hands. Arthur Yamabe "borrowed" a carrot from the kitchen and carved a splendid image of the Buddha.[5]

The ritual to mark the birth of the religion would normally have involved the ceremonial pouring of sweet tea on a statue of the newborn Buddha. Without such items, the Buddhist priests imaginatively recreated the ritual for themselves collecting rationed sugar from other internees, stirring the sugar into coffee to concoct an American approximation of the traditional sweet tea, and pouring it over the carved-carrot Buddha. Making do was, of course, part of the Buddhist tradition. Throughout Buddhist teachings, there are examples of people using whatever ingredients they could assemble. Consider this, for instance, from a thirteenth-century cooking manual written by Zen Master Dōgen, the founder of Sōtō Zen Buddhism in Japan:

> If you only have wild grasses with which to make a broth, do not disdain them. If you have ingredients for a creamy soup do not be delighted. Where there is no attachment, there can be no aversion. Do not be careless with poor ingredients and do not depend on fine ingredients to do your work for you but work with everything with the same sincerity.[6]

Carrots were available. Rev. Rien Takahashi also used one to carve a Buddha for the founder's birthday ceremony several days later at Camp McCoy (Wisconsin), where many Buddhist priests from the Hawaiian Islands were initially incarcerated. In that camp, run by the Army from March to May 1942, priests surrounded the carrot Buddha with "a cherry blossom flower arrangement" crafted by a Nishi Hongwanji priest using beet-dyed toilet paper, while a Jōdo sect priest officiated the intersectarian birthday ceremony at an altar created by transforming bread wrapping paper and labels from canned goods.[7]

THE DHARMA IN THE HIGH-SECURITY CAMPS

Security was tight on the first transfer ships from Hawai'i to the continent. The head priest of the Jikōen Hongwanji in Honolulu recalled how Japanese detainees were prohibited from using the ship's toilets; if they "wanted to use the toilet, they had to use a barrel or can."[8] Several months later, when Rev. Seikaku Takesono of the Wailuku Hongwanji Mission was transferred, he recalled that, "We were put in the bottom decks of the ships, in the cargo holds . . . it wasn't quite as bad. They let us use the ship's toilets. I volunteered to help clean the toilets that the internees used. They had guards all over the ship; they were watching us from the stairwells and other vantage points. Twice a day, they would let us up on the upper deck to get some fresh air."[9]

Detainees typically spent a few days being processed at Fort McDowell on Angel Island before moving east towards the internment camps. After one long journey with little physical movement, Rev. Suijō Kabashima, Buddhist priest and judo instructor, led a group exercise on the island. His loud commands alarmed the American soldiers in the barracks over the next hill, who rushed to quash what they thought was a protest of some kind. They walked away amused after realizing that the Japanese detainees were only doing calisthenics.[10]

The Buddhist priests from both Hawai'i and the west coast then headed eastward to a series of internment camps operated by the US Army and INS, where they encountered Germans and Italian detainees. The earliest of these internment camps had been established prior to Pearl Harbor and the declaration of war, and used to detain German and Italian seamen after several incidents when they had sabotaged their merchant ships as retaliation for US support of the European nations allied against fascism.[11]

The first of the high-security camps was set up just south of Bismarck, North Dakota, at Fort Lincoln and began accepting internees on May 31, 1941, when the German seamen were transferred there. The Italians were moved to a second large facility opened at Fort Missoula in Montana.[12] These two facilities could accommodate up to two thousand Axis seamen and resident enemy aliens if necessary.[13] They marked the beginning of the World War II internment program, in which persons deemed threats would be detained in remote locations, often for the duration of the war. These camps were often under the jurisdiction of the US Army since the "alien enemies" were initially considered civilian prisoners of war, although they would later be referred to simply as "detainees."[14] A year later, the War Department began to shift responsibility for detainees to the DOJ, which meant that these "alien enemies" were frequently transferred between temporary and more long-term detention areas, variously administered by the Army and the DOJ's INS.[15]

Many of the Japanese residing in the continental US and arrested right after Pearl Harbor were also taken to Fort Lincoln and Fort Missoula from temporary detention centers close to where they had been arrested. In Southern California, several Buddhist priests were initially put in the Tuna Canyon Detention Station, located on the site of a former Civilian Conservation Corps (CCC) camp in Tujunga, near Los Angeles. The DOJ took it over on the day of the Pearl Harbor attack and operated it as a temporary holding camp there until October 1943. Roughly 1,700 Japanese detainees and hundreds of Germans and Italians cycled through the camp.[16] One of the Japanese was Rev. Tokumon Aoki of the Los Angeles Nishi Hongwanji Temple. His wife, Hisa Aoki, described his arrest:

> [January 5, 1942]—They finally came. It's the FBI—one glance, and I knew! I politely invited them into the waiting room . . . We had heard . . . that one hundred forty [Christian] missionary families that had spent many years in Japan had returned to the United States as soon as relations became strained, and the majority of them are now working as FBI agents.[17] . . . [Our daughter] Yoko was calmly standing behind us, but [our younger daughter] Sachiko was in the corner of the room and from time to time looking up with terrified eyes . . . shivering like a little bird being glared at by a hawk.
>
> [March 13] Ah, the fateful day has finally arrived. Today my husband was arrested. . . . [He said just before the FBI arrived] "All of the Nishi Hongwanji ministers, with the exception of Revs. Mori and Ishiura, have been taken. With Zenshūji [Zen temple], with the exception of Supervisor Ochi, even Mrs. Suzuki has been taken.[18]

Buddhist priests were not as urgently apprehended on the US continent as in the Hawaiian Islands.[19] Buddhist priests like Rev. Aoki who did not hold high-ranking positions were not prioritized. His arrest came more than two months after the initial FBI home visit in January. And even then, Rev. Aoki was picked up on March 13 primarily because his name appeared on a list of Japanese-language school teachers, 249 of whom were taken that day in an FBI sweep of Los Angeles and several Southern California counties.[20]

Rev. Aoki was allowed visitors at Tuna Canyon two days after his arrest. He had prepared a page-long list of items such as underwear, slippers, eyeglasses, and belts that he hoped his family could secure for him before he got transferred to a more permanent, high-security facility. His wife's diary entry from that day noted that he also asked her "to send Zen Master Hakuin's two books, *Yasenkanna* and *Orategama*." Hisa described how, during the visit, her husband "held the fingertips that the children had extended through the opening in the wire mesh. . . . They say visitations are limited to three minutes, but they didn't put on a time limit and we talked without pause for about seven minutes."[21]

When they returned home, she and her two daughters gathered in front of their home Buddhist altar and chanted verses from the *Shōshinge*, a sacred text in their sect of Buddhism. She wrote in her diary that day:

> Only when praising the virtues of the Buddha am I able to forget the pain in my soul and feel the pleasure of peacefulness. My husband and I are Japanese, and therefore thoroughly enemy nationals, twelve-year-old Yoko and ten-year-old Sachiko are American citizens who are recipients of the blood of the enemy; and Tokuhisa and Kazuo who are studying in Tokyo at Shiba Middle School, because they have US citizenship and in Japan, in the opposite way, will be treated as the enemy and must be undergoing hardship.[22]

Three days later, the implications of her husband's detention at Tuna Canyon seem to have sunk in deeper. "The sad darkness that lies ahead only continues to increase," she wrote. "It has become as if the figure of Amida [Buddha] wrapped in bright lights is nowhere to be seen."[23]

Rev. Daishō Tana, who would later reflect on his move from California to a camp in New Mexico by recalling the prophesy about the eastward transmission of Buddhism, was taken into custody during the same operation that captured Rev. Aoki.[24] He had served as an instructor at the Japanese-language school affiliated with his Buddhist temple in Lompoc. Sent to Tuna Canyon, Tana chronicled his thirteen-day detention there:

> March 15—Woke up at 6 AM. At 6:45 AM, guard inspection, 7 AM, breakfast and room cleaning, 11:45 AM, guard inspection. At noon, lunch, 4:15 PM, guard inspection, 5 PM, dinner, 8:30 PM guard inspection, and 10 PM, lights out. Living in this collective and ordered environment made me think of regimented military life. We had to stay 10 feet away from the barbed-wire fence. Being cut off from the outside is the most painful thing about being in camp.
>
> March 16—[When the detainees first were first brought here], some were forced to change clothes, with photos of them taken from the front and back. Others had their fingerprints taken. And some had their private parts examined. Everyone felt as if they were being treated just like criminals.
>
> March 23—Because of our robes, we Buddhist priests are usually isolated from larger society, but being put in a place like this, we are just regular human beings who experience suffering just like everyone else. Indeed, without this kind of experience we priests should not talk to others about the purpose of life.[25]

During his confinement, Rev. Tana often reflected on the fundamental teaching of the Buddha (sometimes called the "First Noble Truth") that, no matter one's status in society, life necessarily involves suffering. In the teachings, the purpose of a Buddhist life is to discover various forms of liberation from this existential condition. Tana felt that incarceration provided an excellent opportunity for religious leaders to deeply experience isolation and humiliation. It would help Buddhist priests preach to others about the path if they could speak about the nature of suffering from a less rarified position in society.

After a brief period to allow detainees' families to gather clothes or other necessities, the trains to high-security camps began departing. On the four-day trip from Los Angeles to Fort Missoula in Montana, the Japanese were prohibited from speaking to each other and told they would be shot if they lifted the blinds. On the second day of the trip, one man tried to commit suicide by biting off his tongue. Rev. Seytsū Taka-hashi was among those who helped the man. In pitch darkness he found a toothbrush for him to bite down on for the pain and applied a towel to stop the bleeding.[26]

According to Rev. Bunyū Fujimura, armed soldiers on one of the trains kept "the toilet door [open], not to cause us embarrassment, but because our guards were afraid we might commit suicide."[27] He noted:

> In feudal Japan, criminals were transferred from one place to another in what are called *to-marukago*. These are palanquins completely covered over by a bamboo cage, so the criminal had no chance of escaping. I could not help comparing the trains taking us to our unknown destination with *to-marukago*. The windows of the train were covered with iron bars, and the shades were completely drawn at all times.[28]

In an effort to lighten the mood, one priest made everyone laugh by inventing a game in which he improvised comical explanations for why each of them was arrested." He joked that one Bishop, who was known for his love of moxibustion treatments for his health, had been arrested not because of his religious faith or menace to public security, but because he was "a fire hazard."[29]

Describing the arrival of 415 Japanese at Fort Lincoln, North Dakota, on February 9, 1942, the *Bismarck Tribune* reported that "the little yellow men scrambled out of the coaches twenty-five at a time, were put in guarded trucks, and rushed out to the internment camp."[30] With the arrival of a second group of 715 Japanese detainees, two weeks later, the Japanese constituted the majority of the camp's population. Clear demarcations separating the Japanese from the Germans were set up, with a ten-foot lane between the barbed-wire fences of the two compounds.[31]

In that same month at Fort Lincoln, one of the interned Japanese died of a heart attack. In a display of grief rare among Japanese men, his fellow internees "wept openly" at the funeral. Camp rules permitted only two persons to accompany the body out of the barbed-wire compound to Bismarck's crematorium. Rev. Issei Matsuura, of the Guadalupe Buddhist Temple, volunteered to go. The town's mortician later recalled his reaction to hearing the priest recite Buddhist sutras at the crematorium: "What religion is this? This was my first Japanese funeral." Responding to the mortician's curiosity, Rev. Matsuura soon became engrossed in a conversation with him and an armed guard about salvation in Buddhist teachings, and the teaching that beings, including prisoners and guards, were all ultimately Buddhas. The men shook hands at the edge of the barbed-wire fence and expressed hope that they might meet again. Such moments were rare, and they stood out for Buddhists in their difficult circumstances.[32]

Conditions for the Japanese at Fort Missoula were similar to those at Fort Lincoln.[33] At Fort Missoula, the internees began referring to their quarters as Rokushūkan (Six States Hall) after learning that internees from six different US states were assembled there. The rule dictating lights out at 9 PM was strictly enforced, and every night brought a 2 AM check and count of inmates. Making the harsh winter worse, the coal used for heating burned poorly and caused nearly everyone in the fifty-person barracks to suffer repeated coughing fits. One priest noted the new sense of appreciation these community leaders gained for their wives, as many of them found themselves washing clothes for the first time.[34] This was surely less rarified than the life to which they had been accustomed. By experiencing the routines and travails of life in the camps, Buddhist priests were plunged into the muddiness from which a lotus flower would emerge.

After Forts Lincoln and Missoula, the Japanese were eventually sent to five of the other six DOJ / INS run internment camps such as those in Santa Fe and Lordsburg, New Mexico.[35] On one of the many transfers between camps, on July 27, 1942, 148 Japanese were moved from Fort Lincoln to the Lordsburg Internment Camp in New Mexico. After disembarking at the Ulmoris Siding train station, the men were marched two miles through the desert to the camp. Two of the elderly men, Toshiro Kobata and Hirota Isomura, were in poor health and could not keep up with the main group. Along the road to the camp, Private First Class Clarence A. Burleson shot and killed them. According to the official government inquiry that followed, Burleson shot them because they had made a "break and started running" towards the reservation boundary.[36] The other internees strongly doubted that account. Kobata had been quite frail due to long-term tuberculosis, and Isomura had suffered a spinal injury that made it difficult for him to walk, let alone run. The Army refused to allow Japanese doctors in the group to perform autopsies.

The authorities also refused to allow a Buddhist funeral for the two men. In protest, the Buddhists in the camp refused orders to assemble at 4 PM the day after the shooting, stating that they would "pay their respects in their own barracks."[37] After the Japanese complained to the Spanish consul, who was an international monitor charged with overseeing the treatment of Japanese internees, the Army permitted a small funeral, limited to forty people, three weeks later.[38]

Among those who planned the belated funeral were seven Buddhist priests.[39] Rev. Tana, in his diary entry from the day, wrote about the service:

> For flowers, we collected the artificial flowers that people all over the camp had made. Here in the middle of the desert, there are no live flowers except sagebrush. So, we took the wonderfully-colored paper flowers, incense, and candles to offer to the two deceased men who have no proper gravestone. Given that we were able to gather in front of their corpses, it would be a shame not to perform a funeral service on behalf of the entire camp. We let everyone know about our funeral plans and we recited the *Shōshinge*. It was literally a funeral in the midst of the wild.[40]

Priests continued their Buddhist practice by making do in a variety of ways. The Sōtō Zen priest Kōetsu Morita, from Hawai'i's Waiahole Tōmonji Temple, maintained a regular Zen meditation practice from 5 AM to 6 AM, and from 9 PM to 10 PM—just before the military's morning wake-up call and just after lights were ordered out. He used his prison-issued blanket as a *zafu* (meditation cushion), while he meditated and chanted sutras silently. Even some of the younger and not particularly religious men noticed this and one of them offered to make a statue. Rev. Morita recalled that one of them "went to the boiler room, carrying the steel pieces which he had picked up at the dump. There he forged those pieces into five or six chisels. At the time, I doubted a mere mason could carve a statue of a Buddha. Not long after, he brought over a piece of wood and began to carve steadily in the center of the barrack. In a few days, it began to take the shape of a standing Buddha with a halo." The statue ended up as a beautiful, eleven-headed Kannon bodhisattva. Morita was so pleased that he invited the eight Sōtō Zen priests in the camp to hold a dedication ceremony for the new statue. He wanted to involve the younger men and thank them for their efforts, so he "purchased 30 bottles of beer at 10 cents apiece, which made the young men very happy. They were also moved by the chanting of sutras, which they had not heard in many years since leaving Japan."[41]

Rev. Seytsū Takahashi, who was interned at Camp Livingston, adapted his Buddhist practices of meditation and sutra copying to the camp in the swamps of Louisiana. In a letter he sent to the caretaker of his temple in Los Angeles, Takahashi noted his sense of connection to others in Buddhist history who had transmitted the religion while overcoming various obstacles. He wrote:

> I have thought that this lengthy internment life has been pro-vided to me by Heaven and the Buddhas as an opportunity for years or months of Buddhist practice. I return to the quiet and supreme life of walking alongside Kōbō Daishi. As if trying to practice meditation under the moonlit pine, I have been viewing the guard's searchlights as the Buddha's sacred light and have been practicing Kōmyō meditation together with [Kōbō Daishi]. Making the heart-moon [mind-enlightenment] appear, longing after the form of Shakyamuni Buddha, and copying sutras each day has brought delight in the deep Dharmic teachings, which is happiness beyond measure. Further, I have come to appreciate the extreme efforts of those who brought the Buddha Dharma from India to China, and from China to Japan. I am indebted to the connection I had to the place where our founder practiced in Tosa Domain's Murotosaki and I vow as my own practice because of this karmic connection, to recite the Buddha's and bodhisattvas's mantra 2 million times. I wish only to live in this great vow. I believe it is possible to achieve world peace through this practice that benefits oneself as well as others. Further, I pray

for the safety and peace of mind and long life of all of the Daishi (Shingon) followers living here in America.[42]

Takahashi also recorded in his memoir how he used the extreme heat of the Louisiana summer to immerse himself more deeply in Buddhism, especially in classic teachings about employing karmic hindrances to attain liberation. In his first attempts at the traditional practice of *shakyō* (Buddhist sutra copying), he had found the task impossible. The swampy heat inside the barracks caused his sweat to drip onto the paper as he tried to copy Buddhist scriptures using the traditional calligraphic style. Using a handkerchief to lock his elbows into a position that prevented the sweat from dropping onto the paper, Takahashi managed to perfect the writing of the sacred script despite the awkward posture.[43]

The copying of a Buddhist sutra in swampy Louisiana was yet another example of Buddhists practicing their faith in a moment of dislocation. In the movement of the Buddhist tradition from one cultural environment to another, this act of reiterating the teachings of the Buddha, however hostile the situation, was a way to maintain one's traditions and simultaneously to inscribe one's faith onto a new landscape.

The Buddhist priests in the high-security camps made do with whatever was available, both within themselves and outside of themselves, to sustain the hope of liberation while dealing with the uncertain futures of their families and communities. Their improvised American sutra would go on to be replicated across the west coast by lay Buddhists as Japanese Americans found themselves increasingly caught up in mass dislocation and incarceration.

5

SANGHA BEHIND BARBED WIRE

As soon as Hisa Aoki arrived with her two children at Santa Anita Assembly Center, she rushed to the inspection area to ensure that all her luggage came through. She had managed to join an extended "family" composed of several other families of detained Buddhist priests of various sects. That day, she wrote in her diary about standing in front of her new home—Seventh Avenue, Barrack 57, Quarters No. 7:

> We were riveted to the spot! In all probability, we had been assigned to the dirtiest stable in Santa Anita. Furthermore, right in front, there was a street lined with latrines. It is so dirty, so smelly; there is nothing to compare to this I feel faint, and the smell of horse manure makes me want to throw up. . . . I must make an effort to sleep. Unless I do, I will get sick. I cannot fall ill at this time. In the darkness, I held my palms together in prayer and silently intoned Buddhist sutras from memory.[1]

Santa Anita Assembly Center, a converted racetrack in Arcadia, California, surrounded by barbed wire, would eventually house 18,500 Japanese and Japanese Americans. The US Army and its Wartime Civil Control Administration (WCCA) coordinated the waves of movement from each of the 108 zones to the euphemistically named "assembly centers" and "reception centers."

FIGURE 5.1 Arriving at the assembly center in Santa Anita, California.   Photograph by Clem Albers, courtesy National Archives and Records Administration.

The military police of the Fourth Army oversaw the removal. The people being escorted to WCCA centers generally considered them courteous, as were the civilian staff and the nisei volunteers who had gone ahead to help prepare the temporary detention locations. The Santa Anita and Tanforan assembly centers were former race tracks. The Fresno, Merced, Pomona, Puyallup, Salinas, Stockton, Tulare, and Turlock assembly centers were fairgrounds. Mayer was a former Civilian Conservation Corps camp; Marysville and Sacramento were former migrant worker camps; Pinedale was a former lumberyard; and Portland was a former livestock grounds. Only the Owens Valley Reception Center (subsequently known as the Manzanar War Relocation Center) was built from the ground up.

The construction of these temporary facilities was rushed. At the Puyallup Assembly Center in Washington, the Tacoma Building Trades and US Employment Service recruited over one thousand men and, staggering their eight-hour shifts, kept work going around the clock. In one week, they converted the former fairgrounds into facilities to house eight

FIGURE 5.2 The assembly center at Puyallup, Washington.   Courtesy of Museum of History and Industry, *Seattle Post-Intelligencer* Collection, 1986.5.6680.1.

thousand people, with two watchtowers for armed guards and three separate areas that each had a mess hall, latrines, showers, and laundry facilities.[2] One of the volunteers' many jobs was to help the new arrivals make their own beds by stuffing mattress covers with straw.

HORSE STABLE BUDDHISM

En route to the Turlock Assembly Center, in 1942, Rev. Gibun Kimura of the Vacaville Buddhist Temple would write:

> Our family number is 6428 [and we are told to] board the number three train. Both my wife and I wear a tag with this number on it. We feel the same as baggage.... We arrive at the Turlock Station about 2:00. It is still some two miles to the evacuation center so we are grouped in columns of three and marched by a military policeman....

The citizens of Turlock who live on either side of the street stare at us curiously as we walk by. Among them are boys lying on their stomachs and with their chins cupped in their hands. It occurs to me that prisoners of war are paraded in front of the populace like this. . . . [Once at Turlock] our block was a former horse stable with partitions and asphalt for the floor.[3]

In the former stables at Tanforan, the hastily built barracks smelled of dung and were infested with fleas left by the animals. Garter snakes came through cracks in the flooring.[4] Families did their best to make the crude facilities more hospitable. They crafted furniture, used bedsheets brought from home as curtains for privacy, and did their best to decorate the horse stables or barracks. When scrap wood from the ongoing construction of the Centers proved inadequate for making furnishings, residents took lumber from the main woodpiles. One Buddhist priest's wife said that, in her first few weeks in Santa Anita, the noise from people taking lumber from the construction site near her smelly horse stall kept her up all night, especially when the searchlight used by guards to prevent theft shone through the windows of her barrack.[5]

The mess halls offered mass-produced and sometimes stomach-turning meals, and the latrines and showers offered no privacy. The wife of one Buddhist priest (held elsewhere) said of the Tulare Assembly Center: "The showers were just heads jutting out of the walls with no partitions. Delicate and modest ladies waited to take their showers until the wee hours when no one was around."[6] At Santa Anita, numerous women were admitted to the Center's medical facility after developing bowel disorders by avoiding the latrines. Residents themselves finally installed temporary partitions for modest Japanese women.

Hisa Aoki continued her diary entries with a sense of despair. In a June 1942 entry, she wrote:

I have no hope. Husband won't be returning home until the war is over. . . . how long will we be forced to live like this? We have no rights; our freedom is strictly limited; and if we are only going to be fed, it is the same as a dog or a horse. On top of that, presently, thousands have been thrown into unsanitary horse stalls and forced to live there. I wonder if Japan has confined American noncombatants in horse stalls [with] women forced to use toilets with no doors and making people work for eight hours a day at monthly wages of $8, $12, $16, and $18. I want to know.[8]

Her frustrations spilled over several weeks later, when the improperly built latrine system broke down. "Surely they wouldn't have something as dangerous as exposing people to falling into a large pit of human waste." Three days later, she describes her experience of using the latrines in the morning:

> From the hole used to pump out waste, sewage is pouring out, pouring out! On to the road, under the barracks, to any low area, flows this stinky river of human waste. . . . I don't care if I am sent to Japan with only what I am wearing. I want to get out of this insulting, humiliating, melancholy, uncertain life without purpose. . . . if I am allowed to set foot in my homeland, with a feeling of humility, I will start anew from the beginning.[9]

Journal entry

Aoki found comfort from the writings of the medieval Buddhist priest Nichiren and the sounds of "sutra gongs" from a nearby barrack in the early morning.[10] In her diary entry from July 28, she acknowledges contemplating suicide, but writes, "I must not give up. That would be against the will of Buddha. As long as I was given the difficult birth as a human being, to use my own hands to extinguish my life would be a major sin and would require me to carry that infinite sin with me down the yellow path. Although it has slightly dimmed, the protective light which is provided by Kannon [the bodhisattva of compassion] now provides some little support for me."[11]

Others drew hope from both Buddhism and the American promise of liberty. After cleaning and decorating their former stall at the Portland Livestock Pavilion, the Portland Buddhist Temple priest Rev. Tansai Terakawa and his family hung an American flag. Looking at the photo below, one would hardly know that a few weeks earlier, their living space

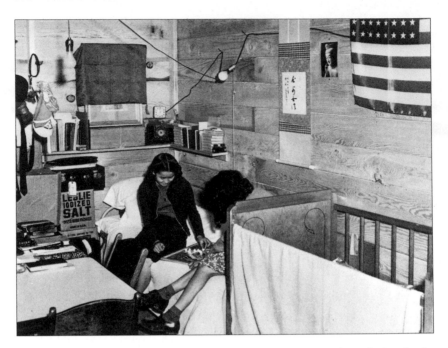

FIGURE 5.3 American flag and Buddha photo displayed in barracks at the Portland Livestock Exposition Building. Shown are Rev. Tansai Terakawa's daughter Hiroko and friend Lilian Hayashi (May 31, 1942).   Courtesy of the *Oregon Journal* Collection, Oregon Historical Society, ORHI-28163.

had been dirty and unfurnished, and smelled of horse manure. Rev. Terakawa would die from kidney failure several months later, but in this photograph one can see Hiroko, his smiling daughter, with a friend in the foreground, and the American flag, a scroll of Japanese calligraphy, and a photo of a Buddha statue hanging on their wall.

The WCCA barely tolerated the practice of Buddhism, and banned groups associated with state Shinto completely, despite its official policy pledging "regardless of sect or denomination, race or creed . . . to tolerate no discrimination against any religious denomination which the Japanese constituency or group within the Center have requested."[12] Assembly Center staff were instructed by the WCCA to monitor religious activities to ensure they were not used to "propagandize or incite the members of the center."[13] Center managers also insisted that camp newsletters include only stories that had been thoroughly vetted. Some managers, worried about the potentially subversive power of Buddhism or Shinto, focused on "screening items announcing upcoming religious services."[14] According to Section 25 of the WCCA Operations Manual, the Japanese language was also banned in the assembly centers, with the exception of dictionaries and Japanese-language Bibles and hymnals, checked by the authorities.[15] *language bans*

Christian sacred books and worship texts thus remained in a protected category. Not only was there a ban on Japanese-language written materials, but spoken Japanese was prohibited in the assembly centers for any gatherings without prior approval and monitoring by a center's administration. This was a particular burden for issei and many kibei, for whom Japanese was their first and sometimes only language.[16] No religious service with a Japanese component could be conducted freely because of the administrators' fear of subversion.

Hisa Aoki became upset when a notice was circulated in English on July 10, 1942: "All printed matter in Japanese (except the Bible, hymn books, English-Japanese dictionary) are to be turned in to the administrative office by 11:00 AM tomorrow. When moved to long-term inland locations, they will be returned." She was furious at being forced to hand in fifty-six books, many of them Buddhist texts. "Really, do white Americans think all they have to do is confiscate written matter, and the Japanese will completely forget how to read Japanese or completely obliterate the contents of what was written?" she wrote in her diary. "How can you eliminate in one swoop what for many decades had been absorbed into your blood, your flesh, your marrow? I want to shout at them in a loud voice—only if you turn the Japanese into ashes can you do that!"[17]

These policies, which stood in stark contrast to the DOJ and Army-run camps holding the Buddhist priests, help explain the initial hesitation many Buddhists felt in overtly practicing their faith. An early survey titled "A Preliminary Report of Japanese Evacuees at Santa Anita Assembly Center" noted that although a great diversity of religious practices existed—including Catholics, Federated Protestants, Episcopalians, Seventh Day Adventists, and Holiness Church among the Christians, as well as several sects of Buddhists (Jōdo Shinshū, Shingon, Jōdo, Nichiren, and Zen)—attendance was lower at Buddhist public worship services

Downplay of buddhism

than at Protestant gatherings.[18] The report observed, "Many Buddhists now residing at the center hesitate to attend services for fear of FBI agents investigating them. . . . [M]embership in Buddhist organizations dropped markedly at the outbreak of the war because most of the members felt that Buddhism was an Oriental religion and that they would probably receive kindlier treatment from Caucasians if they embraced Christianity, an 'American' religion."[19]

A Presbyterian Christian minister at Santa Anita recollected that after the war started, "Buddhists were prohibited to practice [at Santa Anita] because [they] had more [Japanese] nationalistic tendencies. . . . There were no Buddhist services."[20] He was mistaken. While some Christians, both in the administration and in the Japanese American community, exerted subtle pressures against Buddhism or Shinto, there was no official prohibition on Buddhist gatherings in the assembly centers. Indeed, once the initial hesitation wore off, on any given Sunday at Santa Anita, many services were conducted by three Japanese Buddhist priests and the visiting white Buddhist priest, Rev. Julius Goldwater, with thousands in attendance.[21]

As a counterpoint to the Presbyterian minister's recollections, an Episcopalian minister, who served as president of the Santa Anita Federated Protestants, commented in the camp newspaper, the *Pacemaker,* on October 7, 1942, that by sharing the same barracks for religious activities, "Christians and Buddhists have had very good cooperation and understanding in furthering their respective missions and in keeping the morale of the Center life high."[22] At another assembly center in Pinedale, a single barrack was used on Sundays by issei Christians at 9 AM, nisei Christians at 10:30 AM, and Buddhists in the afternoon.[23]

A small but vocal segment of the Japanese American community did hold that public displays of Buddhist faith were inappropriate at a time when the community's loyalty to America was under scrutiny. During his time in the Tanforan Assembly Center, Charles Kikuchi—a Japanese American researcher for the UC Berkeley Japanese American Evacuation and Resettlement Study (JERS) project begun in 1942—wrote an entry about Obon, the major summer ritual held by Buddhists to honor the ancestors. Since the west coast Japanese Americans had moved to these temporary camps in late spring, the summer ceremony was the first major public gathering centered around Buddhism:

> Alex came in this morning and wanted a big write-up [in the camp newsletter] on the Bon [Obon] Odori festival which the Buddhist group is putting on. It is a folk dance and has some connection with the Buddhist religion. We got into a very heated argument when Taro and I said that this was worthy of burial in the most insignificant page. . . . I told [Alex] that the Buddhists should stress Americanism more since the group has been looked upon so suspiciously. Alex contended that the festival was necessary for camp morale. This is a lot of hooey; it is only evidence for the Caucasian public to believe that we cling to Japan and don't want to Americanize, unfair as that may be.[24]

Even prior to the Obon ceremony, Kikuchi had logged a report where one gets an impression that he felt kibei and nisei Buddhists were holding back the true Americanization of the community:

> Got up late this morning and so went to take a shower clad only in my bathrobe and slippers. Had to push through a crowd of Buddhists going to church. They all looked at me so shocked at my lack of dignity. Tonight I went to their dance with a bunch and had to face some of those I saw this morning, but they did not say anything. Met the cutest girl from San Mateo, but have already forgotten her name. About 400 Nisei were present. The Buddhists are a more conservative group of Nisei. Not many outstanding leaders among them except Tad Hirota. Many of them don't even know how to dance so that they announced a special dancing class for their members. A lot of Kibeis are in the group, and even the Nisei Buddhists speak more Japanese than other Nisei groups.[25]

This version of becoming American—through a process of eliminating all traces of Japanese heritage, language, and religion—had been anticipated by Mike Masaoka, the national secretary of the Japanese American Citizens' League (JACL) and a Mormon. In April, just prior to the mass removal to the WCCA camps, he endorsed Assistant Secretary of War John McCloy's idea of treating the incarcerated Japanese Americans as guinea pigs for democratization and Americanization. Masaoka made the case that his organization could work with the War Relocation Authority (WRA) to transform its camps into indoctrination centers promoting "better Americans in a greater America," and help eliminate "those mannerisms and thoughts which mark us apart."[26] Likewise, adherents of the prewar "Americanization as Christianization" movements in Hawai'i and some leaders of the Japanese American Christian movement argued that national belonging necessitated adherence to Christianity. To Masaoka's credit, he believed in the general value of religion and urged authorities to permit the practices of "the most misunderstood of our groups"—those of the "Buddhist faith"—to prevent interfaith conflict. But he also recommended that Buddhist religious activities be confined to "worship only" and exclude any "other sphere of activity," and an absolute ban on Japanese-language schools.[27]

Some Buddhists did convert to Christianity or at least downplay public displays of their faith. Yet, after several months behind barbed wire at the assembly centers—and certainly by the fall, when they had been transferred to the WRA camps—many Buddhists had pushed back. They argued that their religion was not only compatible with life in America, but that the religious freedom enshrined in the Constitution would be undermined if they succumbed to pressures to become Christian.

Efforts to write a new chapter of American Buddhism—from the horse stalls and livestock pavilions—were led by a small contingent of issei Buddhist priests who hadn't been interned at the Army and DOJ camps, wives of issei priests, a handful of nisei Buddhist priests, and several white Buddhist priests. They provided a framework for people to understand their dislocation and to develop confidence that Buddhism was not a hindrance to belonging to an American community.

At the Pomona Assembly Center, four Higashi Honganji Buddhist priests from the Los Angeles temple provided leadership. One of them, although he had been forbidden by government officials to take his

FIGURE 5.4 Buddhist study group at the Fresno assembly center, 1942 (US Army Signal Corps).   Courtesy of San Jose State University Special Collections & Archives, Flaherty (John M.) Collection of Japanese Internment Records, fla_album_102.

Buddhist and Japanese-language books along when he was relocated, defied the order.[28] According to his son, the priest "foresaw the need of them to serve his sangha" and so he took not only these books but also a portable mimeograph machine. Once at the Pomona Assembly Center, he used the machine to print temple notices and a periodic Buddhist newsletter. Ironically, the Pomona Assembly Center's administration borrowed his mimeograph machine to publish its own camp notices until it could acquire printing equipment. In the Stockton Assembly Center, two issei priests led Buddhist activities, including the camp's Sunday school, which soon grew to seven hundred students.[29] In the Santa Anita Assembly Center, the priest and poet Nyogen Senzaki viewed the incarceration experience as the unfolding of a Buddhist scripture. He wrote an open letter to American Buddhists emphasizing the importance of continuing to pay attention to a way of life infused with the

Dharma, even behind barbed wire: "Buddhists should consider that to guard virtues is like defending a fort or a port. If we help America to have few liars, cheaters, and gold-demons, that alone will be something good to her. So you see, fellow students, war or no war, the study of Buddhism must be continued."[30]

The Hawai'i -born nisei Buddhist priest, Rev. Kanmo Imamura of the Guadalupe Buddhist Temple, mobilized the sangha in the Tulare Assembly Center. As the only Buddhist priest at Tulare in early 1942, he brought together seven hundred Buddhists for a Sunday service in the grandstand. His wife, Jane, led the Buddhist choir and his mother-in-law headed the Sunday school.[31] Jane Imamura's work with the choir was enthusiastically supported by Muriel Fiske, a Christian Scientist with an interest in Buddhism who had led the choir at the Guadalupe Buddhist Temple. She and her husband faced disapproval from their white neighbors for their visits and deliveries of fresh lettuce to the center at Tulare. Eventually, the ostracism became unbearable and they moved to New Mexico.[32] Rev. Imamura promoted cooperation across religious boundaries and, in a rare collaboration, on June 21, 1942, a joint Buddhist-Christian meeting was held at Tulare. Raymond Booth of the American Friends Service Committee was the main speaker, while the Buddhist and Christian choirs offered hymns and *gathas*. A second joint service, chaired by the YBA leader Dr. John Koyama, was held with the Rev. Wendell Miller of the Los Angeles University Methodist Church as the main speaker, on the topic of "understanding." The Buddhist and Christian choirs ended the session jointly singing "America the Beautiful."[33]

Another nisei priest, Rev. Eiyū Terao of the Seattle Buddhist Temple, was constantly frustrated in his attempts to reconstitute the temple's sangha in the Puyallup Assembly Center. He was initially limited to section C of the assembly center, though temple members had also been placed in sections A, B, and D. Camp Manager John J. McGovern ordered Rev. Terao not to visit his congregation in other sectors of the WCCA camp except when accompanied by a military policeman, though this was later changed.[34] Historian Ron Magden provides details:

> Camp administrators formally recognized Reverend Terao and
> the Seattle Buddhists in Camp C as a religious body on May 21,

1942. That did not mean, however, that the entire Sangha could reassemble. McGovern repeatedly refused to allow the Buddhists living in camps A, B, and D to attend services in C. Finally, on July 18, 1942, McGovern granted permission for all Buddhists to assemble at Blanc's Cafe in Camp A. But attendees had to obtain individual passes, gather in groups of 20, follow guards to the service, and afterward wait to be escorted back. Still, Reverend Terao's first service attracted hundreds of Washington State Shinshu Buddhists as well as co-religionists exiled from Alaska, Oregon, and California.[35]

A final group that worked to keep up morale among the Buddhists in the WCCA camps was the handful of white priests who were never incarcerated. In Washington State, Rev. Sunya Pratt, who had run the Sunday school program at the Tacoma Buddhist Temple before the war, was the only white female actively leading a Japanese American Buddhist congregation.[36] After receiving permission from WCCA officials in San Francisco, Pratt visited Puyallup Assembly Center daily to continue the services she had led before the war, including holding study groups with nisei and leading the Sunday school program. Together with Rev. Eiyū Terao, she helped conduct Sunday services throughout "Camp Harmony," as the Puyallup center was dubbed by Army officials.[37] At the Tanforan Assembly Center in California, the nisei Rev. Kenryū Kumata coordinated with Rev. Frank Boden Udale to give regular services in English every Sunday.[38]

Finally, in Los Angeles, Rev. Julius Goldwater played a crucial role. A member of the wealthy and powerful Goldwater family (his cousin Barry would later be elected US senator for Arizona and would be the Republican presidential nominee in 1964), he had a trust fund that he used to assist his Japanese American Buddhist friends. These efforts earned him the derision of some who called him a "Jap lover" and defaced his house.[39]

Three temples in Los Angeles County had given Goldwater power of attorney, and this enabled him to do a great deal to help those newly incarcerated in the camps.[40] When he first visited Santa Anita, which held many of those temples' members, he "was dumbfounded to find my people housed in horse stables with dung still about; guards treating the inmates like serfs of the olden English slavery times."[41] Subsequently, he brought Buddhist items, including *ojuzu* (Buddhist rosaries), service books, and even *butsudan* (home Buddhist altars) left by members for safekeeping at the temple.[42] He also visited Santa Anita every Sunday to deliver talks, sometimes with updates on what was going on in the neighborhoods of their temples. At other times, he brought sympathetic Buddhists ordained in lineages other than his—an unusual collaboration given the traditional sectarian divisions that separated Buddhist leaders ritually, doctrinally, and organizationally. Goldwater reasoned that such transsectarian and multiethnic Buddhist shows of solidarity were key to the survival of Buddhism behind barbed wire. Despite their Buddhist sectarian differences, the Nishi Hongwanji Goldwater and the Shingon Buddhist priest Ronald Latimer joined forces to make trips to the Pomona Assembly Center. Together they supported the English-speaking Buddhists, conducting services for those who could not understand the Japanese-language services.[43] Goldwater also believed such collaborations would enhance a sense of Buddhism as universal, and therefore no more Japanese than American in essence.[44] His talks, with titles like "Be Aware of Realism," were mainly attended by nisei youth.[45]

These efforts by a handful of white Buddhist priests could not match the more robust resources and organizational support of those on the outside eager to support Christian worship in the camps. For those Japanese and Japanese American Christian ministers who were incarcerated, there were national-level Protestant church organizations able to keep paying their salaries, allowing them to continue their work as clerics—a type of support unavailable to the Buddhist priesthood in the WCCA camps.[46]

Representatives from the Seattle Council of Churches also secured the help of US Army vehicles to transport "pianos, pulpits, draperies, and communion sets for both Japanese- and English-language services" to support Methodists, Presbyterians, and others in Puyallup.[47] And a number of individuals went out of their way to support the Japanese American Christian community in the WCCA camps. Father Leopold Tibesar of the Maryknoll Mission, who had served Seattle's Japanese Catholic community before the war, had unsuccessfully tried to orga-

FIGURE 5.5 Rev. Julius Goldwater at the September 1942 O-Higan gathering at the Manzanar Buddhist Church.   Courtesy of Manzanar National Historic Site, Shirley Nagatomi Okabe Collection, Nagatomi-033.

nize a voluntary movement of the community to an area east of the restricted Western Defense Command's Military Area 1 and 2, the "free zone," before the enactment of Executive Order 9066. When the forced removals began, he continued his work to support his community by moving into a Catholic rectory in Puyallup so that he could make daily visits to that assembly center.[48] Fluent in Japanese due to his prior service in Manchuria, he had a great influence despite the small Catholic population. This was in part because of his role in converting a leading, if unpopular, spokesperson for the Japanese American community at Puyallup, Jimmie Sakamoto of the JACL.[49]

The Baptist Rev. Emery Andrews also endured tremendous personal sacrifices to make nearly daily trips to the Puyallup camp so that he could continue to minister to his former congregation and bring them items stored at their church's gymnasium in Seattle. When his congregation was transferred to the WRA's Minidoka camp in Idaho, he moved his family and residence to the nearby town of Twin Falls to continue his ministry).[50] Andrews's "Blue Box"—a vehicle cobbled together by mounting the body of the old Japanese Baptist Church bus onto a 1930s Ford chassis and motor stored at the Chinese Baptist Church—made fifty-six roundtrips from Idaho to Seattle to transport items that had been stored at the church.[51] Other Christians helped informally. George Aki, a young Congregationalist seminarian, had been a classmate at the Pacific School of Religion in Berkeley, California, of one of the guards at the Tanforan Assembly Center. The guard helped Aki complete his ordination while incarcerated, which enabled Aki to subsequently serve as one of three Japanese American chaplains of the 442nd Regimental Combat Team.

Given the pressure to conform to presumptions about Americanness as being Christian and the institutional advantages Christians enjoyed in the camps, it was not surprising that some individuals in the temporary WCCA camps maintained their Buddhist affiliation only quietly, or even converted to Christianity. While most of the sangha kept their faith, the full-fledged revival of Buddhist life would only occur with the move to the WRA camps that were built to last the duration of the war.

"BARRACK CHURCHES" IN CAMP

Roughly ninety-two thousand people transferred from the WCCA assembly centers to the ten WRA camps in the summer and fall of 1942.[52] Buddhists constituted the majority population in all ten camps, but because they still represented a minority religion in America, they faced challenges to the free exercise of their religion in ways that Japanese American Christians did not.

Before official houses of worship could be established, the more private practices of chanting, meditation, and other rituals were held in private barracks during the first several months in the WRA camps. In Manzanar, one individual recalled:

I heard a woman in the next room praying to Buddha. How like my mother, I thought. With all the cracks and openings in the wall that ended halfway to the roof and had no ceiling to give privacy to occupants, I could hear the prayer very clearly. The woman prayed for her health, her family's well-being, and for everyone in camp. Later on in the day, her daughter told me that her mother should not pray, for the FBI might arrest her. And her mother told me that she had prayed as long as she could remember and deeply regretted that fear of government reprisal had forced her to burn her Buddha and the tablets of the family dead.[53]

These barracks practices were common even though people did not have proper home altars *(butsudan)* with Buddha statues or ancestral veneration tablets *(ihai).* Informal practices were even found among the priests uncertain of administration support for establishing a communal space for Buddhist activity.

At Heart Mountain, Nyogen Senzaki initially established his routine at Barrack 28-22C with the cooperation of a sympathetic Buddhist family in their shared space. In a letter to a friend on October 15, 1942, Senzaki described his daily practice of morning meditation, reciting sutras, and answering questions about the sutras from the faithful who spontaneously joined him:

> In Los Angeles I had only fifteen chairs in my meditation hall, whereas here in this apartment, twenty by twenty in size, I live with another family, parents and a daughter, and the visitors bring their own chairs or sit on the floor. Ten or twelve of them enjoy the tranquility of their contemplation. They are the happiest and most contented evacuees in this center.[54]

He said he hoped to be transferred to a single-person unit, so that he could conduct Buddhist practice without being a burden to the family whose space he shared. On December 20, 1942, he was fortunate enough to be moved to such a unit, and opened the "Wyoming Zendo" (Zen

Meditation Hall). Here is the temple dedication verse he composed for the occasion:

> The evacuation cramped Japs by heads into the units of barracks.
> Fortunately, the monk could stay with a Buddhist family.
> He called his share of space E-kyo-an, Room of Wisdom Mirror.
> He suffered heat with the family in Santa Anita.
> He suffered cold with the family in Heart Mountain.
> He and the family and a number of Buddhists in the two places
> Meditated together, and recited sutras, and studied Buddhism every
>   morning.
> America gave the monks the alms, a single room, today.
> He now reopens To-Zen Zen-Kutsu, the meditation hall of the
>   eastbound teaching.
> He had it twenty years in California.
> Inviting many Caucasian Buddhists from all parts of world.
> He has to wait exclusively the Japanese Zen students to come,
> In this snow-covered desert of internment, a Wyoming plateau.
> He has nothing to do with the trivialities of the dusty world.
> He rather prefers to sit alone, burning the lamp of Dharma,
> Than to receive any insincere visitors and waste time.[55]

Senzaki's Buddhist practice in his private quarters inspired others to join him there for Zen meditation, study of sacred Buddhist texts, and discussion. Another Zen group was organized as the Poston Bukkyō Jiin—that is, the Buddhist temple at the WRA Poston camp in southwestern Arizona. That group produced a six-page Japanese-language pamphlet in the fall of 1942 promoting *zazen* (Zen meditation) and explaining its practice as "the stillness of one's authentic self." Detailed instructions on how to sit, bow, and chant various Buddhist and Zen texts were included.[56]

Creating spaces for more official Buddhist practice, however, required administrative approval. The first challenge was for Buddhist priests to be recognized by the WRA as professionals on par with their Christian counterparts. This recognition came on August 24, 1942, but with a catch. The policy set forth by the WRA in a guidebook provided to all residents stated that leaders of all faiths "may carry on their religious activities and may hold other WRA jobs at regular rates of compensation. No such workers, however, will receive WRA wages for the performance of religious duties."[57] Since everyone needed income, this meant the wages of religious leaders would have to be covered by outside organizations—in practical terms, a possibility only for Christian denominations. In Manzanar and a few other camps, authorities figured out a workaround by putting incarcerated Buddhist priests, Protestant ministers, and Catholic nuns on the payroll as social workers.[58] Elsewhere, Buddhist priests were forced to do other jobs, limiting their ability to perform ministerial work.

[margin annotation: no options but did sorta begin]

That fall, the Poston Buddhists enlisted the help of issei Presbyterian minister Rev. Sōhei Kowta, who had just been appointed to head the Inter-Religious Council in that camp. Kowta wrote to the WRA's acting director, E. M. Rowalt, on November 3, 1942, requesting cash advances for religious workers. Two weeks later, the request was denied. Rowalt wrote that the WRA appreciated "the morale-building work which the religious groups and their leaders are performing at the relocation centers," and understood "the abnormal circumstances" of the camps "due to the uniqueness of problems at the relocation centers." Yet he insisted that the principle of the "separation of church and state" required the continuation of the current policy, even if it "may work to the disadvantage of some groups whose support from outside sources is not large." He spelled out the implication:

> The Christian church, as you probably know, have indicated their preference and willingness to compensate their pastors on the projects and have agreed among themselves to pay uniform salaries comparable to the WRA cash advances. The main problem will arise, of course, for the Buddhist religious workers for whom outside support will not be so forthcoming.[59]

John Provinse, an applied anthropologist who was hired by the WRA's first director, Milton Eisenhower, to oversee areas such as education, internal security, health care, and community enterprise, served as chief of its Community Management Division. He contested the policy of

prohibiting payments to religious workers, writing to Mark Dawber of
the Home Mission Council in New York:

> Despite agreement on what seem fundamentally sound grounds
> of separation of church and state, our declaration of religious
> freedom for the centers can easily become a mere play on words
> if we in truth stack the cards against those of non-Christian
> faith who happen to lack sufficient outside resources to support
> their ministries. Yet to a considerable extent we are doing just
> this. Support for Buddhist services from outside the centers is
> almost negligible. . . . In truth, I feel here we have a fundamental
> problem of freedom of religious expression which transcends
> sectarian or cult tenets.[60]

President Roosevelt had recently asserted the "four freedoms" America's
government should secure for its citizens—freedom of speech, religion,
fear, and want—defining what America was fighting for in the war.[61]
Provinse's memo invoked those words and pointed to the gap between
them and the WRA's policy. He did not, however, convince WRA administrators. According to historian Michael Masatsugu, this was in
part because the second WRA director, Dillon Myer, saw "cultural assimilation to Christian European American norms as a solution to the
'Japanese problem' . . . [and] viewed Buddhists as non-Christians and
thus an impediment to Americanization."[62]

In the US Congress, Myer's view was shared by the House Un-
American Activities Committee. That committee's initial report on the
WRA, in 1943, demanded the "Americanization" of the internees through
"Americanized recreational activities," such as baseball, basketball, Boy
Scouts, and Girl Scouts. It also urged that Japanese Americans be en-
couraged to join the Young Men's and Young Women's Christian As-
sociations (YMCA and YWCA).[63]

The prejudices of the particular camp directors also affected how
much difference there was in the accommodation of Christian versus
Buddhist and other faiths' needs. Historian John Howard, in his study
of the WRA camps in Arkansas, notes that seventy percent of the residents at the Jerome relocation center were Buddhist and that, according

to the camp administration's weekly reports, Buddhist weekly services typically drew four thousand camp residents, while the Protestants' ten weekly services collectively drew only 2,500 attendees. Hoping to sway issei and nisei to "American" ways of life, Howard writes, "the WRA relied on religious organizing, revivals, and other modes of Protestant evangelism to shape the identity and conduct of their wards. Officials proposed a profound, linked pair of transformations: a nationalist reconciliation facilitated by a personal, spiritual redemption."[64] The WRA administration at Jerome routinely showed favoritism to Christian groups such as the Jerome Community Church and the YWCA by granting them privileges to use camp buildings, Howard notes. Meanwhile, the same administration kicked the camp's Buddhist church out of its space in dining hall 23—a decision that was only reversed after the Buddhists collected five hundred signatures and laid their petition on the desk of camp director Paul Taylor.[65]

Particularly in Arkansas, white Christian leaders viewed the captive Japanese American population as a "home mission" group poised for conversion. Arkansas Southern Baptist President T. L. Harris proclaimed, "Here in our state we have had literally thrust upon us the greatest opportunity for winning to Christ those of pagan faith we have ever witnessed."[66] Buddhism was not banned from the camps like "State Shinto," but American authorities viewed it as a faith unsuitable for the camp's Americanization initiatives.[67]

The legal justification of the ban on State Shinto was that it was not really a religion—a position also taken by the Japanese government. In the work of US intelligence agencies, however, State Shinto was often conflated with "folk Shinto"—traditions that venerated Inari, the fox deity, for example, or Konpira, the guardian deity controlling waters—and with "sect Shinto," the umbrella term used for thirteen newer, Shinto-derived movements, including Konkōkyō and Tenrikyō, that were recognized as religions by the Japanese government.[68] WRA camp administrators were more aware of the distinctions and, for the non-State Shinto groups, more flexible in allowing unofficial gatherings. For example, some WRA camps permitted Seicho-no-Ie—a syncretic new religious movement born in Japan in the 1930s with a loose association with Shinto, Buddhist, and Christian thought—although it was monitored by counterintelligence units. Robert Spencer, a member of the aforementioned JERS project (the study of Japanese American evacuation and resettlement undertaken by researchers at UC Berkeley beginning in 1942), at one point published a report on religion in the WRA Gila River camp. "Naturally, there is adherence to Shintoism on the parts of many of those who are classed as Buddhists," he wrote in it. "Because Shintoism is in accord with the nationalistic policies of Japan, its practice has been banned by the WRA and any meetings that Shinto groups may hold are of course sub-rosa. There are a few followers of the Shinto Tenrikyō definitely in the minority."[69]

By spring 1943, after extended internal discussions, the WRA issued its booklet *The Relocation Program: A Guidebook for the Residents of Relocation Centers.* Included in it was a statement about religious freedom:

> Religion—Like all other residents of the United States, evacuees at relocation centers are free to worship as they please and to conduct any type of religious service of a non-political nature. Because of the critical shortage of building materials, it now seems unlikely that WRA will be able to provide church buildings at relocation centers as originally intended. Space for all denominations, however, will continue to be made available in the recreation halls.[70]

Beyond the recreation halls designated as a place of worship by the WRA's Community Activities Division, Buddhist services and activities were also conducted in individual barracks, mess halls, and other communal locations not specifically designated as Buddhist temples.

One of the first challenges to establishing Buddhism in a more sustainable way was to identify those individuals who were Buddhist and organize them. In the WRA Minidoka camp, Rev. Eiyū Terao was initially the only Buddhist priest. In the ninety-five-degree heat of the summer of 1942, he made rounds throughout the forty-four-block camp caring for Buddhists struck by food poisoning and influenza. After one month in the camp, he himself succumbed to exhaustion. After being discharged from the infirmary, he and an enthusiastic YBA member, Masaru Harada, managed to visit all the barracks in the camp, identifying 5,168 Buddhists and compiling separate lists for former residents of Seattle, Portland, Tacoma, and other smaller communities. They also made notations on who might be eligible for membership in a possible Minidoka YBA.[71]

The few priests in the WRA camps joined forces with the plentiful YBA members to form sanghas. Building a proper altar to place a Buddha statue so as to sanctify a Buddhist temple or church required ingenuity, since the camp administrators provided no assistance. At the WRA Poston camp, Rev. Zessei Kawasaki had carefully wrapped and brought the main Buddhist statuary from the Visalia Buddhist Temple; Rev. Shawshew Sakow had brought the *gohonzon* from the Dinuba Buddhist Church; and Rev. Seijō Onoyama had carried the Buddha from the Reedley Buddhist Temple.[72] The three priests eventually installed their Buddhas in the Poston I, II, and III areas, respectively, within the camp.

At the WRA Gila River camp in Arizona, the Nishi Hongwanji Buddhist Rev. Taigan Hata had brought along a statue of Amida Buddha. Having no experience as a carpenter, he had help from other two other priests and some laypeople installing the statue in one of the recreation halls, and dedicated the hall as a new Buddhist church.[73] Spencer, the UC Berkeley researcher, was an outside observer of the official dedication of the Gila River Buddhist Church. He saw that when the new space was officially opened in Gila River Camp I, the response by the Buddhist community was tremendous. Buddhists in Camp II were banned from attending the dedication, but despite that effort at crowd control, attendance from Camp 1 alone was so great that "two morning services and two afternoon services were held to accommodate the crowds." Spencer makes a special notation in his report that, among the various speeches made, one Buddhist priest gave "thanks to Washington that the Japanese were allowed to practice freedom of religion in the centers."[74]

The Buddhists at the WRA Heart Mountain camp in Wyoming were fortunate to have several master carpenters in their midst. Shinzaburō and Gentarō Nishiura of the well-known Nishiura Construction Company had built a replica of Kyoto's Hongwanji Temple in their home town of San Jose in 1937. These two brothers and several of their company's skilled craftsmen designed and built an impressive and large altar for the camp. An Amida Buddha statue brought along by a man from the

FIGURE 5.6   Rev. Kankai Izuhara next to the Buddhist altar in Heart Mountain crafted by the Nishiura brothers, 1944.   Photograph by George Hirahara, Hirahara Photograph Collection, Washington State University Manuscripts, Archives, and Special Collections, sc14b01f0250n03.

Yakima Buddhist Church was installed in this *shumidan* altar, and in October 1942, the Nishi Hongwanji—the largest of the Buddhist sects— opened the Heart Mountain Buddhist Church at Block 30, formally known in Japanese as the "Daisanjū-ku Nishi Hongwanji Bukkyōkai."

Later in the war, the same team headed by the Nishiura brothers built another large altar for a Buddhist Church located at Block 17, organized by a transsectarian group of Buddhists known as the Heart Mountain Buddhist Federation, or Bukkyōdan.[75] Led by Buddhist priests of four different sects, this became a sanctuary primarily for those who did not belong to the large Nishi Hongwanji organization. Made entirely of left-over wood, great craftsmanship went into building it.[76]

These large altars at Heart Mountain were complemented by many smaller *butsudan* altars made and used by families to enshrine Buddha statues (which included Amida Buddha for the Pure Land sects of Jōdo and the Nishi and Higashi Hongwanji traditions; Shakyamuni Buddha for Zen traditions; and a scroll paying homage to the *Lotus Sutra* for the Nichiren tradition) and ancestral veneration tablets *(ihai)* within their barracks homes. Among the various WRA camps, there was great vari-

FIGURE 5.7 Nishiura family with altar in mid-construction.   Courtesy of the Nishiura Family Collection.

ation in what people could scavenge to make *butsudan*. In some centers, the best materials available were cigar boxes, while at Poston, there was abundant petrified wood.

Once sacred spaces for Buddhist practice were created in the WRA camps, the next challenge was to reformulate Buddhism in such a way as to claim equal standing with Christianity. In the ongoing process of Americanizing Buddhism, the camps served as laboratories for a great number of experiments—not least of which was the activation of a new spirit of cooperation across sectarian lines and in interfaith efforts with Christians. Along with securing religious freedom in America went exercising the freedom to make adaptations to Buddhist traditions, so that Buddhism could ground itself more securely in the American religious landscape.

6

REINVENTING AMERICAN BUDDHISM

THE BUDDHA'S TEACHING that all things are subject to change applies to the religion itself. Chapter Two of the Lotus Sutra explains that all Buddhas "teach the Dharma to sentient beings using incalculable and innumerable skillful means with various explanations and illustrations to benefit many of them and cause them to feel at peace."[1] In the roughly 2,500-year history of the tradition, from its inception in India through its transformation in American camps during World War II, Buddhism has been kept alive by dynamically transmitting the Dharma as it both adapts to and is adapted by its environment. The need to Americanize Buddhism was clear even in the decades prior to the war as the American-born nisei generation and the non-Japanese convert population expanded the sangha. But wartime incarceration brought the question of whether Buddhism could survive in America to a head, dramatically accelerating the natural process of cultural adaptation.

For many young American Buddhists in WRA camps, the sentiments expressed by Misao Yumibe, who was incarcerated in Arkansas, resonated deeply:

> Following the days of Pearl Harbor, doubt, fear and suspicion have arisen, hindering the progress of our religion. . . . [M]any are reluctant to say with pride that they are Buddhists. In spite of all this I still choose Buddhism. . . . It is the newest of religions, brought over by our fathers and mothers from their homeland. . . . What was it that spurred our fathers to carry on? What spirit was it that carried them through

their trials and tribulations? We [nisei], too, can follow the path that He had laid down for us to walk. By our actions and deeds, the American public will come to know Buddhism is nothing to fear and suspect but a religion that will be an asset to a greater and a finer America.[2]

It was a clear statement from a young American that to "still choose Buddhism" was to proactively assert and fulfill America's ideal of freedom. Even those behind barbed-wire fences could make it into "an asset to a greater and a finer America."

To shape Buddhism to America, even in the most inhospitable of situations, Buddhists drew on another key teaching of the Buddha—skillful adaptation (*hōben,* also translated as "skillful means" or "expedient means"). In classic texts, an analogy is proffered that the Buddha's teachings were akin to medicine. Just as a physician would discern the proper dispensation of medicines, appropriate to the condition of the patient, the Buddha as the "great physician" skillfully adapted his teachings to the context of those hearing and receiving the Dharma.

ADAPTING BUDDHISM

This positive outlook on adaptation was reflected in the various efforts of a newly-energized Young Buddhist Association (YBA), led by the nisei in the WRA camps. Many of these young American Buddhists viewed their religion as a powerful repository of the perspectives and practices of their ancestors that needed to be transmitted to future generations of Americans. The YBA was also a community-building organization that sponsored many social activities, including American pastimes such as baseball, dances, and pageants. At the WRA Rohwer camp, Barry Saiki, the editor of *Rohwer Outpost* newspaper and the YBA President for the camp, noted that the major YBA activities in his camp included an "All-Center Oratorical contest, the institution of the Buddhist Basketball and Ping Pong tournaments, the formation of the mixed choir, the celebrations of Hana-matsuri [Buddha's birthday] and O-bon holidays and the Keirokai [a group to support the elderly] for the internees' families."[3]

The mix of Japanese and American social and cultural traditions represented by Saiki's list of YBA activities was common to many of the WRA camps, but the organization's first priority was to establish Buddhist Sunday schools. These weekly programs were designed to teach the basics of Buddhist life, organize social and athletics events, coordinate ritual activities, and offer community services. The Sunday schools were so popular that it was often hard to find enough qualified teachers. At Manzanar, within the first year in camp, the Sunday school service at 9 AM had 650 youths in attendance and the 10 AM Young People's Service regularly attracted seven hundred YBA members.[4] These numbers only grew larger in subsequent years.

Sports had been a big part of prewar YBA activities and it was no different in the camps. The WRA Gila River camp fielded one of the top semi-professional camp teams, made up of players from the Guadalupe Young Men's Buddhist Association (YMBA).[5] In the WRA Tule Lake camp, a crowd of five thousand turned out in the spring of 1942 to watch a baseball game between the Klamath Falls Pelicans, a semi-pro team from the outside, and the Tule Lake All-Stars. A young Buddhist, George Nakagawa, later recalled the game: "Compared to the Pelicans, who were all dressed in the same colorful uniforms, the Tule Lake All-Stars looked ragged, their outfits assembled from a patchwork of different uniforms. However, once the game began, the All-Stars proved to be much the better team and easily won the game by the score of 16–0." He watched the game with a friend along the third base line, and at one point All-Stars third baseman Tak Ikeda charged after a ball and knocked him to the ground: "It was the first time that I had ever had the wind knocked out of me . . . Tak was wearing the purple and white jersey of the prewar Tacoma Bussei (Buddhist Youth) baseball team."[6]

Given the strong impulse to demonstrate a connection between Buddhism and mainstream American society, social dances and even pageants were organized by the YBA. In Heart Mountain, the YBA held a "Bussei Coronation," which was essentially a Buddhist pageant that heralded a queen and her court, chosen for their beauty, composure, sociability—and their understanding of Buddhist teachings.[7]

To capture the momentum of a youth-driven Buddhist movement in the camps, the YBAs organized camp-wide and inter-camp conferences.

At Poston, the first "all-camp" YBA gathering was held in September 1943 when the young Buddhists of Poston Camp 1 took the initiative to bring together Camps 1, 2, and 3 for the conference, which was billed "Gassho: All Units Forum." The gathering featured a standard religious service, with *gathas* (Buddhist hymns) sung by the choir, meditation, and sermons by Buddhist priests, along with discussions on how to run the Sunday school and the YBA movement. The main message of the gathering was that Buddhism could be practiced without all the trappings of the world before camp. Rev. Noboru Tsunoda, in his keynote, proclaimed:

> Buddhism in America is doomed. Such was the impression of many people following the outbreak of war and the resulting evacuation. . . . However, contrary to this pessimistic view taken by the faint-hearted, we find that the very opposite phenomenon has taken place; the hardships and adversities of our faith in the Lord Buddha and His All-embracing Teachings [and] . . . our experience in the relocation centers has shown more than clearly that religion does not consist of beautiful churches and host of clergymen, neither does it consist of dogma as set down by ec-clesiastical authorities; the fundamental basis of religion is in the strength of our faith.[8]

At WRA Gila River's first conference (Unity through Gassho: First Semi-Annual YBA Conference), held in March 1943 in the Canal sector of camp, YBA members living in the Butte sector trekked three miles to attend. The camp's YBA had formed soon after its opening, even before the Buddhist Church was established, when twenty-one former Sunday school youth leaders banded together. They organized a YBA Council with officers similar to those at Poston and a block-by-block orga-nizational structure including youth leaders in every part of camp.[9] The conference, held at the Buddhist churches at blocks 42 and 63, was a day-long affair that began at 8:30 AM and ended with a dance called the Bussei Ball. The ball concluded with the singing of a new Buddhist "hymn" entitled the "Viva Y.B.A. Gatha."[10] It was composed by YBA member Ayako Noguchi, who had long been a columnist for the Los Angeles newspaper *Rafu Shimpo* before the war and was one of the few women newspaper editors in the WRA camps, and its lyrics were sung to the tune of "Auld Lang Syne":

> With joyous hearts we bring to close
> Another perfect day
> We thank thee, Lord, for everything
> And Viva Y.B.A.!
>
> Oh, Viva Y.B.A. we'll sing,
> Oh, Viva Y.B.A.!
> Let's drink a toast of happiness
> To the Followers of His way.
>
> We'll hold this day in memory
> As we join to say
> Namu Amida Butsu
> And Viva Y.B.A.!
>
> Oh, Viva Y.B.A., we'll cheer,
> Oh, Viva Y.B.A.!
> We'll meet again some day, dear friends
> 'Til then, Carry On, Bussei!

The oratory contests, the sports leagues, the dances and pageants, and the religious gatherings were all skillful adaptations of the Buddhist community in camps where one's American loyalties were questioned. A YBA leader in Poston II wrote:

> Those who attend a YBA conference should do at least two things. One is to make friends and the other is to receive religious inspiration and to acquire self-confidence of being a Buddhist. . . . Don't be shy to talk to the one next to you whenever there is a chance. Everyone of them is your friend. In fact, they are all your brothers and sisters in our Buddha's eyes. . . . Today you will see that even in the wilderness of Arizona, Buddha's Mercy and Wisdom are constantly working on us.[11]

The sangha-building dimensions of the Young American Buddhist movement in the various WRA camps combined religious and social activities, and inspired Buddhists to confidently assert their identity despite the generalized antipathy in America towards non-Christian religions.

The "Americanization" of Buddhism also drew on the interracial solidarity with white Buddhists who visited the WRA camps. Rev. Julius Goldwater was the featured speaker at the March 1943 inaugural conference of the Gila River Camp YBA, titled "Strength thru Buddhism." After the service and Goldwater's lecture, an open forum was held to discuss topics like "Buddhism and Relocation," followed by an entertainment hour highlighting vocalists and trumpet players, and then a "quiz show" pitting young Buddhist men in the US Army against young Buddhist women in the Women's Army Auxiliary Corps (WAAC).[12] Goldwater, the leader of the Buddhist Brotherhood of America, an independent organization he had founded in 1928, had long been an advocate for a more "universal" approach to Buddhism. The organization favored a presentation of the Dharma that was less closely linked with Japanese language and culture. Ironically, Buddhist convert priests, including Goldwater, Hunt, Pratt, and others, despite their many assertions about the shortcomings of the Judeo-Christian tradition, mimicked aspects of Anglo-Protestantism in their approach to "Americanizing" Buddhism. Beyond the obvious "Anglicizing" of Buddhism through the increased use of the English language in Dharma or Sunday school curricula, they advocated the introduction of a sermon at Sunday services and the adoption of Christian-originated terms such as "minister" and "reverend" to refer to Buddhist priests and "church" to refer to the temple.

As another aspect of the "Americanization" of Buddhism, the singing of "Buddhist hymns" (*sanbutsuka*) in the "barrack churches" became almost universal in the wartime camps. Prior to the war, the practice had already gained some traction among Japanese Americans and even among small groups in Japan. Some of these Buddhist "hymns" were older Buddhist verses (*gatha*) and Japanese songs that were given Western musical arrangements. Others were newly composed songs to be sung by a Buddhist choir in either Japanese or English, with organ or piano accompaniment.[13] The notion of a "service book" to be used on a Sunday

FIGURE 6.1 Young Buddhist Association (YBA) choir in WRA Amache relocation camp (Granada, Colorado).   Courtesy of the George Ochikubo Collection, Densho Digital Repository, ddr-densho-159-98.

for a worship service, a practice that had slowly developed in the decades prior to the war, was a marked change. Buddhists had not traditionally viewed Sunday as a special day for gathering or used such service books to structure the weekly congregation.[14]

A new publication, *A Book Containing an Order of Ceremonies for Use by Buddhists at Gatherings,* was compiled by Rev. Goldwater and used in Los Angeles, and then later in WRA Buddhist worship.[15] Given the rushed forced removal and limits on luggage people could take with them, few Japanese American Buddhists had brought copies of the original 1939 service book to camp. Goldwater printed and distributed thousands of copies to nearly all the WRA camps, even those in faraway Arkansas.[16]

The project to distribute these service books and to create a more standardized and "Americanized" worship service began after Goldwater's first visit to Manzanar in September 1942, one week after the dedication of the new Manzanar Buddhist Church. The Buddhist community welcomed him with a reception at Barracks 13–15, the location of the temple, after that day's fall equinox Ohigan Service. Later, at a Buddhist Brotherhood of America meeting in Los Angeles, Goldwater would recount his impressions of camp life. He described Manzanar as a "prison" with living quarters that had no furniture except that which "could be made out of apple crates or purchased in the area." His multiracial non-Japanese Buddhist group then resolved to produce a "booklet" for those incarcerated—in Goldwater's words, to demonstrate "how true Americanism is really true Buddhism."[17] This all-English service book aligned with the WRA's interest in an Anglicized Buddhism. By congregating and singing Buddhist "hymns," these Buddhists were skillfully adapting their practice to what was expected in a Protestant Sunday service.

Goldwater managed to deliver these service books to the various WRA camps despite obstacles to traveling to the remote and desolate sites. His requests of friends to share their gasoline coupons with him were repeatedly turned down. Some of them, upset with his sympathetic attitude toward those in camp, called him a "clever traitor." Furthermore, as a Buddhist, he was told he could not take advantage of a discount afforded by railroad companies to Christian clergy.[18] The irony that white Buddhists were ostracized by other Americans while seeking to "Americanize" Buddhism was not lost on the Buddhists who lived within the barbed wire fences. Further, not all Buddhists liked Goldwater's idiosyncratic service book and instead found alternative methods to adapt Buddhist ritual life to the camp environment,

In many camps, grassroots efforts produced new ritual texts for Buddhist gatherings, called "Gatha Books." Printed on mimeographs in the WRA camps, the new books avoided the Christian terminology of "hymnals." Many took a few elements from Goldwater's text, but they more closely resembled prewar styles of ritual texts familiar to the Sangha. At Manzanar, Nob Myose and George Mitsuhata compiled a version of their service book under the direction of Berry Tamura (the YBA President) and distributed 2,500 copies.[19] At Jerome, the Denson YBA produced nine hundred copies of its new *Gathas and Service* books, which included articulations of Buddhist doctrine as well as ritual, written primarily by two longtime west coast journalists employed at the camp newspaper, the *Denson Tribune*. This service book was then

donated by the YBA to Buddhists in other WRA camps.[20] By 1944, after
the official ban on Japanese-language materials in camp had eased, a
hundred-page booklet entitled *Raihai seiten,* which restored many Japanese elements to the service book, was produced at the Poston III Buddhist Church. This text was used at the regular services on Sunday and
by the sutra study group that met every Thursday evening at the barrack church.[21]

The skillful adaptation of Buddhism to the WRA camp context thus
took several directions. Reformatting Buddhism to align with Anglo-
Protestant standards was one strategy to present Buddhism as "nothing
to fear and suspect," in Misao Yumibe's words. At the same time, there
was an impulse to resist mimicry and confidently present the Buddhism
"brought over by our fathers and mothers from their homeland." Young
American Buddhists, during their years in the WRA camps, simultaneously pursued various ways of making the religion "an asset to a
greater and a finer America."

SECT AND TRANS-SECT

Skillful adaptation was required to deal with the physical constraints of
practicing Buddhism behind barbed wire. Because WRA administrators did not want to set aside more public space than necessary for religious practice, they strongly encouraged the many Buddhist sects and
Protestant denominations to merge into "federations"—one for Buddhists and another for Protestants. Just as Protestants from high-church
traditions struggled with holding joint services with Pentecostal-oriented
denominations like the Holiness Church, the Buddhists found it challenging to come together as one sangha given that they belonged to a
multitude of sectarian traditions.[22]

During the prewar period, the small, rural communities that could
not support multiple sectarian Buddhist temples provided a precedent
for gathering various sects under a single roof. But in larger communities with a significant concentration of Japanese Americans, sectarian
differences led to multiple temples, each with its own ritual and organizational styles, and sometimes in competition with each other.[23]

Forming a unified "federation" of Buddhist organizations, even with the best of intentions, proved difficult. But necessity encouraged skillful adaptation and negotiation in the reforming of American Buddhism in the WRA camps.

Priests of every sect corresponded with the members of their prewar temples, who were spread across many different camps, encouraging them to maintain their particular sect's teachings and rituals. Recognizing the severe lack of Buddhist priests in some of the camps, the Nishi Hongwanji secured WRA permission to establish speaker bureaus for coordinating guest clergy who, like Christian ministers, were provided special passes to travel between camps.[24] In Arkansas, Buddhist priests frequently moved back and forth to give sermons or perform services in the two WRA camps there, Rohwer and Jerome.[25]

Traveling priests were particularly important for the smaller sects of Buddhism. The Poston-based Shingon Buddhist priest Ryōshō Sogabe visited his sect's believers, a minority in the Buddhist community, in Gila River (also in Arizona) and Minidoka (Idaho).[26] On occasion, Buddhist priests were even permitted temporary releases to connect with their sect members in the "free zones" east of the wide strip of Pacific coastal land from which all Japanese were restricted. Three Nichiren Buddhist priests, for example, visited their sect's members in the Salt Lake City area to hold services at their homes, since no temple of that sect existed in the region.[27]

The desire to maintain one's sectarian identity and practice was felt by Buddhists and Christians alike. Few Methodists were keen on suddenly adopting Holiness Church worship styles, and few Baptists liked compromising with Episcopalians on theological matters. Likewise, Buddhists wished to retain the characters of their particular sects. It was not surprising that at Heart Mountain, for example, the numerically superior Nishi Hongwanji sect priests and members were intent on maintaining their distinctive worship styles and practices, such as the chanting of the verse "Namu Amida Butsu" to pay homage to Amida Buddha, the central focus of devotion in their tradition.

In most WRA camps, Buddhists instead formed "parallel congregations."[28] They congregated in one space, but each held their distinctive services, Dharma study sessions, YBA meetings, and other gatherings at different times. They agreed to joint services at key moments in the Buddhist ritual calendar, namely Hanamatsuri (the Buddha's birthday), Obon (the summer ancestral festival), Ohigan ceremonies at the spring and autumn equinox, and in some camps Bodhi Day (to celebrate the Buddha's enlightenment) and Nirvana Day (to commemorate the Buddha's passing into *parinirvana*).

At two WRA camps, Poston and Minidoka, further efforts were made at intra-Buddhist cooperation, at least in the realm of chanting, but fell apart.[29] While some traditions of Buddhism, such as Sōtō and Rinzai Zen, did not chant sectarian mantras as a central practice, other sects of Buddhism chanted such verses as a key component of their sectarian identity and worship style. All of the Pure Land Buddhist schools—the Nishi and Higashi Hongwanji Jōdo Shinshū sects and the Jōdo sect—traditionally chanted "Namu Amida Butsu" to pay homage to Amida Buddha of the Western Pure Land, rather than Shakyamuni Buddha, the historical founder of the Buddhist religion. Members of the Nichiren sect chanted "Namu Myōhō Rengekyō," in homage to the Lotus Sutra *(Rengekyō)*, which their medieval founder, Nichiren, believed to be the pinnacle of the historical Buddha's teachings, trumping any other canonical text. Finally, Shingon sect believers chanted "Namu Henjō Kongō Daishi" to honor their sect's founder, Kōbō Daishi.

The newly established United Buddhist Churches at Poston Camp I and at Minidoka attempted to standardize the weekly services into a unified "Buddhist" experience by chanting a common mantra or verse. In those two settings, the United Church determined that no one sect's distinctive chanting would take precedence. Instead, they chanted a verse that no group normally recited—Namu Shakamuni Butsu—to pay homage to the historical Shakyamuni Buddha, from whom they could agree that all lineages of Buddhism originally flowed.[30]

In Poston II and III, this type of unfamiliar ritual practice was frowned upon. One priest noted: "A joint service with different Buddhist denominations raises many problems because someone or other will always raise an objection regarding what to recite during the service. As a result, in Camp I, they compromised with Namu Butsu, which merely means, 'I rely on, or I honor, the Buddha.'"[31]

This priest believed that if the majority of Buddhists in the camp were Nishi Hongwanji members, they shouldn't be forced to adjust their normal Buddhist practice to accommodate other sects.[32] He banded together with other priests of his sect and condemned the experiment in common verse chanting as an inappropriate and "unskillful" adaptation of Buddhism to camp life.[33]

Eventually, the United Church discontinued the chanting of "Namu Shakyamuni Butsu." They did, however, continue some transsectarian cooperation. They held a combined New Year's service in January 1945, for example, with Nishi Hongwanji, Nichiren, and Shingon priests jointly officiating. They also issued the multisectarian Buddhist publication *Hōrin* (Dharma Wheel) to commemorate that collaboration.[34]

The transsectarian effort at the WRA Minidoka camp also failed. George Townsend, the camp's assistant director in charge of community services, had called a forum to discuss the "Place of the Churches in Minidoka" in November 1942. His request of the Buddhists, Protestants, and Catholics was that they all set aside their sectarian differences so that only three religious units might exist.[35] A United Buddhist Church was formed, and priests and lay members from the three sects— Nishi Hongwanji, Nichiren, and Shingon—worked together to establish Sunday services, adult and youth services, and Buddhist Sunday school classes. But the lack of sect-specific chanting during Wesak Week (*Wesak* being the Indic term for the Buddha's birthday) in April 1943, the first major ceremony for Buddhists after being moved to Minidoka, created early murmurs of dissension. The week featured collective religious services, sermons, and many social activities, such as a Young Buddhist Play Day.[36] These uplifting activities could not, however, overcome the deep misgivings that many Nishi Hongwanji Buddhists (representing the majority sect in Minidoka) had about joint services. Though chanting "Namu Shakyamuni Butsu" made some sense when Shakyamuni Buddha's birthday was being celebrated, it still felt foreign to utter verses of that kind, given their sect's tradition of chanting that venerated Amida Buddha.

Dissatisfied, the Nishi Hongwanji Buddhist's Rev. Eiyū Terao led the charge to withdraw from the United Buddhist Church, and formed a

FIGURE 6.2 Shinkurō Ogata's Nishi Hongwanji funeral at the WRA camp at Heart Mountain, Wyoming (July 21, 1943).   Courtesy of David Perley, Migita and Sakahara Collection, Densho Digital Repository, ddr-densho-293-10.

new temple at Recreation Hall 15, the Hunt Buddhist Church, named after a nearby town. There, Rev. Terao prominently installed on the altar a scroll with "Namu Amida Butsu" inscribed in calligraphy."[37] After the Rev. Gikan Kimura of the Shingon sect followed suit to establish his own services, the original federation had only the Nichiren Buddhists, who were then free to follow their own sect's practices.[38] These kinds of sectarian tensions in the WRA camps started with theological or ritual preferences, but sometimes spilled over into struggles over facilities usage and monetary donations.[39] The inter-sectarian contestations of what constituted skillful or inappropriate adaptations of Buddhism in the state of incarceration was ultimately a practical exercise in enculturation.

The emerging American Buddhism from behind barbed wire opened up the possibility of a less sectarian form of the religion that would be accessible to a broader demographic. There could be adaptation of rituals, and a degree of integration with preexisting social conventions in such activities as sports and pageants. The translation and transformation of the religion was therefore not only a matter of language, as English increasingly emerged as the primary medium for transmitting the Dharma. The process of placing Buddhism on an equal footing with the majority religion of the United States would also involve cultural adaptation and increased contact with Christians.

INTERFAITH COOPERATION

Interfaith cooperation was at times encouraged by the WRA authorities. At other times cooperation emerged organically as co-religionists attempted to work together to better the conditions for the camp's population. Projects undertaken for practical and self-interested reasons led to genuine friendships between certain leaders of different religions, despite occasional tensions between faith communities. Many Buddhists observed that white Christian administrators in the WRA camps generally favored Japanese American Christians for positions of authority, and that maintaining good relations with Christians could therefore help the Buddhist cause. And many Christians realized that they were in the minority among Japanese Americans, and that having positive relationships with those of the majority faith was essential to a more harmonious camp life. Thus a combination of idealism and pragmatism gave rise to various forms of interfaith cooperation from the earliest days in the WRA camps.

In the first months of incarceration, with the encouragement of camp authorities, Inter-religious Councils and Inter-faith Ministerial Councils were established. These councils sponsored Buddhist Christian "Religious Forums"—the first was held at Manzanar in November 1942—and joint task forces, such as one at Rohwer, to tackle social issues such as delinquency among youth or the welfare of aged issei.[40]

The WRA Topaz camp, where the Buddhist Mission of North America had its headquarters, became a unique center of such activity after an Inter-faith Church Council was established in September 1942.[41] The Topaz group worked well enough that eventually Buddhists and Protestants shared an old CCC camp building that had been moved to the camp for their services, while the Catholics and Seventh Day Adventists shared another building.[42] Separate from the Council, a Topaz Inter-Faith Ministerial Association was formed with the idea that clerics would attend religious services of other faiths. For example, the

Nishi Hongwanji priest Rev. Itsuzō Kyōgoku, was invited not only to attend, but deliver remarks at, the opening of the Protestant Church of Topaz in November 1942. In his speech, the Buddhist proclaimed, "No matter what the religion or belief, we must have unity and harmony in all our activities and projects here. We should destroy criticisms of each other's faiths, try to understand each other's religion, and enrich ourselves by this added knowledge."[43]

The appearance of Buddhists at a Christian gathering was rare in the prewar Japanese American communities on the west coast, but became routine in the WRA camps. At Manzanar, Rev. Shinjō Nagatomi was given a prominent place in the program for the one-year anniversary of the Manzanar Christian Church celebration on June 13, 1943. He proclaimed there: "The fundamental teachings of Christianity is Love. The fundamental teachings of Buddhism is Mercy. In this great Circle of Love and Mercy we strive to live our daily living harmoniously. Thus, let us stand together regardless of the religion and cooperate peacefully, work and live for the benefit of this Manzanar center."[44]

Buddhists and Christians also tried to come together on important American holidays such as Thanksgiving and Christmas. In the WRA Tule Lake camp, at the first Thanksgiving during the wartime incarceration, a celebration and gala dinner featured produce from the camp's new farms and speakers such as Washington state senator and Quaker activist Mary Farquharson. The Episcopalian minister Rev. Daisuke Kitagawa recalled the good relations between Buddhists and Christians at this event, noting how "Noboru Honda, a distinguished leader of the Buddhist group at Tule Lake and a member of the Community Council, read Psalms 23, and read it beautifully. Christians and Buddhists, Issei and Nisei, Caucasian and Japanese, WRA personnel and evacuees, participated, and the service was as close to the ancient agricultural festival as any Thanksgiving Day I had ever celebrated."[45]

While Christmas was a Christian holiday, many Buddhists (especially children who wished for presents) also viewed it simply as a national holiday. One Buddhist priest reflected in his diary on how Buddhists might want to engage with the Christmas holiday:

> Christmas should not be thought of as a religious event, but rather a national holiday. . . . [W]e Buddhists should celebrate

FIGURE 6.3 Rev. Shinjo Nagatomi giving a talk at the Hanamatsuri (Buddha's Birthday Ceremony).   Courtesy of photographer Tōyō Miyatake, M 0135C.

the Buddha's entrance into nirvana on Christmas. I thought this because, originally, this day had nothing to do with Christ's birthday. As is well known, the day was formerly the winter and still as celebrated by northern Europeans, which was later adopted as Christ's birthday. Christians just took it over. Therefore, if Buddhism is going to spread throughout the world, Buddhist events should be placed into each country's folk customs. Although December 8 is designated as the day of the Buddha's entrance into nirvana, here [in America], if it doesn't fall on a Sunday, we really can't do anything major. Given this, instead of being sad and withdrawn as everyone else celebrates Christmas, we should celebrate the Buddha's entrance into nirvana day on Christmas at every temple. The Bodhi tree could take the place of the Christmas tree and a ball representing the stars in the ten directions could be made into an ornament to represent nirvana. Only the younger generation would get behind a proposal like this, so we'll have to wait for the day when the Young Buddhists can make this happen.[46]

Buddhist parents generally wanted their children to be able to participate in the merriment surrounding the Christian holiday. Deeming Christmas a national civic holiday (or local "folk" custom) became another opportunity to skillfully adapt Buddhism to America.

Christians also viewed Christmas in a similarly broad and inclusive manner. For the first Christmas celebration, in 1942, the Home Missions Council proclaimed the wish to hold "America's Biggest Christmas Party." With the coordination of the Protestant Commission for Japanese Service, the American Friends Service Committee, Fellowship of Reconciliation, and the JACL, it launched a project to bring Christmas gifts to all children in camp regardless of denomination or faith tradition.[47] The Quaker Herbert Nicholson endeavored to collect ten thousand gifts to deliver to the camps.[48] He mobilized a coalition of liberal Christian denominations to participate, noting: "I am ashamed to say that not a single one of [the evangelical Christian] churches or Sunday schools would support this endeavor for fear of 'comforting the enemy'. . . . More liberal churches did cooperate. The Pasadena First Methodist Church gave 5,000 gifts each year."[49] After the first year, more groups contributed, including Chinese American Christians, and Nicholson grew support for the endeavor year by year until 1944, when fifty-seven thousand gifts were delivered. At Tule Lake, Rev. Daisuke Kitagawa recalled how the Committee on Resettlement of Japanese Americans of the Federal Council of Churches mobilized civic groups and churches around the country to send in presents for Christmas 1943. He noted how full the Tule Lake warehouse was, and that "every child, Christian and non-Christian alike, had a Christmas present."[50]

Especially in camps like those at Minidoka and Topaz, where Buddhist-Christian relations seemed most warm, clerics of both traditions worked closely to provide a sense of unity in the face of generational, religious, and regional differences that often caused tensions and affected morale. In Minidoka, Christmas became an occasion for both Buddhists and Christians to celebrate an American civil religious holiday by sharing Christmas cards and decorating the dining hall to achieve a festive moment in a less than ideal environment. A column in the camp's newspaper, *The Irrigator*, noted in 1944 that "the original five members of the Christmas Contest committee . . . were all Buddhists."[51] In Topaz, the close cooperation between Buddhists and Christians was best symbolized by a joint service held in 1944, when by a fluke of the calendar: Easter and Hanamatsuri (the Buddha's birthday ceremony) fell on the same day, so "both congregations held Easter services in the morning and Buddhist services in the afternoon."[52]

One of the more remarkable acts of interfaith cooperation can be found in the 1943 construction of a monument at the WRA Manzanar camp's cemetery to honor the spirits of deceased: the Manzanar Ireitō. The camp's Town Hall Committee, in consultation with Buddhist and Christian ministers, selected the spot in the cemetery to build this monument to honor those who had passed away in camp. Similar to a monument erected before the war in Los Angeles to honor its issei pioneers, the Japanese characters "Ireito" (Monument to Venerate the Spirits of the Deceased) was inscribed on it.[53]

Ryozo Kado, a Catholic landscape architect, gardener, and stonemason, was called on to design and supervise the erection of the monument.[54] He had designed, before the war, the shrine called the "Lourdes of the West" at St. Elizabeth of Hungary Church in Altadena, California, and during the war, Manzanar's entrance sign and stone sentry structures. Rev. Shinjō Nagatomi, a Buddhist, provided the calligraphy for the *kanji* characters—I-Rei-Tō—to be etched into the obelisk. His daughter recalled that her father practiced for hours every day on "large rolls of paper with a huge brush, about 3 ½ inches in diameter, and black paint. . . . Sometimes he was unable to sleep, thinking about his task, and would rise early and tackle the words, *i-rei-to,* until the words seemed to dance off the paper."[55] After several weeks, he was satisfied he had produced a version that could be engraved on the monument in perpetuity.

Each family was asked to contribute ten to fifteen cents to the interfaith Ireitō construction effort, and $1,000 was raised to purchase the concrete for the monument. Among the Buddhists, Rev. Nagatomi, the executive secretary of the Manzanar Buddhist Church, and a kibei YBA leader went around the camp, barrack by barrack, to gather these funds.[56]

FIGURE 6.4 Rev. Shinjō Nagatomi officiating at a Buddhist service at the Manzanar Ireito Monument.   Courtesy of photographer Tōyō Miyatake, M 0285B.

Once the design was complete, the residents of Block 9 and sixty YBA members provided the labor to build it.[57]

Officiating at the Ireitō dedication at the cemetery on the afternoon of August 14, 1943 were both Rev. Nagatomi and the Holiness Church's Rev. Junro Kashitani, and representatives from the various religious traditions were in attendance.[58] For the Buddhists, the choice of August 14 was no accident; the dedication of the Ireitō was closely linked to the Obon festival, an important ceremony in the Buddhist ritual calendar to honor one's ancestors, typically held in mid-August. Indeed, various activities associated with Obon took place on the same day in a firebreak between Blocks 7 and 13, culminating in a major gathering the following day. On August 15, 1943, thousands of Buddhists, including 1,600 dancers, assembled to participate in the Bon Odori (a traditional dance to welcome the spirits of the ancestors).[59]

In Japan and prewar Japanese America, Obon was traditionally held over several days every summer as a festival to honor the spirits of one's family ancestors with the chanting of Buddhist sutras, the lighting of candles or other illumination to guide the spirits, and the Bon dance. At Manzanar, the Buddhist Church members passed out a special publication titled "Obon Festival—Significance of Obon," explaining the proceedings:

> The name "Bon" is a contraction of "Urabon" which in turn is a corruption of the Sanskrit term "ullambana" meaning to salvage souls from the agony of being hanged head down. Various foods and fruits are offered to pay tribute to the souls of the ancestors. Thru offerings made on these days to Buddha and his disciples, the souls of one's ancestors are saved from the miseries in the world beyond.[60]

The WRA administration had an internal memo about Obon, as well.[61]

> Bon or Obon—This is a festival almost equal in importance to New Year's Day. At this time, by Japanese Buddhist tradition, the spirits of the dead return to their former homes. There are special services at the temples and in the homes. Graveyards are visited and tidied up and special offerings are made before the ancestral tablets (ihai) in the household Buddhist shelf (butsudan). Neighbors call on families observing Hatsu Bon or first Bon, i.e., families that have lost a member through death during the past year. In most parts of Japan special dances called Bon Odori are performed at this time which usually commences early in the evening and last many hours.[62]

満砂那佛教会盆踊

一九四三年八月十五日

FIGURE 6.5 Obon dance at the WRA camp at Manzanar, California (1943).   Courtesy of Manzanar National Historic Site, Shirley Nagatomi Okabe Collection, Nagatomi-073.

The massive Obon gathering at Manzanar in August 1943, which coincided with the erection of the Ireito, honored the spirits of both the recently departed and ancestors. The WRA Gila River camp similarly had a massive turnout of 5,000 spectators and 350 dancers for its first Obon in camp.[63] As the WRA report notes about Hatsu Bon (alternately known as Nii-Bon), for the families who had deaths in the previous year at Manzanar, this was a particularly significant ritual to observe.[64]

At one of the main gatherings during the festivities, Manzanar's project director, Ralph Merritt, delivered remarks about Obon from his perspective as a Christian. The speech reflected an unusually sympathetic perspective on Buddhism and religious freedom:

In turbulent times such as these, there is no line to separate men who in common have firm faith in the ethics of life . . . Not long ago a committee, which was said to represent one of the legisla-

FIGURE 6.6 Obon dance sponsored by the Heart Mountain Buddhist Church. Photograph by George Hirahara, Hirahara Photograph Collection, Washington State University Manuscripts, Archives, and Special Collections, sc14b01f0105n03.

tive branches of the State of California, passed a resolution calling for the cancellation of citizenship of those who were members of the Buddhist Church. Such an idea and such a proposal is thoroughly and completely un-American. The FOUR FREEDOMS guarantee freedom of religious worship in America   freedom is the basic concept of Buddhism . . . on this day dedicated by the Buddhist Church to the memories of the past and the honoring of those who have gone before, we all join in gratitude to those who by their sacrifice for us have made possible the light of freedom by which we live today.[65]

Merritt's firm stance that anti-Buddhist legislation was un-American was grounded first and foremost in what he called a "basic principle of America," as underscored by President Roosevelt's wartime assertion of four freedoms worth fighting for: of speech, of religion and worship, from want, and from fear. But Merritt also endorsed, as a Christian, the Buddhist practice during Obon of honoring of the spirits of both the recently deceased and of long-ago ancestors. He viewed it as a way to move through the "turbulent times" toward a more hopeful future. This interfaith understanding during Manzanar's 1943 Obon was also seen in the remarkable all-camp effort with the construction of the Ireitō, involving many individuals of various religious faiths. Were it not for the wartime confinement, it would have been an improbable feat for Buddhists to find enough common ground with Christians to build such a monument. Since the end of the war, the Ireito monument and cemetery have become primary symbols of the WRA Manzanar camp and the mass incarceration.[66]

Cooperation with Christians represented another skillful adaptation for Buddhists in the WRA camps. But their joint efforts, represented by Ireitō, were offset by other, divisive elements that generated tensions, and even violence, between Buddhists and Christians. (The so-called loyalty questionnaire, discussed in Chapter 8, raised particularly divisive issues.) Whether Buddhists found common ground or not with Christians, the WRA camps constituted a new reality in which Buddhists had to negotiate their place in a religiously pluralistic American landscape. On their way to developing a truly American Buddhism, they would also find ways to sever some formal ties with Japan.

ROOTING THE SANGHA

The largest sect of Japanese Buddhism in America was the Nishi Hongwanji tradition which, on the US continent, operated under the auspices of an incorporated organization called the Buddhist Mission of North America (BMNA). In the months after Pearl Harbor, the sect shifted the legal framework of its leadership from the issei to the handful of nisei priests, a dramatic step to demonstrate "Americanization." The national organization, given its displacement from San Francisco, followed its ailing issei bishop, Ryōtai Matsukage, and nisei spokesperson, Rev. Kenryō Kumata, to the WRA Topaz camp. Unlike the bishops of every other sect, the Nishi Hongwanji bishop had not been caught up in the FBI's initial selective incarceration process, which placed Buddhist leaders in Army or DOJ camps.[67] Because Bishop Matsukage was at

Topaz, his residential unit (4-2-C) in that camp automatically became the organizational headquarters of the BMNA.[68]

Almost immediately after he moved to Topaz, Bishop Matsukage pledged loyalty to the United States and against the Axis powers in a pronouncement that was widely circulated within the organization and showcased to WRA authorities. While this riled some issei Buddhist priests who were being held in the Army or DOJ camps, others were sympathetic. One, for example, wrote in his diary:

> it was probably for the best that our organization did not take an anti-American position. Because the North American Buddhist headquarters was originally incorporated under American laws, depending on how the winds blew, it could now either be disbanded by the government or could receive the government's protection. American Buddhism has been nurtured here for roughly fifty years. It is natural that if the organization wants to maintain a long-term existence here and to prosper, it must adopt stances that receive protection from the American government. Thus, we should recognize the necessity of making anti-Axis statements or proclamations of loyalty to America. There are those who complain, "Is our Bishop really Japanese?" But as long as we live here as individuals in America, we must live with the constraints put on us by the US government.[69]

Soon thereafter, as another reflection of skillful adaptation to American democratic practices, a public election was held to select twelve officers for the camp's Board of Directors of Buddhists, from a slate of twenty-two candidates. Polling booths were set up at Recreation Hall 28 from 9:30 AM to 5 PM to encourage a large turnout.[70] This type of democratic arrangement, perceived as more American, was adopted at all the WRA camps to emphasize how each vote weighed equally in the Buddhists' selection of their leadership.[71]

The emphasis on a more democratic organizational structure, and more specifically, one able to distance itself from its headquarters in Japan, was crucial to the BMNA's reorganization in camp. The selection of a nisei spokesperson, Rev. Kumata, was part of this transition. Thanks to the public, pro-American pronouncements in his bulletins and statements, Kumata was able to secure the WRA's support for an emergency nisei Buddhist National Conference, held outside of Topaz in the spring of 1943. The camp was in Utah, and because nearby Salt Lake City was well into the "free zone," far from the exclusion area, delegates of other WRA camps could also receive temporary passes to exit their barbed-wire perimeters and attend. Those assembled selected a popular YBA leader, Tadashi (Tad) Hirota, as the president of the emergency group, and also approved a motion to rename the Nishi Hongwanji organization from Buddhist Mission of North America to the Buddhist Churches of America.[72] The terminological switch to the word "church" was important.

Even more fundamental was a proposal to make a clean break from the authority of the sect's Kyoto headquarters—a clear symbol of the "Americanization" of the organization. It was proposed that the Buddhist Churches of America be run by a nisei board of directors headed by Kumata and composed of forty-seven members. The nisei Buddhist priest was permitted to leave the WRA camp to establish this new organization in the free-zone city of Ogden, Utah.[73] Further, the group decided that English would henceforth serve as the official language of the Buddhist Churches of America.

The measures adopted by the emergency meeting and endorsed soon thereafter by the WRA were ratified in July 1943 by a National YBA meeting, also held in Salt Lake City.[74] With further encouragement by WRA officials, the newly configured, American-citizen-led, national-level organization established local affiliates in several camps.[75] BMNA Bishop Matsukage was at that time experiencing a health crisis and preparing for surgery, yet he did what he could to support the younger generation's efforts. He sent out letters to all Nishi Hongwanji priests encouraging them to Americanize their Buddhism by supporting Rev. Kumata and the new organizational vision.[76]

High-level support like his was vital because this initiative to fundamentally reorganize the largest of the Buddhist sects in America faced opposition from many issei Buddhist priests in the WRA camps. They worried about the consequences of cutting ties to their spiritual home at the Hongwanji Temple in Kyoto, and about the impact on more el-

derly members of the organization of switching the organization's official language to English.[77] Negotiations over the details of this new,
"Americanized" organization came to a head in a major, three-day gathering in late April 1944 within the WRA Topaz camp. According to the
Topaz Buddhist newsletter *Hōmi* (Dharma Taste), the meeting was to
discuss "various issues for the American Buddhist community under
war conditions."[78] A total of forty select representatives attended from
the host Topaz Buddhist Church, the free-zone temples of Ogden, Salt
Lake City, and Denver, and other WRA camps such as Amache (in
Granada, Colorado), Minidoka, Heart Mountain, and Poston I and II.
The group opened with incense offerings, held services and Dharma lectures, and then adopted the new constitution for the BMNA that would
thenceforth govern the priests associated with the new organization, the
Buddhist Churches of America (BCA).[79]

The only concession to the issei priests was to elect former BMNA
Bishop Matsukage temporarily to the newly created BCA board as a lay
president, a position that had formerly been filled by Japanese headquarters appointment.[80] A few days later, one of the nisei BCA leaders filed
the organization's articles of incorporation in California, marking the
formal beginning of an America-centered organization of the largest of
the Japanese Buddhist sects.

Across the 2500-year history of Buddhism, as the religion moved from
one cultural or national context to another, adaptation happened organically, many times creating this kind of independent organization.
Japanese American Buddhists under incarceration, fully cognizant of
the risks of not skillfully adapting to a society that was questioning their
loyalty, accelerated this process. These Buddhists were also encouraged
by white WRA administrators whose perspective on the "Americanization" of Buddhism was framed by the histories of their own European
Christian institutions having transformed in the context of the United
States. At a YBA conference in 1943, Hugo W. Wolter, the acting chief of
community service at WRA Gila River, discussed Buddhism's place in
America as a nation of religious freedom:

> The Buddhist Church has come to a critical point in its history.
> The similar point has been reached in the past by many churches

which have been predominantly made up of people of one or another nationality. Various branches of the Evangelical and Lutheran churches developed among the Scandinavian and German groups in the United States. In the course of time, the languages native to them have almost completely disappeared from their churches. Catholicism uses very little of the original Latin in the carrying out of its services except for ceremonial affairs. Language of necessity and its very nature is not a part of any religious belief. It is merely a means of communicating ideas. It is therefore with great pleasure and understanding that I receive the news of the program of the Gila Young Buddhists to Americanize their program. . . . During the First World War, all groups which spoke German were suspected and criticized. The Japanese people are in that same situation today. . . . Since I have some firsthand experience of the feeling of racial prejudice during the First World War (my home was in Sheboygan, Wis., a predominantly German community), I can appreciate many of the difficulties which you face. . . . A great many people would like to understand much more about the Buddhist religion. I, personally, am one of them. . . . I should be very happy to consult with the leaders of your group and to give them the value of whatever experiences I have had.[81]

Just around the time of this speech, as ritual and organizational "Americanizing" of Buddhism in the WRA camps was speeding up, these skillful adaptations to camp life became interlinked with debates about Buddhists joining the US military. Tens of thousands of Japanese Americans—the majority of whom were Buddhists—served in the US military despite the irony of fighting for freedom while their families continued to be incarcerated in the camps or lived under discriminatory conditions under martial law in Hawai'i. Like many other ethnic communities, Buddhists would find it took the ultimate sacrifice of serving in combat for the United States to earn a recognized place in America.

7

ONWARD BUDDHIST SOLDIERS

"Buddhist Soldiers" was a "hymn" in the World War II service book created by Rev. Julius Goldwater. Composed by Dorothy Hunt, the wife of Goldwater's Buddhist teacher, the hymn sought to teach in song that Buddhist warfare did not involve violence against living beings, but instead the slaying of illusion. It went, in part:

> Have you heard the sound of footsteps
> As of soldiers marching on?
> Have you seen their banners waving?
> Have you heard their battle song?
> Have you watch'd their blazing torches
> Lighting up their columns long?
> [. . .]
> Nay! These are the Buddha's soldiers
> And the foe they seek to slay
> Is illusion's self that hinders
> Mankind's progress day by day
> Righteousness the sword they carry
> Wisdom's torch that lights their way.[1]

Buddhist soldiers didn't use the usual weapons of war. They employed moral righteousness and the light of wisdom as weapons for liberating the self and others from suffering.

But for most people of Japanese ancestry living in the United States during World War II, "Buddhist soldiers" had a different implication.

It referred to the thousands of nisei sons, brothers, and husbands who enlisted and served in the US armed forces. At a time when their country questioned their loyalty, young American Buddhists volunteered by the thousands for military service. Thousands more would be drafted. Just as most Japanese Americans were Buddhist, so too were most of the Japanese Americans who served. After the war, Rev. Newton Ishiura, the executive secretary of the Hawaii Federation of the YBA, discovered that 400 of the 506 Hawai'i-born nisei killed in action during the war were Buddhist.[2]

Many accounts of the Japanese American experience in the US military during World War II focus on the heroics of the 442nd Regimental Combat Team in Europe. But Japanese Americans served in many contexts, including in the Hawaiian Provisional Infantry Battalion (later the 100th Infantry Battalion [Separate]), in a variety of military intelligence units in the Pacific, and even in the Japanese Imperial Army if they were stranded in Japan when the war broke out. With a few notable exceptions, most histories of the Japanese American involvement in the US military also disproportionately highlight individuals who were Christian, despite the fact that the majority who served were Buddhist.

The notion of sacrifice through military service is a common trope in America. But in Rev. Shinjō Nagatomi's memorial sermon for Sergeant Kiyoshi Nakasaki and Private First Class Sadao Munemori, killed in action on the battlefields of Italy on April 5, 1945, those listening to his sermon would have understood his words on another level.[3] He began his address at the memorial service in the WRA Manzanar camp for two nisei soldiers killed in action saying:

> Your sons' life was a short one, but their holy and symbolic spirit of sacrifice now guide and help to preserve the nation's freedom and justice. When the roar of guns cease and the fighting men come home once again, with your strong and determined belief let us continue to keep alive their dedication to the cause: "May the People of the world enjoy everlasting freedom and peace."[4]

As Japanese American Buddhist soldiers, their sacrifice may well have been seen through the lens of the figure of a *bodhisattva* (an ideal

Buddhist practitioner in the Mahayana Buddhist traditions to which the soldiers belonged). *Bodhisattvas* were understood as enlightened practitioners who sacrificed their ultimate liberation by remaining in the world of suffering to assist others to attain freedom. Even at times taking on negative karma to help others, a *bodhisattva* acted always to sacrifice the self for a greater cause of freedom. In a similar way, the nisei Buddhist warriors were seen by many in the WRA camps and on the Hawaiian Islands as serving not only their country, but also, through their sacrifice, the Japanese American community's claim on a place in America. The nisei volunteers and prewar draftees decided to fight fully aware of the karmic debt that killing involved, and despite the irony that their families were incarcerated behind barbed wire or suppressed under martial law by the country they served.

RICHARD SAKAKIDA, AMERICAN SPY

Richard Sakakida, a US Army intelligence officer captured by the Japanese in the Philippines, calculated that his cell in Manila's Bilibid Prison, which he shared with seven prisoners, measured eight feet by twelve feet. The young nisei Buddhist from Hawai'i had spent his first days in captivity laboring in the prison's work detail. He now steeled himself for the worst as the Kenpcitai, the notorious Japanese military "thought police" unit, with their distinctive white armbands printed with the characters "Kenpei," took him to the interrogation room. He knew they would try to beat a confession out of him.

The interrogators tied his hands behind his back and strung him up over a rafter, stripped him naked, and started burning different parts of his body with a lit cigarette:

> He started in the area of my thighs. As the days went on, he went up to the area of my abdomen before finally getting to my genitals, hoping all along that I would crack. The pain, added to the pain in my arms that already felt dislocated, was indescribable. I was subjected to same torture day after day. There were times when I felt like screaming as loud as I could but I refused to give

them that satisfaction. After a while, I began to lapse into a state of extreme nausea compounded by the smell of burning flesh— my own. . . . If I was enraged during the early stages of torture, I was by then, delivered into a state of incandescent fury, particularly as he buried the cigarette into my penis. That was the last straw and I knew that in my state of indescribable rage, my torturer was not about to break the steel-like clamp on my nerves.[5]

Sakakida was the only Japanese American intelligence officer to be captured as a prisoner of war by the Japanese military. During his ten-day ordeal, in which he refused to give up any US military secrets or even admit to being an American agent, Sakakida relied on his Buddhist faith. He said his Buddhist upbringing "made me turn inward, looking for inner strength to counter the pain that had already reached an almost unbearable level. Fortunately, my rebelliousness and Buddhist faith held me in good stead."

Sakakida had entered military service in March 1941 when the US Army Corps of Intelligence Police (CIP)—later known as the Counter Intelligence Corps (CIC)—recruited him in Honolulu. Nine months before Pearl Harbor, the Army had begun preparing for a possible war with Japan by assembling a team to gather information about Japan's intentions. The twenty-year-old was one of two candidates selected from an elite group of thirty nisei. At Central Intermediate High School in Honolulu, he was put through two days of grueling interviews and Japanese language proficiency tests.[6]

Sakakida had been chosen on the suggestion of retired Col. Walter Gilbert, his ROTC mentor at McKinley High School in Honolulu. Gilbert had kept his eye on the young nisei since Sakakida had moved, at a young age, from his plantation roots in Puunene, Maui, to the territorial capital. In his senior year at his multiethnic high school, Sakakida was considered the best cadet at the school and led three regiments as a cadet colonel. He was even offered the opportunity to be the first Japanese American to enroll at the US Military Academy at West Point, which he turned down to honor his mother's objection to a military career.

Sakakida had excellent Japanese language skills, acquired by attending one of the most selective Japanese language schools in Hawai'i, the Buddhist-run Hongwanji Japanese School. The priests also instructed their students in history and ethics, following a curriculum based on one taught in Japan, including the values of filial piety, honor, and integrity—with one difference. "Because the school was run by a Buddhist order," Sakakida said, "the classes on ethics did not stress military values as was the case in Japan during that period. Bushido, the code of the warrior, was ignored in our class on ethics. That was because Buddhism in general stressed compassion and opposition to warlike activities."[7]

Sakakida was elected class president and offered a full scholarship from the Hongwanji Temple in Kyoto to attend the sect's prestigious Buddhist university in Japan. At the end of his coursework, Sakakida would have been eligible for ordination into the priesthood. His widowed mother, a devout Buddhist, hoped her son would become the first Hawai'i-based nisei to become a Buddhist priest.[8] But Sakakida had other ambitions.

Sakakida decided against West Point to respect his mother's wishes. But he was eager to "make it" as an American rather than base himself in Japan. So, immediately after high school, Sakakida went to work at both the Hawaiian Pineapple Company and the radio station KGU as a Japanese-language announcer. Two years later, in March 1941, his ordinary life changed dramatically when he was recruited as a special agent of the US Army's G-2, the intelligence branch at Fort Shafter in Honolulu. Since he was under twenty-one, he needed his mother's permission to join the US military.

Sakakida's ROTC mentor, Colonel Gilbert, visited her at home to plead with her. Resigned to her son's choice, she signed the permission forms, marking them with an "X" because she could not sign her name in English. At that point, neither Sakakida nor his mother knew that he had been recruited to work as an undercover agent in the Philippines. They assumed that he would be sent to the US continent to help translate Japanese documents for the US Army. Sending her young son off, Sakakida's mother gave him a parting message he would never forget: "In the event that my motherland goes to war with America, just remember that America is your country. Your father and uncles all served in the Japanese Army with honor and I do not want you to return from service in the US Army in disgrace."[9]

With his mother's admonition in mind, Sakakida headed to the Philippines to gather intelligence on the Japanese, whose military advances in China and Indochina in early 1941 signaled impending war. Sakakida and fellow agent Arthur Komori—two of only four Japanese American operatives in the CIP at that time—blended in with the crewmembers of *The Republic,* an army transport carrying a reserve unit to the Philippines.[10] When they reached the Philippines in late April, Sakakida developed a cover story that he had jumped ship from an American freighter to avoid being drafted by the US Army, and was looking for a job in Manila. It sounded believable enough to the owner and residents of the Nishikawa Hotel in Manila, where Sakakida checked in. He soon gained the sympathy and trust of the other Japanese in Manila, especially the wealthy proprietor of the hotel and his wife. They were especially impressed by Sakakida's abstinence from meat, following Buddhist custom, on the anniversary of his father's death.

Meanwhile, at the US Army G-2 military intelligence headquarters in Fort Santiago, the Army gave Sakakida his code name, "Sixto Borja," and badge number, "B-16."[11] As US-Japan relations worsened during the fall of 1941, Sakakida's first mission was to identify Japanese nationals in Manila working for Japanese military intelligence.[12] Then, on December 7, the Japanese bombed Pearl Harbor. Between December 10 and 12, they simultaneously attacked US air bases in the Philippines and landed invasion forces at six locations. US headquarters ordered Sakakida to remain with the Manila Japanese community, and he continued gathering intelligence until assigned to nearby Fort Santiago, which sorely needed qualified Japanese linguists. By that time, the US army had fully engaged Japanese forces and was being pushed back into northern Luzon. Sakakida's new responsibilities included "psychological warfare, radio intercepts, cryptology, and prisoner interrogation."[13] But in the face of advancing Japanese troops, Sakakida and the US forces were forced to evacuate Manila. He was ordered to Corregidor and Bataan, where he worked on radio broadcasts urging the Japanese to surrender, translating captured enemy documents and conducting prisoner interrogations.[14]

As US forces retreated farther south on the Bataan Peninsula, the men were put on half-rations and their morale deteriorated. In February 1942, Sakakida analyzed documents found on the body of a slain Japanese officer on the other side of Bataan. Among them he discovered an order for transporting a battalion to Quinauan Point, as part of a major drive with the Japanese troops already established on Luzon. With this intelligence, US forces launched a successful surprise attack against a Japanese flotilla and killed the Japanese battalion commander, whose sword was delivered to General MacArthur as "a memento of our victorious stand against the seemingly unstoppable Japanese invasion force."[15]

Despite this victory, Japanese forces continued their advance, and thousands of US troops were lost in Bataan. In March, military intelligence sent Sakakida to Corregidor, where he was assigned to work with Col. "Tiger" Teague and the Signal Corps to monitor Japanese radio and decipher Japanese codes. By decoding voice communications from Japanese bombers taking off from Clark Air Base, he identified when and where bombing raids would occur, preventing American casualties. Nonetheless, with Japanese control of the air virtually unchallenged, Bataan fell on April 9, 1942. Corregidor was overrun by Japanese troops and hundreds of American POWs died in the long and brutal Bataan Death March.[16]

G-2 had given Sakakida a last-minute opportunity to leave the Philippines for a safer base in Australia, where General MacArthur's headquarters were located.[17] But Sakakida chose to remain, though he knew he would be executed if his role as an intelligence agent were exposed. After destroying documents linking him to army intelligence, he accompanied General Wainwright, the general in command of US forces in the Philippines, to the surrender site as the US translator on May 6, 1942. He went in civilian clothes, posing as a local interpreter.

Almost immediately after Sakakida arrived at the surrender site, a Japanese sergeant major punched him in the face, shattering his glasses. Several former Japanese POWs whom Sakakida had interrogated had identified him as the Japanese American involved with the US propaganda broadcasts.[18] After the formal surrender, the Japanese army seized him and took him to the commander of the notorious Kenpeitai.

Although he was an American citizen, the Japanese accused Sakakida of treason. At the prison, the Kenpeitai viewed a person of Japanese ancestry working for the enemy as a traitor of the worst kind. Their torture of Sakakida—the beatings, the dislocating of his shoulders, and the systematic burning—was particularly brutal. After the torture sessions, they forced him to perform so-called "spiritual exercises" in the prison courtyard, such as collecting pebbles in a container before they were scattered again by the guards, and to clean the latrines used by the prison director and the guards. Through these cruelties, guards taunted that they would cleanse him of his "Yankee spirit."

"They were wrong," Sakakida later said. "All the torture and beating did not dampen my Yankee spirit and whatever spirit it was that was fueling my resistance. They not only rekindled that spirit in prison; they set it on fire."[19]

Sakakida remembered the example of priests at his Buddhist Japanese-language school in Hawai'i. "Their intensity was reflected in the very quiet way they seemed to control every observable facet of their behavior," he said. "They eschewed violence for the sake of violence, but we [students] always sensed that there was a response of fierce intensity waiting to be unleashed if they were provoked. They taught us a great deal about emotional and physical control and endurance."[20] This "*gaman,* or the need to endure even the seemingly unendurable . . . made me a better American in the process."[21]

After the torture sessions failed to break him, the interrogators suddenly informed him on February 11, 1943 (Japanese Empire Day) that the Japanese Imperial Army was graciously dropping the treason charges. They assigned him to work for the judge advocate's office as a translator. One of Sakakida's main tasks was to work on court cases related to Filipino guerrillas fighting for independence and their suspected sympathizers. He served as an interpreter at show trials, where authorities had already determined who would be sent to Mantinlupa Prison and who would be decapitated. The executions, Sakakida said, were "normally performed in groups of ten. I felt helpless knowing that this was going on and able to do nothing."[22] The most he could do was tone down the guerillas' remarks in his translation in the hope that the Japanese judges would show some small mercy toward the prisoners.

Sakakida knew the cases were rigged because he was given the job of running the mimeograph machine to copy trial verdicts before the trials had begun. In his first week of training on the machine, he ran across some scrap paper on which a death verdict for his own treason trial was printed. Later he learned that the Japanese General Takaji Wachi had overturned his death sentence, reasoning that Sakakida could be killed after his language skills had been exploited by the Japanese Imperial Army.

Although Sakakida was constantly under suspicion, he worked well with others in the office, and soon found moments when he was not being watched. Having access to incoming correspondence, he made up his mind both to deliver intelligence to the US side and to escape. The tide of the war in the Pacific was turning and, after several major American victories, Sakakida knew that he would be executed if he did not escape before the Americans came too close.

His first step was to establish a network on the outside that could be trusted to get information to the United States. One day while Sakakida was working, the wife of a prominent guerrilla, Ernesto Tupas, came by the judge advocate's office. Tupas had participated in the Bataan campaign and worked with the US Army G-2. His wife needed a special dispensation from the captain at the office for a visitor's pass. Earlier, Sakakida had managed to use the captain's legal stamp, and left the stamp in an unlocked drawer at night so he could forge several of these passes. He gave them to Mrs. Tupas with an additional authorization allowing her to deliver food parcels to her husband, which had hidden tools the guerrillas later used for a prison break. Mrs. Tupas, grateful to Sakakida, risked her life to serve as the conduit to the guerrillas on the outside, who had obtained several Japanese army uniforms. They smuggled in one officer's uniform to Sakakida so that he could help the guerrillas escape.[23]

Sakakida had also managed to steal an officer candidate's spare insignia. He then concocted an escape plan based on surveillance of the prison's security detail. In August 1944, Sakakida and the Filipino guerrillas went forward with their plot. Sakakida recalled:

> Just before midnight, we moved silently toward the prison gate. We were blessed that night because there was no inspection by the duty officer. We began marching to the gate. As soon as the guard spotted the red sash of the officer of the day, which I was

wearing, he and the other guards bowed deeply. Without a word, we disarmed the guards who were taken completely by surprise. Within five minutes we had the prison office under our control. . . . All of the guerrillas and anyone else wishing to be freed were released from their cells."[24]

Sakakida returned to his quarters as if nothing had happened and the Japanese did not connect him to the bogus officer. Afterward, he delivered sensitive intelligence to the United States through Tupas's group, meeting at night at the Ayala Bridge or at the parking lot at Quiapo Church. One of those messages proved devastating for a Japanese force moving south from Mindanao.

While helping a judge advocate officer pack his bags, Sakakida learned the officer was to accompany a massive convoy headed to the front lines. Sakakida's information confirmed data gathered by MacArthur's code-breaking team, allowing American submarines to lie in wait for the convoy and destroy three transports with 1,290 troops on board. A further 6,800 Japanese troops on other transports and destroyers lost their ordnance and supplies when their ships were sunk.[25]

Sakakida still had to escape. His opportunity came in January 1945. With the Americans advancing, the judge advocate's office was to be withdrawn to Baguio. But with MacArthur's island-hopping strategy in full swing, the Japanese army in Baguio was forced to contemplate a quick retreat into the mountains. While his commanding officer was preoccupied with operational matters, Sakakida, who had become trusted by the Japanese officers, received permission to stay behind for a few days to recover from a bout of malaria and beriberi before joining them. Having planned his escape for some time, he had managed to steal and hide pouches of rice, a mess kit, and a .357 magnum and ammunition to use until he could rejoin advancing US units.

Escaping the largely abandoned base, he entered the jungle. For the first few days, he wandered aimlessly without a compass, surviving by eating edible grasses and fruit. He then wandered into a settlement of the aboriginal Igorot tribe—who, Sakakida had heard, were headhunters. Having narrowly avoided a beheading at the hands of the Japanese military, he wondered if his luck would hold. But rather than a beheading, the Igorot provided him with a hut and a special meal of roast dog, an Igorot delicacy. Sakakida later said he ate with little relish, but great appreciation.

His strength restored, Sakakida pressed into the jungle, a no-man's land between the Japanese and American forces, walking for several weeks with little to eat. At one point, he happened across an abandoned Japanese quartermaster field depot, where he found sacks of rice and other food and prepared what seemed like a feast. After dinner, he decided to have a smoke—a near-fatal mistake. A Japanese artillery unit spotted the smoke and engulfed Sakakida in a barrage of fire. Hit and knocked unconscious, he woke up to a searing pain from shrapnel lodged in his abdomen. He could barely move, and after three days, gangrene set in. Using a razor blade, he removed the last piece of shrapnel, nearly passing out after each cut.

In the ensuing weeks Sakakida recovered thanks to something he remembered from Hawai'i and the samurai movies he watched as a kid—a medicinal paste made of fresh herbs used to heal sword cuts. The herbs did help treat his most pressing wounds, but he was beset with malaria, beriberi, dysentery, and body lice. Delirious, he lost track of time, but kept moving. After nearly five months of aimless wandering along the Asing River, eating rats and whatever he could forage, he ran into an American patrol. Worried that his Japanese face would alarm them, he shouted, "Don't shoot, I'm an American."

They told him that the war had been over for weeks. Shoulted and relieved, Sakakida was nonetheless initially treated poorly. The sentry repeatedly demanded that he hand over the gold watch his mother had given him in Hawai'i, and the master sergeant told him, "Look, you may speak good English but you're still on the other side."[26] Their attitude changed after the commanding officer called CIC and confirmed Sakakida's story.

By mid-September 1945, Sakakida was back in Manila at the CIC headquarters. Here, too, his loyalty was questioned when his debriefing turned into something more akin to an interrogation. But Sakakida's expertise was in such demand that, despite his poor health, he forfeited

FIGURE 7.1 Richard Sakakida tells of his capture and torture at a war crimes trial.   Courtesy of CriticalPast, File No. 65675071358_004255.

the usual convalescence period granted to POWs and was immediately sent to work on the war crimes trials.

Sakakida would spend the next nineteen years in Japan as a career military officer, initially serving as part of the US occupation staff. Offered a commission in the army, he became the chief of the apprehension and interrogation division of the war crimes commission. In that position, he had access to all the POW camps. He decided to track down the Kenpeitai master sergeant, captain, and major who had overseen his torture back in 1942 in the Manila prison:

> I had them brought to Manila and went to see them, wearing dark glasses to hide my identity. Through an interpreter I asked them, "We are looking for a nisei by the name of Sakakida. Did any of you know him?" They each replied in the negative. I removed my sunglasses and [they] showed no traces of the arrogance I had long associated with them. Looking frightened and

guilty, my former torturers prostrated themselves on the ground as if ready to accept any punishment I chose to inflict upon them. But by now I was far too removed from the rage I had felt while in their control; the war was over, and I had no desire to return to bitter hatred and killing.[27]

Instead, tears rolled down Sakakida's face and he offered the three Kenpeitai men cigarettes and candy. In later years, he attributed his forgiveness to his Buddhist faith.[28] After savage torture and the harrowing experiences of war, there remained something serene and compassionate within Sakakida.

Few nisei who served and survived in either the Pacific or European theaters had such dramatic wartime experiences as Sakakida.[29] But many nisei soldiers faced the same dilemma. They wanted to affirm their American identity without abandoning their ethnic and religious heritage—but these tied them to America's enemy, Japan.

THE MILITARY INTELLIGENCE SERVICE

Richard Sakakida was one of roughly three thousand nisei who served in the US military's campaign in the Pacific. Another three thousand served during the immediate postwar years when Japan was under US occupation.[30] Assessing their significance to the Allied cause, Major General Charles Willoughby, the G-2 intelligence chief for General MacArthur, said: "The six thousand niseis saved a million lives, and shortened the Pacific war by two years."[31]

Most of these men were Buddhist, many of them kibei (American citizens educated in Japan). They were recruited for their Japanese language ability, whether acquired from schooling in Japan or in Japanese-language schools run by Buddhist temples in America.[32] Ironically, the bitter opposition of many Japanese American Christian leaders during the 1920s and 1930s to Japanese language schools as an impediment to "true Americanization" limited the ability of Japanese American Christians to assist the American war effort. Owing to their Japanese language ability, the so-called heathen Buddhist nisei and the "unassimilated" kibei would be the ones who primarily contributed to American intelligence operations in the Pacific.

In innumerable instances, their knowledge of Japanese language and culture allowed these soldiers, like Sakakida, to save the lives of fellow Americans through document translation, prisoner interrogation, and interpreting of radio intercepts. Later in the war, they saved thousands more lives of Japanese soldiers, POWs, and civilians using their Japanese-language skills in combat zones and to create propaganda material urging surrender.

Early on, senior military intelligence officers had recognized there would be a need for qualified linguists in the event of war with Japan. A 1942 *Life* magazine piece entitled "The Japanese Language" publically highlighted the "troublesome war shortage" of "non-Japanese American citizens who understand the Japanese language." Viewing the nisei as a suspect group, its author worried about the lack of trustworthy individuals to serve "as interpreters, code-room assistants, and censors." Citing a study by the Office of War Information, he claimed that only "three Americans" (meaning white Americans) had "full command of the language." Even with the requirement reduced to partial ability, "the most optimistic estimates from Washington put the number at less than 100 persons."[33]

While German Americans and Italian Americans already in the US military could provide the requisite language skills to effectively conduct a war on European soil, no branch of the US military could boast more than a handful of white Japanese-language speakers. Military authorities considered these individuals—typically former government and military attachés who had served in Japan or Christian missionaries who had traveled or been born there—to be far more trustworthy than Japanese Americans who could speak Japanese. Especially in the most sensitive areas such as code breaking, the Army entrusted work primarily to white former missionaries and their offspring who had spent time in Japan.[34] Exacerbating the situation was the fact that, prior to the activation of the Selective Training and Service Act in October 1940, the military, with the exception of a few National Guard units, had not permitted the voluntary enlistment of Japanese Americans.[35]

This had changed with the United States' first peacetime draft, requiring able-bodied young men to serve for one year in the armed forces, and for an indefinite term of service if war broke out. Between October 1940 and the attack on Pearl Harbor, roughly three thousand nisei between the ages of twenty-one and thirty-six were conscripted through the selective service system and its local boards.[36] The US Army's contingent of drafted nisei constituted a sizable new pool of potential linguists at a time when military intelligence analysts considered a war against Japan increasingly probable.[37]

In June 1941, the Army embarked on a program to recruit nisei for a Japanese language school that would train men for potential work in cryptology, prisoner interrogation, translation, and psychological warfare. Major Carlisle Dusenbury, a former Japanese language student in the Army's Intelligence Division, and Lieutenant Colonel Wallace Moore, who had been born to Christian missionaries in Japan, proposed the program. They suggested recruiting nisei already in the US military, arguing that culturally-sensitive interrogators could persuade Japanese POWs to reveal information of military value.[38] By early fall 1941, the Fourth Army was selected to open a new school at the Presidio in San Francisco, which was the headquarters of the Pacific command and located near a large concentration of Japanese Americans.

The few Christian Japanese Americans with Japanese linguistic ability were favored. John Aiso was initially recruited as a student, quickly made an instructor, and later became the school's director of academic training. Born in 1909 in Burbank, California, he was regarded as a model of assimilation. His mother hung portraits of Jesus, Lincoln, and Washington in their family living room. He served in the Reserve Officers' Training Corps (ROTC), and was on an award-winning debate team at Hollywood High School. After attending Brown University as undergraduate, he became the first nisei to graduate from Harvard Law School in 1934. After graduation, he worked for an American legal firm with interests in Japan and Manchuria, during which time he mastered not only the Japanese language, but also many aspects of Japanese commercial law. Aiso returned to Los Angeles in 1939, and two years later was drafted into the US Army. Captain Kai Rasmussen discovered him at the Riverside Air

Force Base, working as a parts clerk in the motor pool, and quickly had him transferred to the Presidio.[39]

The Japanese language school, housed in an abandoned hangar at the Presidio's Crissy Field, formally opened on November 1, 1941, about a month prior to the attack on Pearl Harbor.[40] The process of recruiting the first class of sixty students—fifty-eight nisei and two Caucasians already in the army—was shaped by prejudices long held by both army and navy intelligence communities against Buddhists and Japan-educated kibei.[41] During the recruitment period from July to October 1941, the Fourth Army's G-2 decided to neglect Hawai'i-based Japanese Americans in the military and focus its energies on the 1,300 nisei draftees based on the west coast. Interviewing them at their various military posts, Lt. Col. John Weckerling reported to the war department that the majority seemed eager to serve in such a school. He declared, however, that only a small fraction of the nisei, perhaps as few as forty, could be considered both linguistically competent and "of unquestioned loyalty."[42]

The team screened out those who had a parent or sibling living in Japan, those who had made trips to Japan deemed suspicious in some way, or those who belonged to social or athletic clubs that appeared too culturally "Japanese." This screening inevitably reduced the pool, since those most likely to be fluent in both languages and cultures were those who participated in Japanese cultural, religious, and athletic activities. By contrast, Christian nisei on the continent who spoke only English were the candidates least likely to be helpful. It was not until late 1942 that Kai Rasmussen finally, desperately ordered: "Use the Hawaiians!"[43] The sudden wartime demand for Japanese-language speakers loosened the strict and prejudicial screening tests. Provided with a meager budget and three hastily constructed classrooms in the hangar, the Presidio's inaugural class learned how to read and write Japanese at advanced levels, focusing on the familiarity with specialized military Japanese terminology and ability to read cursive handwriting that would be necessary to decipher codes, military orders, and captured documents.[44]

Among those who excelled was a kibei Buddhist, Private Thomas Tokio Sakamoto, who became an instructor at the language school and later interrogated prisoners in combat zones in the Pacific. Sakamoto,

born in San Jose, California, had attended one of San Jose's Japanese language schools "just on Saturdays" where he had studied under a Buddhist minister. "I had considerable knowledge before I went to Japan [in]
1934 [to start] high school all over again. When I returned from Japan I
started a *kendō* school in San Jose," he recalled, referring to the Japanese fencing-style martial art. "The war began, and because *kendō* was
associated with ultra-nationalism the FBI took in many of the parents.
By that time I was already in the Army."[45]

As the eldest of eleven children, Sakamoto remembered worrying,
when he was drafted into the US Army in February 1941, that his family
would not be able to manage its forty-three-acre fruit and vegetable farm
without him. But his father, a veteran of the Japanese Imperial Army,
was pleased to see his son serve *his* country, the United States. Pvt. Sakamoto recalled his send-off at the Santa Clara train station with several
other nisei draftees: "the families waved both the US and Japanese flags,
shouting *banzai* over and over. The echoes of *banzai* stayed with me for
a long time, as we rode the train with mixed feelings."[46] Unlike the nisei
who served later in the European theater, many of these young men knew
that, given their language training, they would likely help prosecute a
war with their parents' and other relatives' homeland.

Pvt. Sakamoto was approached at his Army base, Fort Hunter Liggett
in California, by Captain Rasmussen on one of the latter's early recruitment tours. Rasmussen pulled the prewar draftee Sakamoto aside and
asked him to translate several passages from a Japanese military field
manual on the spot. While many nisei had great difficulty making any
sense of the document, even those who had attended Japanese language
school regularly, Sakamoto recalled that since he "had graduated from
Japanese high school in 1938, reading and translating this textbook wasn't
difficult."[47]

Sakamoto later became one of the first Military Intelligence Service
(MIS) personnel to volunteer to serve in a combat zone. Embedded with
the Texas-based First Cavalry Division in Australia and New Guinea,
he participated in the assault on Los Negros Island, later recalling: "we
climbed over the side with full gear, into a net, and landed on a landing
craft. We were being machine-gunned by the Japanese at the entrance
of Los Negros's small bay as we landed. . . . For three days and three

nights we didn't sleep; there was firefighting all the time."[48] There, thanks to Sakamoto's translation of a Japanese operations order found on a captured solider, the American artillery gained accurate coordinates for firing as well as the dates and times of planned "banzai attacks." He was awarded a Bronze Star for bravery in one battle. On orders from General Chase, he stood up at one point to face a group of Japanese soldiers and urge them to surrender, only to have them fire on him and go on to fight to the last man. Their commander committed suicide.[49] At the end of the war, Sakamoto was one of the nisei who stood on the deck of the USS Missouri to witness Japan's surrender.

George Taketa, who had joined the US Army as a volunteer prior to the war, also became an MIS linguist. Born in Sacramento, California, Taketa had a father who had taught the martial arts of judo and kendō and was an active member of the Japanese Association and a Japanese military support group (the Heimusha). With the outbreak of war, the FBI had immediately arrested the elder Taketa. But it was precisely the immersion in his father's culture that made George Taketa an asset to the US military: "I went to Japanese school twelve years, Boy Scouts, judo, kendō, Buddhist church, basketball, a lot of baseball. Every day, every night was occupied. . . . no time to fool around. [Dad] made us straight and sharp and to the point."[50]

Another prewar draftee who ended up in the MIS was Frank Hachiya, a kibei from Hood River, Oregon. A student at the University of Oregon before he enlisted in the US Army, Hachiya was among the more Americanized of the kibei. Nevertheless, he was highly proficient in Japanese because of his four years of education in his father's hometown of Okayama, Japan. A Buddhist funeral was held for him in the mess hall of Block 37 in the WRA Minidoka camp in 1945, after he was killed in action during the campaign to retake the Philippines from the Japanese. Hachiya had volunteered for forward duty to interrogate prisoners and parachuted deep into the remote mountainous jungles of Leyte with the Thirty-Second Infantry Regiment. Accounts of how he was killed vary. Some news reports of the day attributed his death to a Japanese sniper, while later accounts, such as an editorial in the New York Times, claimed that his fellow American GIs mistook him for the Japanese enemy and shot him dead in the heat of battle.[51]

Yet another early Buddhist MIS recruit was Hawaiʻi-born Akira Ki-kuchi, who had been a college student on the continental US when the war broke out. His father, Rev. Chikyoku Kikuchi of the Naalehu Hongwanji Mission, had been arrested right after the Pearl Harbor attack. Not knowing that his father had been taken away, Kikuchi wrote in the days following the declaration of war: "Father and Mother, you must be at an awful loss, but please try not to worry about me. I am always with the Buddha."[52]

Initially, the loyalty of these young Buddhists to the United States was questioned. Lt. Col. Weckerling himself monitored the Japanese Americans he had recruited. As he wrote at the time:

> I have been so anxious to enroll white Americans, particularly officers, in the school. Upon their graduation such personnel, of unquestioned loyalty, will be available to assign to the headquarters of divisions, corps and army. Their presence there would serve to check the actions of the Japanese translators, and relieve commanders of their apprehensions on being double-crossed by the latter.[53]

After the war, one of the white graduates of the language school, Sheldon Covell, revealed: "We were told our principal mission was to learn sufficient Japanese so that we could be sure the nisei were translating, interrogating, and reporting accurately, and not deceiving our intelligence people with false information."[54]

The suspicion of Japanese American MIS linguists came in part from the fact that many of them had relatives in the Japanese military. Further, of the more than ten thousand nisei living in Japan at the outbreak of the war, roughly three thousand served in the Japanese Imperial Army and Navy.[55] Rev. Jikyō Masaki, a Buddhist priest serving the Jōdo Mission of Hawaii Betsuin at the outbreak of the war, had three sons in the military. One served in the Japanese Imperial Army stationed in China, a second in the US Army as a part of the segregated Japanese-American 100th / 442nd in Italy, and a third in the US Military Intelligence Service.[56] Rev. Masaki himself was arrested immediately after Pearl Harbor. He was housed in Sand Island internment camp in Hawaiʻi before being sent to a series of Army and DOJ-administered camps on the continent, and then deported to Japan on a prisoner exchange ship in 1943. After returning to Japan, he entered the Japanese military as a translator in Singapore, serving his country in a role parallel to that of his own son in the US Military Intelligence Service. Before the family could reunite, the father died when a US submarine sank his ship as it headed back to Japan from Singapore.

The war in the Pacific theater thus required these bilingual and bicultural Buddhist families to sacrifice sons for the American cause. That the security of the nation suddenly turned on the "heathen" Japanese-speaking Buddhist volunteers laid bare the fault in assuming America to be simply an Anglo-Christian nation. Indeed, as the war in Europe began to be fought by American forces, the US Army also began to map out a role for Japanese Americans in that theater of operations. These considerations of how to employ those already in the US military, having volunteered or been drafted before the war, would pave the way to a segregated Japanese American unit in Europe.

DRAFTEES AND VOLUNTEERS

While the Presidio language school accelerated its activities after Pearl Harbor, other nisei already in the US military were on a different trajectory. Brig. Gen. Lewis Hershey, the director of selective service, took the public stance for some weeks after Pearl Harbor that Japanese Americans should still be accepted into the US military through the mandatory draft. But in practice, local boards generally acted to reject them. In Hawai'i, boards immediately stopped inducting draft-age nisei into the military. A great number were reclassified to 4-F, a category defined as "undesirable," most often because of a physical, mental, or moral defect. Only a handful of local boards in the continental US permitted Japanese Americans to join the three thousand nisei who had been drafted prior to the attack on Pearl Harbor. One such board was near the Oakland Buddhist Temple. Writing to the temple's headquarters, one temple official reported that thirteen young Buddhists had joined the armed forces during January and February of 1942, and that the temple had arranged for "send-off parties and gifts in appreciation for the duties they are to perform as American soldiers. In order that they keep up their morale, and to let them know that they are not forgotten, the Older Women's Club are sending gifts twice a year to these boys stationed at the various camps."[57]

Some nisei slipped through the cracks of local boards more interested in filling their quotas than in banning Japanese Americans. But in March 1942, the war department ordered selective service to impose an absolute ban on accepting "Japanese or persons of Japanese extraction, regardless of citizenship status" into the armed forces. By the end of the month, all state directors were informed by selective service that such inductions must be halted.[58] A formal policy was issued by selective service headquarters six months later, uniformly classifying all Japanese-American registrants in the 4-C category of "enemy aliens," regardless of their citizenship status or family history.[59] This was demoralizing to Japanese Americans already in military service, who were retained or discharged according to the wishes of their commanding officers, as well as the thousands of nisei of military age who wanted to be given the chance to serve and prove their loyalty to their country. Given that the military of that time was primarily a citizen's rather than a professional military, being denied the right to serve undermined many Japanese Americans' sense of citizenship.

On the US continent, nisei soldiers were considered suspect. At Fort Lewis in Washington State, they had their rifles confiscated and were sent to their guard posts unarmed. Robert Yoshioka was sent empty-handed to guard the mouth of the Columbia River and told "You'll get your rifle back if there's an attack."[60] The majority of the nisei were reclassified into the DEML (Detached Enlisted Men's List) by March 1942 and reassigned to nonessential jobs such as garbage or latrine details, or were organized into labor units to clean up after other troops passing through camps.

Many prewar draftees ended up in military training at Camp Robinson in Arkansas, where local leaders from nearby Little Rock were hostile to the 901 Japanese American soldiers stationed there. Locals were concerned about Japanese American soldiers interacting with both whites and blacks, and how their presence might affect race relations in the region. White community leaders also complained about their religion. In a letter sent to the war department in March 1942, the Little Rock Chamber of Commerce demanded the removal of Japanese American soldiers, focusing on the fact that Buddhist services had been held in the camp and the ill effects this "pagan religion" would have on the community.[61]

About six hundred Japanese Americans who had undergone basic training in Arkansas were transferred to Fort Riley in Kansas, where the Army declined to issue them firearms and helmets. While two-thirds of this contingent of nisei soldiers were reassigned over the course of about a year to Camp Shelby, Mississippi, to prepare for eventual active duty, many soldiers were kept back in Kansas to perform menial tasks. The most glaring example of Japanese American soldiers being treated as suspect and a potential threat to national security was during President Roosevelt's April 1943 tour of military installations and factories focused on the war effort. Upon his arrival at Fort Riley, the Japanese Americans were marched to a building far away from the parade grounds where all other military personnel were lined up to greet the president. A half-dozen white soldiers aimed .30 caliber machine guns at the Japanese Americans as they filed into the building and another group pointed rifles at them once inside. Ordered to keep their eyes forward and not to speak, the nisei spent the next several hours in silence, contemplating how their country viewed them. US Army officials in Washington became concerned about the camp commander's treatment of them as if they were prisoners in their own military. When a report was issued in response, denying the treatment was discriminatory and claiming it was perfectly reasonable given security concerns, Colonel William P. Scobey, the general staff executive to the assistant secretary of war, raised the following questions: "Was the inspecting officer trying to give protective cover-up to someone? . . . When did the classification of Kibei or Buddhist become conclusive proof of disloyalty? . . . Why were the 72, presumably loyal Japanese Americans, confined?"[62]

Such rejection and discrimination by the military undermined nisei confidence in America's commitment to fair play. In Hawai'i, the state-run Hawaii Territorial Guard was disbanded on January 21, 1942—and reconstituted the following day with all Japanese American guardsmen excluded. A small contingent of nisei associated with the University of Hawai'i's ROTC lobbied for reinstatement. With the assistance of two members of the public morale division in the territorial office of civilian defense, the nisei offered their services in any capacity, and were given a cautious go-ahead.[63] Lieutenant General Delos Emmons permitted 169 nisei former guardsmen to organize as a civilian volunteer force, essentially as a manual labor unit attached to the Thirty-Fourth Combat Engineers Regiment in the US Army Corps of Engineers. In late February, this group was assigned to three barracks at Schofield named Varsity, Victory, and Volunteers, earning the unit its moniker: VVV, or Triple V.

Non-Japanese American officers led the unit, including the Chinese American Captain Richard Lum and several native Hawaiian or half-Hawaiian men. Lum secretly censored all correspondence and provided intelligence reports on the nisei volunteers to the G-2 head at Schofield.[64] The distrust of the nisei remained so high that General Emmons proposed, if a Japanese invasion of Hawai'i were to occur, that any Japanese American in uniform "be shot immediately by the American troops."[65]

For the next eleven months, the young volunteers of the VVV, desperate to demonstrate their loyalty to the United States, took on tasks that required back-breaking labor and for which they had no prior training. For very low pay—especially after paying for their work clothes themselves—the men built prefabricated houses and large warehouses on the Army base, cooked, and strung miles of barbed wire.[66] In his study of the unit, historian Franklin Odo notes that Assistant Secretary of War John McCloy, visiting Hawai'i in late March 1942, was particularly impressed with the hardworking VVV men on a quarry gang who showed real dedication breaking and shoveling rocks in the mountains.'

Among these young men was Ralph Yempuku, an individual Odo calls "the single most important figure in the VVV." He was the second of five sons of a Higashi Honganji Buddhist priest who had served, before the war, at a Buddhist temple on an Oahu sugar plantation. Yempuku said that his upbringing at the Buddhist temple, which included cleaning chores and polishing altar implements, required discipline and acting in a manner that would not bring shame to his family.[67] An early ROTC volunteer and employee in the University of Hawai'i's physical education department, Yempuku played a key role in the formation of the VVV unit. Humiliated by his removal from the Hawaii Territorial Guard, he circulated a letter to those who would form the core of the VVV initiative, which read in part: "In view of the serious situation now confronting the security of these islands, it is urgent that we Americans of Japanese ancestry demonstrate our loyalty in concrete ways. We need the active cooperation of every American of Japanese ancestry and we urgently request that you be present at a meeting called to consider this matter at the Nuuana YMCA auditorium." His call led approximately seventy-five former "Hawaii Territorial Guard Boys" to attend this meeting, which followed a meeting a few days earlier of nearly two hundred "university boys" eager to contribute in some way to the war effort.

Yempuku wished to serve his country even though his Buddhist missionary parents had moved back to Japan and one of his brothers had enlisted in the Japanese Imperial Army. After the VVV unit was formed, Yempuku was assigned to be its civilian supervisor. Based on his strict attitude, he was given the nickname "Nap" for Napoleon, and his men called him "Caesar" and "Dictator" because of his high expectations for the volunteers.[68]

Three other early volunteers for this manual labor unit were former students of the Buddhist Hongwanji "coat school," so called because the Buddhist administrators required boys to wear jackets and ties.[69] In describing the religious background of the families of the VVV volunteers, Franklin Odo observed, "A few were Christians, converted in Japan or shortly after arrival in Hawai'i. Most were Buddhists, including two Buddhist priests who traced their lineages back many generations in that calling."[70]

The father of VVV volunteer Yoshiaki Fujitani, Rev. Kōdō Fujitani, was serving the Moiliili Hongwanji Mission at the outbreak of the war and would become Bishop of Hongwanji in Hawai'i after the war. (The American-born Yoshiaki would later emulate his father and also be appointed the Bishop of the largest Buddhist organization in Hawai'i, in 1975). Fujitani had seen the black smoke from the attack on Pearl Harbor and rushed to join his university ROTC unit in bare feet, wearing only a sweatshirt and corduroy trousers. He spent that first night patrolling the armory. For the next month and a half, his unit gained the distinction of being the only ROTC unit in the country to experience military action while guarding water and gas tanks at Iwilei and the piers of Honolulu Harbor.[71]

Having experienced the disappointment of being dismissed from the Hawaii Territorial Guard, Fujitani relished the opportunity to volunteer with the VVV and contribute to the American war effort, even if he was viewed as an "enemy alien." But when his father was arrested by the FBI and interned at Sand Island in April 1942, a devastated Fujitani quit the VVV in disgust:

> I learned that my father, a Buddhist minister, had been impris-
> oned because he was considered a "potentially dangerous"
> enemy alien. Suddenly, whatever patriotic feeling I possessed
> disappeared. Deep down, I had known that someday this would
> happen, and it finally did. Most of the Buddhist clergy and
> language-school principals were arrested within days of the
> December 7 bombing. Father had been spared, however. He
> enjoyed four extra months of freedom. I am not sure why that
> happened, but I was told that a Nisei officer who served with
> G-2 in the provisional government had vouched for Father's
> behavior during that period.[72]

In time, the young Fujitani did reenlist with the Military Intelligence Service, citing the Buddhist teaching of the four "gratitudes," including gratitude towards one's country.[73]

Both Buddhist priests' sons, like many other bilingual Japanese Americans, put their understanding of Japanese language and culture to use in the war in the Pacific. Fujitani served primarily as a translator at the Pacific Military Intelligence Research Section (PACMIRS) at Camp Ritchie (Maryland) and Yempuku served on a covert team with the Office of Strategic Services (OSS) involved in guerrilla action against the Japanese behind enemy lines in the China-Burma-India Theater.[74]

Before their assignments in the field, Yempuku and Fujitani were among those enrolled in a crash course at the Army's Japanese language school. With Executive Order 9066, the language school, now renamed the Military Intelligence Service Language School (MISLS), was relocated in May 1942 from the Presidio in San Francisco to Camp Savage in Minnesota.[75] Colonel Rasmussen chose the site on the premise that most residents of Minnesota, having never encountered Japanese Americans, would not have formed strong racial prejudices against them. Similarly, a smaller Japanese language program run by the Navy had been concentrated on the west coast in Berkeley, but with two dozen nisei civilian instructors teaching 150 white students, the Navy also had to move out of the Western Defense Command zone, where Japanese Americans were excluded.[76] Due to Colorado Governor Ralph Carr's relatively friendly attitude toward Japanese Americans, the Navy moved its Japanese language school to the University of Colorado in June 1942. It was headed by the Higashi Honganji Buddhist priest Rev. Enshō Ashikaga, who had been professor of Japanese language and Buddhist studies at UC Berkeley prior to the war.[77]

Upon completion of their studies, the nisei were assigned to either a translation center or to one of the combat units in the Pacific.[78] Ultimately more than two thousand nisei linguists served in combat zones translating texts or interrogating captured Japanese POWs.[79] Due to the secret nature of their work, their efforts, despite being awarded with numerous Silver Stars and Purple Hearts, as well as three Distinguished Service Crosses, have often been overlooked.

Although prisoner interrogation had been a major component of the nisei linguists' training, neither Allied nor Japanese troops took prisoners in the brutal combat zones during the early phases of the Pacific war. For American officers and enlisted men, the attitude of "the only good Jap is a dead Jap" led to massacres of enemy soldiers who could have been taken prisoner to gain intelligence. But rewards of ice cream, soda, or three-day passes for those who produced a live Japanese POW eventually had an effect, and American forces began receiving and housing captured enemy soldiers.[80] Ironically, it was the familiarity with the language, culture, and religion of Japan that made these nisei, especially the kibei Buddhists, critical in gathering valuable intelligence. By offering food or cigarettes and otherwise showing empathy and kindness to captured Japanese POWs who had been trained to fight to the death, the nisei were able to win their confidence and get them to talk. The intelligence garnered by the MIS linguists, including names of commanders and officers, battle tactics, enemy positions, and locations of arms caches, helped to formulate battle plans, and repel attacks used to advance the US rollback of the Japanese military in the Pacific.

In contrast to nisei who would later serve in the European theater, many of those in the Pacific found that the fighting provoked complex feelings. A young soldier serving as a translator in the South Pacific wrote to his Buddhist teacher, who was in the WRA Topaz camp at the time, that the battles against the Japanese were horribly brutal. He explained how his life was "hellish" and that he often "drifted between the worlds of life and death," but that his mentor's sharing of Buddhist chanting and singing during his youth kept his hopes alive. The soldier even enclosed five dollars with his letter in appreciation for his incarcerated Buddhist teacher.[81]

Most nisei who served in the Pacific did so, unlike their white comrades, without an extreme hatred of the Japanese opponents on the battlefield. Some, like Sakakida, drew on their Buddhist faith to feel empathy for the captured Japanese POWs or to reconcile using their understanding of the Japanese enemy as a weapon in the Allied cause.

THE 100TH BATTALION

While the war was raging in the Pacific, many nisei were eager to serve in the campaign unfolding in the European theater. Partially due to the efforts of the Victory Varsity Volunteers (VVV), the formation of a segregated Japanese American unit for the European theater began in Hawai'i. On May 26, 1942, Army Chief of Staff General George C. Marshall announced the establishment of the Hawaiian Provisional Infantry Battalion, composed of soldiers from the Hawaii Army National Guard's 298th and 299th Infantry units. Of the roughly 3,000 men in these units, over 1,400 of them were Japanese Americans from Oahu (the 298th) and the other islands (the 299th), 900 of whom had volunteered.[82]

Two days after the announcement, 1,432 Japanese American soldiers gathered at Schofield Barracks to join the new battalion. They were to be trained, according to an order from the operations division of the war department, "for future use as an infantry combat unit to be ready for field service on 10 days notice after September 30, 1942."[83] One week later, this predominantly Japanese American battalion boarded the S.S. *Maui* to undergo training as a segregated unit. When they arrived in Oakland, California on June 12, 1942, they learned that their outfit had been officially activated as the 100th Infantry Battalion (Separate) to be based at Camp McCoy—the "Separate" status indicating that the battalion stood apart from a parent unit.

Once in Oakland, the group—who unofficially dubbed their unit One Puka Puka (the number zero being a "hole," or *puka* in the Hawaiian language[84]—realized that views on Japanese Americans in the continental US, who were then being herded into the WCCA Assembly Centers, were more discriminatory than in Hawai'i. As the Battalion members boarded trains to head towards Camp McCoy in Wisconsin for their infantry training, they were ordered by Army officials to keep their window shades drawn, like many of the trains that transported the Japanese Americans to the WRA camps. The white officials explained that this was to prevent west coast residents from becoming alarmed at seeing large numbers of Japanese Americans in military uniforms.[85]

Once the 100th arrived at Camp McCoy, Wisconsin, for basic training, some unit members grew concerned that they had been tricked and taken to an internment camp. Indeed, a section of Camp McCoy was used as an internment camp for enemy aliens and one of the first orders given to the 100th was to guard the issei detainees allowed out for exercise. One battalion soldier encountered his own father. Like many of the detainees rounded up in Hawai'i, his father had been transferred a month earlier to this camp on the continent.[86]

The nisei underwent basic training from June to December 1942. Knowing that their conduct would be scrutinized closely, they waited to hear if the initiative for an all-nisei military unit would be approved to fight in Europe. They soon earned a reputation for superior performance in the field and for demonstrations of patriotic behavior, such as participating enthusiastically in blood bank drives and purchasing war bonds.[87] Many, even the kibei in the group, avoided using the Japanese language. While the most capable 67 Japanese-language speakers in the 100th Battalion were recruited for the MIS's language school at Camp

Savage, most of the unit continued their training in anticipation of serving on the European front.

Leighton Sumida recalled the pressures in that period to conform to a certain kind of "Americanism" that required the toning down, if not outright rejection, of the Buddhist culture that most of the unit had grown up with. White officers believed that Buddhist amulets carried by some of the soldiers were too closely associated with "Japanese customs" and decided to confiscate and burn them one evening. Sumida reflected, "They didn't burn mine because I didn't give it to them . . . but some people just gave them to the officers and they burned them." Another time, a Buddhist offered up a short prayer before a meal and was yelled at by a white officer to stop despite the soldier's protestations that, "he wasn't doing anything wrong, not preaching and asking people to become Buddhist . . . just asking for blessings."[88]

The locals in the nearby town of Sparta, Wisconsin were generally friendly towards the soldiers, and this in turn inspired Japanese Americans in Hawai'i to look out for soldiers from Wisconsin, welcoming them to the islands with free *luau*.[89] The Texan soldiers of the Second Division, on the other hand, constantly harassed the 100th Battalion soldiers, calling them "Jap" or "Yellow belly." Being from Hawai'i, the men were not used to such insults, and fights between the Texans and the Hawaiians frequently broke out in town. The Texan bullies soon discovered they had underestimated them. Though small in stature, many of the men in the 100th had trained for years in judo, *kendō*, and other Japanese martial arts taught in the Buddhist temples and Japanese language schools in Hawai'i. Black belts in judo, such as Corporal Masaharu Takeba and Private Satoshi Furukawa, continued to train in their Japanese martial arts discipline at Camp McCoy. In one incident, the Texans targeted Private Furukawa and his fellow soldiers. In the ensuing fight, despite being vastly outnumbered, only one Japanese American was injured, while thirty-eight Texans had to spend the night in the camp infirmary.[90] A little over two years later, Pvt. Furukawa gave his life for his country in the battle for Viareggio, Italy.[91]

The Army's higher echelons commissioned daily reports on members of the 100th Battalion to check on the progress of their training at Camp

McCoy, but also, according to historian C. Douglas Sterner, to get information on "the loyalty and suitability for service of individual soldiers, [which was] surreptitiously sent to higher echelons from clandestine mail drops."[92] Despite the presence of several Japanese Americans in the unit who had been commissioned as officers from as early as 1929, the Army instituted a wartime regulation, eventually overturned, that no Japanese American could be an officer in a rifle company. Four such officers were reassigned to headquarters staff, rather than detailing them as commanding officers.[93]

The segregated Battalion's leadership was in the hands of Lieutenant Colonel Farrant L. Turner and his hand-picked executive officer and second-in-command, Major James Lovell. Both men were respected by the nisei because of their long-standing ties to Hawai'i. Although there was initial tension between the nisei men and Second Lieutenant (and later Colonel) Young Oak Kim, a Korean who joined the unit in Wisconsin as the leader of the second platoon, once in combat any historic animosity between Japanese and Korean Americans disappeared.[94] Since they had already undergone basic training in Hawai'i, the unit excelled in the exercises and maneuvers at Camp McCoy, but it remained unclear whether the Battalion would be treated as a legitimate infantry unit and sent to Europe.

During the period of uncertainty, two dozen enlisted men from Company B were selected to board a plane for a special exercise at Mississippi's semi-tropical Cat Island, which was thought by the military to resemble the topography and climate of some islands in the Pacific where the war would be waged. The war department had instituted a program there for dogs to receive combat training as sentries to protect military installations. The men of the 100th Battalion were chosen to participate in this program to teach the dogs to attack Japanese soldiers, noted military historian James McCaffrey, because the Army believed that the Japanese Americans had a distinctive smell akin to the enemy:

> The Japanese American soldiers were to place meat around their necks as the dogs got trained to ferociously attack the neck— when the trainer commanded "Kill!" the animal lunged at the soldier's throat [and the Nisei had wrapped burlap around their

arms to protect themselves]. Among the Nisei, most thought the experiment a failure; one recalled, "We didn't smell Japanese. We were Americans, even a dog knew that!"[95]

In early January 1943, all the men of the 100th Battalion left the cold of Wisconsin for the heat of Mississippi, to receive further training at Camp Shelby. After they arrived, the nearby Hattiesburg newspapers editorialized "Japs Not Wanted," while signs with "Go Home, Japs" abounded in the town.[96] This prejudice and hostility contrasted with their experience in Wisconsin, but was somewhat eased by the kindness of a handful of Hattiesburg individuals, notably local rancher-businessman Earl Finch. He invited up to three hundred nisei soldiers for home-made meals, arranged for shipments of rice, soy, and tofu from New York for men desperate for Japanese food, and organized buses to take the soldiers to the WRA Rohwer and Jerome camps in Arkansas to meet with Japanese American women at dances.[97] While initially permitted to use the white USO Club in Hattiesburg, the Japanese American soldiers found that very few white women in Mississippi would dance with them.[98]

The USO (United Service Organization) had been formed in early 1941 by six separate entities to provide privately funded centers for soldiers to relax during off-duty hours. These hospitality centers often had free coffee and snacks and sponsored dances. But in Mississippi, because of the strongly-held notions of racial segregation, four separate USO centers were established: one specifically for the Japanese Americans from Hawai'i named the Aloha Center, and the others for whites, Jews, and blacks.[99]

The USO, to its credit, worked with local Christian churches to assist with efforts to find temporary housing for the wives and children of the enlisted men of the 100th Battalion during their time in Mississippi. But, as historian John Howard has noted, these efforts came alongside a not-so-subtle effort to Christianize the nisei. The Hattiesburg USO distributed Bibles to the Japanese Americans, including Buddhists, and encouraged enlisted men to attend Christian worship services through their "Go to Church" program.[100]

The main counterpoint to the pressure to Christianize was the work of nisei Buddhist priest Rev. Tadao Kouchi. He had served at the Lanai

Hongwanji Mission at the outbreak of the war and was one of the few American citizens arrested by the FBI the day after Pearl Harbor. Spending time in the Haiku Camp and at Sand Island, he was eventually transferred to the WRA Rohwer camp in Arkansas. The authorities, with encouragement from Chaplain George Aki, gave permission for Kouchi to go to Camp Shelby soon after his arrival in the American South and to perform Buddhist services for the Buddhist Japanese American GIs there.[101] His children recalled, "There were many from Hawaii, who were homesick . . . missing their food and family. The boys were not a happy group. So, Reverend Kouchi went back to the Rohwer Camp and had the young ladies there make little gifts for the boys, and he took a few girls at a time and the gifts to the GIs. A few of them even married eventually, with Reverend Kouchi conducting the wedding ceremony!"[102] Among the young Buddhist women were those who, according to the *Sangha News* newsletter from Rohwer, served as senior hostesses whose task was to "select and organize a group of qualified junior hostesses who will co-operate w/the USO movement as YBA reps."[103] The 100th Battalion's visits to the WRA camps in Arkansas involved joint activities such as dances and baseball games. The visits also gave the nisei from Hawai'i a first-hand look at the situation of their fellow Japanese Americans on the continent, and the stark difference between selective and mass incarceration.

THE 442ND REGIMENTAL COMBAT TEAM

The outstanding performance of the 100th Battalion in marksmanship, marching, and hand-to-hand combat while at Camp Shelby so impressed war department officials that on January 28, 1943, they made the announcement that a new all-Japanese American segregated combat unit—the 442nd Regimental Combat Team (RCT)—would be formed. President Roosevelt formally authorized this development on February 1, 1943, stating, "The principle on which this country was founded and by which it has always been governed is that Americanism is not a matter of race or ancestry. A good American is one who is loyal to this country and to our creed of liberty and democracy."[104] Despite such noble words, as with the 100th Battalion, the war department's initial decree was that all officers of this regiment down to the company commander level were to be "white American citizens."[105]

The newly designated 442nd RCT, with which the 100th Battalion would eventually merge, was widely discussed in Hawai'i, where nearly ten thousand nisei eagerly volunteered to join, including the VVV members. They requested three days after the announcement that their unit be deactivated so that they could join the new unit. Indeed, Ralph Yempuku sent a memo to all VVV members that the "Army intends to give preference to the boys of the V.V.V., in the Volunteer Combat Regiment," encouraging them to sign up immediately. Another 442nd volunteer, Charles Oda, recalled that Yempuku, the Buddhist priest's son, "glorified war and returning as heroes. We got taken in by that. . . . Actually I didn't feel I had to volunteer but did so because Yempuku told us we should."[106]

In Hawai'i, the Army's call for 1,500 volunteers was exceeded multifold. In an initial recruitment drive, 2,645 men were inducted into the segregated infantry unit. These men, including a young Stanley Masaharu Akita, were greeted by a massive crowd of supporters on March 28, 1943 when they marched in front of the iconic Iolani Palace in Honolulu. Akita was a rare adult Sansei (third-generation Japanese American). His nisei father had served as the President of the YBA in Honomu and as a first sergeant in Hawaii National Guard as early as 1934. Akita had grown up in a devout Buddhist and military family and had been sent away from his hometown of Honomu to the Hongwanji Buddhist dormitory in Hilo for his Japanese language school studies. Akita joined, like many of his friends, because of patriotism, excitement, and not wanting to miss out on an opportunity to be like any other American.[107]

Many volunteers also received less elaborate, but equally important, send-offs from their local communities.[108] On the Big Island, Mrs. Shigeo Kikuchi, the wife of an interned Buddhist priest, was always called on to deliver the "sendoff speech" for the nisei volunteers from the Naalehu and Hilo regions. She recalled:

> The volunteers who sat at the table with their parents were mostly nisei, only 17 or 18 years of age. They were all my students

who were until recently sitting at their classroom desks with their boyish faces. Of these boys who are going to the war front, how many of them will return safely, I wondered. My heart was filled with apprehension and sadness, but I had to suppress such feelings to deliver the sendoff speech. And when the sendoff party was over I would go home and in the privacy of my room weep loudly. . . . I told each young man, "The Buddha is always with you" and gave them a Buddhist rosary, but whatever "nenju" [rosary] I had at hand soon were all gone. I could only grasp the hands of the remaining boys and say, "The Buddha is always with you no matter when or where. When you are lonely or when you're in trouble, repeat 'Namu Amida Butsu.' Even if you cannot repeat His name, He will always be with you, so don't worry."[109]

The exuberance of nisei willing to volunteer in Hawai'i was in stark contrast to the reactions of nisei on the US continent. Many men who had been eager to serve when the war began had changed their attitude after they and their families were incarcerated in WRA camps. Military recruiters had set a quota of three thousand volunteers, but only received interest from twelve hundred nisei, disappointing Army leaders.

Volunteering, or even responding positively to being drafted, while leaving behind parents and siblings who would continue to be denied their freedom was a hard choice. Ultimately, the vast majority of Japanese Americans eligible to enlist would do so. They served their country on either the Pacific or European fronts, but not before a contentious debate about freedom and loyalty ensued as splits emerged within families contemplating their futures whilst behind barbed wire.

8

LOYALTY AND THE DRAFT

IN 1943, the Buddhist priest Rev. Shinjō Nagatomi wrote an open letter to young Japanese American Buddhists. "Today," he wrote, "I believe you are faced with deciding whether you will show your loyalty to the US as US citizens or to Japan as Japanese." His missive continued:

> you can deceive other people but cannot deceive yourself. You cannot deceive the Amida Buddha who sees all. . . . It is said that a mother lion drops her cub from a cliff to the bottom of a ravine when it is just three days old to test the cub's physical abilities. Today you are like the lion cub. Do not bear a grudge against the mother lion that pushes you down to the ravine. You have to realize that you are at the bottom of the ravine and must stand up on your own feet

His message came at a critical moment in the lives of those in the WRA camps.[1] Especially for those eligible to serve in the US military, the question of loyalty to America was filled with an irony that the nisei in Hawai'i did not face. They were asked to serve in the military of the government that had imprisoned them and their family members. The Army had recently changed its policy to allow nisei to volunteer for military service. Although the Army would not begin drafting nisei for another year, recruitment officers traveled to the WRA camps in February 1943 seeking volunteers. Nisei men age seventeen and older were asked to fill out a selective service form altered specifically for them, titled "Statement of United States Citizen of Japanese Ancestry."

The procedure for volunteering for the army from within the camps, initially proposed by a committee headed by Deputy Army Chief of Staff General Joseph McNarney, involved filling out a loyalty questionnaire to ascertain a prospective inductee's background and views. A military Joint Board would then rule on each person's candidacy after a review by military intelligence and the FBI.[2]

This initiative was seized upon by the WRA to expedite "leave clearance"—a program to release as many "loyal" individuals as possible from the camps. Even during the early days, in the Wartime Civil Control Administration Assembly Centers, conditional releases to areas outside the Western Defense Command zone were granted for those willing to work on agricultural projects deemed essential to national security (for example, to harvest beets in Idaho necessary for sugar production) and for college students who had been enrolled in west coast schools to transfer to colleges east of the Rocky Mountains.[3]

With the January 1943 announcement that the army would seek nisei volunteers, WRA Director Dillon Myer proposed that the War Department broaden the scope of these loyalty examinations to include all men and women seventeen years old and older, and issei as well as nisei. In the following two months, the government produced two questionnaires: one developed by the Office of Naval Intelligence and administered by the army (DSS Form 304A—"Statement of United States Citizens of Japanese Ancestry") for male nisei and one produced by the WRA (Form WRA-126, Rev., "War Relocation Authority Application for Leave Clearance") for everyone else.[4]

THE LOYALTY QUESTIONNAIRE

On both forms, Questions 27 and 28 became the most contentious. The army form's Q27 for male nisei read: "Are you willing to serve in the armed forces of the United States on combat duty, wherever ordered?" Its Q28 asked: "Will you swear unqualified allegiance to the United States of America and faithfully defend the United States from any or all attack by foreign or domestic forces, and forswear any form of allegiance or obedience to the Japanese emperor, or any other foreign government, power, or organization?" The WRA form, perhaps in part because it was intended to include nisei women, read slightly differently but with the same purposes. Its Q27 asked: "If the opportunity presents itself and you are found qualified, would you be willing to volunteer for the Army Nurse Corp or the WAAC [Women's Army Auxiliary Corps]?" And for Q28, it asked simply: "Will you swear unqualified allegiance to the United States of America and forswear any form of allegiance or obedience to the Japanese emperor, or any other foreign government, power, or organization?"

As soon as the forms were sent to the WRA camps, Myer realized the problem inherent in asking issei to forswear allegiance to the only country to which they had nationality. Issei had not been allowed to naturalize in the United States due to citizenship restrictions, and were obliged to remain Japanese subjects. Myer contacted the camps and told WRA staff to allow issei to ignore Question 28 and await a revised question.

The next day, the WRA sent out new copies with a revised question stapled over the original question on the form. This one read: "Will you swear to abide by the laws of the United States and to take no action which would in any way interfere with the war effort of the United States?" But by then, many issei were confused and insulted by the questionnaire. When some WRA officials refused to allow issei to meet and discuss how to fill out the questionnaire, many felt even more inclined to answer "no" to the most important of the "loyalty" questions.[5]

A rumor circulated that those answering "no" to the two questions would be sent to a "segregation" camp for "disloyals," splitting up families—a rumor that proved true when Tule Lake was designated a segregation camp. Among the nisei, most felt it wrong not to coordinate and discuss their answers with their issei parents. Others chose to answer "no" to one or both questions on the grounds that their constitutional rights as Americans had been violated, and they refused to unconditionally answer the call to military service until their rights had been restored. A report produced in 1946 by the WRA succinctly lists the various reasons why some Japanese Americans in the camps did not answer with an unconditional "yes" to these questions:

> the No of protest against discrimination, the No of protest against a father interned apart from his family, the No of bitter

antagonism to subordinations in the relocation center, the No
of a gang sticking together, the No of thoughtless defiance, the
No of family duty, the No of hopeless confusion, the No of fear
of military service, and the No of felt loyalty to Japan.[6]

While a large majority of both issei and nisei ended up answering "yes"
to Q28 on allegiance, there was still a sizeable segment of the community that answered with a qualified "yes," a "no" on one of those two
questions, or even a straight "no, no" on both questions.

Some scholarly observers from that period claimed that Buddhists,
especially issei and kibei, tended to answer "no, no" on these questionnaires in greater numbers than Christians. One researcher found that
"nisei were more likely to answer 'no' if they had been educated in Japan,
were Buddhist (rather than Christian or nonbelievers), if they had come
from an American area unfavorable to Japanese before the war, or if their
previous occupations had involved little contact with Caucasians."[7]
While these analyses may have been accurate, in fact more nisei Buddhists than nisei Christians served in the US military, and the performance of these Buddhists soldiers demonstrated that assumptions about
the (dis)loyalty of Buddhists were misguided.

TULE LAKE SEGREGATION CENTER

Once the loyalty questionnaires had been administered, the US Senate
passed a resolution on July 6, 1943 instructing the WRA to separate those
who had not affirmatively recorded their loyalty to the United States.[8]
Given the largely negative responses from the WRA camp at Tule Lake,
it was designated as the "segregation camp" for the "disloyals" or "no,
nos," and twelve thousand individuals who had been deemed "disloyal"
were transferred from the other camps into the newly renamed Tule Lake
Segregation Center. Roughly 6,500 "Old Tuleans" who had responded
"yes, yes" were transferred out to other WRA camps.

During the administration of the loyalty questionnaire, tensions ran
high between those whose opinions differed, particularly at Tule Lake.
In February 1943, the executive secretary to the Tule Lake "city council"

and a liaison between the issei and nisei, wrote about a young nisei relative who volunteered for the 442nd regimental combat team (RCT):

> It was unbearable for him to languish helplessly at Tule Lake while his homeland was being attacked by foreign countries. Moreover, he wanted to get even with the anti-Japanese officials who regarded him and his family as unpatriotic and threw them into the internment camp. His parents did not discourage him from enlisting. Both parents were devout Aki [Hongwanji] Buddhists who had taught their Nisei children that their obligations to Buddha and their country were boundless. Predictably, four of the seven children willingly came to the aid of their country.[9]

An older brother of this volunteer had already enlisted in the army prior to the war and his two younger sisters joined the Women's Army Corps. This was considered an overly pro-American stance by the Japan-oriented nationalists in Tule Lake. The family was ostracized and made to sit separately in the mess hall at a table marked *"inu"* or dog (a colloquial term for informant or traitor). Heavy peer pressure from pro-Japan factions was applied to individuals urging them to refuse to register or fill out the questionnaire, or to answer "no" to the loyalty questions. Indeed, of the 3,254 individuals who refused to register (out of an eligible 77,842 from all the WRA camps), 3,218 resided in the Tule Lake camp.[10] Frank Miyamoto noted how those seen as too cooperative with the WRA administration were given the "silent treatment," had signs posted on their barracks doors calling them *inu*, or had pictures of dogs captioned "white man's dog" slipped under their doors.[11]

Opposite pressure to fill out the questionnaires came from the WRA Tule Lake project director, Harvey Coverley. He threatened those who refused with fines of $10,000 and twenty-year jail sentences under the Espionage Act—a threat subsequently found to have no legal basis. On February 21, 1943, the director called in the soldiers of the Fourth Army armed with machine guns to force about thirty-five nisei in Block 42 to fill out the forms. A week earlier, this group had publically proclaimed their refusal to participate in the loyalty questionnaire process. According

FIGURE 8.1 Volunteers inducted into the 442nd Regimental Combat Team in the WRA camp at Minidoka, Idaho (March 20, 1943).   Courtesy of the National Archives and Records Administration, Densho Digital Repository, ddr-densho-37-663.

to one report, the infuriated director sent "soldiers with bayonets [to] search the barracks one by one. They rounded up those who refused to register and tossed them into the back of a truck. . . . Stunned at seeing the prisoners hauled away in trucks, people stood there and shouted, 'Banzai! Banzai!' over and over again. There was no time to think of anything else to shout."[12] A young Buddhist detailed what happened when soldiers surrounded Block 42 with bayonets and machine guns:

> Old men stood by helplessly, their eyes wet, dimmed, their lips hard pressed by angry teeth. . . . I decided not to register. If they were treating those boys like prisoners for refusing to register— then I would join them too. With deep conviction in the righteousness of my cause and with firm reliance on the protection of divine providence, I acted against registration. . . . My brother had volunteered and enlisted in the American army almost a year before Pearl Harbor. For my brother's sake and because America is my birthplace, I harbor no ill will towards this country. . . . My father, mother and sister are now residing in

Japan; that is the basic reason why I will not fire a gun against Japan. . . . Of a certainty I will gladly work for America on the production front but I will not bear arms against my father's country. I will not bear arms against America either.[13]

This attitude was considered so extreme by the WRA authorities that this young man was taken along with the other nisei from Block 42 to a secret, high-security detention center outside the WRA camp. This battle between US government authorities and pro-Japan inmate factions produced a growing number of harsh and even violent incidents in the WRA camps. Much of the violence was split along religious lines. Though Buddhists were not immune to these attacks, Christians were most often the targets of the violence that seemed to resist cultural assimilation as much as military service.

One Christian in Tule Lake recalled, "At Tule Lake we had some pro-Japan people. We Christians were branded as spies for America and were tormented. Some were beaten up."[14] In Poston, another said, "certain people hated me in the camp at that time, probably because they thought I was overdoing many things in a Christian way, or they might have thought I was too Americanized or something. . . . [There were] incidents where human excrement was scattered in front of the houses of some Christians."[15] The Congregationalist Rev. George Aki, who volunteered from the Jerome camp to serve as the only chaplain for the 442nd RCT from within the WRA camps, recalled in his memoir that he "was the most hated clergyman in the 10 relocation camps. My accusers were bitterly angered by the fact that I had the audacity to volunteer for the country that forced all Japanese into concentration camps away from our livelihood, our school and our homes. I could not blame them."[16]

Christian ministers were especially targeted by the pro-Japan factions for harassment, intimidation, and even beatings. During the controversy over the loyalty questionnaire, there were only Christian ministers in the WRA Tule Lake camp, despite its overwhelmingly Buddhist population. That situation held until later that year when about a hundred Buddhist priests were transferred there as "disloyals." Both the Episcopalian and Presbyterian clergy in camp felt threatened enough that groups of young men served as bodyguards in the evening, with the Division of Internal Security even posting policemen for protection.[17] It would turn out to be the Methodist and the Salvation Army leaders who were set upon; they were severely beaten by five men with pro-Japan sentiments.[18] In the aftermath of these attacks, when those who had answered "yes, yes" had the opportunity to relocate to another WRA camp, "most of the [Christian] church people petitioned to move as a group."[19]

These attacks were not confined to Tule Lake. While Buddhist priests were not subject to this kind of violence, a number of Christian ministers faced bodily harm. The earliest case involved a Methodist minister at the WRA Topaz camp, whom the administration relied on to mediate the rising tensions between the Japanese-speaking issei and kibei and the English-speaking nisei. The camp authorities believed that he could "settle down the troublemakers," but soon discovered that some youth simply viewed him as an "inu," which led to the first case of violence against a Christian minister.[20] After he was removed from the camp for his safety and transported to the "free zone" of Denver by the WRA, the administration turned to a retired Nishi Hongwanji priest to help calm tensions.[21]

One of the best-known incidents was memorialized by the eminent painter Henry Sugimoto. The director of the WRA Jerome camp had requested the assistance of Episcopalian minister Rev. John Yamazaki in translating various government announcements from Japanese to English. After he helped two US Army colonels translate the "loyalty questionnaire," Rev. Yamazaki became a target. And on March 8, 1943, he was beaten so severely by a gang of seven youths that he had to be admitted to the hospital.[22] He later recalled:

> Before they beat me, they said, "Reverend, take off your glasses." I took off my glasses. I didn't resist so they couldn't beat me too much. I was knocked down near a fence, where there was nobody. I fell to the ground. "Stop," cried the leader, and when they were leaving a voice said, "Reverend, don't forget your glasses."[23]

From the Jerome Center Hospital, he wrote a letter to Charles S. Reifsnider, the Episcopalian Bishop charged with assisting Japanese

FIGURE 8.2 Painting by Henry Sugimoto entitled *Reverend Yamazaki Was Beaten in Camp Jerome.* Courtesy of the Japanese American National Museum (Gift of Madeleine Sugimoto and Naomi Tagawa), 92.97.6.

Americans of that denomination, opening with: "I am in trouble. A very serious one."[24] The camp director swiftly arranged for Yamazaki's release to Chicago, a "free zone," with his wife and daughter.[25] He also wrote a traditional Japanese *waka* poem after the assault:

> When I received the blow I felt
> as my own child hitting me
> for they were of my own kind
> Each blow reminded me of God's will
> who taught me of our own lack of suffering.[26]

Amidst these beatings, it became clear that it was not just pro-Japan sentiment that held back support for the nisei to volunteer for the US Army. Some issei parents feared that a segregated battalion "would only be used for the most dangerous of missions to spare white soldiers' lives" and were firmly convinced "that the ultimate intention of the government was to exterminate nisei on the battlefield and make the issei men without a country."[27] Such rumors and fears were not completely baseless. Even before Executive Order 9066 was issued, the secretary of the JACL, Mike Masaoka, in an attempt to avert the mass removal, recommended to authorities the formation of "a volunteer 'suicide battalion' which would go anywhere to spearhead the most dangerous missions" while "the families and friends of the volunteers would place themselves in the hands of the government as 'hostages.'"[28]

Amidst the ugly atmosphere that enveloped the camps in early 1943, a number of nisei Christian pastors exhorted young men to sign up. One encouraged those who committed to serve: "Soon you will be donning the Army Khaki in place of your 'civvies.' God grant you might also don the Lord Jesus Christ on your spiritual selves as naturally as you would wear your everyday apparel. . . . the type of armor a Christian soldier must wear to stand fast in the thick of battle."[29]

In contrast, many nisei Buddhists, including Minoru Kiyota, gave neither the WRA authorities nor the radical pro-Japan factions their full support.[30] Kiyota had grown up in a devout Buddhist family, spent some time in Japan living at a temple, was a dedicated practitioner of the martial art of *kendo,* and after the war became an eminent professor of Buddhist studies at the University of Wisconsin, Madison. When it came time for him to make a decision on the loyalty questionnaire, he found the "ingratiating, opportunistic attitude" of some excessively pro-American nisei annoying and answered "no" on Question 28, which prompted his transfer to Tule Lake.[31] Later, he wrote poignantly in his memoir about the complex feelings he and others experienced. He reflected on a family he knew that had one son in the Japanese Imperial Army and another considering volunteering for the American 442nd RCT, and imagined "brother pitted against brother as enemies fighting one another on the ephemeral stage of a global war. This was not some fictional scene from Dante's *Inferno* or an imaginary description of the Buddhist hells related by the monk Genshin in his *Essentials of Deliverance*. It was a real situation created by a war between Japan and the United States in the very twentieth century that advocates love for humanity and prides itself on rational, scientific thinking."[32]

In the end, few from the WRA camps volunteered for the 442nd RCT. Of the 1,208 men who voluntarily enlisted from the WRA camps, 308 came from Minidoka; 236 from Poston; 152 from Amache; 116 from Topaz; 101 from Gila River; 100 from Manzanar; 59 from Tule Lake; 54 from Heart Mountain; 42 from Jerome; and 40 from Rohwer.[33] Even within Minidoka, which was populated primarily by former Pacific Northwest residents who were considered by some to be more integrated into the broader American community than Californians, one of the leaders within the camp's self-government recalled that the "majority of the Japanese people at Minidoka were against" his encouragement of nisei military service. One day he found a mock grave inscribed with his name on it.[34] Eleven of the early volunteers, each of whom was given a Christian Bible by the Minidoka Parent-Soldier Association as a send-off gift, had to leave the camp in secret at night to avoid trouble.[35]

The disturbances caused by the radical pro-Japan groups, especially at Tule Lake, were led in many cases by a small clique of Buddhist priests—certain pro-Japan issei priests and American nisei priests who had grown disillusioned with America. One of them was the Hawai'i-born Buddhist priest Rev. Shizuo Kai who was transferred to Tule Lake after he was expelled from the United (Denson) Buddhist Church in the WRA Jerome camp by the pro-American majority of the sangha. (He

FIGURE 8.3 US Border Patrol guards forcibly moving "lie-down" strikers in the WRA camp at Tule Lake, California, June 1945.   Courtesy of the National Archives and Records Administration, Densho Digital Repository, ddr-densho-37-193.

had formed a new splinter organization called the Daijō Buddhist Church, made up of pro-Japan individuals opposed to cooperating with the US military effort.)[36] Rev. Kai and his followers were transferred to the Tule Lake Segregation Center, where he became a spokesperson for the "no, no" residents and was marked by officials as a "troublemaker."

Rev. Kai was one of the leaders of the November 1943 Tule Lake "Jap riot," as the local newspaper dubbed it, reacting to the camp administration's refusal to permit a campwide Buddhist funeral for a nisei who died on the job—killed by a fall from a truck when camp detainees were taken out to harvest potato and barley. After the protest, the American Buddhist priest was severely beaten by US Army guards, who had been asked by Tule Lake Project Director Raymond Best to take over the security of the camp.[37] Rev. Kai and other leaders of the riot were placed in a prison within the prison, known formally as "Area B" or the "surveillance area," and colloquially called the "stockade."[38]

About four hundred people were placed in Area B, which required the construction of six barracks and four observation towers with armed guards.[39] The inmates in this isolation unit were held without charges or hearings, some for nearly a year.[40] Inside the stockade, further trouble brewed as the prisoners refused US Army orders to come out for roll call. When challenged to openly disobey the order, the first to step forward was Kōji Todoroki, the nisei son of Fresno priest Rev. Shisei Todoroki, who had been arrested by the FBI. Branded one of the seven leaders of the riot, Todoroki's disdain for the authorities intensified his harsh treatment. He had already been severely beaten before being placed in the stockade but, given his defiance, he and the others were then denied food and water for twenty-four hours and had all their personal items confiscated.[41] In time, those people considered most disruptive to the camp's order were transferred to the DOJ's Santa Fe camp or the army camps at Fort Lincoln and Fort Stanton.[42]

Another nisei Buddhist priest similarly removed was one of the three leaders of the Sokoku Kenkyū Seinendan (Young Men's Association for the Study of the Mother Country).[43] Later known as the Hokoku Seinendan (Young Men's Organization to Serve the Mother Country), it was associated with another pro-Japan youth group, the Seinendan Hōkōkai, co-led by the nisei son of a Jōdo sect priest who had served the Ko'olau Jōdoshū Kyōkaidō in Hawai'i.[44] The resentment against the US government because of the sudden arrests and disappearances of their Buddhist priest fathers seems to have fueled much of the pro-Japan sentiment of these American-born priests or sons of issei priests.

The Seinendan Hōkōkai and the Hokuku Hoshidan (also known as the Hokukudan or Patriot's Association) were the two large organizations of ultra-nationalistic Japanese with significant followings at Tule Lake. Many members sported military haircuts and wore shirts emblazoned with the Rising Sun while doing morning calisthenics that were akin to close-order drills. The latter organization also had as its chief advisors (komon) two issei Buddhist priests.[45] The original purpose of the Hokuku Hōshidan was to help prepare those in Tule Lake intending to go to Japan after the war through intensive immersion in Japanese social and culture mores.[46] Finally, there was a smaller organization called the Shichishō-kai (Association of Seven Lives), whose members vowed to be reborn seven times to serve their homeland of

Japan, that had as its chief advisor the prewar leader of the Zenshūji Sōtō Zen Mission in Los Angeles.[47]

While pro-Japanese factions existed in all WRA camps, after the transfers of thousands of individuals to Tule Lake, the tense, intra-community clashes over nisei military service in the Army died down considerably in most of the camps. Eventually, most issei and nisei Buddhist leaders came to either tacitly accept nisei service to the United States or even actively encourage it. Nyogen Senzaki, the Rinzai Zen Buddhist priest in the WRA Heart Mountain camp, gave an interpretation of loyalty based on the Japanese concept of *bushidō* (the way of the warrior) in his commencement speech to the camp's high school students: "Nisei soldiers take the straight course which is simple and primitive. They love America as their birth-land and they fight for it. Japan appreciates their noble feeling and righteous action. No one in the Mikado's land will blame Nisei about this."[48]

LEAVE CLEARANCE AND THE DRAFT

In administering the questionnaire, the military was looking for suitable volunteers for military service. By contrast, the WRA intended the loyalty questionnaire to determine "loyalty" for organizing the release of as many as possible from the camps. This was a type of parole system in which a joint military board would assess the relative risk of releasing an individual to areas outside of the exclusion zone on the west coast. Though the process was cumbersome, eventually a majority of the camp population obtained permission to resettle.[49] The others spent the entirety of the war behind barbed wire.[50]

With the leave clearance program, as was so often the case, Buddhists faced barriers beyond those experienced by their Christian counterparts. They faced scanter employment opportunities in Chicago, Denver, New York, and other cities, and fewer educational opportunities at the six hundred college and university campuses in the east, where nearly four thousand nisei students were released.[51] Among the college students, Christians received more generous financial aid than Buddhists.[52] They even faced obstacles obtaining work in agriculture, which desperately needed to replace the men who had joined the war effort overseas.

Christians also found it easier to fulfill the requirement for a sponsor outside the camps during their "parole," since there were many more Christian organizations, and their natural tendency was to give preference to those of their faith.[53]

Moreover, the US government's criteria for leave clearance systematically favored Christians. Although questions 27 and 28 of the "loyalty questionnaire" have received the most attention, the WRA took the entire questionnaire into account in considering leave clearances, including questions relating to religion. As legal historian Eric Muller notes, because reviewing roughly forty thousand Japanese Americans' files was such a massive undertaking, the army hired statistician Calvert Dedrick of the Census Bureau to oversee analysis of this huge data set.[54]

Dedrick's formula to discern "loyalty" involved setting aside as many individuals as possible as "disloyal," so that the Japanese American joint board reviewing the cases could focus their attention on individuals deemed worthy of review. He devised a plus-and-minus points system to make quick work of pegging someone as disloyal. The point system explicitly considered Christians more trustworthy and "American" than Buddhists, and Buddhists more trustworthy than Shintoists. An answer to the religious affiliation Question 16 of "Shintoist" was grounds for automatic rejection. An answer of "Buddhist" reduced one's loyalty score one point, while two extra points were awarded for identifying oneself as a "Christian.[55]

Religion was not the only factor determining loyalty, of course. Among the questions that could immediately block release were Q14 (asking if the "subject has travelled to Japan 3 or more times"), Q23 (asking if the "subject made substantial contributions to organizations connected with Japanese Army, Navy, or kindred agencies"), and Q26 (asking if the "subject himself has ever applied for repatriation"). Other questions presenting the greatest demerit risk (minus 3 points) were designed to flag any individual with a father who was interned (Q11) or who had family in Japan (Q12). Muller observes that there was a certain absurdity to Dedrick's point system: "If Japan had recruited spies among the nisei before the war, it surely would have encouraged them to minimize rather than maximize the public's perception of their connections with Japan. Yet Dr. Dedrick's point system principally indicted those who behaved least like spies."[56]

The point system was discontinued after five weeks and replaced with an approach that sorted individuals into three color-coded categories: "white" for automatic and immediate indefinite leave, "brown" for borderline cases, and "black" for automatic rejection. In this new system, any of three criteria led to immediate categorization as black: suspicion of affiliation with the Japanese military, a "no" on the infamous Q28, or a prior interest in repatriation or expatriation to Japan.

Membership in or affiliation with "a Buddhist church" would disqualify one from leave clearance if paired with Japanese-language school attendance at a Buddhist-run school, or with one or more trips to Japan, even if for less than six months. Attendance at a Japanese-language school was considered less problematic if it was run by Christians instead of Buddhists, Shintoists, or secularists, and was not disqualifying if the Christian hadn't made a trip to Japan. The terminology used by reviewers was to refer to answers in the questionnaire as either "derogatory" or "nonderogatory"—and being an American Buddhist or Shintoist was considered "derogatory."[57] Muller's examples of rejected Buddhists include a Los Angeles-born, football-playing nisei Buddhist who had had never visited Japan and had a brother in the US Army; and a young woman born in Betteravia, California, who was a round-the-clock caregiver to her ailing mother, had a brother in the US Army, and had answered "yes" to both Questions 27 and 28.[58]

The WRA, unlike the military agencies that dominated the Japanese American joint board, was more circumspect in its evaluations of individual cases, but its decisions were regularly overturned. To develop its recommendations, the WRA used a loyalty point system of its own devising that placed less emphasis on affiliations with Japanese cultural organizations. Even so, the WRA point system made distinctions based on religious belonging, assessing minus-two points for nisei who had become Buddhist priests, minus-three points for those who had found their calling as Tenrikyō priests, and simple rejections for any who reported their occupation as Shinto priest. It awarded a plus-one point to any nisei who wrote down Christian as their religious affiliation.[59]

A short while after those in the WRA camps learned whether they would be granted leave clearance, another major shock hit. On January 20, 1944, Secretary of War Henry L. Stimson announced that nisei would be eligible for the draft. Any Japanese American man aged eighteen to forty-five could be ordered to report for military duty, whether he had volunteered or not. Having been removed from selective service eligibility right after Pearl Harbor, some nisei found it ludicrous now to be compelled to register for military service.

Stimson's announcement triggered another crisis within the camps. About two hundred individuals risked their futures by resisting the draft and refusing to report for preinduction physical exams.[60] At Poston, roughly a hundred individuals refused to register for the draft. The eighty-eight resisters in Heart Mountain had the most organized group, which called itself the Heart Mountain Fair Play Committee.[61] And among the thirty-eight resisters at Minidoka, fifteen belonged to the Seattle Buddhist Temple before the war.[62] Judge Chase Clark processed this group from Minidoka, Idaho, in assembly-line style, making sure that the resisters could not mount any serious defense or be allowed proper deliberations with juries.[63] Charged with conspiracy to evade selective service, many of the resisters were swiftly sent to federal prison or work camps.[64]

While the draft issue roiled those in the WRA camps, the segregated unit that included the Japanese Americans (the 100th / 442nd RCT) was facing heavy losses on the battlefields of Italy. When reports of these casualties reached the WRA camps or the Hawaiian Islands, concerns shifted to questions of how to deal with their deaths. Would their dog tags identify them as Buddhists? Would Buddhist chaplains be admitted to the US military to perform their last rites? What kind of memorial services could be held for Buddhist soldiers behind barbed wire or under martial law?

9

COMBAT IN EUROPE

HARU MATSUDA was well known in the Japanese American community in Kona, Hawai'i, for her original and creative songwriting in the folksong style popular in her native Yamaguchi Prefecture.[1] One song she wrote, however, called "Gunka (A War Song)," was decidedly different from her usual compositions. Its highly personal lyrics were about the death of her son Gorō, also known by his American name, Carl. Haru, like so many other women during World War II, became a Gold Star Mother—someone who had lost a child in uniform. As the song laments:

> Thousands of miles away from home
> under the far off bright red sunset in Italy
> My beloved child is buried under stone.
> Even though he rushed ahead of everyone to charge the enemy
> to say he was a brave soldier is too sad.
>
> . . .
>
> Oh, how fierce the fighting must have been.
> His fellow soldier suddenly fell.
> Carl ran over for he could not leave his friend
> Though the strict military rule prohibits acts without orders
> Carl went over to encourage him, to hold him
> to bandage him in the middle of the battlefield.
> It was then that Carl was shot
> and there he fell.
>
> . . .

finally you have come back to us loving parents
who have waited and waited for your return to your homeland,
Hawaiʻi.
You have come back guided by the compassionate hands of
  America.
You have come back silently. You have come back silently.
Namu Amida Butsu, Namu Amida Butsu.

After being informed of Gorō's death in combat in Italy, the Matsuda family received a package from the Army containing his bloodstained uniform. His sister was shocked by it. "I remember my mother opening the package, and I was there, too. The whole living room was filled up with the smell of old blood from the stained uniform. He was shot. I don't understand why it was sent home to us. Months later his ashes came back. And after that we had a memorial service."[2]

In the intervening period between the initial news of his death and the eventual return of his cremated remains, the Gold Star Mother composed a song based on Buddhist folk song rhythms. She made reference to being guided in both life and death by Amida Buddha's "compassionate hands," but replaced the Buddha's hands with "the hands of America."

DOG TAGS

Both in Hawaiʻi and on the US continent, as the combat deaths of Japanese Americans in the 100th / 442nd began to mount, the Buddhist community became less embroiled in the controversies of military service and the draft and focused more on the care and spiritual support of the sangha members fighting as part of the segregated unit in Europe.

These combat deaths took place in Italy, France, and Germany. The 100th Battalion's campaign began in Oran, North Africa, when it was attached to the "Red Bull" Division of the Fifth Army just as it joined the fight in Italy, pushing two hundred miles from the beachhead of Salerno toward Naples with the objective of liberating Rome. Although the Italians had surrendered to the Allies on September 8, 1943, the

100th Battalion faced crack German troops, their snipers hidden behind high ridges in wooded areas and in stone farmhouses. Messerschmitts and Nebelwerfer rockets called "screaming Mimis" rained death from the sky.

In October, facing the German defensive positions along the Volturno River referred to as the Volturno or Viktor Line, the Japanese American unit from Hawai'i broke through the heavily defended lines and crossed the river. Taking heavy losses, they were turned back in their first assault. On the second, one sergeant called out the order to "fix bayonets." It was the first American bayonet charge in Italy during World War II, and featured troops yelling "Banzai!" as they overran the stunned Germans.[3] Fighting aggressively in daily battles, they then took one hill after another in an advance toward Naples, suffering a nearly 25 percent casualty rate in the first six weeks of combat.[4] Four months after the Battalion arrived in Europe, the 1,400-man unit was down to 832 men.[5]

Further heavy losses were sustained in January 1944, when the unit was ordered to take Cassino, near the Rapido River, where the Monte Cassino monastery overlooked the region. By the time it was ordered to withdraw, the unit had been reduced to 517 men, earning it the moniker "the Purple Heart Battalion."[6] In fact, so many were killed or wounded that it could no longer act as a combat unit. Volunteers from the 442nd, who had responded to the call for the combat team, began arriving as replacements. By December 1943, 524 enlisted men and 31 officers from the new unit had become members of the 100th. As a segregated Japanese American unit, the 100th Battalion could not take replacements from any other division. Unlike other units, it had to wait for replacements from the 442nd volunteers to conclude their basic training at Camp Shelby in Mississippi.

Among those who died in the Italian campaign was Technical Sergeant Kiyoshi Jimmie Shiramizu, one of the few members of the original 100th Battalion raised on the US continent. He had been drafted in July 1941 and, as a tech sergeant, he would normally have stayed at the relatively safe battalion aid station. But given the shortage of medics in B Company, he had volunteered to help attend to the wounded men who needed to be brought back to safety. In January 1944 he had ventured into open terrain to rescue fallen comrades when he was caught in a mortar barrage and sustained an injury to the abdomen that proved fatal four days later.[7] The chaplain assigned to the 100th Battalion, a Lutheran named Israel Yost, later recalled the conversation he had had with Shiramizu just before, during the long hike to a forward aid station:

> Jimmie shared with me what he called his "one gripe" against the US Army. "Chaplain," he said in a confidential tone, "I still can't forget that when I entered the army they wouldn't put a 'B' on my dog tags."
>
> "Jimmie, are you a Buddhist?" I responded.
>
> "Yes, Chaplain, I am, and I can't see why the military did not give me the right to believe what I want."
>
> "Jimmie, I had no idea you were not a Christian. You always attend my services, and you conduct yourself like I think a Christian would."
>
> "I like your services," he replied, "and I can understand what you preach. But I am still a Buddhist."
>
> "I agree with you that you should be allowed to believe what you want . . ."
>
> As we talked of other things I inwardly rebuked myself for never having opened a discussion about faith with him. I had simply assumed by his good life that he must be a believer in Jesus.[8]

As the war in Europe progressed, Buddhist soldiers increasingly called for the US Army to officially recognize their faith by issuing dog tags and assigning chaplains specifically for them. Military historian Franz Steidl comments on memorial services held by a Christian chaplain assigned to the 442nd, where "Christians and Buddhists prayed side by side, reflecting on their own lives, mindful of the irony inherent in fighting for a country that kept their families in internment camps, and stamped the Buddhists' dog tag[s] 'Protestant' as a matter of expediency."[9] The military at that time permitted only "P" for Protestant, "C" for Catholic, "H" for Hebrew (or Jewish), and "blank" for no religious affiliation.[10]

Many members of the 100th / 442nd had their first encounter with the Army's prejudice against their Buddhist faith when they registered for their dog tags. In Hawai'i, one volunteer reporting to Draft Board No. 7 was asked: "What is your nationality?" But when he replied "Japanese," the person in charge of processing his dog tag corrected him. He learned "that the army's classification for us was 'Mongolian.'" When asked "What is your religion?" his answer was "Buddhist"—a response that also prompted a correction. The newly inducted soldier was informed "the army's classification for us would be 'Protestant.' So, all during my time in the army, I was a 'Mongolian-Protestant.'"[11]

When another young Buddhist asked that his dog tag be marked "Buddhist," a "scornful Caucasian officer [said] 'Let me tell you that we don't have the Buddhist religion in the American army. Pick another one.' [I] then chose Protestant, and when the officer asked [me] why I selected Protestant, [I] said, 'Because I protest!'" The angry officer then assigned him to latrine duty.[12]

In the field, Chaplain Israel Yost had a complex relationship with his non-Christian soldiers, including his close friend Shiramizu, with whom he had been billeted during the entire Italy campaign. Yost had a deep desire to "save" the Japanese American Buddhists in his unit and convert them to Christianity. Despite his obvious admiration for Shiramizu, Yost expressed concern in a letter to his wife about his recently killed friend: "Some good friends are gone—one was a Buddhist. It's worried me since that he died a Buddhist and not a Christian."[13] He also preached on the battlefield about "why God spares some of us; it is for our conversion to his way or to do his work."[14] At the first Sunday service he officiated for the 100th, he bemoaned the fact that only three hundred of its thousand men attended, and that among those who turned up only eight were Christians and received Holy Communion.[15] In a speech after the war, he remarked, "Not all of our dead were Christians, that I know; but now from out the grave they cry that we have faith in God, the loving Father whom we know alone through Christ."[16]

Despite his theological views, Yost was sympathetic to non-Christians in his unit and often intervened on their behalf. He wrote to Colonel Farrant Turner on behalf of Staff Sergeant Heiji Fukuda in Company B, who had valiantly served with the 100th Battalion since its inception, inquiring about the possibility of freeing Fukuda's nisei stepfather, the Shinto priest Rev. Yoshio Akizaki. That effort was unsuccessful, but a thoughtful letter Yost wrote to his wife gives a sense of how sincerely he believed non-Christian Battalion members:

> some of the Hawaiians have relatives [some] who are even citizens by birth, still in internment, and the soldiers here cannot even find out why they are still being held. Our wonderful America! We rave about Niemöller's imprisonment, yet one fellow here has a stepfather who is a Shinto priest, citizen by birth, who has been imprisoned for three years, so far as the stepson knows solely because he is a Shinto (not state Shintoism). . . . There's no other land I'd rather live in, but there's lots of housecleaning to be done back home.[17]

In the allied advance on Rome, the 100th was selected as the forward team of "Task Force Singles." Under the command of Lieutenant Colonel Gordon Singles, the task force was organized to ensure that the Americans would reach Rome before the British. Despite its forward role in the advance, taking the cities and the highway on the march to liberate Rome, and its role in the battles of Cassino and Anzio, the unit was held back by US Army officials at the last moment. Despite the heroism and sacrifice of the nisei during this campaign, the unit was not given the honor of entering Rome first on June 4, 1944. Many of the men figured that Army strategists wanted white troops to be the face of the Allied liberators of Rome.[18]

Finally, on June 15, 1944, by special order of General Charles Ryder and General Mark Clark, the Army recognized the valiant fighting and sacrifice of the 100th Battalion. And when it was attached on August 2 to the 442nd regimental combat team, it was allowed to retain its 100th Battalion designation, for purposes of morale and in recognition of its historical significance, rather than being redesignated as the 442's First Battalion.

During the rest of the campaign in Italy, advancing from Rome to Arno, the 100th / 442nd continued to suffer heavy losses. It also received the first of three Presidential Unit Citations, recognizing extraordinary heroism in action, after taking the town of Belvedere in only three hours—in the process, killing 178 Germans, taking 73 prisoners, and

FIGURE 9.1 442nd Regimental Combat Team jeep patrol in Leghorn (Livorno), Italy (July 19, 1944).   Courtesy of the Seattle Nisei Veterans Committee and the US Army, Densho Digital Repository, ddr-densho-114-179.

capturing two tanks and 42 enemy vehicles.[19] In June 1944, the 100th Battalion's liberation of Livorno, considered second only to Naples in its strategic importance, stood in contrast to its experience outside Rome. This time, it was first to march into the city. The Second and Third Battalions also led the way when they liberated and entered the historic city of Pisa. During the Rome-Arno Campaign, the 100th / 442nd suffered an extraordinarily high 1,300 casualties, roughly 25 percent of its total strength.[20]

Two Buddhists from Southern California, Technical Sergeant Ted Tanouye and Staff Sergeant Kazuo Masuda, died in this campaign in July 1944. Tanouye, who was killed by an exploding land mine near San Mauro Cilento, had earned the Distinguished Service Cross a month earlier. Despite being wounded by a grenade, he single-handedly wiped out six German machine-gun nests that had pinned down his unit for

FIGURE 9.2 442nd Regimental Combat Team machine gunner in area of St. Die, France (November 13, 1944). Courtesy of the Seattle Nisei Veterans Committee and the US Army, Densho Digital Repository, ddr-densho-114-90.

two days at Hill 140, northeast of Cecina, Italy.[21] His siblings and parents, incarcerated at the WRA Jerome camp, had to wait to honor him with Buddhist death rites until after the war, when a service was held in the Hongwanji Temple in Little Tokyo, Los Angeles.

Staff Sergeant Kazuo Masuda also received the Distinguished Service Cross for his actions at Hill 140, when he fought the enemy for twelve hours from a stranded position in an exposed area. Rather than wearing his steel helmet, he had filled it with dirt so that it could serve as a makeshift base for firing mortars. The precision aim he achieved with this impromptu setup held off three successive German counterattacks. The next month, however, Masuda was killed near Florence when he and two of his men came upon a German outpost manned by soldier with a Spandau light machine gun. Masuda opened fire with his Thompson submachine gun at point blank range, allowing his men to escape and survive, but leaving himself open to be riddled with bullets. One of the men in his unit noted, "Sgt. Masuda died true to his word. He always said, 'Not a step back. Never! You can't win by going backwards.' He lived and died by his belief."[22] Kazuo's older brother, Takashi, who had been a replacement member of Company A in the 100th, requested and was granted a transfer to Kazuo's place in the Fourth Platoon, where he served until he was wounded on November 3, 1944. Two younger brothers, Masao and Mitsuo, also served in the US military, Masao in the Pacific theater with the military intelligence service.

CHAPLAINS

Although the majority of the unit were Buddhists, all of the chaplains associated with the 100th / 442nd were Christian. In addition to Chaplain Yost, the First Battalion was served initially by the Presbyterian Rev. Ernest Eells and then by Congregationalist Chaplain George Aki, who replaced Yost in July 1945.[23] As a result, the fallen could not be given Buddhist death rites on the battlefields of Europe. Chaplain Yost said he never attempted to conduct a Buddhist religious rite, but he "prayed with any solider who wanted a prayer."[24] This was the best he could do despite the official policy issued by the chief warrant officer of the regimental headquarters stating that "it will always be assumed that a Chaplain of the deceased's faith officiated at the burial. . . . It is important that the correct faith be mentioned except when the deceased's record show his religious preference as "none" or when such records are incomplete in this respect."[25]

The first memorial service that Yost had to perform on the battlefield was for a Buddhist soldier in D Company in early October 1943. The request came from the well-respected Capt. Jack Mizuha of D Company, who assembled his men to meet the chaplain, saying, "Chaplain, I don't believe the same things you do, but my men want a memorial service for their buddy, and I want them to have it." Telling the story later, Yost reflected on the fact that "no provision was made for the spiritual care of Buddhists and Shintoists, the faiths of many of the men of the 100th."

As Yost got to know Mizuha better, he came to deeply respect him. "I was not convinced that he was as antagonistic to Christian beliefs as he appeared to be," he wrote. "Before long I realized that Jack was indeed a fine man." Mizuha would receive multiple wounds from German machine-gun fire. As he was being carried from the field, he saw Yost and told him, "Chaplain, don't go near those German heavies; they are deadly accurate." Jack Mizuha survived his injuries and became a Hawai'i Supreme Court justice after the war.[26]

Yost's standard letter of condolence must have appeared odd to those Buddhist families he wrote to notify of their sons' deaths. It always included a card imprinted with the Bible verse John 15:13 and the following sentences: "May the heavenly Father give you His comfort and strength in your hours of sorrow. Whenever we gather for church services we remember in prayer the loved ones of our fallen comrades. We seek to honor their memory by carrying on as they would have us do until peace is won; in the day of victory their sacrifice will not be forgotten."[27] Christian condolences were sent by even the Japanese American chaplains assigned to the unit.

The chaplain for the Third Battalion, Rev. Masao Yamada, was the first Japanese American chaplain commissioned in the US Army. A convert to Christianity, he had been serving the Hanapepe Japanese Christian Church in Kauai when the war broke out. "Chappie," as he was known to the men, related more closely to the volunteers and draftees from Hawai'i, many of whom, like Yamada, had come from rural plantations and spoke Pidgin English. He was dedicated to the men, whether Buddhist or Christian, and continually accompanied them to the front lines. Yamada was seriously injured when his jeep hit a mine as he crossed the Arno River on his way to recover fallen soldiers' bodies. He was the only man to survive the incident.[28]

Soldiers who lost their lives, whether Buddhist or Christian, ended up in Christian gravesites. One such site was described by a medic in a letter to his wife as "a bare new plot of ground where many of our boys lie. . . . There were rows and rows of mounds, seeming naked in their newness. But, a few months will see the green sod covering the graves and white crosses will dot that acre."[29] The Second Battalion's chaplain, the Congregationalist Hiro Higuchi (a nisei from Hawai'i), described how he handled battlefield rites in a letter to his wife: "We don't get to perform the funeral service as we are at the front all the time and the bodies are interned in the rear echelon. However, some chaplain takes care of the funeral services. We go back when we can to say a prayer for them."[30]

Even before news reached grieving families of Buddhist soldiers dying on the battlefield and being buried under Christian crosses, there were calls from the Buddhist sangha to appoint a Buddhist chaplain to the US Army. At the outbreak of the war, the Army had 40 Regular Army, 298 National Guard, and 1,040 Reserve chaplains on duty. The need for chaplains grew during the war, and by its last day, over 8,000 chaplains had been on active duty, among them 311 Jewish chaplains, 247 black chaplains assigned to segregated units, and one Greek Orthodox chaplain assigned to an all-Greek unit.[31] None were Buddhist. The religion was not one of the group that Deborah Dash Moore calls the three "fighting faiths of democracy" (Protestantism, Catholicism, and Judaism)—a tri-faith collective conceived from the battles of World War II.[32]

As early as February 1943, US Army recruiters who visited the WRA camps received appeals to appoint a Buddhist chaplain. At Gila River, chief recruiter Captain Norman Thompson passed the request up the chain of command, where it was initially endorsed by the War Office.[33] Colonel William Scobey wrote to the 442nd's commander: "I suggest that you determine the number or percentage of Buddhist and . . . . should you discover that fifteen or twenty percent are Buddhist, a Buddhist chaplain will be provided." But his letter also revealed that the Army's Chief of Chaplains, William Richard Arnold, had already declared there were "not sufficient Buddhists in the combat team to warrant the commissioning and detailing of a Buddhist chaplain to the unit."[34] Arnold's claim was blatantly false, given that the majority of the unit was Buddhist. Still, Assistant Secretary of War John McCloy ultimately ruled against adding a Buddhist chaplain. According to the JACL's Mike Masaoka, McCloy believed "since there was widespread suspicion of, as well as ignorance about Asian religions, it would be better public relations to approve only Christian chaplains for the 442nd."[35]

Some Japanese American Christians also opposed Buddhist chaplains, including Rev. John Yamazaki, an Episcopalian, who implored his bishop to confidentially urge the army not to induct Buddhist priests because he believed non-Christian clergy represented a force against Americanization. The recipient, Bishop Charles S. Reifsnider, then wrote to the army's intelligence division suggesting "if a Japanese Chaplain or Chaplains are to be appointed for the Japanese Combat Unit, that they should be Christian ministers, whether the majority of the Unit are Christian or not."[36] Hiro Higuchi and Masao Yamada, who were both Christian chaplains in the 100th/442nd RCT, also voiced their opposition to appointing a Buddhist chaplain to their unit.[37]

Buddhist hopes rose briefly when Army Chief of Chaplains Arnold reversed his position, apparently under political pressure from the Adjutant General, and reached out to the Buddhist Mission of North America. Arnold wrote BMNA's bishop in the WRA Topaz camp that the army would be "pleased to consider a clergyman of your faith" who could be "assigned to a unit a majority of whose members are Buddhist."[38] The bishop recommended the BMNA spokesperson, Rev. Kenryō Kumata, whom the JACL had already encouraged to apply directly to McCloy.[39] In May 1943, the camp's *Bussei Life* newsletter reported on Arnold's decision that Rev. Kumata would be the army's "first chaplain of Japanese descent" attached to the 442nd.[40] Unfortunately, Kumata did not pass the army physical due to his poor eyesight, and no other candidates were accepted that year.[41]

The following March, the Young Buddhist Association at the WRA Gila River camp was inspired to take up the initiative.[42] That month, the WRA camps screened a newsreel, *Go For Broke,* which reported that although 70 to 80 percent of the soldiers in the 442nd were Buddhists, no progress had been made to secure a Buddhist chaplain. A Gila River YBA leader wrote to the deputy bishop of the BMNA that it was vital to "contact the War Department, so that several Buddhist ministers could be accepted in Chaplain corps of the US Army. We feel that due to no Buddhist Churches or ministers in the Armed forces of America, that eventually, the Young Buddhists will either turn to Christian or Catholic churches to obtain their enlightenment."[43] In his reply, the deputy bishop conveyed his own eagerness to see Buddhist chaplains serve in the armed forces, but explained that efforts to meet the strict criteria set by the Army Chaplain Corps—that candidates be nisei, physically fit, and otherwise qualified—had so far yielded no good prospects.[44]

Of the twenty ordained Buddhist priests who were male, military-age, and nisei, only half had completed the requisite ministerial training at a Buddhist "seminary," such as at the Hongwanji in Kyoto. Others failed the physical requirements. The commanding general of the Hawaiian Department had forwarded the names of two Buddhist priests who had participated in the ROTC program at the University of Hawai'i and his wife had recommended the white Buddhist priests, Rev. Ernest Hunt and Rev. Julius Goldwater, but none of these suggestions led to an appointment.[45]

The Congregationalist George Aki, the third Japanese American chaplain and the only one from the WRA camps, was then assigned to the unit. Aki was more sympathetic to the Buddhists. He wrote in his memoir that during his time training at Camp Shelby, "It was told to me that when the enlisted men volunteered, in their application on religious specification, most of them put down, Christian, for to put down Buddhist might not be acceptable since Japan and Buddhism signified the enemy. But knowing that the vast majority were Buddhists, I contacted a Buddhist clergy friend from the Jerome, Arkansas camp to hold services one week-end."[46] Although this was not the combat chaplain that many Buddhists had hoped for, the open-mindedness of Rev. Aki was welcomed by the young Buddhist soldiers and their families.

At this juncture, the army preferred to train existing chaplains on how to deal with the Buddhist soldiers. In March 1944, the Office of the Chaplain (Second Army) wrote to the BMNA bishop asking for guidance on how existing army chaplains could ensure that Buddhists could practice any "religious obligations" demanded of them, minister to them in the case of serious illness, and attend to any "religious ministration" when Buddhists died while on active duty.[47]

Though no chaplain of their faith was attached to the 100th / 442nd RCT, Buddhists in the camps and elsewhere actively supported those sent into overseas combat. As the sacrifices made by the segregated unit became increasingly well known in 1944, community support for them grew, even among those who had initially opposed nisei joining the military. In Poston, where opinions about registering for the draft were split, Block 43 organized a program to provide a traditional farewell gift (*senbetsu*) of five dollars for all inducted nisei, but also gave the same amount to draft resisters headed to the jail in Yuma, Arizona.[48]

Buddhists not only sponsored farewell parties, but also provided amulets, *senninbari,* and other traditional good-luck items to afford protection for the soldiers. Popularized during Japan's war with China in 1894, *senninbari*—literally, "thousand person stiches"—are handkerchief-sized cloths with a thousand knots or stitches sewn onto the cloth by groups of women. The campaign to gather the many stitches was often headed by the soldier's mother, sister, or wife, and represented his entire community's wishes of good luck and protection from harm on the battlefield.[49] Just before he left for Camp Shelby for basic training, Minoru Tsubota received a *senninbari* from his widowed mother, who had invited women throughout their WRA camp to each sew one small stitch of red thread on it.[50] "Somehow she wanted to . . . protect me," Tsubota recalled. "Any woman [born] in the year of the tiger could put as many as her age . . . so a sixty-year old lady could put sixty, but most of the time just one."[51] His mother was in Tule Lake, where many were opposed to having nisei fight for the US Army. "She probably had to stand out there and ask each lady to sew one dot," he said. "She never told me but I heard from others that had them that some people refused to sew in that one red dot." Since Tsubota couldn't wash it, he rolled it into a plastic case and carried it with him through France, Italy, and Germany.

Even some non-Buddhists appreciated the symbols of spiritual protection given to them. Mickey Makio Akiyama, for example, appreciated his *senninbari* and the party his coworkers at the Manzanar garment factory took up a collection to throw. In the October 1944 battle to rescue the "Lost Battalion," which had been trapped by German forces in the Vosges Mountains, Akiyama was wounded in the head by a sniper's bullet. He attributed his survival to his *senninbari* and a photo of his daughter that he kept in his helmet.[52]

More common than *senninbari* were protective amulets provided by the Hongwanji Buddhist Temple to nisei Buddhist soldiers.[53] In the WRA

FIGURE 9.3 Senninbari (thousand-stitch belt) with Dharma name and verse praising Amida Buddha.   Courtesy of the Tsubota Family Collection, Densho Digital Repository, ddr-densho-105-8.

camps Jerome and Gila River, the Buddhist women's group (Fujinkai) took the lead in creating *o-myōgō* scrolls extolling Amida Buddha with the phrase "Namu Amida Butsu" to protect departing nisei soldiers.[54] These amulets were miniaturized to enable soldiers to easily carry them in their wallets.

In the WRA Topaz camp, another kind of amulet was mass produced featuring an image of the Buddha. Called *go-ezō,* these were sent through a YBA in the free zone, in Denver, to forty Colorado-based Japanese American Buddhist soldiers leaving for the European front.[55] The YBA responded with a letter stating "we know that our members in the Army will carry them close to their hearts with their faith in Lord Buddha."[56] They were also shipped to the Poston WRA camp's Buddhist Church, which distributed them to the soldiers and encouraged barracks with Buddhist families to buy them at fifty cents apiece to support the cause.[57]

In the camps, YBA groups and women's associations also sent care packages called *imonbukuro,* including *go-ezō* amulets and candy bars, to those serving on the front. By the time the 442nd RCT had reached France—already renowned for its bravery in Vosges Mountains battles, its liberation of Bruyères, and its rescue of the so-called "Lost Battalion"—the soldiers appreciated anything that could alleviate, even just temporarily, the brutal realities of war. One of the seven 442nd servicemen who received a care package from the WRA Poston Buddhist Church, Tayoshi Munakata, wrote a letter in Japanese in January 1945 to the "barrack church" members:

> Thank you for the heart-filled care packages *(imonbukuro)* sent to me by the Bussei group, which I received one week ago. I have no words of thanks to express how much it means that you sent this to me even though we are not very closely tied. Right away, I opened one bag and ate its contents with my fellow soldiers. I cannot say how much we appreciated the tasty candy. I had heard about the care packages, but now that I have actually received one, this is something I really appreciate. I left the United States last August to go to Italy. After about one month there, we moved to southern France and spent some time at the [cannot reveal] front lines. It must be the help of the Buddha that I came out of that without a scratch. Right now, I am in a less dangerous part of southern France. At the beginning of January, it began to snow and it is quite cold. I write to you with pen in hand hoping that in the near future, peace will come to this world.[58]

Later in 1945, the Buddhist Churches of America headquarters sent hundreds of pamphlets, including ones entitled "Salvation," to Buddhist soldiers overseas.[59] Correspondence was also a key way to encourage the nisei soldiers. Bilingual individuals helped issei sangha members with sons on the front compose English-language letters.[60] Likewise, the young men in the 442nd RCT often attempted to write to their parents in camp in broken Japanese to reassure them that they were still alive and that, as American soldiers, they had not forgotten the importance of their Buddhist faith. One, for example, wrote as follows:

> Dear Mama and Papa,
>   It's me. Tonight, I'm finally being sent to the front. Thank you for loving me all these years. Mama, and Papa too, there's no need to worry. I'll be back soon. I'll rush back to where you are just as soon as I get back. Both of you stay in good health till then, all right? Since everything's set to go, I've not got nothing else left to say except good-bye. Take care, Mama and Papa. Good-bye, good-bye. Oh wait, I'd forgotten, there is something else Mama. That story, you know, the one you used to tell me all the time when I was a kid. The story about the Buddha. I remember that really well so you can put your mind at ease. The Buddha will always be with me, even when I'm sent to the front. I'm not sad at all because the Buddha will protect me. Mama and Papa, don't worry about me because I remember that story really well. Well, I've got to be off so you two take care of yourselves. Good-bye."[61]

Of course, many Buddhists did not make it back. Sergeant Jimmie Toshio Shimizu of F Company was praised by fellow soldiers for fighting "without intimidation" throughout the French campaign. On what would be his last combat mission in October 1944, Shimizu asked the company cook to keep his wallet to send to his sister in the WRA Minidoka camp if he didn't make it. A few weeks after receiving her brother's wallet, she wrote back asking exactly when Jimmie had died. On October 29, 1944, the day her brother had passed away in France, a candle she had lit on the *butsudan* (Buddhist altar) in her barrack flickered out three times. She had taken it as an omen of her brother's death.[62]

FALLEN SOLDIERS

Private rituals at a family altar in a barrack were complemented by public Buddhist services for the fallen members of the 100th / 442nd and military intelligence service. In the Poston WRA camp, hundreds gathered at an outdoor auditorium in August 1944 for a public memorial of two nisei killed in action. Rev. Bunyū Fujimura, formerly of the Salinas Buddhist Temple, delivered the sermon:

> [That the two] died for their country in a hail of bullets while in the prime of their lives, is something their families can take pride in. Theirs is truly the Bodhisattva Way in the Buddhist teaching. [But] sadness also exists. . . . For over twenty years, their sons were always at the forefront of the parents' minds. . . . the beloved child they raised to adulthood has now been transformed into a single telegram informing the parents of his death. . . . Shakyamuni Buddha raised his voice and cried in sorrow at the sight of the dead. Trying to discard sorrow is a lie. Telling someone not to cry is unreasonable. . . . In one drop, and then in another drop, of tears, of blood, is where the Buddha sobs his tears. This is what I believe. I believe the great land that has been soaked bright red with Yamamoto and Shiomitsu's blood, and the heart-rending tears of their bereaved family, is the sacred sacrifice that will in the near future sound the bell of the dawn of peace in the entire world. Namu Amida Butsu.[63]

In Manzanar, Rev. Shinjō Nagatomi used a similar language of sacrifice and the sadness of families in his public addresses at memorial services for the nisei killed in Europe. For example, after the news of two 442nd soldiers' combat deaths reached their Buddhist parents, he spoke at their memorial service at the Manzanar Community Auditorium. Concerned about large gatherings where anti-American sentiments might be expressed, camp authorities had assigned staff member Margaret D'Ille to translate the speech into English. But far from inciting anti-Americanism, Rev. Nagatomi captured the complex and heartfelt feelings of loss, loyalty, and identity felt by many families:

> Today, we are gathered here at this Memorial Service being held in the honor of Sgt. Kiyoshi Nakasaki and PFC. Sadao Munemori under the sponsorship of the Manzanar USO and the

FIGURE 9.4 Shingon Buddhist memorial service with altar photos of fallen nisei soldiers in the WRA camp at Minidoka, Idaho.   Courtesy of the National Archives and Records Administration, Densho Digital Repository, ddr-densho-37-732.

residents of Manzanar. These two honored heroes of 25 and 22 years of age died in action on the battlefield of Italy on April 5, 1945. Although the lives of Sgt. Nakasaki and PFC. Munemori were brief (young and in the prime of their life) their struggles and sacrifices were dedicated to the teachings and traditions of the Japanese people. We are gathered here without distinction of an Issei or a Nisei, but in behalf of the 110,000 Japanese people. . . . To you, the family members and relatives of the deceased: Since the first day of the call for service of your sons and brothers I am sure you must have prepared yourself for this ill tiding news of your loved ones. With the official notices of their death, along with their enlarged pictures which are enshrined at the altar taken while they were in active duty, you cannot help but recall the many childhood passing years of your beloved sons and the numerous memories left behind by them for you

FIGURE 9.5 Three Buddhist priests conducting a nisei soldier's memorial service in the WRA camp at Rohwer, Arkansas.   Courtesy of the Japanese American National Museum (Gift of the Walter Muramoto Family) 97.293.8.

to cherish. . . . Your sons' life was a short one, but their holy and symbolic spirit of sacrifice now guide and help to preserve the nation's freedom and justice. When the roar of guns cease and the fighting men come home once again, with your strong and determined belief let us continue to keep alive their dedication to the cause: "May the People of the world enjoy everlasting freedom and peace."[64]

Rev. Nagatomi's issei perspective was representative of many older community members, who viewed the nisei soldiers' courage and spirit of sacrifice as derived from a Japanese warrior spirit with an honorable tradition. In this way, he gently reminded the nisei not to forget their Japanese roots, and affirmed that the nisei soldiers' sacrifice would earn a place for those of Japanese descent in America.

During the war, Buddhist soldiers' sacrifices for America were rarely publicly honored on the US continent, except in these gatherings in the

WRA camps. Most Nisei soldiers who received the Medal of Honor were recognized and honored only after many years had passed and much painstaking research and lobbying had been done gain the acknowledgment of their sacrifices. One exception was Private First Class Sadao Munemori, who was posthumously awarded a Medal of Honor in 1946 for heroically diving onto a grenade to save the lives of his fellow 442nd soldiers. A US Army transport ship was named after him in 1947, and more recently, a hall in the US Army Reserve Center in West Los Angeles, in 1993. In 1994, the always-busy interchange between the Interstate Highway Routes 105 and 405 in Los Angeles was named the Sadao S. Munemori Memorial Freeway Interchange.[65]

In the Hawaiian Islands, such public acknowledgment of the sacrifices of nisei soldiers—400 of the 506 Hawai'i-born nisei killed in action during the war were Buddhist—was one of the main avenues for reviving Buddhism.[66] Since sixty-three percent of the Hawai'i-born soldiers who died in combat were of Japanese heritage, the military government felt compelled to loosen its ban on Buddhist gatherings at temples.[67] One nisei recalled that he attended "memorial services at the Hongwanji temple almost every Sunday for many of the local boys who were killed in action."[68]

It took numerous appeals to the military government to gain general permission for such gatherings at Buddhist temples. A young nisei of the Paia Buddhist Church's Women's Association in Maui sent a letter to Brigadier General Donald J. Meyers in March 1944 requesting the ability "to conduct regular services once a month for these boys who have died in action and also prayers for the boys who are fighting in the front."[69] She asked permission to officiate the services herself. Her letter prompted a report, which noted that all Buddhist priests of that sect on the island of Maui had been interned, and highlighted that the Buddhist Women's Association at Paia had donated money to the US Army and Navy Relief funds in the past. It concluded: "neither petitioner, nor any of the church-goers interviewed, are engaged in any subversive activity . . . and that the few prayer gatherings held at the temple to date, in honor of soldiers who died in their country's defense, were duly authorized and permitted by the local Provost Marshal's Office."[70] Despite this promising initial assessment, Colonel R. C. Morrison, an executive of the Judge Advocate General's Department, denied the request:

> The petitioner in this case is probably all right but once religious services are permitted to be resumed by the Japanese, opportunity is presented for subversive gatherings. It is felt that while Christian services present much the same opportunity to gather, the Japanese espousing the Christian religion are less likely to promulgate pro-Japanese matters. [Further, it is the] general policy of this office to discourage the resumption of Japanese religious activities other than Christian. This attempt to revive Buddhist Services should not be approved at this time.[71]

Many Buddhist families were forced to hold services at a Christian church instead. When one nisei who came from a very devout Sōtō Zen Buddhist family was killed in action serving with the 442nd, his sister recalled, "It was the saddest moment when one day, two military officers knocked on our door and informed Okaasan [Mother] that 'your son was killed in action on July 14, 1944.' As there were no Buddhist ministers available, a Christian service was held and he was interred at the National Memorial Cemetery of the Pacific at Punchbowl."[72]

There were a handful of exceptions to the general inability to honor those who had made the ultimate sacrifice for their country with Buddhist services. Rev. Mitsumyō Tottori of the Haleʻiwa Shingon Mission, one of the few priests not interned, fulfilled multiple requests for prayers from the families of nisei soldiers. His daughter recalled:

> He offered many prayers on their behalf. In addition, he personally made *toba* (wooden memorial tablets) for those Hawaiʻi AJA [Americans of Japanese Ancestry] men who gave their lives for their country . . . [after his death, his successor] found the 420 *toba* Reverend Tottori had personally dedicated to the Hawaiʻi Nisei killed in combat. [In a notebook with all the names of the dead], the first entry was that of Sgt. Shigeo Takata of Waialua, the first Nisei casualty from Hawaiʻi, who died on September 29,

FIGURE 9.6 Pvt. Walter Kanaya's Silver Star medal posthumously awarded by
Chaplain (Colonel) Corwin H. Olds to his Buddhist family in Honolulu
(1945).   Courtesy of the Seattle Nisei Veterans Committee and the US Army, Densho Digital
Repository, ddr-densho-114-147.

> 1943. My father gave him his posthumous [Buddhist] name:
> "Yu-mon-in Chu-sei Ho-koku Ko-ji," which means "For the sake
> of America, he gave his life."[73]

During the course of the war, Tottori served members of the Buddhist
community at large, bringing sect-specific sutras to conduct private
home memorial services for the many non-Shingon Buddhist families
who lost sons in combat. He even created Buddhist memorial tablets for
Christians who perished as part of the 100th / 442nd as he learned of each
death on the battlefields of Europe. Immediately after the war, he made
an unusually large memorial tablet for the main altar of his temple,
which he dedicated to all soldiers, from both the American military and
Japanese Imperial Army, who lost their lives during the war. Inscribed

on the tablet was a prayer to end the animosity between the two nations and a wish that all who passed would swiftly attain enlightenment.[74]

On the Big Island, other families were also able to hold Buddhist services for their lost soldiers at the Naalehu Hongwanji Mission. Shigeo Kikuchi, the wife of the interned Rev. Chikyoku Kikuchi, was implored by a family whose son had been killed in action in Italy to conduct a Buddhist service in his honor.[75] Having agreed to do so, Kikuchi was joined by Rev. Ernest Hunt, who happened to be visiting the Big Island from Honolulu at that moment. This unusual situation led to a sanctioned Buddhist funerary service with even military officials in attendance. She recalled:

> High officials, the Army Band, the elite of the Kaʻu district, residents and various representatives attended the funeral rites. The main hall [of the temple] was filled and more than half of the people gathered had to stand outside the hall. This was the first time that a funeral for an American casualty was held together with the military in Naalehu Hongwanji [Temple]. Besides the military music on the program, I added a Buddhist *gatha* to be sung by the choir and conducted a very solemn ceremony.[76]

After setting this precedent, Ms. Kikuchi went on to perform all the funerals in the Kaʻu district on the Big Island for the duration of the war. By the war's end, Buddhist temples headed by the wives of interned Buddhist priests, often assisted by the women's association, reacquired some of their prewar role as community centers, though limited to memorializing deceased Buddhist nisei soldiers. The irony remained that young nisei sacrificed themselves for a country that considered their families less than fully American. Yet the visible process of memorializing Buddhist soldiers made a critical public declaration that one could be both Buddhist and American.

As the war wound down and ended, in Europe in May of 1945 and in the Pacific in August, the sangha rebuilt itself on the sacrifices of the nisei soldiers. They had perished in places from the jungles of Pacific islands to the forests of northern France, but it was resolved in the immediate postwar period that they would be remembered. The poem "Silent Crosses" by Lieutenant Barry Saiki, who was an active youth leader in the WRA's Rohwer camp and a cofounder of the Chicago Young Buddhist Association during the war, suggests a silent suffering by Buddhist soldiers buried under Christian crosses:

> They crossed the death-filled foreign vales
> Through heavy fire of leaden hails
> They cleared the hills that barred the way
> And breached the woods where snipers lay. . . .
> Yet all who went did not come back
> For some were lost in each attack. . . .
> Again on foreign soil there lie
> Silent crosses where men did die.
> To mark the graves of those who said,
> "Are all men free though we be dead"

The poem was published by *Nirvana,* a journal of the Eastern Young Buddhist League, New York City Chapter.[77] It ends with a poignant question of whether the nisei soldiers' deaths secured freedom for those left behind.

The military service and sacrifice of the roughly thirty-three thousand Japanese American men and women in the armed forces during World War II did improve how they were treated in the postwar military.[78] Several years after the war, a soldier in Private First Class Jitsuo Matsubara's unit, stationed in Germany, was mysteriously murdered. Investigating the crime, headquarters ordered the entire company strip down for inspection.[79] As the young soldier was taking off his trousers, a Buddhist amulet that he always kept on him dropped to the floor. The sergeant in charge demanded to know what it was. Matsubara explained that it was an amulet given it to him by his mother that contained sacred words extolling the Buddha, *Namu Amida Butsu.* The white sergeant, who had served in the Pacific theater during the war, angrily tore up the paper amulet. Early in the war, incidents like these were not uncommon. But when Matsubara brought the incident to the attention of his company commander, he reported it to the division commander—and the two commanders offered an apology to the nisei private for this regrettable conduct. They further ordered the sergeant court-martialed for violating the Buddhist soldier's religious freedom, and sentenced him to six months in prison without pay, followed by a dishonorable discharge. The regimental commander of all military operations in Germany cited this case as a standard for religious freedom that all soldiers should bear in mind. Japanese American newspapers and Buddhist magazines of the period also covered this incident.

Another sign of progress was the successful advocacy effort launched in 1948 by the National Young Buddhist Coordinating Council (NYBCC) to urge the US military to include a "B" designation on Buddhists' GI identification tags—the "B for Buddhism" campaign. As the nisei leaders of the NYBCC earned political backing from mainstream political entities, including the Los Angeles County Board of Supervisors, and Joseph Rider Farrington, the Republican delegate to Congress representing the Territory of Hawai'i, the US Army responded with a compromise they found acceptable: a dog tag with an "X" on the standard tag to designate a religious tradition that was not one of the three used previously ("P" for Protestant, "C" for Catholic, and "H" for Hebrew or Jewish), and an additional metal identification tag with the specific designation for Buddhists. The NYBCC and the Hawaii Federation of the YBA also succeeded in having the military symbolically recognize Buddhism at military cemeteries by placing the Dharma Wheel on the tombstones of fallen Buddhist soldiers. A section of the Punch-bowl National Cemetery in Hawai'i was designated to honor Buddhist veterans of World War II. Eight Bodhi trees, symbolizing the Eightfold Noble Path and the tree under which the Buddha attained enlightenment, were planted there.[80]

These postwar measures to recognize Buddhism would never have secured the support of military leaders and the public if it hadn't been for the service of Japanese American men and women during World War II. Even the mainstream media began covering issues and events related to the Buddhists. In May 1948, the *Los Angeles Times* covered the "last rites" of Private First Class George Gushiken of the 442nd, killed in action in France in 1944 and finally given proper rites after the war:

The East was there—expressed in the mystic ritual of the ages-old Buddhist faith . . . .

The West was there. It was high officers of the Army of the United States. It was Mayor Bowron. It was the trim precision of the military guard of honor.

It was, above all, in the fierce pride and loyalty that marked the hero's parents, Mr. and Mrs. Tom Gushiken, 413 E 7th St.[81]

Japanese American Buddhists welcomed these public acknowledgments by city mayors and military officials, but still faced tremendous difficulties in the aftermath of war. For most, returning home meant traveling by train from the WRA and DOJ camps to the west coast homes from which they had been forcibly removed, or by ship to their homes in Hawai'i. Some, embittered by their incarceration or concerned about keeping their families together, opted to journey further westward to Japan—the issei as repatriates and the nisei as expatriates, some of whom had never lived in their parents' homelands. For others, including those who had previously moved to the "free zones," resettlement meant new lives in Chicago, Denver, New York, and other east coast cities. In an important respect, the resettlement was like their prewar migration from Japan to the Americas, and their wartime movement into prisons and camps. It was a moment of dislocation, when they would once again need to draw on their faith, family, and community and start a new life.

10

THE RESETTLEMENT

WHEN THE DAY CAME to close the Wyoming Zendo, the Zen Buddhist community in the WRA Heart Mountain camp, it was coincidentally the same day, August 15, 1945, that a message from the Emperor was broadcast across Japan announcing its surrender. Presiding priest Nyogen Senzaki chose his words well:

> Fellow students:
> Under Heart Mountain
> We formed a Sangha for three years
> And learned to practice
> The wisdom of Avalokitesvara.
> The gate of the barbed wire fence opens
> You are now free
> To contact other students,
> Who join you to save all sentient beings
> From ignorance and suffering.[1]

The Japanese characters for the taking of the precepts to live a Buddhist life or "taking refuge" in Buddhism literally mean "relying" on "a return." For Buddhists, to take refuge in the Buddha, Dharma, and sangha can be thought of as a form of homecoming—a return to a reliable place that orients them toward seeing and living a life of awakening and community.

Before his incarceration three years earlier, Senzaki had administered the Buddhist precepts to Ruth Strout McCandless and conferred on her the Dharma name "Kangetsu" (Cold Moon). With the closing of the camp, he traveled to Pasadena, California, and stayed at her home, where he had stored his Buddhist book collection. Two months later, he returned to his prewar neighborhood in Los Angeles and lamented: "Being a mere returnee from the evacuation / I could establish no zendo."[2] But shortly thereafter, one of his disciples, the owner of the Miyako Hotel in Little Tokyo, offered Senzaki a place to live and run a small Zen meditation hall.[3] Senzaki was more fortunate than most. For the majority of the Japanese Americans who had been confined in the WRA and DOJ camps, the return journey to their prewar homes was filled with travail and uncertainty.

As far back as September 1943, President Roosevelt had said, "We shall restore to the loyal evacuees the right to return to the evacuated areas as soon as the military situation will make such restoration possible."[4] Even before the United States dropped atomic bombs on Hiroshima and Nagasaki in August 1945, government authorities had begun to release individuals from internment. With the end of the war, the WRA camps began closing, one after the other. To the issei in their fifties and older who had lost everything, returning and starting all over again was a particularly daunting prospect.

In Jerome, the YBA formed the Buddhist Home Program to assist Buddhists—both those in the Arkansas camp and those in the military—in planning their next moves as that camp's closure was approaching.[5] At Topaz, where the wartime headquarters of the Buddhist Churches of America (BCA) was located, the organization "directed an aggressive program of relocation and housing assistance for [its] members."[6] And in Manzanar, Rev. Shinjō Nagatomi and his family stayed to take care of both Buddhists and Christians—whoever lacked the resources to make the move back—and left in November 1945 as the last family out of that camp.[7] Despite these efforts, the historian Greg Robinson notes, "the WRA had to evict a number of Japanese and Japanese Americans left in the camps at the war's end and it took until December 1945 to close down all the WRA camps except Tule Lake, which only closed its gates in March 1946."[8]

For many, leaving the camps was bittersweet. The communities they had built were disbanded as they went their separate ways to an uncertain future. Senzaki's poem to his fellow Zen Buddhist travelers, declares they are "now free." It expresses the hope that his fellow Buddhists have learned during their confinement to practice wisdom and compassion, which will help them orient themselves, whatever their futures hold. It urges them, once they are beyond the "gate of the barbed wire fence," to help all beings.

RETURN TO A HOSTILE WEST COAST

Though their freedom was precious, returning home was fraught. Many faced the difficulties of trying to recover homes or businesses they had sold, and living alongside neighbors who had supported their forced removal. Ever since their incarceration, they had heard worrisome rumors of possible violence if they ever returned to the west coast. In June 1943, for example, the WRA Amache camp newspaper had quoted a warning from the Los Angeles evangelist Aimee Semple McPherson that the return of the Japanese American community would "incense the people and create riots and even bloodshed."[9] Echoing other west coast politicians, California Governor Earl Warren (later to become US Supreme Court chief justice) told reporters in that same month that the return of the Japanese would be a "body blow" to the nation's security: "I believe the evacuation of the Japanese at the time it occurred was one of the things which saved our state from terrible disorders and sabotage to wreck our industry."[10] After the US Army lifted the exclusion orders, Japanese Americans legally returning to California had reason to fear they would not be welcomed home.

Other political and community leaders continued to oppose the return of Japanese Americans to the west coast because of intense political pressure from ordinary citizens. By 1944, citizens had organized groups against the return, such as the Remember Pearl Harbor League formed by farmers in the Washington state towns of Kent and Auburn.[11] A 1944 pamphlet entitled *The Japs Must Not Come Back!* warned that "Samurai-indoctrinated" Japanese-American citizens "will have the right after the war to settle next door to us and consort with our daughters unless something is done to stop them." Its author, Lambert Schuyler, proposed shipping anyone of Japanese descent to the South Pacific "Japanese Man-dated Islands," where they would be far away from white women.[12] And in San Benito County, California, a group called the California Preser-vation Society was formed to oppose the return of Japanese Americans "by all lawful means."[13] The county's Board of Supervisors went on record opposing a return: "We are in no position to judge the emotions of the Japanese inasmuch as they have maintained their own schools and reli-gion, and in many cases, dual citizenship with their main allegiance to the Emperor of Japan."[14]

In a well-publicized incident in Hood River, Oregon, in late 1944, the local American Legion removed the names of sixteen nisei soldiers who had served or were still serving from a Second World War memorial wall in front of the county courthouse. The American Legion restored the names only after the chapter and town were roundly criticized by mili-tary officials and the press from around the country. The US Army news-paper, *The Stars and Stripes,* reported comments from white GIs, in-cluding this one: "Those Legion people ought to sell their property and give it to these Nisei. They deserve it more. If these Japanese-Americans are good enough to die for their country, they ought to be good enough to live in it."[15] Still, when Japanese Americans from Hood River returned home, they found shopkeepers unwilling to sell to them and barbershops unwilling to serve them.[16] Local newspaper ads proclaimed: "We should never be satisfied until every last Jap has been run out of these United States and our Constitution changed so they can never get back!"[17]

Nonetheless, a few Japanese Americans had started quietly returning to the west coast in early 1944, with US Army permission going initially to families of nisei soldiers.[18] By the end of August 1944, only thirty-seven people had returned to California, and those returning to Oregon and Washington had moved mainly to areas outside the "exclusion zone."

In September 1944, Kaoru Ichihara, a nisei Christian woman, became the first person from the camps to return to Seattle, an exclusion zone. Douglas Dye, in his study of the Seattle Council of Churches during the war, notes that Ichihara "must have seemed like an ideal choice to present the Japanese return as not a threat."[19] Since she had been a secretary with the Seattle Council of Churches before the war, her return brought her back to one of the few organizations in the city that publicly welcomed returning Japanese Americans. Christians such as Ichihara were thought less likely to provoke racist responses.

A handful of individuals deemed highly "assimilated" were successfully moved back to the west coast. After a tip that the US Supreme Court might rule on constitutionality of the mass exclusion of Japanese Americans in the Korematsu and Endo cases—two legal interventions filed on behalf of Fred Korematsu, who had violated the military order by not reporting to an assembly center, and Mitsuye Endo, who challenged the exclusion and incarceration through a habeas corpus petition from within the camps—the commanding general of the Western Defense Command announced the dissolution of the exclusion zone on December 17, 1944. This determination was made a day prior to the court handing down its rulings on both cases.[20]

Rev. Gikan Nishinaga used that opportunity to act. Tapped by members of the former Seattle Buddhist Church to lead its reopening, he returned in late February 1945. Rev. Nishinaga and other Buddhists faced a more contentious return to the west coast than Christians did. Upon arriving in Seattle, the US Maritime Commission, which had taken a four-year lease on the temple property as a training site and housing unit for their seamen, did not honor its agreement to vacate on schedule. The Commission had removed stored belongings of temple members from the gymnasium, and many items were stolen. The temple had been damaged and defaced, including in the main Buddha hall.[21]

In fact, most former Seattleites in the camps were reluctant to abruptly cut ties to the religious communities they had formed and move back. At a February 1945 "All Centers Conference" in Salt Lake City, attended by WRA Director Myer and representatives from the various camps, the delegates agreed to a ten-point statement that included: "(8) Practically every Buddhist priest is now excluded from the west coast. Buddhism has a substantial following, and the members obviously prefer to remain where there are religious centers."[22] James Sakoda finds that the "rate of departure from Minidoka was quite selective by generation, religion, and gender. . . . In each generational category, Buddhists were more likely to stay behind [in camps] than Christians."[23]

Buddhist temples all the way from Tacoma, Washington, to San Diego, California, had been vandalized in the course of the war. The

FIGURE 10.1 Returning to find vandalism at the Los Angeles Nichiren Buddhist
Temple.   Courtesy of the National Archives and Records Administration, Densho Digital Repository,
ddr-densho-37-283.

break-in at the Nichiren Buddhist Temple in Los Angeles caused so much
damage that it caught the attention of the WRA. The government arranged for one temple member at Colorado's Amache camp to return
temporarily to Los Angeles and inspect the damage. She reported:
"Nothing was untouched, sewing machines were ruined, furniture
broken, mirrors smashed to smithereens, broken glass from breakable
articles, household goods scattered helter-skelter, trunks broken beyond
repair."[24]

The concerns about violence were justified. A War Department memo
from June 1945 notes that roughly 3,500 Japanese Americans had returned to the Pacific coast states and details eighty incidents of violence, such as shooting attacks and arson cases, against resettlers since
the beginning of that year.[25] Japanese American newspapers reported
these incidents with some regularity.[26]

Fortunately, Secretary of the Interior Harold Ickes made strong comments against these types of incidents. In one statement, he declared:

In the absence of vigorous law enforcement, a pattern of planned terrorism by hoodlums has developed. It is a matter of national concern because this lawless minority, whose actions are condemned by the decent citizens who make up an overwhelming majority of West Coast residents, seems determined to employ its Nazi storm trooper tactics against loyal Japanese Americans and law-abiding Japanese aliens in spite of the state laws and Constitutional safeguards designed to protect the lives and property of all of the people of this country.[27]

One "threatening visit" was paid to Mary Masuda when she was granted a short-term break from the WRA Gila River camp to check on her family home in Orange County, California, in May 1945. Masuda was the nisei sister of staff sergeant Kazuo Masuda, one of the Buddhist soldiers who died in action with the 442nd in Italy. When Mary reached the house in Talbert, she discovered it had been occupied by another family who had hurriedly departed just before her arrival and who had farmed their land although her family did not grant permission for that or gain compensation from it. Staying with neighbors, Mr. and Mrs. Albert Trudeau, Mary found herself targeted by self-described "patriots" affiliated with the Native Sons of the Golden West, who told her to get back to camp. Mary refused to be intimidated.[28] Her sister June later recalled her attitude: "I came this far, I must fight for what Kazuo and all the rest of the soldiers fought for."[29] With that determination, Mary Masuda and her entire family came back in September 1945.

In an important public display, General Joseph W. Stilwell went to the Masuda's Orange County farm home a few months later to present Kazuo Masuda's Distinguished Service Cross to the family. The four-star general traveled three thousand miles to pin a medal on Mary in person.[30] Joining the general were several Hollywood celebrities, including the motion picture actress Louise Allbritton, who spoke about how the 442nd had saved the "Lost Battalion" from her home state of Texas, and the young actor and future president of the United States, Ronald Reagan.[31]

TEMPLES AS HOMES

With tens of thousands of Japanese Americans returning to their prewar locations, a pressing issue was finding new homes and new places of belonging for a people whose livelihoods, farms, businesses, and residences had been lost to them. Despite the news of hostilities, some Buddhist priests took the lead in returning and reestablishing their communities. In WRA Gila River, Rev. Issei Matsuura insisted to authorities that his family should be allowed to return to Guadalupe, California. The request was denied after an investigation found that townspeople strongly opposed Japanese returning there, but Rev. Matsuura pleaded to the camp officer, "I must return to Guadalupe. There are several hundred graves of our fellow Japanese buried [there] and I suspect no one has tended to them for over four years during our absence. As a minister, I am bound to return. I can endure the hostile winds of prejudice."[32] Disinclined to argue against this, the officer granted permission.

Immediately upon their return to the Guadalupe Buddhist Temple, Rev. Matsuura and his wife Shinobu established a hostel, turning the temple's classrooms and main hall into temporary housing for those returning to the farming community. Shinobu Matsuura was grateful to the Regalado family, who had lived in and cared for the temple during the war and warmly greeted the Matsuuras on their arrival from the rail depot. Entering the temple dissipated the feelings of estrangement from home they had felt during the camp days: "Although it was late at night, we opened the altar which had been nailed shut, and entered from the back. When we placed the Amida [Buddha] in the altar, our great relief and delight were emotions I shall never forget."[33]

In those early days of the return, Mrs. Matsuura helped prepare meals for nearly a hundred people every day:

> In this small town, there were only a few shops. And to face their refusal to sell us anything was exasperating. Some of the white people who had been friendly before the evacuation would not even speak to us and they even held back commodities from us. In fact, once someone shot into a room where many of us were sleeping . . . However, among them, some showed kindness, and

brought us vegetables and fish. The important thing was that among the returnees, everyone was under the same stressful condition together so everyone became united, helping one another. The hostel evolved into one big family.[34]

The idea of a big family or new sangha where the temple served as a shelter and spiritual home recalled the earliest days of the migration from Japan and the formation of Buddhist communities in the Americas. This temple and others simultaneously provided temporary homes and revived Buddhist religious activity. "Over half the temple hall was taken up by personal belongings from the camps, piled high almost to the ceiling," Mrs. Matsuura said. "Despite the congestion, services were begun, and Sunday School, YBA, and other gatherings began to grow again. Little by little, jobs and housing were found, and a year and half later, most of the hostel members had resettled into the surrounding area. Only those too ill or too old remained."[35]

Most hostels were not designed for housing resettlers long-term, but finding homes was not always easy. In rural Vacaville, California, the Buddhist temple limited its religious services for six years to accommodate those who had no means to restart their former lives.[36] In San Jose, California, after numerous break-ins and arson cases in the Nihonmachi (Japantown) section, the WRA helped establish a secure hostel at the San Jose Buddhist Temple.[37] The temple offered its main hall and annex to the WRA as temporary housing for the returnees despite the facilities being vandalized in May 1945.[38] Most returnees stayed, on average, for two weeks, and residence on any given day was as high as 370 people. This joint effort with the Buddhist temple, the JACL, and the San Jose Council for Civic Unity was run by the WRA until March 31, 1946, the date when government support for hostels ended. By that point, 1,423 people had spent time living at the temple. The Buddhist Church maintained the hostel until 1955, when an apartment complex was built for issei still requiring housing.[39]

In Los Angeles, the WRA calculated a need for thirty housing centers, but the city built only five to accommodate the estimated four thousand returnees needing temporary housing. Of those, 1,300 were subsequently placed in trailers at the Winona emergency housing project, established by the Federal Public Housing Authority.[40] Nearly thirty hostels, most affiliated with Buddhist temples or Christian churches, managed to house most of the resettlers.[41] As in other locations, the coordinated efforts of sympathetic white Christian organizations and individuals enabled Christian resettlers to return earlier. They found housing at the Pasadena Hostel run by the American Friends Service Committee (AFSC), the Evergreen Hostel in Boyle Heights, jointly organized by the AFSC and the Presbyterian Church, and other locations. Evergreen was one of the largest of the Los Angeles hostels and, after the WRA forwarded unused furniture from the camps, increased its capacity to nearly 150.[42] Unlike other Christian hostels, such as the West LA Methodist Church, which tended to cater to its own members, the Evergreen Hostel became well regarded for its openness to members of any religious affiliation.[43]

Coordination with white sympathizers, as in the camps, came easier for Christians, but white Buddhists, including Rev. Sunya Pratt and Julius Goldwater, were also helpful in assisting the returning Buddhists. In Seattle, Rev. Pratt, who had cared for and safeguarded the Tacoma Buddhist Church during the war, opened a hostel for returnees in March 1945.[44] That same month in Los Angeles, Rev. Goldwater established two Buddhist hostels, at the Senshin Buddhist Temple and the Gardena Buddhist Temple. A third he attempted to establish, the Nishi (Hompa) Hongwanji Betsuin, fell through due to a dispute with its board members.[45]

The Senshin Buddhist Temple, located near the University of Southern California, was one of the largest Buddhist hostels. The temple was a key religious institution set among the largest residential concentration of Japanese Americans in the city; Little Tokyo, farther north, was the commercial center. The hostel opened in April 1945 after the temple's Japanese-language school was converted into a new sanctuary open to those of any faith.[46] The WRA provided some cots and beds, and Goldwater "contacted his friends in Beverly Hills, who kindly donated loads of assorted furniture. In this way, the hall was transformed into a living area with quality but mismatched furnishings."[47] For his efforts, he was called a "Jap lover" and his home defaced.[48]

Along with Goldwater, YBA leader Art Takemoto and Rev. Kanmo Imamura and his wife, Jane Imamura, served as managers of the hostel. Four rooms and cellar spaces were converted into rooms to house eight persons each. Takemoto recalled that "assistance was provided for the evacuees, arranging for their food ration coupon books, gas ration books, arrangements with the WRA, and making arrangements for jobs, housing, and transportation. Because of the number of returnees, every attempt was made to get them settled within a week to ten days. Room and board was at its bare minimum—$2.00 per day and increased to $3.00 after ten days."[49]

"Arthur literally wielded a hammer to make the partitions for the sleeping quarters, makeshift showers, and toilets," said Rev. Goldwater, and Jane Imamura "cooks, slaves, cleans, shops with me for food."[50] Just securing food was quite the daily task for both Buddhist priests and the YBA leader, who "gathered ration stamps, then pulled a shopping cart to haul the ample amounts of food from nearby stores. Three meals a day had to be prepared for fifty ever-changing residents."[51] One family had tried to move back to their farm in Lancaster, but immediately returned to the temple hostel after vigilantes shot at their home during their first night there.[52] Sympathetic African American neighbors also contributed to the sanctuary. Roy Loggins, who ran a food catering company for the film studios, brought leftover food to the temple.[53] When most white businesses refused to hire the returning Japanese, he offered part-time work to hostel residents, including Art Takemoto's father.[54]

While acts of kindness infused Los Angeles's Senshin temple, other Buddhist hostels faced hostility. Los Angeles County officials imposed property taxes on the Kōyasan Temple for its "non-religious" use of the temple to store its members' belongings while they were in camp, and declared it $5,000 in arrears.[55] Similarly, the Salinas Buddhist Temple was taxed by the city council, despite its incorporation as a religious body, because of the temple's use as a hostel.[56] Worse, in September 1945, the temporary homes at both the Watsonville and San Francisco Buddhist temples in California were attacked. In Watsonville, flares were thrown at the building housing the returnees. In San Francisco, vigilantes hurled rocks, plaster, and beer bottles through the windows at

FIGURE 10.2 Senshin Buddhist hostel in 1945.   Courtesy of Ryo Imamura.

the 150 people staying at the hostel.[57] The *Los Angeles Daily News* called the attack one of the "first acts of terrorism against the Japanese in San Francisco."[58]

These acts of violence were a sequel to vandalism during the war. Only a handful of temples were fortunate enough to have a white Buddhist priest as caretakers or kind neighbors to watch over temples.[59] The main Buddha image was stolen at the Bakersfield Buddhist Temple and temple members' precious belongings were stolen from many temples, including the Higashi Honganji Temple and Nichiren Buddhist Temple in Los Angeles.[60] At the largest of the Zen temples on the US continent, the Zenshūji Sōtō Zen Mission in Los Angeles, trouble began immediately after the mass removal. Though the temple had paid real-estate broker F.W. Kadletz & Co. to protect the temple, in September 1942 Zenshūji members received a letter from Kadletz about looting: "The Mission has been broken into two or three times since you left. I have spent considerable money for locks and keys. The police have in jail now one gang of boys that broke in and their trial is coming up soon. I was down there again last night and found they had broken in again. They had broken the glass and reached in and opened the lock. I have sent a man down this morning and have had it boarded up."[61] During the three years of vacancy, great damage had been done. An investigative report compiled at war's end described the conditions of the temple as "deplorable." It found that "vandals had broken into the place, chopped open boxes, trunks, etc., and scattered the contents all over the place and we suppose stole what they wanted . . . fully 65% of the property [left] cannot be identified."[62]

Before anyone could move back into the temple, the Los Angeles Department of Building and Safety had to confirm with the WRA that building code violations had been corrected. Further, Kadletz reported to temple leaders that they were required to evict the "colored people" who had occupied the temple's first floor on a wartime lease agreement.[63] The "colored people" in Kadletz's letter referred to a sizable African American community that had grown during the war years in the Little Tokyo area where Zenshūji was located, sometimes referred to as Bronzeville.[64] Like San Francisco's Western Addition/Fillmore district, which was a Japanese American enclave (Nihonmachi) from the 1906 earthquake until the mass removal in 1942, Bronzeville had become a home for African Americans from the South who had thronged to wartime industrial jobs in California.

Many of the predominantly white neighborhoods that had restrictive housing covenants barring the Japanese also excluded African Americans, leaving few places for either group to live. In Los Angeles, 95 percent of the city had such housing restrictions. The repopulation of Little Tokyo began promptly after the forced removal of Japanese Americans. By October 1943, the African American community had grown so large that Leonard Christmas, one of the founders of the Bronzeville Chamber of Commerce, declared that the neighborhood should no longer be referred to as Little Tokyo. The acute shortage of housing for the tens of thousands of new African American arrivals—populating a neighborhood that had probably housed only seven thousand Japanese American before the war—forced people into makeshift living quarters, including Buddhist temples, the Zenshūji Sōtō Zen Mission, and Christian churches.[65]

Bronzeville's short-lived existence came to an end as resettlers from the camps returned to Little Tokyo. In some cases, building owners did not renew lease agreements with African Americans. In others, the returning Japanese Americans bought out the business leases for their former stores from Bronzeville merchants, sometimes paying "50, 75, 100, 200 percent more for the stores," according to one report.[66] Although the two communities generally coexisted without incident, relations became strained during the transition. A lawsuit filed in Los Angeles Superior Court, *Providence Baptist Association v. L.A. Hompa Hongwanji Buddhist Temple*, centered on the right to use the main temple (*Betsuin*) in Los Angeles associated with the Buddhist Churches of America. Members of the Nishi (Hompa) Hongwanji Temple returned to Los Angeles's Little Tokyo to find their temple occupied by African Americans. To maintain the temple during the war, Rev. Goldwater had leased the temple and its facilities to the Providence Baptist Association on January 1, 1944 for a one-year period. Anticipating that the sangha would be able to return in 1945, Goldwater declined to renew the lease in December 1944 and the heads of the Providence Baptist Association agreed that the premises would be vacated by the end of January. Instead, the congregation's pastor, L. B. Brown, continued to hold Christian theology classes at the Buddhist temple, disregarding the agreement. The *Los Angeles Times* reported on the conflict in an article on December 31, 1944 entitled "Japs Plan Return to 'Little Tokyo': Court Battle Looms as Negroes Receive Notice to Vacate Temple":   *Yikes*

> First attempt of returning Japanese-Americans to oust the Negroes and regain possession of Little Tokyo—a move to evict the Providence Baptist Church from the Hongwanji Buddhist Temple—was made yesterday and immediately gave indication

of becoming a court battle. Following disclosure that the church and the 75 Negro war workers now housed in the temple, located at First St. and Central Ave., have been given until January 5 to vacate the structure, Dr. L. B. Brown, pastor of the First Street Baptist Church and president of the Providence Baptist Institute, announced that the church group has retained an attorney.

An attorney for the Providence Baptist Association told another newspaper that the Army's order proclaiming the west coast open to returnees did not apply to the Buddhists because they were not "American born persons of Japanese descent and proven loyalty" and that therefore the lease still held.[67]

Though the lawsuit was seemingly without merit, the jury's verdict went against the Buddhist temple in May 1945. The attorney for the temple filed an appeal, arguing that the unjustified verdict had been reached "under the influence of passion and prejudice." Judge Myron Westover and the District Court of Appeal concurred with the Buddhist temple's attorney and agreed to a new trial. The Baptists, apparently aware of the weakness of their case, dropped the suit. According to testimony, one of the leaders at the Providence Baptist Association with whom Goldwater had negotiated had said "that the Japanese were a minority people like they themselves, they had no wish to deprive them of their own property, and that they could understand the situation."[68] With the end of the legal case, the temple members were finally able to come home.

While most Buddhist temples regrouped and restarted their activities, several temples in California were looted or vandalized, including those in Brawley, Isleton, and El Centro, which were forced to shut their doors.[69] Others fell victim to arson. The Delano Buddhist Church in California was burned to the ground in February 1945.[70] In Sebastapol, arsonists tried to destroy the Enmanji Buddhist Temple and chopped down the small orchard of flowering cherry trees surrounding the temple.[71]

On January 19, 1943, someone set fire to the San Diego Buddhist Temple after breaking in and stealing temple members' belongings,

FIGURE 10.3 Arson to cover up theft: fire damage to the San Diego Buddhist Temple.   Courtesy of the Japanese American Historical Society of San Diego.

causing extensive damage to the altar section and second floor.[72] While members held many discussions about whether to sell the burned temple, they ultimately determined to restore it. They leased the usable portion of the temple to the USO, and set aside $200 out of each month's $250 payment to rebuild the temple.[73] But upon the Buddhists' return to San Diego, the USO refused to vacate the premises, and occupied the building for another two years. In the meantime, Rev. Guzei Nishii lived in a shed with his family in Chula Vista and tried his hand at farming, while temple members held services at their residences or at the Benbough Mortuary.[74]

With the loss of personal belongings and their temples, the west coast returnees found the homecoming a stark reminder of what the wartime incarceration had wrought. Meanwhile, although there had been no mass incarceration in Hawai'i, the effort to reestablish Buddhism after martial law was equally challenging.

RESETTLING IN HAWAI'I AND JAPAN

In 1948, Margaret Miki recalled a conversation her mother had with a friend during the war, when gatherings at Buddhist temples were generally prohibited by the military authorities governing Hawai'i :

> Mother: Don't you think it's a pity to die now? One can't even be buried decently.
>
> Friend: It just doesn't seem final without the smell of incense, the temple gong, and the chanting of the prayers at funerals. These haole services are so incomplete and cold. There almost seems to be no respect for the dead. What is this world coming to?
>
> Mother: I don't want to die until the temples are reopened and the priests return from the internment camps. Then I'll be assured a *decent* funeral."[75]

The dialogue was emblematic of the distress these restrictions inflicted on religious people. Miki writes that the "lost look on Mother's face was pitiful" when she saw Christians dressed in their "Sunday best" for church.[76] Even "the jubilation of V-J Day was not complete for Mother until the news came that the priests were returning once more and the temples would be reopened. This was the real end of the war for her."[77] Her issei mother and other women of that generation threw themselves into temple activity as soon as the Buddhist priests returned. The women gossiped and laughed together, enjoying the contrast from their wartime stresses every time they attended services at the Buddhist temple, where previously only periodic memorial services for dead nisei soldiers had been held.

In Hawai'i, the returnees—soldiers from military service and civilians from their confinement by the selective incarceration arrests—were fewer in number and their homecoming did not spark the public resistance seen on the west coast. But the reopening of the Buddhist temples proved problematic.[78] Pressure to close temples and Japanese-language schools permanently had been high during the war.[79] In August 1944, the government had sent the Shinshu Kyokai Mission a letter advising it to dissolve its temple unless it could show it was a viable religious organization. This was absurd given that the government had prohibited any regularized temple activity and gatherings at Buddhist temples. To prevent the closure of the temple, seventy-two members defied the prohibition and staged a meeting to demonstrate the temple's viability, and their tactic worked. The government issued license #14974 for the temple as a duly recognized corporation in the Territory of Hawai'i.[80]

After the war ended, some groups doubled down on the wartime Americanization campaigns, such as the "Speak American" movement and other attempts to rid Hawai'i of Japanese customs, religious traditions, clothing, and food. The January 3, 1946 editorial in the *Honolulu Advertiser*, entitled "The End of a Phony Religion," specifically warned Shinto priests returning from the camps that "the door is slammed on their racket." The editors also put Buddhists on notice, saying the days "of beating gongs and burning punk" were over.[81]

In May 1946, the Honolulu Council of Churches, representing thirty-six Protestant churches on the islands, took a more moderate stance. They issued a statement that, while not endorsing Buddhist activities on the islands, declared that if returning Buddhist priests acted "solely as religious leaders," they did have a legal and moral right to give guidance to their followers and perform services.[82]

One major undertaking was the rebuilding of temples destroyed or vandalized, such as Pahala Hongwanji on the Big Island and the Ewa Jōdo Mission on Oahu, both targets of arsonists. Recalling a meeting at Pahala temple to consider raising funds for a new facility, the temple priest's wife noted that the members were hesitant to take on such a financial commitment: "Perhaps everyone felt the gravity of the responsibility in being the first person recorded on the list. Then suddenly Mr. Tanaka stood up and said, 'It seems the big land owners and high salaried persons present seem to hesitate to sign first. It is presumptuous of me but I pledge [undisclosed dollar amount], which is the most that I can do within my ability. I humbly request that the rest of you do the same and individually donate the greatest amount you can within your own capabilities.'"[83] Starting with Mr. Tanaka's pledge, one more Hawai'i Buddhist temple rose from the ashes.

At the Hilo Hongwanji Temple, which the US Army occupied during the war, valuable temple equipment and documents had gone missing.

One long-time temple member spent the first year after the war negoti-ating with the army for compensation so that the temple could restart, and finally settled for eighty percent of the dollar amount of the dam-ages.[84] On Maui, in an ironic twist of fate, members rebuilt the Paʻia Rinzai Zen temple with lumber hauled in from the nearby military base and took over an abandoned navy building in Puunene for a new main temple hall.[85]

While many Buddhist priests returned from the camps to join these efforts, a significant group within the priesthood and the community believed their future lay in Japan. After returning to Honolulu, one priest noted that among his brethren who had journeyed with him back to Hawaiʻi, over half returned to Japan.[86] Most had personal and family rea-sons to return to Japan, though a handful of influential priests belonged to a group known as the kachi-gumi or katta-gumi ("the winner group"), who believed that Japan had won the war.[87] This small, ultra-nationalist group was unwilling to conceive of a defeated Japan, and attributed news of the atomic bombings and Japan's surrender to US propaganda. They physically assaulted others who dared to suggest that Japan had lost the war.[88] According to a contemporary account, a group arriving at the port of Seattle to head westward across the Pacific "had expected Japanese ships, flying the Rising Sun, to pick them up in Seattle. Still clinging to hope, they claimed that we would soon learn the truth when we encoun-tered the three hundred Japanese battleships currently surrounding Oahu. It was useless to talk to them."[89]

Of course, these delusions were lifted for most when they realized Japan had not in fact occupied either the west coast or Hawaiʻi. Still, a couple of individuals, including Sōtō Zen Buddhist priest Rev. Jishō Yamazaki, actively organized gatherings urging all Japanese and even Japanese Americans to have faith in Japan's eventual victory.[90] Incred-ible as it may seem that speeches denying the end of the war and Japan's surrender could have been made in Honolulu in spring 1946, Rev. Yamazaki attracted several hundred people to his speeches, as well as the attention of the media and authorities.[91]

The vast majority of Buddhists were astounded by these pronounce-ments. Several Buddhist priests returning from camps on the continent took firm measures to oust fanatical katta-gumi members, including former temple members.[92] One 442nd Regimental Combat Team veteran published pieces in Buddhist magazines denouncing Rev. Yamazaki. In the 1946 issue of *The Forum*, for example, produced by the Hongwanji Young Men's Buddhist Association, he wrote: "It is regrettable that the good name of the lord Buddha should have been so grossly exploited. . . . Such remarks only tend to arouse suspicion and alienate the cause of Buddhism in the eyes of the public."[93] Issei Buddhist priests also condemned Yamazaki. One said:

> He asked while he was in camp to be repatriated to Japan. I hope he will be. He will be happier there, although persons like him may not be appreciated in Japan either. But his presence in Hawaii is harmful for all Japanese who want to cooperate and live according to American customs and ideas. [A] priest's responsibility is to help people face reality squarely and to give them the strength in suffering and to guide them in the right direction. Reverend Y is doing everything contrary to this and is misleading the people.[94]

While *katta-gumi* members were extreme and marginal even among those who considered themselves pro-Japan during the war, Buddhists, like any religious community, held a diverse range of perspectives on social, political, and global issues. The sector of the community that insisted on returning to Japan having fully accepted the reality of its defeat did share a common feeling of disillusionment or bitterness about an America that had pronounced them and their families unwelcome because of their race and religion.[95] Especially for those in the Crystal City Internment Camp, where families intending to return to Japan were placed, and for others that shared their sentiments, the journey to Japan represented freedom from American racism.[96] After the war, nearly five thousand Americans of Japanese ancestry resettled in Japan, as did roughly four thousand from Canada.[97] The number would have been even higher if not for the efforts of attorney Wayne Collins and others who fought to reverse a government decision to deport several thousand Nisei in Tule Lake who had renounced their American citizenship during the war.[98]

Those who chose to repatriate played an important role in reestablishing trans-Pacific connections between Japan and Japanese America in the immediate postwar period.[99] Many returned to their prewar homes in rural regions of Japan, such as Hiroshima, Yamaguchi, Wakayama, and Okinawa. Ironically, quite a number of Buddhists and other returnees ended up working for Allied Occupation authorities because of their bilingual capabilities. In especially high demand were the kibei, who also knew Japan's customs and language. This occurred despite the strong pro-Christian bias of the Supreme Commander for the Allied Powers (SCAP), General Douglas MacArthur. Reflecting on his time in Japan, MacArthur later noted his "duty as a soldier of God to attempt to restore and revive religion in Japan."[100] He thus urged the leaders of the Federal Council of Churches to fill Japan's "spiritual vacuum" because "if you do not fill it with Christianity, it will be filled with Communism. Send me one thousand missionaries!"[101]

Historian Ray Moore argues that, despite the official stance of the Potsdam Declaration and the Initial US Post-Surrender Policy, which established that occupation forces would guarantee freedom of all religions, "neither MacArthur at SCAP nor the government in Washington was serious about supporting the principles of these documents."[102] In MacArthur's words, "I have many times publicly stated my belief that Christianity . . . offers to the Japanese a sure and stable foundation on which to build a democratic nation and have expressed the hope that a Bible can be placed in the home of every family group in this land."[103] When Ruth Sasaki—the Caucasian wife of a Buddhist priest who died in 1945 during internment—attempted to gain entry to Japan as a Buddhist missionary, her application was initially denied. SCAP's Religions and Cultural Resources Division ruled that allowing her to enter under their missionary policy "would be an extension of that policy to a purpose for which it was not intended."[104] (She was later allowed to travel under the category of "research in social cultural fields.") That division included US officials who were less zealous than MacArthur, but they certainly gave "material and moral support" to Christian missionary efforts during the Occupation.[105]

MacArthur's efforts were counterbalanced by other individuals who enacted a broader and more complex policy of religious freedom that would set the course for post-war religious life in Japan.[106] Yet the enduring notions of manifest destiny and westward expansion were clearly alive and well during the Allied occupation of Japan. Meanwhile, in contrast, the fulfillment of the Buddha's prophecy that the Dharma would inevitably migrate eastward was happening under the radar on the US continent.

BUDDHISM IN AMERICA'S HEARTLAND

In 1945, in his final days of his internment at WRA Poston, Rev. Bunyū Fujimura published his sentiments in the camp's Buddhist newsletter, *Jikō*:

> Now that our camp is about to close, those we have become so close to, will go their own ways; some to the west, some to the east, and others to the north and south. And the result will undoubtedly be tears that will soak our sleeves at parting.[107]

The narrative of *bukkyō tōzen*—the ever-advancing eastward transmission of the Dharma prophesized by the Buddha—reinforced the building of a new sangha in the Americas through migration, both during the war and its aftermath. In this new migration, many Japanese American Buddhists left the camps and carried the Dharma with them to the midwest and the east coast, swelling the numbers of Buddhists in those areas. The eastward resettlement of Buddhists was even supported by some American authorities. Charles Ernst, the director of the WRA Topaz camp, proclaimed as early as 1943 that his agency had "signaled its willingness and its desire to cooperate with leaders of the Buddhist Church in their plans for providing opportunities for persons who relocate from the centers to continue their worship as Buddhists." Ernst framed the resettlement of Buddhists to the midwestern and eastern states as an opportunity for a new start for the spread of Buddhism. He noted that "Americans living in these sections of the United States know very little about the Japanese or about Buddhism," and relocating Buddhists could change that. "Men and women of character and courage are having their chance to now introduce themselves to America." Ernst concluded that "the extension of persons of the Buddhist Faith and the extension of the relocation of persons of Japanese ancestry will go hand in hand in the joint effort to develop a stronger America."[108]

The nisei priest Rev. Kenryō Kumata, urged the 350 young Buddhist delegates gathered at the first Intermountain YBA Convention held in Salt Lake City, where Ernst's remarks were highlighted, to rise to that challenge. They could take what he called the "upward path" of spreading Buddhism to regions of the United States unfamiliar with the tradition:

> We have come to the fork in the road. One, a comparatively easy road, leads downward toward oblivion. The other, an upward path beset with hardships, leads to the happiness of mankind, the Ideal of Buddhism. Need I say, Carry on, Bussei?[109]

Yet many were disinclined to relocate once again, especially to regions of the country unaccustomed to religious and racial differences. Even in the most welcoming places, they knew they would face resistance from not only white Christians but assimilationist Japanese American Christians, as well.

Dorothy Swaine Thomas, a UC Berkeley sociologist among the first to study Japanese American resettlement in the midwest, characterized the resettlement process as the broad dispersal of "the most highly assimilated segments of the Japanese American minority"—which were the "college-educated Christian nonagricultural men."[110] Though Buddhists were the majority within the Japanese American community, they were a minority of those who resettled in the midwest and east coast, partly by design—since the leave clearance process assigned negative points to Buddhists or Shintoists, but not Christians—and partly because, as within the camps, the organic connections between sympathetic white Christians and Japanese American Christians simply made for easier transitions.

Chicago was the most popular destination. By the end of the war, nearly twenty thousand people of Japanese heritage, almost all of them nisei citizens, were living in a city where the prewar population had been only several hundred.[111] Chicago's labor shortage helped drive the migration, as Japanese Americans joined African Americans from the South in filling new industrial jobs central to the war effort. And like African Americans, nisei had difficulty finding homes. In 1944, YBA leader and future Buddhist priest Art Takemoto had moved to Chicago with the issei Buddhist priest Rev. Gyōdō Kōno to assist with the resettlement of young nisei Buddhists released from the WRA Rohwer camp.[112] Because Rev. Kōno could not speak English well and was under constant FBI surveillance, the bilingual Takemoto conducted all external relations with others, including a mandatory visit to the FBI office every Monday to provide a translation of Rev. Kōno's Sunday sermon. Before long, the FBI agent assigned to the Buddhist priest warmed up to Takemoto. Takemoto later recalled:

> And then, he began to ask me certain things. "Why do all the Japanese Americans live in these kinds of places?"—like Clark Street, or La Salle, or whatever the area. He said, "You know, these are dangerous places—these are places where . . . some of these Mafia people hung around, and you people are living here?" I said, "Well, look, where else can we live?" It didn't dawn on him. "Where else can we live?" Who would rent a room or an apartment or a house to a Japanese American except in an area where you might say, it's blighted?[113]

More difficult than finding residential housing was finding anyone willing to lease or sell property for a Buddhist temple. Unlike Japanese American Christians who could attend preexisting churches with predominantly white congregations, Buddhists had no network of coreligionists to rely upon. Ethnic and lineage differences with Buddhists in the Chinese American community and the negligible number of white American Buddhists made it impossible to have any substantial links with Buddhists more broadly. So the creation of a sangha in the city of Chicago had to start from scratch.

The first challenge was with the WRA itself. Despite Ernst's encouragement, WRA officials in Chicago tried to persuade YBA representatives and military veterans Barry Saiki and Tom Shibutani not to try to start a Buddhist temple. While the officials could not legally prohibit them from doing so, they made clear they would prefer "the Japanese American people not to congregate at all . . . their hopes were to disperse people to different areas of the city to assimilate them."[114] During that meeting at the University of Chicago, WRA staff suggested that Buddhists might instead keep up their faith through something like a mail correspondence course.[115]

Japanese American Christians and well-meaning white liberals were also an obstacle to establishing a temple. As early as June 1943, a memo titled "Proposed Plan for Nisei Integration in the City of Chicago" called for a resettlement approach called "Complete Integration." Backed by white Christian religious groups and sociologists, it argued against the formation of any "transitional groups" of nisei, instead recommending that "every Japanese coming from the centers should be immediately channeled into some Caucasian organization." Buddhist temples dominated by nisei were, of course, precisely the kind of non-Caucasian organization the memo wished to prevent, since they were spiritual homes for a religion with a long-standing tradition, hardly a transitional cultural artifact. A Buddhist temple would certainly "be hindering rather than helping the integration program."[116] The memo also noted that Christian organizations including the American Friends Service Committee, Federal Council of Churches, and the Brethrens Home were also invested in the concept of "complete integration."[117] Their goal was not only to assist resettlers in finding homes, but "to introduce them to church organizations of their denomination."[118]

In fact, a month after this memo was written, the YBA leader and former US Army officer Barry Saiki was once again put on the defensive, this time at a meeting hosted by Mrs. Elmer L. Sherrill, the wife of the first acting director of the WRA Tule Lake camp. Historian Michael Masatsugu shares an observer's notes from that meeting regarding the idea of the formation of a YBA:

> the Sherrills and Niseis expressed concern [to Saiki, the only Buddhist present] that Buddhists were leaving themselves vulnerable to public relations attacks by right-wing conservative Hearst reporter Ray Richards who had just arrived in Chicago. They noted that Richards had published an article the day

before the meeting in which he claimed that former West Coast Japanese subversive organizations were now reorganizing in Chicago. Those attending the meeting charged that Buddhists were "courting danger" by organizing a local YBA, permitting a priest who did not speak English to deliver sermons, and by meeting on the South Side of Chicago, in a predominantly African American neighborhood. With regard to the third point, Mrs. Sherrill noted that most Americans remembered Japanese wartime propaganda targeting African Americans in efforts to spread racial war.[119]

The newly-formed African American neighborhoods were often more welcoming to Japanese American Buddhists. The Midwest Buddhist Church, affiliated with the Buddhist Churches of America (BCA), was established in 1944 at the South Parkway Community Hall in the predominantly African-American South Side neighborhood.[120]

Buddhists in Chicago attempted to advance their own formulation of assimilation, one that was nonsectarian and open to members of all races. A few months after the BCA temple was established, San Francisco–born nisei priest Rev. Gyomay Kubose, of the Higashi Honganji sect, using money borrowed from his father, bought a defunct Protestant church on South Dorcester Avenue, and established the Buddhist Temple of Chicago. Independent of doctrinal or organizational affiliations, Rev. Kubose advocated for a transsectarian "American Buddhism" that brought together roughly four hundred members. Though smaller than the BCA-organized temple, it was evidence that transsectarian forms of Buddhism could succeed in a city like Chicago, which did not have a lengthy history of multiple sects of Buddhism as the west coast did.[121]

These efforts to take the "upward path" echoed Rev. Kumata's early exhortation for nisei Buddhists to bring Buddhism to the midwest, the east coast, and other regions. The temples created new homes for Japanese American Buddhists while opening up the possibility for people of other ethnic backgrounds to encounter the tradition; even before the war, the New York Buddhist Church had twelve white Americans among its seventy members, and the Buddhist Society of America founded by the Rinzai Zen priest Sōkei-an was composed almost entirely of non-Japanese Americans.[122] Indeed, multiethnic Buddhist temple membership was more likely outside the west coast and Hawaiʻi in Japanese ethnic enclaves.

The several thousand Japanese American Buddhists who ended up in midwestern and east coast cities did so as minorities of a minority. But by migrating beyond ethnic enclaves, they served as a vanguard in building new Buddhist sanghas across the United States. Bridging the sectarian divides of the prewar and wartime periods, they ushered in a new era of postwar American Buddhism that would prove to be increasingly multiethnic and transsectarian.

EPILOGUE

The Stones Speak: An American Sutra

"Stone can also preach the Dharma. What is this?"

—Guṇabhadra (394–468 CE)

IN 1956, NEAR THE ABANDONED camp cemetery at Heart Mountain, a worker named Bill Higgins, employed as a heavy equipment operator with the Bureau of Reclamation, hit something hard just below the surface with his road grader.[1] Though he had been told that the Japanese Americans buried at the camp cemetery had been transferred to the local town cemetery in Powell, Wyoming, or to the west coast, Higgins's first worry was that he had disturbed a casket.

To his relief, he instead found a large metal drum filled with hundreds of small stones. Looking more closely, he saw that each stone had a single character painted on it. Unable to read the Japanese script, Higgins informed Les and Nora Bovee, who owned the ranch where he'd discovered the drum. The Bovees had been awarded their homestead in a lottery run by the Bureau to give away the land occupied by the former WRA camp.

The Bovees stored the stones in their barn in the portion of the metal drum still intact, and for the next thirty-five years, the stones remained there. Occasional visitors, including former Japanese Americans incarcerated at Heart Mountain, were shown the mysterious stones, but no one was able to ascertain what they were. Over the years, Les and Nora gave hundreds of stones away to the visitors and to friends. Then in 1994, the Bovees donated the remaining 656 stones to the Japanese American National Museum in Los Angeles.[2]

Seven years later, Sōdō Mori, the eminent scholar of Indian Buddhism, visited the museum and noticed the Heart Mountain stones on display. Some of the stones were included in an exhibit on the wartime incarceration experience, but its curators offered no explanation of what the artifacts were or represented. Indeed, the museum's publications had dubbed the stones the "Heart Mountain Mystery Rocks."[3]

Two years later, and now retired from his university, Mori returned to the museum to take a closer look at the full collection of the stones. Since the museum would not permit photography, he painstakingly hand-copied each character. His gut instinct was that when combined and placed in the correct order, the characters represented something coherent, perhaps a Buddhist text because he had discovered characters that combined to form Buddhist terms such as "bodhisattva" and "samādhi."

To check his hypothesis, Mori turned to Professor Kenryō Minowa at the University of Tokyo. Minowa was a member of the SAT Daizōkyō Text Database Committee, a project to make one of the largest Buddhist canonical collections, the *Taishō shinshū daizōkyō*, digitally available and searchable. Containing 5,320 separate texts, many consider it the authoritative edition of the Sino-Japanese Buddhist canon.

The researchers' initial hunch was that the Heart Mountain stones represented a Buddhist text produced by copying a sutra with one character per stone *(ichiji isseki kyō)*. But they also noticed something else: a number of stones had *kanji* characters that appeared frequently in the *Lotus Sutra*. This Buddhist scripture is one of the most popular in East Asian Buddhism and central to Nichiren Buddhism, a tradition in which Minowa was ordained as a priest.

With so many character combinations, Minowa needed a computational analysis to identify the text with certainty. He first eliminated texts that did not contain the *kanji* characters on the steel-drum stones. He then narrowed his search by making the assumption that the stones were from a single text (not a random and mixed collection of multiple texts) and that it was likely to be a relatively popular scripture used in one of the major sectarian traditions of Buddhism in America (an obscure text would have required access to a canonical collection unavailable in a Wyoming camp).[4] Given that the Bovees had given away several hundred stones and that a number of the extant ones were illegible, Minowa ultimately developed a dataset of 302 distinct characters with certain characters on multiple stones.[5] Running these through the canon's database, he found that the only text containing these characters was the *Lotus Sutra,* and more specifically the first six volumes of the eight-volume edition of the scripture.[6]

But who would have written out a massive portion of the *Lotus Sutra* on stones and buried them in a large metal drum at the cemetery—and for what purpose? Several years after they met, Minowa and Mori had reported their findings in an obscure Japanese Buddhist journal.[7] They concluded that the calligraphy on the stones was the work of the Nichiren Buddhist priest Nichikan Murakita (camp ID number 5198B). They believe he had painted the stones during the first year of the war, undetected by camp authorities and possibly with the quiet help of others in Heart Mountain.[8]

Murakita was the only priest in the camp of the sect that venerated the *Lotus Sutra* and would have been familiar with the sutra copying tradition. In a practice that could be traced back to the late seventh to early ninth centuries in Japan, the ritualized copying of scriptures was seen as meritorious, both for the scribe and to whomever the scribe dedicated the text.[9] Some scriptures, including the *Lotus Sutra,* even extolled the merits of copying itself as evidence of virtuous Buddhist practice. The *Lotus Sutra,* for example, states: "if anyone [should] write and transcribe the *Scripture on the Blossom of the Fine Dharma* [the *Lotus Sutra*] . . . [such a person] will surely be able to become a Buddha in a future age."[10]

Further, Murakita was a master calligrapher and taught calligraphy in the camp. In 1943, Murakita and the students in his calligraphy association put on an exhibit in camp that ran for three days and featured roughly eight hundred pieces.[11] But in August of that year, Rev. Murakita and his wife Masako left the camp for Japan as part of an exchange of civilian detainees with Japan. Minowa and Mori attributed the mystery of the stones and the incomplete transcription of the *Lotus Sutra* to his early exit from Heart Mountain. After the war, Murakita eventually attained the second highest rank (Gon-Daisōjō) of his sect of Buddhism in Japan, having left the stones' teachings, without fanfare, literally entrusted to American soil.[12] If not for Bill Higgins, the heavy equipment operator clearing the land near the Heart Mountain cemetery in 1956, this sacred Buddhist text might have disappeared forever into a Wyoming field.

◆   ◆   ◆

In medieval Japan, many Buddhists believed that they were living in a "Degenerate Age of the Dharma" *(mappō)*—a time when the Buddha's teachings had lost their power and the world was in a state of disarray, conflict, and destruction. Hoping for a brighter future when the "future Buddha," Maitreya (*Miroku*), would reappear to reinvigorate the teachings and save the world from confusion and chaos, many Japanese Buddhists adopted the practice of burying Buddhist scriptures and artifacts in underground *kyōzuka* (or "sūtra mounds"). Their expectation was that these texts would be unearthed by the future Buddha to deliver his inaugural sermons.[13] It was a ritual practice not just for individual salvation, but for saving an entire religion.[14]

The stone copy of the *Lotus Sutra* unearthed from a Wyoming camp's cemetery should probably not be thought of as a direct reenactment of the medieval practice of building sutra mounds for the future Buddha. But the priest who planted the Buddha's words into American soil quite possibly hoped that their retrieval would signal the dawn of a better future—a time of peace—when they and their fellow Japanese American Buddhists could resume the lives that had been disrupted by war.

The Heart Mountain stones preach the Dharma.

American Sutra shares a multitude of stories and teachings buried in the memories of people who were often too modest or hurt to recount their experiences. These Buddhists faced hostility and suspicion before Pearl Harbor, recrafted their sangha in desolate camps behind barbed wire and under martial law in Hawai'i, and served and sacrificed on the battlefields of the Second World War.

This book began with the Zen priest Nyogen Senzaki's 1942 poem written in the form of a Buddhist scripture, using the phrase "Thus have I heard." By 1945, with the end of the wartime incarceration in sight, Senzaki composed another poem in the same camp where the stone scriptures were buried.

> Land of Liberty!
> People of Independence!
> The Constitution is beautiful.
> It blooms like the spring flower.
> It is the scripture by itself.
> No foreign book can surpass it.
> Like the baby Buddha,
> Each of the people
> Should point to heaven and earth, and say,
> "America is the country of righteousness."[15]

Here was an assertion of boundless faith not only in Buddhism, but in America. For Senzaki, the US constitution is a scripture that protects religious liberty and continuously reemerges like a spring flower. Indeed, the constitution became a new scripture for Buddhists in America, one that would protect their freedom to practice the Dharma in the land of liberty they called home. As Senzaki hoped, the wartime experience forged a new American Buddhism, manifesting the possibility of being both fully Buddhist and fully American.

ACKNOWLEDGMENTS

NOTES

INDEX

ACKNOWLEDGMENTS

When a manuscript is the culmination of seventeen years of research and writing, as this one is, it can be hard to enumerate all the sources of help one has had along the way. My acknowledgments must begin with Professor Masatoshi Nagatomi and his wife Masumi (Kimura) Nagatomi, who provided inspiration and assistance on so many levels that I gladly dedicate the book to them.

A number of scholars reviewed the various iterations of this book and provided critical guidance throughout the process of research and writing. Chief among them were Michihiro Ama, Patricia Biggs, Anne Blankenship, Steven Doi, Jane Iwamura, Tetsuden Kashima, Michael Masatsugu, Tomoe Moriya, Greg Robinson, and Paul Spickard. To them I perform nine bows.

Others who provided substantial feedback and encouragement over the years include Barbara Ambros, Naofumi Annaka, Roger Daniels, Russell Endo, Charles Hallisey, Helen Hardacre, David Kyuman Kim, Reed Malcolm, Charles Prebish, Sharon Suh, Lon Kurashige, and Richard Seager. The anonymous reviewers of the manuscript for Harvard University Press also gave key pointers toward the end of the process. If errors still lurk in the book despite their collective assistance, I am naturally responsible.

I cannot name all the hundreds of Japanese American and Buddhist community members who assisted with interviews and the sharing of family history. But I must at least acknowledge the support of Rev. Shingetsu Akahoshi, Rev. Don Castro, Rev. Marvin Harada, Carole Hayashino, Patti Hirahara, Rev. Chishin Hirai, Sat Ichikawa, Jane Kurahara, Sadako Tottori Kaneko, Rev. Shūmyō Kojima, Rev. Shūgen Komagata, Rev. Seimoku Kosaka, Ron Magden, Irene Mano, Eiko Masuyama, Archie Miyatake, Allyson Nakamoto, Togo Nishiura, Nancy Oda, Dakota Russell, Kanji Sahara, Akira Tana and other members of the Tana family, Rev. Arthur Takemoto, Jerald Takesono, Joyce Terao, Sakaye Tsuji, and Sadie Yamasaki.

A number of editors over the years were instrumental in my being able to deliver a manuscript worthy of the subject. They include Dave Harris, who patiently worked through very rough chapters and refined the writing at later stages; developmental editor Kerry Tremain, who contributed tremendously to recasting the manuscript for a broader readership; and Andrew Kinney and Julia Kirby, my editors at Harvard University Press.

Others to whom I owe great debts in the editing and production of the book include Jason Bacasa, Michelle Chihara, Robert Dewhurst, Colleen Lanick, Nicky Schildkraut, Patricia Wakida, Holly Watson, and Olivia Woods. The staff of the USC Shinso Ito Center—Kana Sugita, Shannon Takushi, and Vanessa Haugh—were also instrumental to the completion of the manuscript.

Institutional funding for research behind this book came from the Japan Foundation, the California Civil Liberties Public Education Program, the Shin-nyo-en Buddhist Order, an Advancing Scholarship in the Humanities and Social Sciences Grant from the University of Southern California (USC) Office of the Provost, the USC Dornsife Dean's Office, the USC Shinso Ito Center for Japanese Religions and Culture, a Project Grant from the UC Berkeley–Mellon Foundation, a Research Bridging Grant from the UC Berkeley Townsend Center, a Faculty Research Grant from the UC Berkeley Committee on Research, a grant from the UC Irvine Academic Senate Council on Research, Computing, and Library Resources, and a Research and Travel Grant from the UC Irvine School of Humanities. Several Buddhist magazines, including *Tricycle*, *Lion's Roar*, and *Dharma World*, also supported this project by publishing interviews or short essays about the themes of the book.

Much appreciated support also came from Carol Lynn Akiyama through a fund to honor her father, Makio Mickey Akiyama. Moral support came from my Zen teacher Ogasawara Ryūgen of Kōtakuji Temple in Matsumoto, Nagano Prefecture, and from family members both alive and deceased, including my mother, Tsutae Iikubo Williams; my brother, Nigel Williams; my father, Stephen Williams; my father-in-law, Hong Yung Lee; my mother-in-law, Whakyung Lee; and my sister-in-law, Sonia Lee.

Finally, my gratitude goes to my wife Sunyoung Lee, who fully understood what was at stake with this research and never failed to offer encouragement whenever doubts arose that this manuscript would be completed.

NOTES

PROLOGUE

Nyogen Senzaki's "Parting," Zen Studies Society, *Like a Dream, Like a Fantasy: The Zen Teachings and Translations of Nyogen Senzaki* (Somerville, MA: Wisdom Publications, 2005), 51. Copyright © 2005 by Zen Studies Society. Reprinted by arrangement with The Permissions Company, Inc., on behalf of Wisdom Publications, Inc., wisdompubs.org.

1. Recognition of the importance of a Pacific approach to retelling American religious history can be found in Laurie F. Maffly-Kipp, "Eastward Ho! American Religion from the Perspective of the Pacific Rim," in *Retelling US Religious History*, ed. Thomas A. Tweed (Berkeley: University of California Press, 1997), 117–267.

2. The transition from the prevalent conception of the United States as a Protestant nation to a Judeo-Christian or "Tri-Faith" America is discussed by Kevin M. Schultz, *Tri-Faith America: How Catholics and Jews Held Postwar America to Its Protestant Promise* (Oxford: Oxford University Press, 2011).

3. A survey of the religious activities in the camps by the Methodist minister Lester Suzuki was an early work that touched on Buddhism in the wartime WCCA and WRA camps. See Lester Suzuki, *Ministry in the Assembly and Relocation Centers in World War II* (Berkeley, CA: Yardbird Publishing, 1979). More recent work on Christianity, primarily in the WCCA and WRA camps, by Anne Blankenship and Beth Hessel, makes significant additions to the Christian aspect of the story. See Anne Blankenship, *Christianity, Social Justice, and Japanese American Incarceration during World War II* (Chapel Hill, NC: University of North Carolina Press, 2016) and Beth Hessel, *"Let the Conscience of Christian America Speak": Religion and Empire in the Incarceration of Japanese Americans, 1941–1945* (PhD diss., Texas Christian University, 2015). For Buddhism, also see the compilation of anecdotes, photographs, and other artifacts from the wartime camps by Eiko

Masuyama and others associated with the Los Angeles Nishi Hongwanji Betsuin. Eiko Masuyama, *Memories: The Buddhist Church Experience in the Camps, 1942–1945*, 2nd rev. ed. (Los Angeles: Nishi Hongwanji Betsuin, 2007).

4. Nyogen Senzaki, *Like a Dream, Like a Fantasy: The Zen Writings and Translations of Nyogen Senzaki* (Somerville, MA: Wisdom Publications, 2005), 51.

5. Senzaki, *Like a Dream*, 5. His initial ordination was into the Sōtō Zen Buddhist tradition, whereupon he received his Dharma name "Nyogen." Senzaki's own account from an essay written in Heart Mountain in 1942, states: "My foster father, a Japanese scholar-monk, picked me up at the death bed of my mother, who was, I was told later, Japanese. (I look more Chinese than Japanese.) In those days the Japanese census was not very strict, so I was booked as the first-born baby of the Senzaki family. The Senzakis live near the temple of my foster father." Senzaki, *Eloquent Silence*, 306.

6. Kazuaki Tanahashi and Roko Sherry Chayat, *Endless Vow: The Zen Path of Soen Nakagawa* (Boston: Shambala, 1996), 145.

7. His undated essay "Zen and American Life." See Senzaki, *Like a Dream*, 87–88. He elaborated on his views while incarcerated in Heart Mountain. In his essay dated October 15, 1942, he writes: "What is philosophical in Buddhism is no more than a preliminary step toward what is practical in it. William James's pragmatism, a well-known interpretation of true Americanism, is nearest in thought to Buddhism. Emerson and Whitman had ideas that were congenial with Buddhism, too, without realizing it." See Nyogen Senzaki, *Eloquent Silence: Nyogen Senzaki's Gateless Gate and Other Previously Unpublished Teachings and Letters* (Somerville, MA: Wisdom Publications, 2008), 307.

8. For scholarship on the stock opening phrase "Thus have I heard," see John Brough, "Thus Have I Heard . . . ," *Bulletin of the School of Oriental and African Studies* 13, no. 1 (1949): 416–426; B. Galloway, "'Thus Have I Heard': At One Time . . . ," *Indo-Iranian Journal* 34 (1991): 87–104; Frank J. Hoffman, "*Evaṁ me sutaṁ*: Oral Tradition in Nikāya Buddhism," in *Texts in Context: Traditional Hermeneutics in South Asia* ed. Jeffrey Richard Timm, (Albany, NY: State University of New York Press, 1992), 195–219; and Jonathan Silk, "A Note on the Opening Formula of Buddhist *Sūtras*," *Journal of the International Association of Buddhist Studies* 12, no. 1 (1989): 158–164. Many thanks to Charles Hallisey for sharing various interpretations of this phrase as found in Buddhaghosa's classic commentary.

9. This gathering, sometimes referred to as the first Buddhist Council, was purported to have been held at Rājagṛha during the first rainy season

following the Buddha's death or *parinirvāṇa* ("complete extinction"). Scholars are divided on how to date or assess the significance of this gathering. Gombrich has proposed that this gathering should be understood as the stuff of legend (and that only the so-called second council held at Vaiśālī is historically documentable). See Richard Gombrich, "Dating the Buddha: A Red Herring Revealed," in *Die Daiterung des Historischen Buddha: Vol. 2*, ed. Heinz Bechert (Göttingen, Germany: Vandenhoeck and Ruprecht, 1992), 237–259. For scholarship on this gathering, see Étienne Lamotte, *History of Indian Buddhism*, (Louvain-la-neuve, France: Institute Orientaliste, 1988), 124–126; Charles Prebish, "A Review of Scholarship on the Buddhist Councils," *Journal of Asian Studies* 33, no. 2 (1974): 239–254; and Jean Przyluski, *Le concile de Rājagṛha* (Paris: Paul Geuthner, 1926).

10. The teachings of the Buddha were transmitted in an oral tradition before becoming codified in written manuscript form sometime during the first century BCE. See Steve Collins, "On the Very Idea of the Pali Canon," *Journal of the Pali Text Society* 15 (1990): 76 and James P. McDermott, "Scripture as the Word of the Buddha," *Numen* 31 (1984): 22–38.

11. The Japanese characters for "shukke" or priestly ordination literally means "leave home."

12. Reprinted in Senzaki, Nakagawa, and Shimano, *Namu Dai Bosa*, 13; Senzaki, *Like a Dream*, 51.

13. Old Māgadhī is considered one of the many Prakrit or Middle Indic vernaculars spoken in the region where the Buddha resided; it is not a literary language. Scholars have noted that the earliest extant, written records of the Buddha's discourses were produced in Gāndhārī (based on scrolls discovered in the first century CE). And Pali was a non-vernacular language used to memorize and transmit the Buddha's teachings that would come to serve as a critical language for written transmission in the ordination lineage that is known today as Theravāda. See Heinz Bechert, *Die Sprache der ältesten buddhistischen Überlieferung* (Göttingen: Vandenhoeck und Ruprecht, 1980) and Oskar von Hinüber, *The Oldest Pāli Manuscript: Four Folios of the Vinaya-Pitaka from the National Archives, Kathmandu* (Stuttgart, Germany: Steiner, 1991). In certain commentarial traditions, Māgadhī seemed to have a status beyond being the most likely vernacular language used by the historical Buddha. One analysis of the *Vibhanga* states: "If again, a person in an uninhabited forest in which no speech (is heard) should intuitively attempt to articulate words, he would speak the very Māgadhī. It predominates in all regions, such as hell, the animal kingdom, the petta sphere, the human world; and the world of the devas. . . . Even Buddha who rendered his tepitaka words into doctrines, did so by means of

the very Māgadhi; and why? Because by doing so it was to acquire their true significations. Moreover, the sense of the words of the Buddha which are rendered into doctrines by means of the Māgadhi language, is conceived in hundreds and thousands of ways by those who have attained the Patisambhidā, so soon as they reach the ear, or the instant the ear comes in contact with them . . ." Cited in Robert Spence Hardy, *The Legends and Theories of the Buddhists, Compared with History and Science* (London: Williams and Norgate, 1866), 22–23.

14. Nyogen Senzaki's "Leaving Santa Anita," © 2008, Zen Studies Society, *Eloquent Silence: Nyogen Senzaki's Gateless Gate and Other Previously Unpublished Teachings and Letters* (Somerville, MA: Wisdom Publications, 2008), 12. Reprinted by arrangement with The Permissions Company, Inc., on behalf of Wisdom Publications, Inc., wisdompubs.org.

15. Iori Tada, *Nihon ryōiki to bukkyō tōzen* [The *Nihon ryōiki* and the Eastward Advance of Buddhism] (Kyoto: Hōzōkan, 2001).

16. Minoru Tada, *Bukkyō tōzen: Taiheiyō o watatta bukkyō* [The Eastward Advance of Buddhism: Buddhism That Crossed the Pacific Ocean] (Kyoto: Zen Bunka Kenkyūsho, 2001).

17. He had originally used this name a decade earlier for his Zen meditation center in Los Angeles. Senzaki, Nakagawa, and Shimano, *Namu Dai Bosa*, 14; Senzaki, *Eloquent Silence*, 9, 13, 382–383.

Rev. Daishō Tana was another priest who espoused the notion that the incarceration was a fulfillment of the Buddha's prophesy of the eastward transmission of Buddhism. In his diary entry from April 8, 1942, Tana describes spending the Buddha's birthday, typically celebrated on that date, in the remote camp located the furthest east he had ever gone in the United States: "It brings tears to my eyes to think of the profound words 'the eastward advance of Buddhism' [*bukkyō tōzen*] as I reflect on the fact that Buddhists on the Pacific coast have carried the Buddha all the way here; to a place where we can see the Rocky Mountains as we celebrate the birth of the Buddha. While it may be true that the Buddhist organizations on the Pacific coast have been decimated, the Buddha seeds that have now flown on the winds of this war will eventually move eastward and take root before flowering into authentic Dharma flowers." Daishō Tana, *Santa Fe, Lordsburg senji tekikokujin yokuryūsho nikki: Vol. 1* [The Wartime Internment Diaries of an Enemy Alien in Santa Fe and Lordsburg] (Tokyo: Sankibō Busshōrin, 1976), 136. The translation is mine.

18. "Masatoshi Nagatomi: Faculty of Arts and Sciences Memorial Minute, *Harvard Gazette*, February 24, 2005, http://news.harvard.edu/gazette/story /2005/02/masatoshi-nagatomi/.

19. I was working with my new advisor and mentor, Helen Hardacre, to complete my dissertation and transform it into a monograph.

20. Several of these International Red Cross letters are located in the Nagatomi Collection housed at the Manzanar Interpretive Center. One dated September 2, 1943 from Rev. Nagatomi included a message for his son: "Be healthy until we meet after the war." Thanks to Patricia Biggs for bringing these postcards to my attention.

21. They were shooting at the ancient Buddhist symbol called the *manji*, which represents an aerial view of a *stūpa* (a Buddhist shrine), and which adorns many Buddhist temples around the world. An ancient Indian symbol, the *manji* coincidentally—and unfortunately—resembles a German Nazi swastika (though often reversed in orientation and predating the swastika by thousands of years). For other incidents targeting the *manji*, see Ron Magden, *Mukashi Mukashi Long Long Ago: The First Century of the Seattle Buddhist Church* (Seattle: Seattle Buddhist Church, 2012), 104; Thomas Heuterman, *The Burning Horse: The Japanese-American Experience in the Yakima Valley, 1920–1942* (Cheney, WA: Eastern Washington University Press, 1995), 114; and Eric Walz, *Japanese Immigration and Community Building in the Interior West, 1882–1945* (PhD diss., Arizona State University, 1998), 185.

22. Yoshii notes numerous cases of doll burnings as well as one family's success in hiding the Girl's Day dolls. See Michael Yoshii, "The Buena Vista Church Bazaar: A Story within a Story," in *People on the Way: Asian North Americans Discovering Christ, Culture, and Community,* ed. David Ng (Valley Forge, PA: Judson Press, 1996), 47. In Waipahu, Hawai'i, Deanne Nakamoto recalled how she had a large collection of Japanese dolls that her parents ordered her to destroy right after Pearl Harbor. See Michael Yamamoto, Nina Sylva, and Karen Yamamoto, *Waipahu Recollections from a Sugar Plantation Community in Hawai'i* (Honolulu: Michael Yamamoto, 2005), 108.

23. The Kimura family's story comes from four interviews with Masumi (Mary) Nagatomi (née Kimura), Cambridge, MA (May 27, 2002, June 15, 2002, and February 15, 2008 home interviews and February 12, 2003 telephone interview).

This was the first of over ninety interviews I conducted with Buddhists who were detained in the wartime camps, lived under martial law in Hawai'i, or served in the US military during World War II. In order to supplement, corroborate, and enrich the oral histories, I consulted diaries, letters, camp newsletters, government reports, confidential records of the US Army's G-2 (intelligence) section, FBI files, Office of Naval Intelligence documents, and other primary historical sources, including over 1,800 documents from collections maintained by Buddhist temples, government agencies, and other archives in the United States, Canada, and Japan. Notable archives include the Buddhist Churches of America Archives at the Japanese American National Museum, the UC Berkeley Bancroft Library Japanese American Evacuation and Resettlement Records, the UCLA University Library Manzanar War Relocation Records, the University of Hawaiʻi Hamilton Library Special Collections, and collections at the National Diet Library in Tokyo.

1. AMERICA

1. Although it is difficult to make an exact accounting of the religious affiliations of the Japanese American community in December 1941, my best estimate would be that the issei were 83 percent Buddhist, 16 percent Christian, and 1 percent other; and the nisei were 71 percent Buddhist, 28 percent Christian, and 1 percent other. These numbers refer only to the Japanese American community in the continental US and not the larger community in the territory of Hawaiʻi, where the percentage of Buddhists on the islands was higher. My estimates on the continental US are extrapolated from the assumption that at least 95 percent of those interned in the Army and DOJ camps were Buddhist and Shintoist, with only a handful of Christians in those camps. As for the WRA camps, there are two wartime surveys taken by US government authorities. A 1942 WRA survey of the mass incarceration camps estimates that 55.5 percent were Buddhist; 28.9 percent Protestant; 2.0 percent Catholics; 0.4 percent Tenri-Kyo and similar sects (popular Shinto); and 13.2 percent did not name a religious preference. See Wartime Relocation Authority, *The Evacuated People: A Quantitative Description* (Washington, DC: Wartime Relocation Authority, 1942), 72, table 24: Religious Preference by Nativity, Under 14 and 14 Years Old and Older: Evacuees to WRA in 1942, http://npshistory.com/publications/incarceration /evacuated-people.pdf. The second data source for the WRA camps is a 1944 survey based on a 25 percent sampling of the ten camps. It revealed that among the issei, 68 percent were Buddhist; 23 percent Protestant and Catholic; 0.8 percent other (including .04 percent Tenrikyo); and 7.6 percent named no religious preference. Among the nisei, 48.5 percent were Buddhist; 34.8 percent Protestant and Catholic, 0.4 other; and 16.3 percent named no religious preference. See War Relocation Authority "Buddhism in the United States," Community Analysis Section's Report No. 9 (May 15, 1944), UCLA Special Collections C-1297-p10-bu. There were also camp-specific statistics, such as those compiled by anthropologist Robert F. Spencer for his report on

the Gila River relocation center, where he estimated 80 percent of the population to be Buddhist. See Robert F. Spencer, "Religious Life in the Gila Community" (Japanese American Evacuation and Resettlement Study, November 2, 1942—BANC MSS 67/14 c, folder K8.51, UC Berkeley, Bancroft Library), 1.

2. In his famous "infamy" speech to Congress, Roosevelt declared, "Yesterday, December 7, 1941—a date which will live in infamy—the United States of America was suddenly and deliberately attacked by naval and air forces of the Empire of Japan."

3. Chiye Sumiya recounted this story under her married name Chiye Itagaki. See Hawaii Sōtōshū Kaikyō Sōkanbu [Hawaii Soto Mission Bishop's Office], ed. *Gokurosama (Thank you very much for your hard work)* (Honolulu: Hawaii Soto Mission Bishop's Office, 2005), 16–17.

4. They included Janet Yumiko Ohta (age three months), killed alongside her mother and aunt when a shell hit their family home in Honolulu; Shirley Kinue Hirasaki (age two) in Honolulu; Yaeko Lillian Oda (age six) in Ewa; and Nancy Masako Arakaki (age eight) in Honolulu.

5. With heavy black smoke still rising from the attack, teenager Diane Hirotsu rushed towards her home in nearby Waipahu from the morning YBA meeting at a Buddhist temple in Honolulu. She managed to get to safety, but learned that her Japanese immigrant grandfather had been taken to the hospital, critically injured in the attack. See Michael T. Yamamoto, Nina Yuriko Ota Sylva, and Karen N. Yamamoto, *Waipahu: Recollections from a Sugar Plantation Community in Hawaii* (Albuquerque: Innoventions, 2005), 112. Also, Japanese fishermen out at sea at the time of the attack found themselves under fire from American machine gunners when they returned. A number of them were killed, and those who survived were taken into custody. Suikei Furuya, *An Internment Odyssey: Haisho Tenten* (Honolulu: Japanese Cultural Center of Hawai'i/University of Hawai'i Press, 2017), 37. Regarding the total number of civilian deaths, the sources are far more varied. The Remembrance Exhibit at the USS *Arizona* Memorial Visitor Center includes forty-eight civilians. Meanwhile, the Hawaii War Records Depository (HWRD) includes a document (HWRD 12) dated January 25, 1950 that lists seventy-four civilians killed—but appears to duplicate two names. Of its seventy-two unique names, thirty-two are Japanese surnames. See Yasutarō Soga, *Life Behind Barbed Wire: The World War II Internment Memoirs of a Hawai'i Issei* (Honolulu: Japanese Cultural Center of Hawai'i/University of Hawai'i Press, 2008), 24. Others have cited lower numbers. Masayo Duus states that sixty-eight civilians died, in *Unlikely Liberators: The Men of the 100th and 442nd* (Honolulu: University of Hawai'i

Press, 1987), 13. Gwenfread Allen states that states that fifty-seven civilians died, in *Hawaii's War Years: 1941–1945* (Westport, CT: Greenwood Press, 1971).

6. R. Jean Gray, "Our Man of Peace in a Time of War: SAC Honolulu Robert Shivers during World War II," *The Grapevine* (the monthly magazine of the Society of Former Special Agents of the FBI), December 2016, 9.

7. Hearing the radio announcement that all military personnel were to report to their posts, he was on his way to Schofield Barracks from his family home in Honolulu when killed by friendly fire. Private Migita had been spending his leave from the base with his mother Setsu Migita, a devout member of the Shinshū Kyōkai, a Buddhist temple in Honolulu established in 1914. Yoshiko Tatsuguchi and Lois A. Suzuki, *Shinshu Kyokai Mission of Hawaii, 1914–1984: A Legacy of Seventy Years* (Honolulu: Shinshu Kyokai Mission of Hawaii, 1985), 58.

8. The precise number of military personnel who died in the attack is disputed, but all accounts are close to the total of 2,340 (Navy, 1,998; Army, 233; Marines, 109) recognized officially by the official National Park Service at the USS *Arizona* Memorial at Pearl Harbor, https://www.nps.gov/nr/twhp/wwwlps/lessons/18arizona/18charts1.htm

9. Stuck in between two nations suddenly at war, Private Migita's father was able to arrange for the Buddhist funeral service for his dead American son only after discovering the whereabouts of Rev. Egen Yoshigami, spared from the initial dragnet because of his American citizenship. Tatsuguchi and Suzuki, *Shinshu Kyokai,* 58.

10. He was Rev. Goki Tatsuguchi.

11. Biddle subsequently sent a written order to FBI Director J. Edgar Hoover, who issued the following instruction to the FBI agents in charge of all fifty-six field offices around the nation: "Immediately take into custody all Japanese who have been classified in A, B, C categories in material previously transmitted to you." See Louis Fiset, *Imprisoned Apart: The World War II Correspondence of an Issei Couple* (Seattle: University of Washington Press, 1997), 30. The December 7 arrest warrant from Biddle to Hoover stated: "In pursuance of authority delegated to the Attorney General of the United States by Proclamation of the President of the United States dated December 7, 1941, I hereby authorize and direct you and your duly authorized agents to arrest or to cause the arrest of each of the following alien enemies, whose addresses are set forth following their respective names, and whom I deem dangerous to the public peace and safety of the United States." Lists of names followed, organized by different areas of the country. The signature of

Attorney General Francis Biddle appears under the concluding lines: "Each of such persons is to be detained and confined until further order. By order of the President." See http://www.foitimes.com/internment/Arrest30.pdf.

12. The head priest, Rev. Goki Tatsuguchi, was arrested toward the end of the day at the McCully Japanese-Language School, where he was assisting people impacted by the attack. He had brought food from the temple and was cooking it when he was taken into custody at dusk. See Roland Tatsuguchi, "'Friendly Fire' and 'Collateral Damage,'" *Gassho* (newsletter of Shinshu Kyokai Mission, Honolulu), December 2015, 4–7. Gail Honda states that 391 individuals were arrested on December 7 to 9, 1941. Japanese Cultural Center of Hawai'i, *The Untold Story: Internment of Japanese Americans in Hawai'i*, DVD, directed by Ryan Kawamoto (Honolulu: Kinetic Productions, 2012).

13. Gary Okihiro, *Cane Fires: The Anti-Japanese Movement in Hawaii, 1865–1945* (Philadelphia: Temple University Press, 1991), 210, 213. On the legal dimensions of the declaration of martial law and the suspension of the privilege of the writ of habeas corpus in the Hawaiian Territory, see Harry Scheiber and Jane Scheiber, *Bayonets in Paradise: Martial Law in Hawai'i during World War II* (Honolulu: University of Hawai'i Press, 2016); and Amanda L. Tyler, *Habeas Corpus in Wartime: From the Tower of London to Guantanamo Bay* (Oxford: Oxford University Press, 2017), 212–222.

14. The head priest was Rev. Kōgan Yoshizumi. Hawaii Sōtōshū Kaikyō Sōkanbu, *Gokurosama*, 50–51.

15. The Nichiren Buddhist priest was Rev. Jōei Ōi. Furuya, *An Internment Odyssey*, 8–9.

16. Ibid.

17. Soga, *Life Behind Barbed Wire*, 26.

18. Ibid., 31. The newspaper editor, Yasutarō Soga, mentions Revs. Buntetsu Miyamoto and Ryūten Kashiwa in this episode. Yoshihiko Ozu, the proprietor of the Ozu Hat Store in Honolulu, also recalled that first evening at the Immigration Station:

> "Oh, you're here too," Bishop [Gikyō] Kuchiba of Hongwanji Temple greeted me. As I glanced around the room, I saw about 20 leaders and VIPs of the Japanese society all looking downcast and depressed. They were Bishop [Kyokujō] Kubokawa of Jodo [Buddhist] Mission, Totarō Matsui of Taiheiyo Bank, Mr. [Toratarō] Onoda of Sumitomo Bank, Mr. Sugita of [Yokohama] Shokin Bank, and Mr. [Kenji] Kimura of [Nippon] Yusen Company.
>
> I was on the top level of the bunks along with Rev. [Shigemaru] Miyao of Izumo Taisha [Shinto Shrine] where we could see Pearl Harbor with oil tanks burning furiously.

Yoshihiko Ozu, "The Day the US-Japan War Began," excerpts from a
wartime account, translated by Leslie Iwatani and edited by Shirley Iwatani,
in Center for Oral History Social Science Research Institute, *Unspoken
Memories: Oral Histories of Hawai'i Internees at Jerome, Arkansas* (University of Hawai'i at Mānoa, March 2014), 392–397 (quote from 393). https://
scholarspace.manoa.hawaii.edu/bitstream/10125/33185/4/unspokenmemories
_12_iwatani.pdf.

19. Bishop Kyokujō Kubokawa was taken in his Buddhist robes.

20. For example, Rev. Nisshū Kobayashi was arrested alongside two
Buddhist laymen as they were building the peace tower at Hokekyōji Temple
on Oahu. They were not afforded the opportunity to return home to retrieve
any clothes or belongings. Eijō Ikenaga, "Honolulu Myōhōji: Bussari
Heiwatō, Peace Tower," in *Hawaii Nichirenshū hachijushūnen no ayumi: A
History of Nichiren Buddhism in Hawaii,* ed. Nichiren Mission of Hawaii
(Honolulu: Nichiren Mission of Hawaii, 1982), 36. Others, including Rev.
Jūkaku Shirasu of the Hilo Hongwanji Betsuin, were picked up in the middle
of the night—in Shirasu's case, while he and his wife slept with gas masks at
the ready beside their bed. Eiko Irene Masuyama, *Memories: The Buddhist
Church Experience in the Camps, 1942–1945* (Sacramento: California Civil
Liberties Public Education Program, 2007), 29.

21. Louise Hunter, *Buddhism in Hawaii: Its Impact on a Yankee Community* (Honolulu: University of Hawai'i Press, 1971), 189.

22. The priest was Rev. Chikyoku Kikuchi. Shigeo Kikuchi, *Memoirs of a
Buddhist Woman Missionary* (Honolulu: The Buddhist Study Center Press,
1991), 35.

23. "Terminal Island Isolated as Defense Precaution," *Los Angeles Times,*
December 8, 1941, F1.

24. The priest was Rev. Bun'en Ikeda of the San Pedro Kōtaiji Temple.
Naomi Hirahara and Geraldine Knatz, *Terminal Island: Lost Communities of
Los Angeles Harbor* (Santa Monica, CA: Angel City Press, 2015), 249.

25. "Takahashi (Reverend Seytsu), Dept. of Justice Internment Camps,
Internee Experience," Oral History 1616, interview conducted December 16,
1978 by Mariko Yamashita and Paul F. Clark (California State University
Fullerton, Oral History Program, Japanese American Project), http://texts
.cdlib.org/view?docId=ft6290068d&doc.view=entire_text.

26. Presidential Proclamations 2525, 2526, and 2527 (December 8, 1941)
designated Germans, Italians, and Japanese nationals as enemy aliens. This
was based on a long-standing law dealing with such individuals during times
of war (the Alien Enemies Act, originally enacted in 1798 and revised in 1918 as
Section 21, Title 50 of the US Code). John Christgau, *Enemies: World War II*

Alien Internment (San Jose, CA: Authors Choice Press, 2001), 33; and Tetsuden Kashima, *Judgment without Trial: Japanese American Imprisonment during World War II* (Seattle: University of Washington Press, 2003), 50.

Many of the Germans detained were associated with pro-Nazi groups like the German American Bund (which had gained increased visibility, for example, through a 22,000-person rally in New York's Madison Square Garden in 1939). Arnold Krammer has noted the wildly disparate estimates of the German American Bund's membership. While the FBI estimated 6,500 members, US congressman Martin Dies (of the Dies Commission—later the House Committee Investigating Un-American Activities) believed it had as many as 400,000 sympathizers on top of 25,000 active members. The leader of the Bund itself, Fritz Kuhn, also gave rather different numbers of his organization's membership depending on whom he was addressing: from 8,299 to 230,000. Krammer himself concludes that total membership was about 10,000. Arnold Krammer, *Undue Process: The Untold Story of America's German Alien Internees* (Lanham, MD: Rowman & Littlefield, 1997), 4–5. Other groups that were considered dangerous included the Association of German Nationals, Friends of the New Germany, the German American National Alliance, German-American Vocational League, and the various Kyffhaesuser organizations. Krammer, *Undue Process,* 45–46.

In contrast, the Italians detained tended to be former soldiers, such as members of the Ex Combattenti (Federation of Italian War Veterans), people involved in Italian-language newspapers and radio, and consulate-supported Italian-language school instructors. Rose Scherini, "When Italian Americans Were 'Enemy Aliens,'" in *Una Storia Segreta: The Secret History of Italian American Evacuation and Internment during World War II,* ed. Lawrence DiStasi (Berkeley, CA: Heyday Books, 2001), 11.

About a fourth of Germans and Italians were swiftly released without even a hearing, while only 4.25 percent of the 5,181 Japanese arrested up until May 5, 1943 were released. Over time, not only did the Japanese aliens have a lower rate of parole, those who were "released" often were sent on to WRA camps, unlike the Germans and Italians, most of whom were paroled into the greater society. For example, among the 1,500 Italian nationals rounded up, only 257 were interned behind barbed wire for the duration of the war. See the first chart of FBI's *Disposition of German, Japanese, and Italian Alien Enemy Cases as of May 5, 1943* (FBI File #100–2, section 186), prepared by D. M. Ladd for Director Hoover on June 1, 1943. On the number of Italians detained and interned, see Lawrence DiStasi, "Morto il Camerata," in *Una Storia Segreta: The Secret History of Italian American Evacuation and Internment during World War II,* ed. Lawrence DiStasi (Berkeley, CA:

Heyday Books, 2001), 3. Others have reported the number of interned Italians at 228, 250, or 277. Scherini, "When Italian Americans Were 'Enemy Aliens,'" 13.

For descriptions of the Alien Enemy Control Unit hearings that determined release, parole, or further internment, see Kashima, *Judgment without Trial*, 58–63; and Gloria Ricci Lothrop, "Unwelcome in Freedom's Land," in *Una Storia Segreta: The Secret History of Italian American Evacuation and Internment during World War II*, ed. Lawrence DiStasi (Berkeley, CA: Heyday Books, 2001), 167. The Group Presidential Warrant that US Attorney General Francis Biddle forwarded to J. Edgar Hoover on December 8, 1941 included the names of nearly three thousand Japanese, Italians, and Germans. The FBI's A-B-C lists initially included thousands of Japanese individuals, although thousands of individuals of Japanese heritage were eventually interned as enemy aliens without warrants. Christgau, *Enemies*, 54. For the numbers on the Japanese, Germans, and Italians in the DOJ camps, see Roger Daniels, "Words Do Matter: A Note on Inappropriate Terminology and the Incarceration of the Japanese Americans," in *Nikkei in the Pacific Northwest: Japanese Americans and Japanese Canadians in the Twentieth Century*, ed. Louis Fiset and Gail Nomura (Seattle: University of Washington Press, 2005), 193.

27. See Kōno Kawashima, *Kōyasan beikoku betsuin gojushūnenshi: Koyasan Buddhist Temple, 1912–1962* (Los Angeles: Kōyasan Beikoku Betsuin, 1962), 176–179; and Masuyama, *Memories*, 102.

28. Takahashi interview; and "Rikita Honda," Densho Encyclopedia entry, http://encyclopedia.densho.org/Rikita%20Honda/. The two individuals identified by Takahashi were Dr. Rikita Honda, the head of the Nanka Teikoku Gunyūdan (a Japanese veteran's organization); and Ms. Umeya, the female proprietress of a Japanese confectionary in Little Tokyo. Some questions have been raised about whether Dr. Honda actually committed suicide. Harry Ueno reported rumors that Dr. Honda may have been tortured by the FBI despite the official report (FBI File No. 100-8514) that noted the suicide as occurring on December 14 in INS custody in San Pedro, California. Harry Yoshio Ueno, *Manzanar Martyr: An Interview with Harry Y. Ueno*, interview conducted October 30, 1976 by Sue Kunitomi Embrey, Arthur Hansen, and Betty Kulberg (Fullerton, CA: Oral History Program, California State University, 1986), 51.

29. Seytsū Takahashi, *Amerika kaikyō: Shōwa no mikkyō tōzen* [The American Buddhist Mission: The Eastward Advance of Esoteric Buddhism during the Shōwa Period] (Osaka: Tōhō Shuppan, 1990), 3–4; and Takahashi interview.

30. Some were taken and then placed in a series of prisons and then internment camps run by the US Army and the Department of Justice's Immigration and Naturalization Service (INS). For more on the breakdown of those arrested in the selective internment process (Army/DOJ camps) versus the mass incarceration (WRA camps), see this book's website: www .americansutra.com/. The breakdown for the Army/DOJ arrests was 170 Buddhist priests (out of 231 total priests who were incarcerated), 44 Shinto priests (out of 44 total priests), and 27 Christian ministers (out of 160 total ministers). The Christian ministers were most often either language school instructors or *toritsuginin* (unpaid consular officials); *toritsuginin* constituted about half of the nearly two thousand Japanese Americans ultimately rounded up in Hawai'i.

31. The authorities targeted Shinto priests, as well as virtually all the high-ranking priests of all the major sects of Japanese Buddhism in America—Jōdo, Higashi Honganji, Nichiren, Nishi Hongwanji, Shingon, and Sōtō Zen. One exception was the frail Ryōtai Matsukage, North American Bishop of the San Francisco-based Nishi Hongwanji, initially left untouched perhaps due to his health condition, although he would eventually be incarcerated at WRA Topaz as part of the mass incarceration following President Roosevelt's executive order. A second exception was Dōjun Ochi, Bishop of the North American Sōtō Zen Buddhism sect, mentioned in Aoki's diary as Supervisor Ochi. He was arrested a few days after the diary entry and sent to the Santa Fe internment camp in New Mexico. On the Hawaiian Islands, Mitsumyō Tottori, the priest of Kōshōji (Haleiwa Shingonshu Buddhist Mission) was also spared arrest. According to FBI records, he had written two articles in Buddhist publications, *Hawaii Mikkyō* and *Kōyasan Jihō*, during 1941 that expressed pro-American views for the nisei generation. One stated, for example, that "our children should have the courage to grasp their guns and aim them at Japan for the sake of the USA." Under questioning by FBI agents about what he would do if ordered by Japanese officers to render assistance to potential Japanese Imperial Army invaders of the Hawaiian Islands, he is said to have replied that "he would rather die than obey an order for such a person" given his belief that a Japanese officer "should be sufficiently imbued with true Yamato spirit to realize that the (subject) should not be called upon to take arms up against a land which has been kind to him." It is speculated that such strong pro-American views preempted Tottori's arrest. National Archives, FBI File of Mitsumyo Tottori, report by John Harold Hughes, October 2, 1942.

32. The FBI's Shivers, generally more levelheaded about the "grab lists," held deep suspicions of the *toritsuginin*. John Michael Gordon, *Suspects in*

*Paradise: Looking for Japanese "Subversives" in the Territory of Hawaii,
1939–1945* (M.A. thesis, University of Iowa, 1983), 41.

33. In retrospect, concerns about fishermen and consular officials had
some validity: some of the most vital intelligence used by the Japanese Navy
in the Pearl Harbor attack was collected by Takeo Yoshikawa, a Japanese
naval intelligence officer who arrived in Honolulu in March 1941. Going by
the name Tadashi Morimura and using a job as a Japanese Consulate clerk as
cover, he sent detailed information to Tokyo. He also posed as a Filipino to
gain employment as a busboy at the Pearl Harbor Officers Club to gather
information for the air attack. To gain information for the midget submarine
attack, he acted as a local fisherman and cast fishing lines to determine the
depth of the seabed in the area around Pearl Harbor. For more on Yoshikawa,
see Edwin M. Nakasone, *The Nisei Soldier: Historical Essays on World
War II and the Korean War* (White Bear Lake, MN: J-Press Publishing,
1999), 13–15.

34. National Archives, RG 389, Entry 380, Box 1723, 1942–1946.

35. Lt. Colonel George W. Bicknell, Memorandum to Army Contact Office
(Honolulu), Seizure and Detention Plan (Japanese), November 21, 1941 [FBI
file, 100-2-1777].

36. For the December 4 FBI list, see Kashima, *Judgment without Trial*,
71–72.

37. Since Christianity was still viewed as a social force that could undermine
the stability of the Japanese nation (the religion was illegal in Japan until
1871), the Japanese government allowed emigration only on the condition
that any migrant would reject any attempts to convert them to Christianity.
Thus, the first Japanese passports for these migrants included the phrase
"never convert to another religion." Publication Committee of "A History of
Japanese Immigrants in Hawaii," *Hawaii Nihonjin Iminshi* [A History of
Japanese Immigration in Hawaii] (Honolulu: United Japanese Society of
Hawaii, 1964), 226.

38. Dorothy Hazama and Jane Komeiji, *Okage Sama De: The Japanese in
Hawai'i, 1885–1985* (Honolulu: Bess Press, 1986), 8–11.

39. The greatest number came from regions known for devout Buddhist
populations such as the Aki Monto (Jōdo Shinshu Buddhist followers from
the Hiroshima region, which was the prefecture that sent the largest number
of immigrants to Hawai'i, the continental US, and Brazil); the Gōshū Monto
(Jōdo Shinshu Buddhist followers from Shiga Prefecture that also sent large
numbers of migrants to Canada); and Sōtō Zen Buddhists (who made up the
majority of those from Fukushima Prefecture who ended up most frequently
in Hawai'i). Although Buddhist immigrants hailed from a variety of sec-

tarian traditions, Jōdo Shinshu Buddhists would come to play a disproportionate role in the formation of early Buddhism in America because of their sheer numbers. In addition to those deeply devout Buddhist regions of Japan, most of the other immigrants initially hailed from Yamaguchi, Kumamoto, and Fukuoka Prefectures (these prefectures plus Hiroshima account for over 90 percent of all Japanese who emigrated in the early decades) where Jōdo Shinshu Buddhism was also a major part of life. Several decades after the first major wave of Japanese migration came a substantial migration from Okinawa, which also became a major "emigration prefecture," despite the fact that that these southern islands had only recently been annexed by Japan. See Tomonori Ishikawa, "Okinawa imin kankei shiryō tōkei, zuhyō, chizu," [Okinawa Emigration Documents: Tabulations, Charts, and Maps] *Shin Okinawa bungaku* [Okinawa Literature] 45 (1980), 149; Yukiko Kimura, *Issei: Japanese Immigrants in Hawaii* (Honolulu: University of Hawai'i Press, 1988), 47; Stewart Lone, *The Japanese Community in Brazil, 1908–1940: Between Samurai and Carnival* (Hammondmills, England: Palgrove, 2001), 30.

40. Quoted in Michihiro Ama, *Immigrants to the Pure Land: The Modernization, Acculturation, and Globalization of Shin Buddhism, 1898–1941* (Honolulu: University of Hawai'i Press, 2011), 34–35.

41. The pattern of moving from residences to temples continued as late as the 1930s. See Walz, *Japanese Immigration*, 142.

42. Land ownership for issei immigrants was also an issue and in many places Buddhist temple land had to be put in the name of American-born nisei. For example, for the Los Angeles Nichiren Temple, "since a non–American citizen could not buy land, the temple board asked to use the name of Mr. & Mrs. Sanji Kinoshita who were born in Hawaii." Los Angeles Nichiren Buddhist Temple, ed. *90th Anniversary Nichiren Buddhist Temple, 1914–2004* (Los Angeles: Los Angeles Nichiren Buddhist Temple, 2004), 10. Similarly, in 1937, the land for the new headquarters of the Shingon Buddhist sect, the Kōyasan Betsuin Temple in Los Angeles, was purchased in the names of the sons (American-born US citizens) of temple lay leaders. See Richard K. Payne, "Hiding in Plain Sight: The Invisibility of the Shingon Mission to the United States," in *Buddhist Missionaries in the Era of Globalization*, ed. Linda Learman (Honolulu: University of Hawai'i Press, 2005), 108. On Rev. Sunya Pratt, one of the first convert women ordained as a Buddhist priest, see Michihiro Ama, "'First White Buddhist Priestess': A Case Study of Sunday Gladys Pratt at Tacoma Buddhist Temple," in *Buddhism Beyond Borders: New Perspectives on Buddhism in the United States*, ed. Scott Mitchell and Natalie Quli (Albany, NY: State University of New York Press, 2015), 59–74.

43. Quoted in Hunter, *Buddhism in Hawaii*, 94.

44. Quoted in Michael Angevine and Ryo Yoshida, "Contexts for a History of Asian-American Presbyterian Churches: A Case Study of Japanese-American Presbyterians' Early History," in *The Diversity of Discipleship*, ed. Milton Coalter, et al. (Louisville, KY: Westminster / John Knox Press, 1991), 299.

45. Jennifer C. Snow, *Protestant Missionaries, Asian Immigrants, and Ideologies of Race in America, 1850–1924* (New York: Routledge, 2007), 70–72.

46. Sidney Gulick, *Mixing the Races in Hawaii: A Study of the Neo-Hawaiian American Race* (Honolulu: The Hawaiian Board Book Rooms, 1937), 199–200.

47. Gary Scharnhorst, "'Ways That Are Dark': Appropriations of Bret Harte's 'Plain Language from Truthful James,'" *Nineteenth-Century Literature* 51:3 (1996), 377–399.

48. Quoted by Lon Kurashige, *Two Faces of Exclusion: The Untold History of Anti-Asian Racism in the United States* (Chapel Hill, NC: University of North Carolina Press, 2016), 37.

49. Izumi Hirobe, *Japanese Pride, American Prejudice: Modifying the Exclusion Clause of the 1924 Immigration Act* (Stanford: Stanford University Press, 2001); and James Q. Whitman, *Hitler's American Model: The United States and the Making of Nazi Race Law* (Princeton: Princeton University Press, 2017), 34–37.

50. Hiromi Monobe, *Shaping an Ethnic Leadership: Takie Okumura and the "Americanization" of the Nisei in Hawai'i, 1919–1945* (Ph.D. diss., Stanford University, 2004), 96, 100.

51. Okihiro, *Cane Fires*, 131.

52. Quoted in Hunter, *Buddhism in Hawaii*, 129–130.

53. Henry Judd, "The Repaganization of Hawaii," *Friend* 89 (1920): 188.

54. Quoted in Hunter, *Buddhism in Hawaii*, 159.

55. Translated in Noriko Shimada, "Social Cultural, and Spiritual Struggles of the Japanese in Hawai'i: The Case of Okumura Takie and Imamura Yemyo and Americanization," in *Hawai'i at the Crossroads of the US and Japan before the Pacific War*, ed. Jon Thares Davidann (Honolulu: University of Hawai'i Press, 2008), 161.

56. US National Archives, 1936, Box A8-5 / EF37 / EG12 (5–22): Lyhan, W. K. [Kilsoo Haan], "Letter to Cordell Hull," May 22, 1936. Lyhan claimed in a letter to Secretary of State Cordell Hull that he had been the executive secretary of the Korean Information Bureau under the Korean National Association before working with Lt. Raymond and Major Muir of the Army G-2 since 1931. He also notes in this letter to Hull that he had been keeping

tabs on Bishop Gikyō Kuchiba of the Nishi Hongwanji Betsuin in Honolulu as a possible pro-Japanese person of interest. For more on Kilsoo Haan, see Richard Kim, "Managing the 'Foreign' and 'Domestic': Kilsoo Haan, Korean Diasporic Nationalism and US Liberal State, 1931–1945," *Seoul Journal of Korean Studies* 19:1 (2006): 15–59; and Michael Macmillan, "Unwanted Aliens: Koreans as Enemy Aliens in World War II," *Hawaii Journal of History* 19 (1985), 196.

57. Lyhan also noted that these "Japanizing" factors and the Japanese consulate would likely mobilize fishermen (442 Japanese-owned sampans are noted in the report), Japanese domestic servants (to "poison" their employers), and Japanese contractors and masons, who Lyman alleges have been hoarding dynamite for future use, to attack American interests. Kim, "Managing the 'Foreign,'" 27.

58. Jeffrey M. Dorwart, *Conflict of Duty: The US Navy's Intelligence Dilemma, 1919–1945* (Annapolis, MD: United States Naval Institute, 1983), 180.

59. Quoted in Roger Daniels, *The Politics of Prejudice: The Anti-Japanese Movement in California and the Struggle for Japanese Exclusion* (Berkeley: University of California Press, 1962), 70.

60. Ibid., 77.

61. Ibid., 106–107.

62. Ibid., 107.

63. These reports include the 1926 Military Intelligence Department (MID) study *A Survey of the Hawaiian-born Japanese in the Territory of Hawaii*; the 1929 MID report *A Survey of the Japanese in the Territory of Hawaii*; and the 1933 Hawaiian Department G-2 *Estimate of the Situation— Japanese Population in Hawaii*. The FBI issued further reports, such as the 1933 *Survey of the Japanese Situation in Hawaii*; and the extensive 1941 *Hawaii's Japanese Problem*.

64. Captain C. C. Cavender, "Loyalty of Immigrants in the Event of War," report to the Adjutant General, War Department (September 1, 1939; Box A8-5 / EF37 / EG12), 1–2.

65. On Robert Shivers and his connections with the Japanese American community in Honolulu, see the documentary *The First Battle: The Battle for Equality in Wartime Hawai'i*, DVD, directed by Tom Coffman (San Francisco, CA: Center for Asian American Media, 2006); and Gray, "Our Man of Peace."

66. For a book-length treatment of Burns, see Dan Boylan and T. Michael Holmes, *John A. Burns: The Man and His Times* (Honolulu: University of Hawai'i Press, 2000).

67. Quoted in Boylan and Holmes, *John A. Burns*, 33–34.

68. Gordon, *Suspects in Paradise*, 39.

69. Counter Subversion Section, Office of Naval Intelligence, Report to all Navy Districts, FBI, State Dept.: "Japanese Intelligence and Propaganda in the United States During 1941," December 4, 1941, National Archives, A8-5), 23–24.

70. Alan Hynd, *Betrayal from the East: The Inside Story of Japanese Spies in America* (New York: Robert McBride & Co., 1943), 93.

71. Brian Hayashi, *Democratizing the Enemy: The Japanese American Internment* (Princeton: Princeton University Press, 2004), 39; Greg Robinson, *A Tragedy of Democracy: Japanese Confinement in North America* (New York: Columbia University Press, 2009), 36; and Ronald Seth, *Secret Servants: A History of Japanese Espionage* (New York: Farrar, Strauss and Cudahy, 1957), 193.

72. All eleven persons eventually convicted of espionage in relation to the Pacific war were white and not of Japanese heritage. Robinson, *Tragedy of Democracy,* 46. While this evidence suggests that US officials were not entirely misguided in their concerns, no evidence has turned up suggesting such subversive activities by Japanese or Japanese American Buddhists in the United States.

73. In a rather hyperbolic book published in 1943 (and in 1945 made into a Hollywood film), journalist Alan Hynd claimed there was an extensive network of Japanese spies, in collusion with German spies, who used the Furusawas, the Kōyasan Buddhist Temple, and Shinto shrines as venues for their espionage. Alan Hynd, *Betrayal from the East: The Inside Story of Japanese Spies in America* (New York: R. M. McBride, 1943), 19–20, 93–94, 129–131, 155.

74. The notion of inserting operatives in the guise of other occupations seems to have been routine. In the case of Japanese espionage efforts in Russia, Sinkiang, Tibet, and Mongolia, for instance, James Boyd has convincingly argued that the Nishi Hongwanji cooperated with the Japanese military and used their priestly networks to gather intelligence. See James Boyd, "Undercover Acolytes: Honganji, the Japanese Army, and Intelligence-Gathering Operations," *Journal of Religious History* 37:2 (2013), 185–205.

75. Yuji Ichioka, *Before Internment: Essays in Prewar Japanese American History* (Stanford: Stanford University Press, 2006), 206–209, 219.

76. On agency investigations into these two plots, see Hynd, *Betrayal from the East,* 93–95, 123–131.

77. For more on the sending of *imonbukuro* and *sennin-bari* from Japanese America to the Sino-Japanese war front, see Yuji Ichioka, "Japanese Immigrant Nationalism: The Issei and the Sino-Japanese War, 1937–1941," *California History* 69:3 (1990), 260–275, 310–311.

78. Publication Committee of "A History of Japanese Immigrants in Hawaii," *Hawaii Nihonjin Iminshi*, 84; Hunter, *Buddhism in Hawaii*, 178; and John Fee Embree, *Acculturation among the Japanese of Kona, Hawaii*, Supplement to *American Anthropologist* 43:4:2 (1941), 42.

79. Receipts from the Japanese Imperial Army to the Buddhist Mission of North America headquarters and those made out to the groups in Fresno and San Jose to acknowledge donations are filed in the Buddhist Churches of America Archives, Box 13 (June 20, 1939; July 29, 1939). Sometimes Buddhists, along with a considerable issei Christian contingent, participated in broader efforts to support the Japanese military. Shinobu Matsuura, the wife of the priest at the Guadalupe Buddhist Temple in California, organized the preparation of hundreds of care packages and raised thousands of dollars for the Japanese military as a devout supporter of the secular Aikoku Fujinkai (Women's Japanese Patriotic Association). That association was founded by Ioko Okumura, the sister of the Higashi Honganji Rev. Enshin Okumura, who had founded his sect's mission temple in Korea. Historian Eiichiro Azuma notes that the Federation of Southern California Japanese Women's Associations organized a campaign to send five thousand *imonbukuro* to Manchuria; the Los Angeles Buddhist women's associations made up a thousand of those bags. See Eiichiro Azuma, *Between Two Empires: Race, History, and Transnationalism in Japanese America* (Oxford: Oxford University Press, 2005), 165; and Shinobu Matsuura, "Kaikyōshi no tsuma ga mita nikkei imin," [Japanese Emigrants as Seen by a Buddhist Missionary's Wife] in *Issei to shite Amerika ni ikite*, [Living in America as an Issei] ed. Takao Kitamura (Tokyo: Sōshisha, 1992), 220.

80. While these issei immigrants simultaneously felt a strong kinship and sympathy with America, the fact that issei Christians were also very active in these efforts, according to the historian Brian Hayashi, "was shaped in part by concerns that had little to do with their religion." See Hayashi, *"For the Sake of Our Brethren,"* 104–106.

81. In the United States, at the Northwest Young Buddhist League annual meeting in 1937, even as older speakers passionately urged the young nisei to support the Japanese imperial cause (with Shōji Okamura from the Japanese consulate providing the Japanese government's perspective on the war), the convention refused to adopt a public position on this issue. Indeed, by mid-1941, as the clouds of war seemed to loom ever closer, the General Assembly at the Young Buddhist Federation of North America convention in April adopted three resolutions declaring: 1) the loyalty of young Buddhists to the United States; 2) Buddhist support for America's national defense program; and 3) cooperation with the Japanese American Citizens' League

(JACL). See Ron Magden, *Mukashi Mukashi Long Long Ago: The First Century of the Seattle Buddhist Church* (Seattle: Seattle Buddhist Church, 2012), 99.

82. Lothrop, "Unwelcome in Freedom's Land," 164.

83. Ibid., 118.

84. F.D.R. Memorandum for the Chief of Operations, August 10, 1936. For more on the significance of this memo, see Greg Robinson's Densho Encyclopedia entry "FDR Memo," http://encyclopedia.densho.org/FDR_Hawaii _Memo/

85. Michael Slackman, "The Orange Race: George S. Patton, Jr.'s Japanese-American Hostage Plan," *Biography* 7:1 (Winter 1984), 1–22. The word "orange" in the title of the plan was a code word for "Japan" among military planners.

86. Ibid., 7. Patton's "Plan Orange" identified Pearl Harbor as a potential target of a Japanese aerial attack, but this plan was supplanted by the "Rainbow 3" and "Rainbow 5" war plans. The fact that these assigned more likelihood to Japanese attacks on islands closer to Japan like Wake, Guam, Midway, and the Philippines, and to British and Dutch possessions, accounts for the surprise of the Pearl Harbor attacks.

87. Dorwart, *Conflict of Duty*, 121.

88. These minutes of the July 29, 1940 meeting on "Joint Coverage of Japanese Activities" can be found in National Archives, *Memorandum of Pearl Harbor Attack and Bureau's Activities Before and After, Volume II: Reference Material to Volume I, Part I* (December 6, 1945). For sections on Buddhism and Shintoism, see 34–36.

89. Quoted in Okihiro, *Cane Fires*, 182.

90. In one of the first postwar analyses of the "grab-list" in Hawai'i, sociologist Andrew Lind wrote in 1946 that "Shinto priests in so far as they were active exponents of the divinity of the Japanese emperor and of Japanese nationalism, although few in number in Hawai'i prior to the war (probably less than forty), obviously constituted a potential menace to morale. The Buddhist priests and priestesses, numbering about a hundred, were less directly associated in the propagation of Japanese nationalism; but most of them were recent products of the educational system of Japan, and it had to be assumed that their outlook and sentiments tended to be more or less sympathetic with the objectives and ideals of the military regime in Japan." Andrew W. Lind, *Hawaii's Japanese: An Experiment in Democracy* (Princeton: Princeton University Press, 1946), 74.

91. Kashima, *Judgment without Trial*, 29. Stephen Fox notes that Special Defense Unit (SDU) lawyers devised a "scheme to show the reliability of FBI

information. If a person was 'most dangerous' but the source unreliable, the suspect was classified 'A-2.' Similarly, a 'less dangerous' individual, for whom there was 'acceptable (reliable) information, was classified 'B-1,' and so forth." Stephen Fox, *America's Invisible Gulag: A Biography of German American Internment and Exclusion in World War II* (New York: Peter Lang, 2000), 5. Fox also explains the greater differences among the British A-B-C classifications and how much the American system differed from its counterpart in the UK.

92. Kashima, *Judgment without Trial*, 30–31, 229. See in particular the names of twelve organizations said to have been targeted by the SDU.

93. Kashima notes that for the SDU in February 1942, Shinto shrines (mistakenly called "temples" in the government documents) and so-called "sect Shinto" groups like Konkōkyō were listed as "B" category organizations. Kashima, *Judgment without Trial*, 229–230.

94. Wegars notes the confusion in the existing literature about which categories of persons belonged to which group, possibly in part due to the secrecy surrounding the ABC lists. Wegars notes that scholars such as Bob Kumamoto, Greg Robinson, and Peter Irons place Buddhist priests in Group A, but that the *Report of the Commission on Wartime Relocation and Internment of Civilians* does not. See Priscilla Wegars, *Imprisoned in Paradise: Japanese Internee Road Workers at the World War II Kooskia Internment Camp* (Moscow, ID: Asian American Comparative Collection Research Reports, University of Idaho, 2010), 1. The commission's report is available in book form as Tetsuden Kashima, ed., *Personal Justice Denied: Report on the Commission on Wartime Relocation and Internment of Civilians* (Seattle: University of Washington Press, 1997). While the DOJ and units within it were taking precautions in case of war, the War Department, which did not trust the DOJ, created the Provost Marshal General's Office on July 3, 1941 to oversee operations related to prisoners of war and enemy aliens should war break out. For a detailed discussion of the relations between the Justice and War Departments, as well as the creation of DOJ's Special Defense Unit, in discussing their respective responsibilities for "controlling selected individuals after the United States entered the ongoing war," see Kashima, *Judgment without Trial*, 23–29. Although such classification by potential danger and guilt by association was eventually deemed distorting, particularly when applied to citizens, by even US government officials, they were influential in the initial incarceration experience of many Japanese nationals, including Buddhist priests. On July 16, 1943, US Attorney General Francis Biddle issued a memorandum to both the DOJ and the FBI to halt the use of these lists, stating that they were "inherently unreliable." Hoover did not fully heed

Biddle's memorandum and continued to keep lists on security suspects. Christgau, *Enemies*, 82–83.

95. Kashima, *Judgment without Trial*, 22.

96. Among such resident aliens were over one million Japanese, German, and Italian nationals (695,000 Italians, 315,000 Germans, and 91,000 Japanese), who would be designated as "enemy aliens" after Pearl Harbor, mandated to always carry an alien registration certificate, which also served as a photo identity card. Other sources state the number of registered "enemy aliens" as low as 1.1 million and as high as 5 million. See Christgau, *Enemies*, 10; Fiset, *Imprisoned Apart*, 28; Krammer, *Undue Process*, 26; and Wegars, *Imprisoned in Paradise*, 4. For the exemptions, see Hyung-ju Ahn, *Between Two Adversaries: Korean Interpreters at Japanese Alien Enemy Detention Centers during World War II* (Fullerton, CA: Oral History Program, California State University, Fullerton, 2002), 9.

2. MARTIAL LAW

1. Jay Cocks and Martin Scorsese, *Silence*, DVD, directed by Martin Scorsese (Los Angeles: Paramount, 2016). http://www.cinefile.biz/script/silence.pdf

2. "Mr. David Kobata: Memoirs of a Buddhist in Hawai'i—an Interview, 5 February 1993" ch. 8, text 44, in Esben Andreasen, *Popular Buddhism in Japan: Shin Buddhist Religion and Culture* (London: Routledge, 2014), 158–161; 161.

3. Ibid.

4. In an encoded dispatch to all FBI offices. FBI Director Hoover instructed all field offices to furnish to the Bureau "the names concerning persons of American citizenship, either by birth or naturalization, who you believe should be considered for custodial detention." Arnold Krammer, *Undue Process: The Untold Story of America's German Alien Internees* (Lanham, MD: Rowman & Littlefield, 1997), 35. In Hawai'i, 468 kibei nisei were picked up and detained for interrogation despite their American citizenship. Roland Kotani, *The Japanese in Hawaii: A Century of Struggle* (Honolulu: Oahu Kanyaku Imin Centennial Committee, 1985), 91. Tetsuden Kashima states the lower figure of 92 males for nisei arrested or interned from Hawai'i. Tetsuden Kashima, *Judgment without Trial: Japanese American Imprisonment during World War II* (Seattle: University of Washington Press, 2003), 78. In contrast to the significant number of American citizens of Japanese heritage in Hawai'i who were targeted, especially those of Buddhist and Shinto affiliations, only two American citizens of Italian heritage were

ever registered and interned as enemy aliens. See http://
worldhistoryconnected.press.illinois.edu/8.3/forum_rosenfeld.html.

5. Office of the Chief of Military History, Special Staff, US Army, "United
States Army Forces Middle Pacific and Predecessor Commands World War II,
7 December 1941–2 September 1945: History of G-2 Section," Classified
document from the Historical Sub-Section, G-2 Historical Manuscript File
Collection, US Army (8-5.6 AA v. 10, pt. 2, September 1, 1950).

6. The statistics on Hawai'i's incarcerated Japanese and Japanese Americans are not absolutely clear. Okihiro cites roughly 1,875 Japanese (1,118 who
were placed in WRA camps and 757 in DOJ camps) and Hazama and
Komeiji have it as 1,444 persons (979 Aliens, 525 nisei, mainly kibei).
Kashima has suggested 733 during the period from December 7, 1941 to
March 30, 1942 and more recently, has noted a higher number—2,392
individuals from Hawai'i detained, with all but 300 of them detained in
facilities on the continental United States (of the 2,092 detained on the
continent, he breaks the group down as 875 issei and 1,217 nisei). Gary
Okihiro, *Cane Fires: The Anti-Japanese Movement in Hawaii, 1865–1945*
(Philadelphia: Temple University Press, 1991), 244–245; Dorothy Hazama and
Jane Komeiji, *Okage Sama De: The Japanese in Hawai'i, 1885–1985* (Honolulu:
Bess Press, 1986), 132; and Kashima, *Judgment without Trial: Japanese
American Imprisonment during World War II* (Seattle: University of Wash-
ington Press, 2003), 78.

7. The fourteen factors were listed in this order: Family (in Japan), Time
Spent in Japan, Education, Citizenship, Religion, Organizations, Financial
Interest, Attitude Toward the Emperor, Donations, Visiting Japanese Public
Vessels, Military Deferment, Americanization, Positive Reactions (to US war
efforts), and Expressed Sentiments (about the war).

8. Office of the Chief of Military History, Special Staff, US Army, "United
States Army Forces Middle Pacific and Predecessor Commands World War II,
7 December 1941–2 September 1945: History of G-2 Section," 815. With regard
to "Religion," the memorandum urged nuance, citing as problematic the
many instances that agents had hitherto listed as an "unfavorable factor"
simply that the "Subject is a Buddhist." In setting policy that seemed intended to ameliorate the hitherto biased attitudes and rash actions of agents
on the ground, the memo also warned that a subject's Buddhist faith "in
itself, should not be classified as adverse information. It is as natural for a
Japanese to be a Buddhist as it is for an Irishman to be a Catholic." For future
targeting of Buddhists, the memo encouraged a more nuanced attention to
the sectarian affiliation of the subject, noting that belonging to the Nichiren
Buddhist order should be "considered an adverse point" for hearing subjects

because that lineage, along with most all Shinto organizations, ought to be classified as "nationalistic Japanese sects." It is likely that the Nichiren Buddhist tradition was singled out because of well-known ultranationalist Nichiren-affiliated organizations in Japan, such as Kokuchūkai, that used Buddhist ideology to argue that Japan's imperial ambitions were part of a spiritual mandate given to Japan to spread Nichiren Buddhism around the world.

9. Among them were Revs. Takeo Akizaki (Moilili Inari Jinja), Masao Arine (Maui Jinja), Shigeo Fujino (Lihue Daijingū), Shinkō Hirai (Honolulu Fudō'in Temple), Yoshizoe Kawasaki (Hawai'i Daijingū), Tadao Kouchi (Lanai Hongwanji Mission), Takeo Eshō Miura (Puunene Hongwanji Mission), Yazō Satō (Hawai'i Izumo Taisha), and Kenjitsu Tsuha (Ewa Hongwanji Mission). The Buddhist priest and US citizen Rev. Tadao Kouchi, for instance, was arrested the day after Pearl Harbor and initially incarcerated at Haiku Camp before being transferred to the WRA camps of Rohwer and Jerome in 1943. Meanwhile, his family was forced out of the two-story Buddhist temple in Lanai by the authorities because, according to his son, "the Christians wanted a large church. We moved to a two-bedroom house on a plantation." Eiko Irene Masuyama, *Memories: The Buddhist Church Experience in the Camps, 1942–1945* (Sacramento: California Civil Liberties Public Education Program, 2007), 166. Another individual arrested was Shigeo (Robert) Muroda, the secretary of the Waianae Youth Men's Buddhist Association, whose initial hearing before the Military Governor's Reviewing Board focused on his donations through "comfort kits" to support the Japanese military in the prewar period; his leadership in the Nishi Hongwanji Buddhist organization; the fact that he held his Shinto-style wedding at the Izumo Shrine; and unsubstantiated rumors that he discouraged Filipinos from buying American war bonds. But the main concern, even though he had never visited Japan, might have been that Muroda had never completed the paperwork to renounce the Japanese nationality that he automatically acquired as child of a Japanese citizen. Even without a direct connection to Japan, the combination of that dual citizenship and his association with both Buddhist and Shinto organizations seems to have made up the minds of those assessing his internment that he was "Japanese in attitude and reactions and he failed to Americanize himself" on top of his being "an officer and member of several pro-Japanese societies." These comments about Muroda are noted in the margin of the transcript of his interview with the review board on October 27, 1943, included in his "Basic Personnel Record: Alien Enemy or Prisoner of War," which I have in my possession. In contrast, on the continent, just a handful of citizens were rounded up in this initial

detention process. The arrest of Sumio Higashida of the Tenrikyō Church of Los Angeles, in the early roundup in the continental United States, fit the pattern of suspicion of Shinto and Buddhist nisei priests. But in this initial roundup in Los Angeles, two US citizens who would normally have been seen as "Americanized" (given their Christian faith and Japanese American Citizens' League affiliation) were also arrested: Eiji Tanabe (a JACL senior officer) and Togo Tanaka. Tanaka was the English-language editor of the *Rafu Shimpo* and may have been a person of concern given the power of the media to potentially spread subversive propaganda. Unlike most of the nisei arrested in this program, he was swiftly released without explanation after twelve days. Togo Tanaka, "How to Survive Racism in America's Free Society: A Lecture by Togo W. Tanaka," in *Voices Long Silent: An Oral Inquiry into the Japanese American Evacuation,* ed. Arthur Hansen and Betty Mitson (Fullerton, CA: California State University, Fullerton Oral History Program / Japanese American Project, 1974), 94.

10. Rather than transport them to DOJ and Army camps on the US continent—where they might file lawsuits, given that they were not provided appropriate due process of law—US authorities kept many American citizens of Japanese ancestry detained in Hawai'i. Brian Niiya and Sheila Chun make this point about the Honouliuli camp in an introduction to Suikei Furuya, *An Internment Odyssey: Haisho Tenten* (Honolulu: Japanese Cultural Center of Hawai'i / University of Hawai'i Press, 2017), xxxiv.

11. Tsuda was also known as Shinsho Hirai at different points in her life. See Furuya, *An Internment Odyssey,* 40, 313–314; and Amy Nishimura, "From Priestesses and Disciples to Witches and Traitors: Internment of Japanese Women at Honouliuli and Narratives of 'Madwomen,'" *Social Process in Hawai'i* 45 (2014), 213.

12. Quoted in Nishimura, "From Priestesses," 213. Tsuda's incarceration continued despite her testimony that she got up every day at 5:30 AM to pray for the safety of the Japanese American soldiers fighting in Italy, who were sons of her congregation's members. Another nisei, Helen Shizuko Nakagawa, took over the responsibility of caring for the forty- to fifty-member congregation after Tsuda was interned. Tsuda also attracted a certain notoriety by smuggling letters to the outside, defying camp rules by trying to communicate with her followers. Nakagawa, her main disciple, managed to move the temple from the McCully district in Honolulu to a new location in Palolo Valley, before she was also detained. On Tsuda and Nakagawa, also see Linda Nishigaya and Ernest Oshiro, "Reviving the Lotus: Japanese Buddhism and World War II Internment," *Social Process in Hawai'i* 45 (2014): 180–181. The original documents can be found at the National

Archives document RG 494, Entry 19, Box 257, 1943 and RG 494, Entry 19, Box 305–306, 1944.

Tsuda had directed the Fudō'in Temple (which changed its name in 1948 to Tōdaiji Hawaii Betsuin, as a branch temple of the well-known Kegon Buddhist headquarters in Nara) prior to the war and was well known for her *danjiki* fasting practice. Using the pretext of a hunger strike, she was able to continue her Buddhist ascetic practice of fasting during her incarceration. See Eijō Ikenaga, "Honolulu Myōhōji: Bussari Heiwatō, Peace Tower," in *Hawaii Nichirenshū hachijushūnen no ayumi: A History of Nichiren Buddhism in Hawaii*, ed. Nichiren Mission of Hawaii (Honolulu: Nichiren Mission of Hawaii, 1982), 35–38; and Hirochika Nakamaki, *Nihon shūkyō to Nikkei shūkyō no kenkyū: Nihon, Amerika, Burajiru* [Studies in Japanese Religions at Home and Abroad: Japan, America, and Brazil] (Tokyo: Tōsui Shobō, 1989), 293–294.

13. Female clerics in both the Buddhist and Shinto traditions in Hawai'i were generally detained. While mostly male community leaders were targeted, a number of female religious leaders, Japanese-language school instructors, newspaper correspondents, and wives of male targets were also caught up in the early dragnet. In addition to those mentioned above were the Sōtō Zen nun Kanzan Itō, of Mantokuji Temple in Maui; Kegon sect leader Helen Shizuko Nakagawa among the Buddhists; Yukiko Miyao and Yoshie Miyao of the Izumo Taisha Shrine in Honolulu among the Shinto priestesses; and leaders of sect Shinto new religions, including Tenrikyō female leaders Miyuki Kawasaki of Waipahu and Shizuyo Yoshioka of Honolulu, and Konkōkyō leaders Kiku Horibe from Kauai and Haruko Takahashi of the Konkō Church of Wahiawa. While at Sand Island, the Japanese women were placed together with a handful of German and Italian women. During their time at Sand Island, the women appear to have been better treated by Mary Lou Eifler, the wife of Commander Eifler, with whom the men had many clashes. See Furuya, *An Internment Odyssey*, 39–40; and Yasutarō Soga, *Life Behind Barbed Wire: The World War II Internment Memoirs of a Hawai'i Issei* (Honolulu: Japanese Cultural Center of Hawai'i/ University of Hawai'i Press, 2008), 46–47.

14. Kotani, *The Japanese in Hawaii*, 91. At least publicly on December 8, 1941, the US military tried to calm what they called "unfounded rumors," with a radio announcement by US Army Colonel Butch Felder stating that there was no desire "on the part of the authorities to organize mass concentration camps." See the documentary film, *The First Battle: The Battle for Equality in Wartime Hawai'i*, DVD, directed by Tom Coffman (San Francisco, CA: Center for Asian American Media, 2006).

15. Emphasis in original. Quoted in Greg Robinson, *By Order of the President: FDR and the Internment of Japanese Americans* (Cambridge, MA: Harvard University Press, 2001), 148. Also see Greg Robinson, *A Tragedy of Democracy: Japanese Confinement in North America* (New York: Columbia University Press, 2009), 116–119.

16. Kashima, *Judgment without Trial*, 76–77; Robinson, *By Order of the President*, 150–155.

17. De Soto Brown, *Hawaii Goes to War: Life in Hawaii from Pearl Harbor to Peace* (Honolulu: Editions Limited, 1989), 72–73; Mackinnon Simpson, *Hawaii's Homefront: Life in the Islands during World War II* (Honolulu: Bess Press, 2008), 114–115; Soga, *Life Behind Barbed Wire*, 25.

18. Soga, *Life Behind Barbed Wire*, 74–77, 82–85.

19. Masuyama, *Memories*, 166.

20. Gaku Kinoshita, *Us, Hawai'i -Born Japanese: Storied Identities of Japanese American Elderly from a Sugar Plantation Community* (New York: Routledge, 2006), 179.

21. Hazama and Komeiji, *Okage Sama De*, 128.

22. Ibid., 128.

23. Kotani, *The Japanese in Hawaii*, 102.

24. Okihiro, *Cane Fires*, 240.

25. Simpson, *Hawaii's Homefront*, 86.

26. University of Hawai'i Special Collections File 181.

27. Richard T. Miyao, *Saga of a Church in Hawaii: 90th Anniversary of the Izumo Taishakyo Mission of Hawaii* (Honolulu: Izumo Taishakyo Mission of Hawaii, 1996), 80.

28. Okihiro, *Cane Fires*, 226–227, 234.

29. Louise Hunter, *Buddhism in Hawaii: Its Impact on a Yankee Community* (Honolulu: University of Hawai'i Press, 1971), 191.

30. Shizue Seigel, *In Good Conscience: Supporting Japanese Americans during the Internment* (San Mateo, CA: AACP Inc. and Kansha Project, 2006), 256.

31. Yukiko Kimura, *Issei: Japanese Immigrants in Hawaii* (Honolulu: University of Hawai'i Press, 1988), 156.

32. Yoshiko Tatsuguchi and Lois A. Suzuki, *Shinshu Kyokai Mission of Hawaii, 1914–1984: A Legacy of Seventy Years* (Honolulu: Shinshu Kyokai Mission of Hawaii, 1985), 60.

33. Similarly, the wife of Rev. Enjō Kobayashi took the role of officiating priest at the temple in Hawi, Big Island after her husband was in the Fort Missoula internment camp, while the nisei female priest, Yoshiko Shimabukuro, based out of the Eleele Hongwanji Mission, took care of Buddhist

funerals for the entire island of Kauai. At the Hilo Mission, Hakuhōzan Taishōji, the US military confiscated the temple's official registry, with the result that formal services could not be held, but permitted a lay member, Iwajirō Miyashita, to serve as the caretaker of the temple. With prior approval, he and other lay members were able to meet every third Sunday for their Kannon-kō gatherings, as well as to organize funerals and memorial services, collect donations, and carry out mundane tasks as termite fumigations. In applications to the US military for exemptions to the general prohibition on Buddhist gatherings, temples including the Hokekyōji Mission of Hawaii emphasized in their requests to the US Army that they would not hold their regular Buddhist sermons, so as to assuage the military's concerns about "Japanese propaganda" being spread by the temples. See Hawaii Honpa Hongwanji Kyōdan [Honpa Hongwanji Mission of Hawaii], ed. *Gomonshu no junkyō kinen Honpa Hongwanji enkakushi* [A Short History of the Honpa Hongwanji on the Occasion of the Visit of His Eminence the Gomonshu] (Honolulu: Hawaii Honpa Hongwanji kyōdan, 1954), 8; Gail Honda, *Family Torn Apart: The Internment Story of the Otokichi Muin Ozaki Family* (Honolulu: Japanese Cultural Center of Hawai'i and the University of Hawai'i Press, 2012), 80; Hawaii Sōtōshū Kaikyō Sōkanbu [Hawai'i Soto Mission Bishop's Office], *Sōtōshū Hawaii kaikyō nanajū shi (1903–1978)* [Seventy Years of Soto Zen Buddhist Propagation History in Hawai'i, 1903–1978] (Honolulu: Hawaii Sōtōshū Kyōkai, 1978), 95; Letter from Y. Yamashita to Colonel Thomas H. Green, February 13, 1942. Cited in Tara Ogden, *Gambarimashō! Religion Among the Japanese in America during World War II* (M.A. thesis, University of California, Santa Barbara, 1995), 33.

34. Shigeo Yoshida, "The Job Ahead," speech, Oahu Conference of Americans of Japanese Ancestry, Sponsored by the Emergency Service Committee, January 28, 1945, http://digitalassets.lib.berkeley.edu/jarda/ucb/text/cubanc6714_b317w02_0464_2.pdf. Quoted in Kotani, *The Japanese in Hawaii,* 104.

35. Takakazu Maeda, *Hawaii no Jinjashi* [A History of Shinto Shrines in Hawai'i] (Tokyo: Taimeidō, 1999), 30.

36. Tatsuguchi and Suzuki, *Shinshu Kyokai,* 59.

37. Dennis M. Ogawa, *Kodomo no tame ni (For the Sake of the Children): The Japanese American Experience in Hawaii* (Honolulu: University of Hawai'i Press, 1978), 317; Okihiro, *Cane Fires,* 230, 234–235.

38. Nakamaki, *Nihon shūkyō,* 268.

39. Hawaii Honpa Hongwanji Kyōdan, *Gomonshu no junkyō,* 8.

40. The fire occurred on January 18, 1943. After the fire, the Women's Association (Fujinkai) of the Pahala temple pleaded with the temple priest's

wife to remain on the island to continue organizing Buddhist activity, rather than joining her husband, who had been interned on the continental United States. She told them, "We're all together with the Buddha. Let us help each other," and stayed to perform her religious duties. Shigeo Kikuchi, *Memoirs of a Buddhist Woman Missionary in Hawaii* (Honolulu: Buddhist Study Center Press, 1991), 51.

41. Ibid.

42. Ibid., 61.

43. They included the Jōdo Shinshū Puna Hongwanji, Kapaa Hongwanji, Nichiren Buddhist Hokekyōji in Honolulu, the Jōdo Buddhist Haleiwa Kyōkaidō and Hawi Kyōkaidō, and the Sōtō Zen Buddhist Kona Daifukuji, the Sōtō Mission of Aiei Taiheiji, Hilo Mission Hakuhōzan Taishōji, and Waiahole Tōmonji. See Ikenaga, "Honolulu Myōhōji," 2, 36; Kinoshita, *Us, Hawai'i -Born Japanese*, 179; and Hawaii Sōtōshū Kaikyō Sōkanbu, *Sōtōshū Hawaii*, 103.

44. Hawaii Sōtōshū Kaikyō Sōkanbu [Hawaii Soto Mission Bishop's Office], ed. *Gokurosama (Thank you very much for your hard work)* (Honolulu: Hawaii Soto Mission Bishop's Office, 2005), 132–133.

45. For a discussion of the takeover of about half of all public parks by the military to build storage depots or other structures needed by the military, see Brown, *Hawaii Goes to War,* 69. Ultimately the Army alone controlled a third of the island of Oahu.

46. Okihiro, *Cane Fires,* 230.

47. The woman who chased the soldier away was Hisako Sakamoto. Hunter, *Buddhism in Hawaii,* 187.

48. Senchū Murano, "Hawaii Nichirenshū hachijūnen no ayumi," [The Eighty-Year Path of Nichiren Buddhism in Hawai'i] in *Hawaii Nichirenshū hachijushūnen no ayumi: A History of Nichiren Buddhism in Hawaii* (Honolulu: Nichiren Mission of Hawaii, 1982), 45–47. After its head priest was interned, a nun took care of the temple with its Buddha's relics inside.

49. Okihiro, *Cane Fires,* 214–216, 221.

50. Kōetsu Morita was the Zen priest. See Kōetsu Morita, "Internment Camp Buddhism: Memoirs of Rev. Koetsu Morita," *Turning Wheel: The Journal of Socially Engaged Buddhism* (Fall 2000), 26.

51. Soga, *Life Behind Barbed Wire,* 36.

52. On Eifler and Sand Island, see Kotani, *The Japanese in Hawaii,* 92.

53. The initial group included four priests (the leader, Ōi of the Nichiren sect, Morita of Sōtō Zen, Kuroda of Higashi Honganji, Masaki of Jōdo), along with two laymen. Kotani, *The Japanese in Hawaii,* 92.

54. On Kubokawa, see Furuya, *An Internment Odyssey,* 32; Soga, *Life Behind Barbed Wire,* 38.

55. On the Sand Island vegetable garden, see Furuya, *An Internment Odyssey*, 32; Morita, "Internment Camp Buddhism," 26.

56. Soga recalls that this "spoon incident" occurred around February 15, 1942. See Soga, *Life Behind Barbed Wire*, 44.

57. Okihiro, *Cane Fires*, 216–217, 309. Three accounts by detainees of this incident include Furuya, *An Internment Odyssey*, 17–18; Honda, *Family Torn Apart*, 21; and Soga, *Life Behind Barbed Wire*, 31.

58. Furuya, *An Internment Odyssey*, 18.

59. Marumoto was the rare exception of a prominent Buddhist community leader who remained at liberty after Pearl Harbor. As a young man, he had to wake up at 5 AM to wash up before sitting with his father in front of his home's Buddhist altar to chant sutras to start the day. In 1930, Marumoto gained some renown as the first Asian-American graduate of Harvard Law School, where his education costs were partially funded by the efforts of Nishi Hongwanji Bishop Yemyō Imamura. Marumoto was also a strong advocate on behalf of Japanese-language schools, including the Kona Hongwanji Japanese School that he attended. But Marumoto was a rare Buddhist who had the respect of people in the US government, and had even testified at the 1937 Congressional Hearings for Hawai'i statehood. Most attribute his non-incarceration to his relationship with the FBI's Robert Shivers, the head of the FBI's Honolulu office. He met Shivers in May 1940, soon after the FBI office opened, at a function on the new Japanese luxury liner *Nitta Maru* and quickly established a close personal relationship. Marumoto's wife, Shigeko, a Japanese-language school instructor at two Buddhist-run schools, also became friends with Shivers's wife, Corinne, and with the family of Colonel Morrill Marston, assistant chief of staff for military intelligence in Hawai'i. These connections with Shivers paid off for Marumoto. He became Shivers's main conduit to the Japanese community in Honolulu, and introduced him to other leading nisei who would serve as advisers during the war years. After Pearl Harbor, Marumoto was even invited to serve as a member of the Emergency Service Committee (ESC), a subsection of the Morale Section of the Military Government of Hawai'i, in February 1942, which he did for the subsequent fifteen months. For more on Marumoto, see Furuya, *An Internment Odyssey*, 33; and Ogawa, *Kodomo no tame ni*, 11–16, 41–51, 69–88. Beyond Marumoto, Shivers had six nisei advisers in his inner group initially. One of them, Masatoshi Katagiri, came from a devout Jōdo Buddhist family (his parents were active members of the Hale'iwa Jōdo Mission), but during his college years, he become very involved with the Christian YMCA. See Tom Coffman, *How Hawai'i Changed America: The Campaign for Equal Treatment of*

Japanese Americans in the War Against Japan (Honolulu: EpiCenter, 2014), 189–190, 195.

60. Ogawa, *Kodomo no tame ni*, 81–85.

61. Furuya, *An Internment Odyssey*, 11.

62. Furuya, *An Internment Odyssey*, 30; Soga, *Life Behind Barbed Wire*, 31.

63. Soga, *Life Behind Barbed Wire*, 41.

64. Ibid., 37. Although the detainees at Sand Island increasingly found ways to communicate with each other as camp rules eased over time, they were prohibited from interacting with either the roughly fifty Japanese POWs or the roughly eighty German and Italian detainees picked up in the early days of the war. Curiously, the only exception was the Buddhist priest mentioned above, Rev. Jōsen Deme, who after spending several months with the Japanese detainees, was suddenly transferred to the Immigration Office in Honolulu and placed with German detainees; authorities mistakenly believed "Deme" was a German name and assumed his first name was actually "Josef." He would eventually end up in the continental US camps, experiencing great difficulty living among Germans, unable to understand German. Eventually he was reunited with his fellow Japanese Buddhists in Santa Fe. Also see Furuya, *An Internment Odyssey*, 18.

65. The translation is mine. Jōdoshū Kaigai Kaikyō no Ayumi Henshū Iinkai [Editorial Committee for the History of Overseas Jōdoshū Missions], ed. *Jōdoshū kaigai kaikyō no ayumi* [A History of Overseas Jōdoshū Missions] (Tokyo: Jōdoshū Kaikyō Shinkō Kyōkai, 1990), 200–201.

66. Hull asked the Japanese to do the same with regard to civilian detainees. The Axis powers eventually agreed, despite Japan's not having ratified the original convention. The original Geneva Convention, Geneva I (1864), resulted in a treaty to protect wounded and sick on land; Geneva II (1906) drew up rules for those wounded and sick at sea and shipwrecked; Geneva III (1929 / 1949) created rules for prisoners of war, which during World War II extended to civilian internees; and Geneva IV (1949) resulted in protections for civilians. Louis Fiset, *Imprisoned Apart: The World War II Correspondence of an Issei Couple* (Seattle: University of Washington Press, 1997), 43.

67. Kashima discusses Class I and II categories of Geneva Convention regulations around required labor versus voluntary or paid labor. Kashima, *Judgment without Trial*, 197.

68. Among the other stipulations, according to historian Louis Fiset, were "guarantees of food, hygiene, healthfulness, and medical treatment for all those needing it . . . access to authorities, including local camp administration, international relief societies, and their own governments via neutral

countries representing their interests." In the case of the interned Japanese in the United States, the consul general of Spain in Washington, DC was charged with looking after the rights of the Japanese detainees, who would often send requests to his office. Fiset, *Imprisoned Apart*, 43.

69. Regarding Geneva Convention violations of forced labor, this continued to be an issue for the continental US camps, as well. In one incident, internees at Camp Livingston refused to clear a forest area for a US military airfield, and lodged a formal complaint that using their labor to assist American military efforts was in violation of the Geneva Convention. Furuya, *An Internment Odyssey*, 112.

70. Honda, *Family Torn Apart*, 44.

71. Rev. Chikai Odate was released temporarily from the Kalaheo Stockade on Kauai to officiate at the funeral. Soga, *Life Behind Barbed Wire*, 59–60; Okihiro, *Cane Fires*, 218.

72. Kashima, *Judgment without Trial*, 106.

73. Soga, *Life Behind Barbed Wire*, 226. Among these detainees, a sizeable group was later transferred to the WRA camps and even later to the DOJ-run Crystal City Alien Enemy Detention Facility in Texas.

74. Nishigaya and Oshiro, "Reviving the Lotus," 180.

75. The drum was discovered in February 2017 by Naofumi Annaka, a Risshō University researcher of Nichiren Buddhism in the Americas. Rev. Komagata's name is inscribed on the drum along with three other internees as celebrants of the August 15, 1944 Obon service at Honouliuli. The drum had originally been donated to the Nichiren Mission of Hawaii in 1921 by Masao Sakamoto. In 2018, the bishop of the Nichiren Mission of Hawaii, Chishin Hirai, speculated that a relative of Sakamoto might have taken the drum from the temple to give to then Nichiren Bishop Kanryū Mochizuki in Sand Island so that he could maintain some semblance of Buddhist practice—and that Mochizuki in turn might have asked the Sōtō Zen Bishop Komagata to safeguard the drum for him when he was selected for transfer to the continental United States. Chishin Hirai (bishop, Nichiren Mission of Hawaii), in discussion with the author, January 13, 2018). Hirai elaborates in an unpublished paper: Chishin Hirai, "Hawaii Nichirenshū betsuin to Honouliuli kankinsho" [The Nichiren Buddhist Mission and the Honouliuli Internment Camp] (2018).

76. Zenkyō Komagata had been brought into the Immigration Station briefly during the initial wave of detentions and then released before his re-internment at Honouliuli. Bishop Komagata was thought to be a threat to national security because of his prewar service as a Buddhist chaplain for the Japanese Imperial Army in China. He viewed his incarceration in the

Hawaiian detention camp as an opportunity to continue and further his Buddhist practice, volunteering to clean the camp toilets, symbolic of his daily Zen practice of cleansing his heart. Soga, *Life Behind Barbed Wire*, 180–181.

77. For the list of the Buddhist priests in this category, see this book's website: www.americansutra.com/.

78. The only Buddhist priest on the Big Island not interned, Rev. Zenyū Aoki of the Hilo Hongwanji Betsuin, had become friendly with a chief agent of the FBI on a voyage from the continent to Hawai'i in August 1941, who then vouched for him. Kiyoshi Matsukama, "A Minister Survives World War II in Hilo: Reverend Zenyu Aoki," in *Hilo Hongwanji: Recalling Our Past: A Collection of Oral Histories*, ed. Nobuko Fukuda, Midori Kondo, Motoe Tada, and Lillie Tsuchiya (Honolulu: Honpa Hongwanji Hilo Betsuin, 1997), 31–32. Another theory on why he was not arrested was that he had come to Hilo from Canada just before the outbreak of the war and records documenting his status as a Buddhist priest were not available. Furuya, *An Internment Odyssey*, 39. Rev. Reichi Mohri of the Los Angeles Honpa Hongwanji Betsuin temple was able to slip through the dragnet because he used a different spelling of his Japanese name (Mohri) than what was on the custodial detention list (Mori). Others avoided the initial selective incarceration for reasons unknown. On Rev. Mohri's non-arrest, see Masuyama, *Memories*, 13; Mary Nakamura, *White Road of Thorns: Journalist's Diary—Trials and Tribulations of the Japanese American Internment during World War II* (n.p.: Xlibris, 2015), 64.

79. For Shinto priests, I am including those affiliated with the new religions associated with "sect Shinto" such as Konkokyō and Tenrikyō (Seichō no Ie affiliation more generally treated by US authorities as if they were Shinto-related, as well). Breaking down the Army and DOJ arrests, there were 170 Buddhist priests (out of 231 total priests who were incarcerated), 44 Shinto priests (out of 44 total priests), and 27 Christian ministers (out of 160 total ministers).

80. Suikei Furuya, for example, expressed surprise upon learning that the elderly Christian minister Rev. Shuntarō Ikezawa, a voluntary consular agent (*toritsuginin*), had been detained. He was "arrested when he went to see Vice Consul Otojiro Okuda, his close friend, who had been under house arrest at the time." Furuya, *An Internment Odyssey*, 16. The Christian Rev. Takie Okumura is a good example of an influential issei leader who was not detained. Known for his prewar movement to "Americanize and Christianize" the Japanese, he was perhaps not arrested, a number of scholars have suggested, because he (along with his son, Umetarō) had been working as a

secret informant for the ONI in a relationship that may have begun as early as 1918. FBI reports dating back to 1923 praise Okumura as a "consistent worker among the Japanese for Americanization and Christianization." Masayu Duus, *Unlikely Liberators: The Men of the 100th and 442nd* (Honolulu: University of Hawai'i Press, 1987), 295. By 1938, Okumura was working closely with US military intelligence in the surveillance of Japanese Buddhists; he informed the agencies, for example, that Nishi Hongwanji Bishop Gikyō Kuchiba was a threat to American national security. After Pearl Harbor and the imposition of martial law, Okumura would continue to work closely with Captain Wales and Lieutenant General Emmons to alert them to those who, in his view, presented a threat. Hunter, *Buddhism in Hawaii*, 179; Tomoe Moriya, "Buddhism at the Crossroads of the Pacific: Imamura Yemyō and Buddhist Social Ethics," in *Hawai'i at the Crossroads of the US and Japan before the Pacific War,* ed. Jon Thares Davidann (Honolulu: University of Hawai'i Press, 2008), 197; Fusa Nakagawa, *From Tosa to Hawaii: The Footsteps of Takie Okumura* (Kōchi, Japan: Takie Okumura and the Japanese Hawaiians Exhibition Committee, 2000), 118–120.

81. Rev. Shinpei Gotō, a Christian minister from Windward Oahu, for instance, was released from Sand Island on Christmas Day (December 25, 1941). Furuya, *An Internment Odyssey,* 18, 37.

3. JAPANESE AMERICA UNDER SIEGE

1. Bunyū Fujimura, *Though I Be Crushed: The Wartime Experiences of a Buddhist Minister* (Los Angeles: The Nembutsu Press, 1995), 45–46.

2. Fujimura was released from the DOJ camp into the WRA Poston camp in 1944.

3. Revs. Kōyo Tamanaha and Hōshin Fujikado were also arrested on the same day as Fujimura. A facsimile of the news article is included in Fujimura, *Though I Be Crushed,* 53.

4. Ibid., 52.

5. Laurence Davis, "West Coast Widens Martial Law Call," *New York Times,* February 12, 1942.

6. As cited and accompanied by a facsimile of the article in Fujimura, *Though I Be Crushed,* 53.

7. Ibid., 57–58.

8. Ibid., 55–56. Another question from the FBI included: "You are Reverend Tamanaha's superior even though he is older than you. Why is that?" Rev. Fujimura answered, "Do you mean to tell me that no one working in Washington DC is older than President Roosevelt?" To these somewhat

cheeky replies, the FBI agent in charge shouted, "I am the one who is questioning you. There is no need for you to ask me questions!"

9. Quoted in Brian Niiya, ed. *Japanese American History: An A to Z Reference from 1868 to the Present* (New York: Infobase Publishing / Facts on File, 1993), 12.

10. Quoted in Eileen Sunada Sarasohn, *The Issei: Portrait of a Pioneer, An Oral History* (Palo Alto, CA: Pacific Books / Issei Oral History Project, 1983), 155.

11. Prominent issei Christian leaders like Dr. Kikuwo Tashiro, medical doctor and member of the Gardena Baptist Church, would be overlooked, while Rev. Hohri, who had served in the Methodist Church prior to the war, was told at his parole hearing in Fort Missoula after his arrest, that "his membership in the Veteran's Association above referred to, and the fact of his trip to Japan, Korea, and Manchuria in 1940, makes him potentially more dangerous than if he were a farmer, a storekeeper, or the like." William Minoru Hohri, "A Parable," in *Triumphs of Faith: Stories of Japanese American Christians during WWII*, ed. Victor N. Okada (Los Angeles: Japanese-American Internment Project, 1998), 28.

12. Daisuke Kitagawa, *Issei and Nisei: The Internment Years* (New York: Seabury Press, 1967), 5, 41. Kitagawa reported that he "even paid a visit to the FBI office, simply to let them know that I was available as an interpreter in cases where they might encounter language difficulties. Subsequently I did assist in that capacity on several occasions." Quoted in Stan Flewelling, *Shirakawa: Stories from a Pacific Northwest Japanese American Community* (Auburn, WA: White River Valley Museum, 2002), 172.

13. On some of the differences between Oahu and the outer islands or between Hawai'i and the continent in terms of arrest squads, see Tetsuden Kashima, *Judgment without Trial: Japanese American Imprisonment during World War II* (Seattle: University of Washington Press, 2003), 71. There were also rare cases of Buddhists who also managed to evade arrest because of friendships with influential white businessmen or government officials. In San Diego, a teacher at a Buddhist-temple-affiliated school was not arrested because her husband's "Caucasian business friends spoke up" and vouched for the family. See Kay Keiko Murakami, "I Remember . . . and Give Thanks," in *Triumphs of Faith: Stories of Japanese American Christians During WWII*, ed. Victor N. Okada (Los Angeles: Japanese-American Internment Project, 1998), 81.

14. Sarasohn, *The Issei*, 178.

15. Ibid., 184–185.

16. On the US continent, they included the minister Jingorō Kokubun (who ran two Japanese-language schools in California's Imperial Valley) and

Fuki Kuida's mother, who was imprisoned at the Terminal Island Prison for Women. Kei Kokubun, "Trusting God," in *Triumphs of Faith: Stories of Japanese American Christians During WWII*, ed. Victor N. Okada (Los Angeles: Japanese-American Internment Project, 1998), 67–68.

17. The language school teacher was Hanako Sano; as recalled by her daughter, Pat Aiko Amino. See Japanese American Historical Society, ed. *REgenerations Oral History Project: Rebuilding Japanese American Families, Communities, and Civil Rights in the Resettlement Era* (Los Angeles: Japanese American Historical Society, 2000), 10.

18. Klancy Clark De Nevers, *The Colonel and the Pacifist: Karl R. Bendetsen, Perry H. Saito, and the Incarceration of Japanese Americans During World War II* (Salt Lake City, UT: University of Utah Press, 2004), 147–150, 173. Even the handful of Christian ministers who weren't paroled immediately, such as Rev. Daisuke Hohri, found that their Christian affiliation engendered considerable sympathy. During his Enemy Alien Hearing Board discussions, Rev. Hohri's membership in the Japanese military's Veteran's Association and his 1940 trip to Japan, Korea, and Manchuria, were said to mark his "pro-Japanese" tendencies. Further, his leadership position in the community might make him "potentially more dangerous than if he were a farmer, a storekeeper, or the like." But the hearing board members were sympathetic to him, stating in their report that "the subject is a preacher and it is a hardship to deprive his church of its minister." Rev. Hohri was released in just a few months from internment and paroled to join his family in the WRA Manzanar camp, unlike most of his Buddhist counterparts, who would typically spend over a year interned in an Army or DOJ camp before being allowed to rejoin their families in one of the mass incarceration camps. Hohri, "A Parable," 28; Densho Encyclopedia, "William Hohri," entry, http://encyclopedia.densho.org/William_Hohri/. Other well-known Christian ministers paroled from the Santa Fe DOJ camp included Rev. Hisanori Kano and Rev. Takeshi Ban, while Rev. Paul Osumi, who had served the Lihue Christian Church, was released relatively swiftly from the Army's Lordsburg camp. For the process of Rev. Osumi's release and the supporting letter from his Christian colleagues, see Norman H. Osumi, *Today's Thought: Rev. Paul Osumi—The Man and His Message* (Honolulu: Legacy Isle Publishing, 2013), 43–59.

19. Herbert V. Nicholson and Margaret Wilke, *Comfort All Who Mourn: The Life Story of Herbert and Madeline Nicholson* (Fresno, CA: Bookmarks International, 1982), 83.

20. Salem Leadership Foundation, "Japanese Community Church and the Japanese Community in Salem," July 17, 2017, https://www.salemlf.org/2017/07/17/japanese-community/.

21. Takashi Tsujita and Karen Nolan, *Omo i de: Memories of Vacaville's Lost Japanese Community* (Vacaville, CA: Vacaville Museum, 2001), 98.

22. Kenjitsu Nakagaki, *Manji to hakenkreuz* [The Manji and the Hakenkreuz] (Tokyo: Gendai Shokan, 2013).

23. On the Washington state cases, see Michael Masatsugu, *Reorienting the Pure Land: Japanese Americans, the Beats, and the Making of American Buddhism, 1941–1966* (PhD diss., University of California, Irvine, 2004), 41, 44–45.

24. San Diego Buddhist Temple, ed. *Kansha in Gassho: Fiftieth Anniversary, San Diego Buddhist Temple, 1926–1976* (San Diego, CA: San Diego Buddhist Temple, 1976), 35.

25. Flewelling, *Shirakawa*, 184–185.

26. Ron Magden, *Mukashi Mukashi Long Long Ago: The First Century of the Seattle Buddhist Church* (Seattle: Seattle Buddhist Church, 2012), 117.

27. Louis Fiset, *Camp Harmony: Seattle's Japanese Americans and the Puyallup Assembly Center* (Urbana, IL: University of Illinois Press 2009), 35; Magden, *Mukashi Mukashi*, 120.

28. Magden, *Mukashi Mukashi*, 120.

29. The American-born priest was Rev. Ryōshō Sogabe. See Kōno Kawashima, *Kōyasan beikoku betsuin gojushūnenshi: Koyasan Buddhist Temple, 1912–1962* (Los Angeles: Kōyasan Beikoku Betsuin, 1962), 176–179; Eiko Irene Masuyama, *Memories: The Buddhist Church Experience in the Camps, 1942–1945* (Sacramento: California Civil Liberties Public Education Program, 2007), 102.

30. Tetsuden Kashima, *Buddhism in America: The Social Organization of an Ethnic Religious Institution* (Westport, CT: Greenwood Press, 1977), 49.

31. See Kenryō Kumata to Naval Intelligence, January 15, 1942, BCA Archives Collection, Japanese American National Museum (JANM); also see Masatsugu, *Reorienting the Pure Land*, 22.

32. The Catholic priest Father Hugh Lavery, associated with the Maryknoll mission in Los Angeles, reportedly "baptized more Japanese people in early 1942 than in each of the previous years," but this hardly signaled the disbanding of the Buddhist sangha. See Yuki Yamazaki, "St. Francis Xavier School: Acculturation and Enculturation of Japanese Americans in Los Angeles, 1921–1945," *US Catholic Historian* 18:1 (2000), 64.

33. Kenryō Kumata, "Serve in Silence,'" bulletin, March 5, 1942, BCA Archives Collection, JANM; reprinted in Masuyama, *Memories*, 5.

34. Kenryō Kumata, "Cooperate in the Defense of the United States of America," bulletin, December 19, 1941, BCA Archives Collection, JANM; Kenryō Kumata, "A United America in Action" bulletin, December 23, 1941,

BCA Archives Collection, JANM. Also see Masatsugu, *Reorienting the Pure Land,* 25–26.

35. The Oakland Buddhist Church letter is in the collection of Rev. Tetsurō Kashima and is quoted in Kashima, *Buddhism in America,* 49.

36. Quoted in Masatsugu, *Reorienting the Pure Land,* 39–40. In Honolulu, the Women's Association of Honolulu's Shinshū Kyōkai Temple sponsored a Red Cross bandage-folding program. Yoshiko Tatsuguchi and Lois A. Suzuki, *Shinshu Kyokai Mission of Hawaii, 1914–1984: A Legacy of Seventy Years* (Honolulu: Shinshu Kyokai Mission of Hawaii, 1985), 60.

37. Masatsugu, *Reorienting the Pure Land,* 44.

38. Ibid., 27.

39. Ibid., 37–38.

40. Douglas Dye, *The Soul of the City: The Work of the Seattle Council of Churches during WWII* (PhD diss., Washington State University, 1997), 114 and Louis Fiset, *Imprisoned Apart: The World War II Correspondence of an Issei Couple* (Seattle: University of Washington Press, 1997), 34.

41. Sarah M. Griffith, *The Fight for Asian American Civil Rights: Liberal Protestant Activism* (Urbana, IL: University of Illinois Press, 2018), 108.

42. Fiset, *Imprisoned Apart,* 34.

43. Life Magazine, "How to Tell Japs from the Chinese" *Life,* December 22, 1941: 81–82.

44. Carol Van Valkenburg, *An Alien Place: The Fort Missoula Montana Detention Camp 1941–1944* (Missoula, MT: Pictorial Histories Publishing, 1995), 44.

45. Hyung-ju Ahn, *Between Two Adversaries: Korean Interpreters at Japanese Alien Enemy Detention Centers during World War II* (Fullerton, CA: Oral History Program, California State University, Fullerton, 2002), 2.

46. The sociologist Andrew Lind reported that on the Hawaiian Islands, policemen and social workers of Japanese ancestry were met with remarks like, "I'm a Filipino. My country was invaded by you Japs. I want to kill you, you Jap" or "I'll choke all the Japs I meet like this." Andrew W. Lind, *Hawaii's Japanese: An Experiment in Democracy* (Princeton: Princeton University Press, 1946), 58.

47. Sarasohn, *The Issei,* 160.

48. Tamotsu Shibutani, *The Derelicts of Company K: A Sociological Study of Demoralization* (Berkeley, CA: University of California Press, 1978), 42.

49. Fujimura, *Though I Be Crushed,* 49.

50. Matthew Estes and Donald Estes, "Further and Further Away: The Relocation of San Diego's Nikkei Community, 1942," *The Journal of San Diego History* 39:1–2, 1–31.

51. Fujimura, *Though I Be Crushed*, 53–54.

52. The Tana diaries were written in Japanese and, as edited and published after his death, run to about 1,600 pages. I thank Akira Tana for originally sending me a copy of the four-volume printed edition published in Japan: Daishō Tana, *Santa Fe Lordsburg senji tekikokujin yokuryūjo nikki* [The Wartime Internment Diaries of an Enemy Alien in Santa Fe and Lordsburg], Vols 1–4 (Tokyo: Sankibō Busshōrin, 1976–1989). By chance, Akira Tana was also a student of Professor Masatoshi Nagatomi at Harvard. Over the past decade or so, I have translated for the Tana family a decent portion of the diary, focusing on days when major events occurred or entries where the diarist reflected on Buddhist life in camp. Only a few scholars have employed this diary as a resource—among them, Michihiro Ama. See Michihiro Ama, "The Transnational Development of Japanese Buddhism During the Postwar Period: The Case of Tana Daishō," *Pacific World: Journal of the Institute of Buddhist Studies* (Third Series) 14 (2013), 1–26; and Michihiro Ama, "A Neglected Diary, A Forgotten Buddhist Couple: Tana Daishō's Internment Camp Diary as a Historical and Literary Text," *Journal of Global Buddhism* 14 (2014), 45–62. Tana's diary and other Japanese-language letters, memoirs, and oral histories—many presented and translated for the first time in this book—are critical to telling a more complex and comprehensive story of America. Yuji Ichioka first emphasized the need for Japanese American studies, especially "internment studies," to incorporate Japanese-language materials written by issei and kibei. Yuji Ichioka, "A Historian by Happenstance," *Amerasia Journal* 26:1 (2000), 46, 50–52.

53. Diary entry from February 24, 1942 of Tana, *Santa Fe Lordsburg*, 88.

54. Thomas Ken Walls, *The Japanese Texans* (San Antonio, TX: Institute of Texan Cultures, University of Texas, 1987), 151–152.

55. Tsujita and Nolan, *Omo i de*, 101.

56. According to Lothrop, these policies affected the lives of 38,171 Japanese, 52,008 Italians, and 19,417 German nationals. Gloria Ricci Lothrop, "Unwelcome in Freedom's Land: The Impact of World War II on Italian Aliens in Southern California," *Southern California Quarterly* 81:4 (1999), 508.

57. Tsujita and Nolan, *Omo i de*, 105–106.

58. Ibid., 106.

59. DeWitt's Public Proclamation No. 3, issued on March 24, 1942, extended restrictions that had applied only to noncitizens to "all persons of Japanese ancestry." Two Christian nisei—Gordon Hirabayashi and Minoru Yasui—deliberately violated the curfew and questioned its legality as applied to American citizens. Yasui went to a police station in Portland to turn

himself in. Hirabayashi grew up in the so-called Mukyōkai (non-church) movement and, as a college student, was a leader in the University of Washington YMCA chapter. Hirabayashi not only violated the curfew numerous times as a volunteer for the American Friends Service Committee (AFSC), he also turned himself into the Seattle office of the FBI when his turn to "evacuate" came, refusing to register for what he believed was an undemocratic order. He was one of only a few among the roughly 110,000 "evacuated" from the west coast who refused to register. Hirabayashi explicitly cited his refusal as an act of Christian conscience. Yasui's and Hirabayashi's challenges to the various restrictions both ultimately ended up in the US Supreme Court. In the cases *Hirabayashi* v. *United States* and *Yasui* v. *United States,* the justices sided with the government. For more on the Hirabayashi and Yasui cases, see Anne Blankenship, *Christianity, Social Justice, and Japanese American Incarceration during World War II* (Chapel Hill, NC: University of North Carolina Press, 2016), 22–24; Sidney Fine, "Mr. Justice Murphy and the Hirabayashi Case," *Pacific Historical Review* 33 (1964): 195–209; Arval Morris, "Justice, War, and the Japanese-American Evacuation and Internment," *Washington Law Review* 59 (1984): 843–862; and Jacobus Ten Broek, "Wartime Power of the Military Over Citizen Civilians Within the Country," *California Law Review* 41 (1953): 109–175.

60. Japanese American Historical Society, *REgenerations,* 391.

61. Fiset, *Imprisoned Apart,* 33.

62. Fujimura, *Though I Be Crushed,* 46.

63. Lauren Kessler, "On the Home Front: When the Shadow of WWII Fell on Portland's Japanese Americans, Reed Remained a Ray of Light," *Reed Magazine* 78:5 (1999), 6.

64. US Congress House Select Committee Investigating National Defense Migration, 77th Cong., 2nd sess. *National Defense Migration* [Tolan Committee Report]. (Washington, DC: US Government Printing Office, 1942), 11,042.

65. Cited in Roger Daniels, *Concentration Camps U.S.A.: Japanese Americans and World War II* (New York: Holt, Rinehart & Winston, 1971), 28; and Michi Weglyn, *Years of Infamy: The Untold Story of America's Concentration Camps* (Seattle: University of Washington Press, 1996), 55.

66. One line of scholarship argues that the mass incarceration can be best understood as an attempt by the US government to secure a "hostage barter reserve" for prisoner exchange or as a bargaining chip for potential future negotiations regarding the treatment and release of Americans rounded up by the Japanese government. This idea is certainly consistent with both Patton's plan mentioned earlier and Dingell's memo to Roosevelt. For

example, see Brian Hayashi, *Democratizing the Enemy: The Japanese American Internment* (Princeton: Princeton University Press, 2004), 83–84; Weglyn, *Years of Infamy*, 54–66.

67. Munson concluded that he did not believe that the Japanese "would be any more disloyal than any other group in the United States with whom we went to war." For more on the Munson Report, see Daniels, *Concentration Camps U.S.A.*, 28; Greg Robinson, *By Order of the President: FDR and the Internment of Japanese Americans* (Cambridge, MA: Harvard University Press, 2001), 65–71; Greg Robinson, *A Tragedy of Democracy: Japanese Confinement in North America* (New York: Columbia University Press, 2009), 55–56; Weglyn, *Years of Infamy*, 33–53.

68. Three days after Pearl Harbor, the US Army Chief of Staff George C. Marshall, Jr. declared the west coast a "theater of operations." Daniels, *Concentration Camps U.S.A.*, 39–40; Robinson, *A Tragedy of Democracy*, 69.

69. Quoted in Daniels, *Concentration Camps U.S.A.*, 40.

70. Ibid., 44–45.

71. For these detailed studies of the processes that made possible the mass incarceration and EO9066, see Daniels, *Concentration Camps U.S.A.*; Robinson, *By Order of the President*.

72. Daniels, *Concentration Camps U.S.A.*, 49–50; Robinson, *By Order of the President*, 95–96.

73. Daniels, *Concentration Camps U.S.A.*, 50.

74. Ibid.

75. A small number of Germans and Italians—as of July 1, 1943, only 268 people (including 76 from the Eastern Defense Command)—were "excluded." Most of these "enemy aliens" were Germans, many of them naturalized American citizens. Arnold Krammer, *Undue Process, The Untold Story of America's German Alien Internees* (Lanham, MD: Rowman & Littlefield, 1997), 61, 67.

76. Daniels, *Concentration Camps U.S.A.*, 54. Two memos from Attorney General Francis Biddle to President Roosevelt clarified these matters. One, dated February 20, 1942, states: "The order is not limited to aliens but includes citizens so that it can be exercised with respect to Japanese, irrespective of their citizenship." (Memorandum, Letter from Biddle to President; OF 4805, FDR Library) The other, crafted on April 17, 1943, states: "You signed the original executive order permitting the exclusion so the army could handle the Japs. It was never intended to apply to Italians and Germans" (Memorandum, Letter from Biddle to President; OF 10, 1943, FDR Library).

77. More fully, DeWitt wrote: "In the war in which we are now engaged racial affinities are not severed by migration. The Japanese race is an enemy

race, and while many second and third generation Japanese born on United States soil, possessed of United States citizenship, have become 'Americanized,' the racial strains are undiluted. . . . It, therefore, follows that along the vital Pacific Coast over 112,000 potential enemies, of Japanese extraction, are at large today." United States Congress, Japanese Evacuation from the West Coast, 1942: Final Report, by John L. DeWitt (Congressional Document, Washington: US Government Printing Office, 1943), 34. For discussion, see Fine, "Mr. Justice Murphy," 200.

78. DeWitt uttered these words about a year later, in response to a congressional committee's questions. Testimony before House Naval Affairs Subcommittee, April 13, 1943. NARS. RG 338 (CWRIC 1725–1728). For context, see Commission on Wartime Relocation and Internment of Civilians, *Personal Justice Denied: Report of the Commission on Wartime Relocation and Internment of Civilians* (Seattle: University of Washington Press / The Civil Liberties Public Education Fund, 1997), 65–66.

79. Quoted in Daniels, *Concentration Camps U.S.A.*, 62.

80. Ibid., 70.

81. Ibid., 62.

82. Quoted in Robinson, *By Order of the President,* 91. Robinson notes that Roosevelt "paid close attention" to these types of letters from the west coast, to "[track] public opinion," although there is no evidence that he read this particular letter. Ibid., 93.

83. Daniels, *Concentration Camps U.S.A.*, 65–67; Robinson, *A Tragedy of Democracy,* 89.

84. Robinson, *By Order of the President,* 106.

85. Ibid., 112–124. This negative view came despite personal connections to and even admiration for a handful of Japanese individuals, including those he had met while a student at Harvard and during his service in the US Navy. Robinson suggests that Roosevelt did not "share popular racist views of Asians as innately menacing or uncivilized. Still, despite his friendships with Japanese and his genuine interest in Japanese culture, Roosevelt adopted an increasingly wary position toward Japanese power during the first decade of the twentieth century." Ibid., 11. By 1936, Roosevelt had contemplated the supposed danger of the Japanese American community in case of war with Japan and had read reports produced by military intelligence that worried about an attack on Oahu by the Japanese Navy. Roosevelt's comment on one such report was that, "every Japanese citizen or non-citizen on the island of Oahu who meets these Japanese ships should be secretly but definitively identified and his or her name placed on a special list

of those who would be the first to be placed in a concentration camp in the event of trouble." Quoted in Ibid., 57.

86. Roger Daniels, *The Decision to Relocate the Japanese Americans* (Malabar, FL: Robert E. Krieger Publishing Co., 1990), 23.

87. Stephen Fox, "The Relocation of Italian Americans in California during World War II," in *Una Storia Segreta: The Secret History of Italian American Evacuation and Internment during World War II*, ed. Lawrence DiStasi (Berkeley, CA: Heyday Books, 2001), 43.

88. On the Terminal Island removal of persons of Japanese heritage, see Naomi Hirahara and Geraldine Knatz, *Terminal Island: Lost Communities of Los Angeles Harbor* (Santa Monica, CA: Angel City Press, 2015), 246–254; Robinson, *By Order of the President*, 106–107; Robinson, *A Tragedy of Democracy*, 89.

89. Kawashima, *Kōyasan beikoku*, 176–179.

90. Naofumi Annaka, "Senjika Amerika ni okeru Nichirenshū no tenkai [Developments in North American Nichiren Buddhism during the Pacific War]," *Indogaku bukkyōgaku kenkyū* 63:2 (2015), 109.

91. Hirahara and Knatz, *Terminal Island*, 265; Shizue Seigel, *In Good Conscience: Supporting Japanese Americans during the Internment* (San Mateo, CA: AACP Inc. and Kansha Project, 2006), 257; Tsukasa Sugimura, *Quiet Heroes: A Century of Quakers' Love and Help for the Japanese and Japanese-Americans* (n.p.: Intentional Productions, 2014), 120.

92. From the occasional newsletter of the Los Angeles Hongwanji Betsuin temple, "Stories from the Past: Rev. Julius A. Goldwater," *Betsuin Jihō*, March 1, 1990, 3.

93. The Canadian nisei Rev. Jitsuo Morikawa was also on staff at the Terminal Island Baptist Church.

94. Virginia Swanson and Walter Balderston, "Eviction from Terminal Island," http://ryono.net/terminalisland/eviction1.htm.

95. Julius Goldwater, "Draft of Speech Given at Senshin Buddhist Temple, LA" (undated): 4; BCA Archives, Hisatsune Family Papers (Rev. Julius A. Goldwater); Interview with Ritsu Uyeno Nabeta, San Diego Buddhist Temple (January 26, 2004; Duncan Williams).

96. http://www.nikkeiheritage.org/nh/fvxin1.html.

97. Sugimura, *Quiet Heroes*, 60–61.

98. On the day of Roosevelt's executive order, the American Legion in California adopted a statewide resolution calling for the immediate mass arrest and incarceration of all aliens on the Pacific coast. A few days later, the Los Angeles Council of California Women's Clubs made a similar

recommendation to place them in concentration camps. Similarly, the Young Democratic Club of Los Angeles approved a resolution calling for a mass removal from the Pacific coast, regardless of citizenship. Lothrop, "Unwelcome in Freedom's Land,'" 179; Robinson, *By Order of the President,* 90.

99. Daniels, *Concentration Camps U.S.A.,* 74-75; Robinson, *A Tragedy of Democracy,* 106-107.

100. Krammer, *Undue Process,* 58.

The Tolan committee hearings proved to be critical in the determination that Italian and German American community would not experience the mass incarceration of the Japanese Americans. Fox, "The Relocation of Italian Americans," 45.

101. "Testimony of Hon. Ronald E. Jones, Oregon State Senator, Brooks, Oreg.," Hearings before the Select Committee Investigating National Defense Migration, House of Representatives, Seventy-Seventh Congress (Washington, DC: US Government Printing Office, 1942), 11314, https://archive.org /details/nationaldefensem3ounit. For context, see Morton Grodzins, *Americans Betrayed: Politics and the Japanese Evacuation* (Chicago: University of Chicago Press, 1949), 408.

102. Warren regretted his stance after the war. See http://www.vqronline .org/essay/unacknowledged-lesson-earl-warren-and-japanese-relocation -controversy

103. "Testimony of Hon. Earl Warren," Hearings before the Select Committee Investigating National Defense Migration, House of Representatives, Seventy-Seventh Congress, (Washington, DC: US Government Printing Office, 1942), 11011, 11015, https://archive.org/details/nationaldefensem29unit. For context, see Van Valkenburg, *An Alien Place,* 22.

104. "Testimony of Mayor Harry P. Cain, of Tacoma, Wash.," Hearings before the Select Committee Investigating National Defense Migration, House of Representatives, Seventy-Seventh Congress (Washington, DC: US Government Printing Office, 1942), 11415, https://archive.org/details /nationaldefensem3ounit. For discussion, see Daniels, *Concentration Camps U.S.A.,* 78; Fiset, *Camp Harmony,* 42.

105. "Testimony of Miss Azalia Emma Peet, Methodist Missionary, Gresham, Ore.," Hearings before the Select Committee Investigating National Defense Migration, House of Representatives, Seventy-Seventh Congress (Washington, DC: US Government Printing Office, 1942), 11386, https://archive.org/details/nationaldefensem3ounit. For discussion, see Ellen Eisenberg, "'As Truly American as Your Son': Voicing Opposition to Intern-

ment in Three West Coast Cities," *Oregon Historical Quarterly* 104:4 (Winter 2003), 542–565: 547.

106. "Testimony of Floyd W. Schmoe and Bernard G. Waring, American Friends Service Committee," Hearings before the Select Committee Investigating National Defense Migration, House of Representatives, Seventy-Seventh Congress (Washington, DC: US Government Printing Office, 1942), 11527, https://archive.org/details/nationaldefensem3ounit.

107. "Testimony of Rev. Harold V. Jensen, Representing Seattle Council of Churches," Hearings before the Select Committee Investigating National Defense Migration, House of Representatives, Seventy-Seventh Congress (Washington, DC: US Government Printing Office, 1942), 11564, https://archive.org/details/nationaldefensem3ounit. For discussion, see Blankenship, *Christianity, Social Justice*, 47 and Fiset, *Camp Harmony*, 103. For more other voices of opposition to mass "evacuation" at the Tolan Committee meetings, see Blankenship, *Christianity, Social Justice*, 21–22, 47; Eisenberg, "'As Truly American as Your Son,'" 542–565; Sarah M. Griffith, *The Fight for Asian American Civil Rights: Liberal Protestant Activism* (Urbana, IL: University of Illinois Press, 2018), 110; and Beth Shalom Hessel, "Let the Conscience of Christian America Speak: Religion and Empire in the Incarceration of Japanese Americans, 1941–1945" (PhD diss., Texas Christian University, 2015), 120–127, https://repository.tcu.edu/handle/116099117/8635.

108. Hessel, "Let the Conscience of Christian America Speak," 122.

109. "Testimony of Rev. Frank Herron Smith, in Charge of Methodist Japanese Missions West of the Mississippi River," Hearings before the Select Committee Investigating National Defense Migration, House of Representatives, Seventy-Seventh Congress, (Washington, DC; US Government Printing Office, 1942), 11549, https://archive.org/details/nationaldefensem29unit.

110. Greg Robinson, "Norman Thomas and the Struggle against Japanese Internment," *Prospects: A Journal of American Culture Studies* 29 (2004): 419–434.

111. This was despite Lt. General DeWitt's initial intention to use EO9066 to apply to a number of German and Italian enemy aliens and even one American citizen of Italian heritage, Remo Bosia, managing editor of the pro-fascist newspaper, *L'Italia*. Scherini, "When Italian Americans," 25.

112. Memo, J. Edgar Hoover to Francis Biddle, February 2, 1942, U.S. Commission on Wartime Relocation and Internment of Civilians Papers 4: 138–142; 5: 465–474. Discussed further in Stephen Fox, "General John DeWitt

and the Proposed Internment of German and Italian Aliens during World War II," *Pacific Historical Review* 57:4: 407–438.

113. Memo, Lt Col William A. Boekel to Col Karl R. Bendetsen, May 4, 1942, Western Defense Command-Civil Affairs Division file 014.31: Aliens. For discussion, see Krammer, *Undue Process*, 58.

114. Masuyama, *Memories*, 150. Interview of Rev. Akira Hata, San Diego (January 28, 2004, Duncan Williams).

115. Fiset, *Camp Harmony*, 50; Robert C. Sims, "The "Free Zone' Nikkei: Japanese Americans in Idaho and Eastern Oregon in World War II," in *Nikkei in the Pacific Northwest: Japanese Americans and Japanese Canadians in the Twentieth Century*, ed. Louis Fiset and Gail Nomura (Seattle: University of Washington Press, 2005), 237.

116. Nakamura, *White Road of Thorns*, 83.

117. Ibid.

118. Hessel, "Let the Conscience of Christian America Speak," 130–132.

119. Suzuki, *Ministry in the Assembly*, 112. My thanks to Patricia Biggs for pointing out that the construction company would not hire Japanese Americans because they were not union members.

120. Yamazaki, "St. Francis Xavier School," 64.

121. Blankenship, *Christianity, Social Justice*, 40–41.

122. "83 Workers Leave for Manzanar This Morning to Prepare for Others," *Kashū Mainichi (California Daily News)*, March 21, 1942, 2.

123. Robert J. Maeda, "Isamu Noguchi: 5-7-A, Poston, Arizona," in *Last Witnesses: Reflections on the Wartime Internment of Japanese Americans*, ed. Erica Harth (New York: Palgrave, 2001), 155–157, 164; Robinson, *A Tragedy of Democracy*, 85.

124. Lavery's sermon delivered at Manzanar on March 12, 1943. See Suzuki, *Ministry in the Assembly*, 124. In a separate plan organized by Bishop Walsh as the national head of the Maryknoll community, orders were issued to both Father Lavery in Los Angeles and Father Leopold Tibesar in Seattle to organize and accompany Japanese Catholics to St. Louis, Missouri. This failed, too, but in this case, nearly seven thousand families signed up for the program. Fiset, *Camp Harmony*, 54. Thanks to Anne Blankenship for pointing out the relative success of this program compared to Southern California.

125. Eileen H. Tamura, *In Defense of Justice: Joseph Kurihara and the Japanese American Struggle for Equality* (Urbana, IL: University of Illinois Press, 2013), 52.

126. Kenryō Kumata memo to Buddhist Churches of America, February 9, 1942. Japanese American National Museum (BCA Archive Collection). Also cited in Masatsugu, *Reorienting the Pure Land*, 48. Kenryō Kumata memo to

FBI, San Francisco. February 9, 1942. Japanese American National Museum (BCA Archive Collection).

127. Fiset, *Camp Harmony*, 55.

128. Fiset notes cases of deferments or evasions of the forced removal by individuals with tuberculosis, mumps, or other conditions like advanced stage heart disease. Ibid., 91–92.

129. By August, Military Area No. 2, the rest of California, had also been cleared. Daniels, *Concentration Camps U.S.A.*, 88; Weglyn, *Years of Infamy*, 78.

130. Weglyn, *Years of Infamy*, 76–77.

131. Ann Breed's Diary, April 30, 1942 (Bancroft Library Archives, UC Berkeley). Cited in Sumio Koga, *A Decade of Faith: The Journey of Japanese Christians in the USA (1936–1946)* (New York: Vantage Press, 2002), 38–39.

132. Weglyn, *Years of Infamy*, 77 cites the 80 percent number for goods "privately stored." Historian Greg Robinson describes the evolution of the hastily drawn-up government program to have an alien property custodian (prior to the war under the auspices of US Attorney General Biddle, and after the declaration of war, under Leo Crowley, the director of the Federal Deposit Insurance Corporation) deal with properties of enemy aliens. The issue of Japanese American citizens' property, which did not technically fall under "alien property," muddied the waters as to how the government would deal with the sudden and now mandatory removal of all persons of Japanese heritage from the west coast, and the confusion was multiplied by the various government agencies vying for control of the program. The various agencies ultimately settled on the Federal Reserve Bank in San Francisco to specifically deal with west coast "evacuee property" by opening up offices in areas with concentrations of Japanese Americans to help them dispose of (not care for) properties so as to prevent "fraud, forced sales, and unscrupulous creditors." But these measures were minimal and too late. As Robinson has noted, since the program was voluntary to get around the issue of the government handling Japanese American citizens' property, the Federal Reserve lacked enforcement power and the "bank's representatives were rushed into service, ill-trained and in some cases hostile to the evacuees" which resulted in only one of ten Japanese Americans being able to use the government program. Unable to effectively intervene when the "fire sales" occurred, the government "encouraged forced sales by imposing a deadline for evacuation. . . . the army took no responsibility for the items thus stored, and the Federal Reserve did not insure the warehouses." Robinson, *By Order of the President*, 134–139, 144.

133. Robinson, *By Order of the President*, 84.

134. "A Pair of Suggestions" and "Hongwanji To Help in Storage," *California Daily News*, March 21, 1942, 1–2. For items that Japanese Americans in

Los Angeles could not store, the Nishi Hongwanji Temple's YBA opened and operated a temporary store in Little Tokyo, which offered somewhat better prices than those offered by unscrupulous scavengers who went from house to house. See Honpa Hongwanji Los Angeles Betsuin, ed. *Honpa Hongwanji Los Angeles Betsuin, 1905–1980* (Los Angeles: Honpa Hongwanji Los Angeles Betsuin, 1980), 83. Kōyasan Buddhist Temple's main hall and basement also became a safe house for members' belongings that could not be taken to the Assembly Centers. Temple records note that they "piled up as high as the ceiling in both the hall and basement." With the help of others, the nisei Buddhist priest who remained to take care of the temple "sealed all the windows with wire netting as a burglar-proof measure. He also disconnected the gas, running water, and electricity supply." Kawashima, *Kōyasan beikoku*, 176–179. In San Francisco, the Buddhist temple helped provide storage for equipment used by Grace Fujimoto Oshita's family-run miso-making business. See Sandra Taylor, *Jewel of the Desert: Japanese American Internment at Topaz* (Berkeley, CA: University of California Press, 1993), 51. People also entrusted their rental property or their possessions to Christian neighbors. Sometimes those sympathetic friends proved trustworthy, but in other cases neighbors never returned the items. Some acted to take full possession of businesses, farms, and properties. The tenant farmer Tsuguo Nagasawa, who had converted to Christianity in the prewar period, had an experience so jarring that he returned to the Buddhist faith. The Christian minister who owned Nagasawa's farm forced him to abandon his lease. "I converted from Christianity to Buddhism, and that Christian minister was the reason I converted," he wrote. Sarasohn, *The Issei*, 104.

135. Honpa Hongwanji Los Angeles Betsuin, *Honpa Hongwanji*, 83.

136. They include the wives of Revs. Nichikan Murakita and Reikai Nozaki.

137. The "family" included the wives and children of Revs. Gikō Abiko, Daitetsu Hayashima, Jōkai Kow, Bunpo Kuwatsuki, Kōrō Maehara, Reichi Mohri, Jōtetsu Ōno, Miyoshi Okita, and Gikō Yamamoto. Officially headed by the Kibei leader Yutaka Shinohara, the nisei Buddhist priest Rev. Newton Ishiura, and the issei Rev. Reichi Mohri (who had been able to avoid the initial roundup because the FBI had him on their arrest list with the more common spelling of "Mori"), they were able to comfort each other in the upheaval of removal. Masuyama, *Memories*, 12–15.

138. Robinson, *A Tragedy of Democracy*, 127.

4. CAMP DHARMA

1. Bunyū Fujimura, *Though I Be Crushed: The Wartime Experiences of a Buddhist Minister* (Los Angeles: The Nembutsu Press, 1995), 64.

2. For this account of the Buddha's birthday in camp, see Kōetsu Morita, "Internment Camp Buddhism: Memoirs of Rev. Koetsu Morita," *Turning Wheel: The Journal of Socially Engaged Buddhism* (Fall 2000), 26–27.

3. Ibid.

4. Rev. Zesei Kawasaki wrote an essay during his incarceration that describes how freedom is found in the heart of suffering: "Usually religion is thought of as a way to escape suffering, but this is 'shallow religion.' In the Mahayana [school of Buddhism], we realize that we cannot leave suffering, but must attain nirvana while in the midst of desire and delusion. In fact, where there is no desire and delusion, there is no Buddha." Kawasaki, unlike the other priests discussed in this chapter, was incarcerated in a WRA camp. Zesei Kawasaki, "Shūkyō ni motozuku jinsei" [A Life Rooted in Religion], *Hāto Maunten Bungei* [Heart Mountain literary magazine] 3 (April 1943), 2.

5. Bunyū Fujimura, *Though I Be Crushed*, 64. The passage is from his April 1942 memoir entry for the Buddha's Birthday in Fort Lincoln Internment Camp, North Dakota.

6. Dōgen, "Tenzo Kyokun: Instructions for the Tenzo [chief cook]," trans. Anzan Hoshin and Yasuda Joshu Dainen, in Anzan Hoshin, ed., *Cooking Zen: Zen Master Dogen's Instructions to the Kitchen Master and on How to Use Your Bowls* (Ontario: Great Matter Publications, 1996), http://wwzc.org/dharma-text/tenzo-kyokun-instructions-tenzo.

7. Suikei Furuya, *An Internment Odyssey: Haisho Tenten* (Honolulu: Japanese Cultural Center of Hawai'i / University of Hawai'i Press, 2017). For more on Camp McCoy, see Peggy Choy, "Racial Order and Contestation: Asian American Internees and Soldiers at Camp McCoy, Wisconsin, 1942–1943," in *Asian Americans: Comparative and Global Perspectives,* ed. Shirley Hune, Hyung-chan Kim, Stephan S. Fugita, and Amy Ling (Pullman, WA: Washington State University Press, 1991), 93.

8. Rev. Jikai Yamasato was the head priest.

9. Interview with Seikaku Takesono, March 11, 1982, Japanese Internment and Relocation Files: The Hawai'i Experience, 1942–1982, University of Hawai'i at Manoa Library, box HWN-240, transcript 437.

10. Furuya, *An Internment Odyssey,* 55.

11. John Christgau, *Enemies: World War II Alien Internment* (San Jose, CA: Authors Choice Press, 2001), 14–18; Arnold Krammer, *Undue Process:*

The Untold Story of America's German Alien Internees (Lanham, MD: Rowman & Littlefield, 1997), 23; Carol Van Valkenburg, *An Alien Place: The Fort Missoula Montana Detention Camp 1941–1944* (Missoula, MT: Pictorial Histories Publishing, 1995), 8.

12. Christgau, *Enemies*, 8.

13. Louis Fiset, *Imprisoned Apart: The World War II Correspondence of an Issei Couple* (Seattle: University of Washington Press, 1997), 39.

14. Ibid., 44. See the flow chart documenting the arrests and release options for Japanese, German, and Italian detainees.

15. Indeed, the dual jurisdiction between the Army's Provost Marshal General's Office and the DOJ's INS meant that detainees were frequently registered twice: first with the DOJ, which had taken them into custody, and then by the Provost Marshal General's Office, which received them for internment. Kashima notes that the three-part process for most long-term detainees involved an initial processing at DOJ holding centers, followed by internment at a US Army-run facility, and finally the 1943 return of most of these internees to the jurisdiction of the DOJ. Tetsuden Kashima, *Judgment without Trial: Japanese American Imprisonment during World War II* (Seattle: University of Washington Press, 2003), 105.

16. My thanks to Russell Endo for the information on Tuna Canyon.

17. On former Christian missionaries employed as translators for the US government and intelligence agencies, see Furuya, *An Internment Odyssey*, 35; Lauren Kessler, "On the Home Front: When the Shadow of WWII Fell on Portland's Japanese Americans, Reed Remained a Ray of Light," *Reed Magazine* 78:5 (1999), 5.

18. Mary Nakamura, *White Road of Thorns: Journalist's Diary—Trials and Tribulations of the Japanese American Internment during World War II* (n.p.: Xlibris, 2015), 20–21, 65–66. Note the adjustment to the translation to conform to my transliteration style and because the name of the Zenshūji Supervisor was Rev. Ochi, not Etchi as in the original translation.

19. In the Pacific Northwest, for example, authorities waited as late as April to round up a number of Buddhist priests in the Seattle area. As the historian Ron Magden relates:

> [On] April 27, 1942, two federal agents appeared at the [Seattle Buddhist Temple] Hondo [main hall] front door. The FBI waited until Reverend [Tatsuya] Ichikawa finished marrying Hisato Mizuki and Haruko Hirayama. The moment the service was over, Ichikawa was searched. The federal agents placed in a property envelope Ichikawa's wallet containing his driver's license and a ten-dollar bill, two keys, one penknife, a pair of scissors, and a Dharma book. Later a G-man called on Yasashi [Rev.

Ichikawa's wife]. She was told to pack ten razor blades, a safety razor, and a shaving mirror into a handbag. Then the government official asked her to pack a suitcase with cold-weather clothing for her husband.

Ron Magden, *Mukashi Mukashi Long Long Ago: The First Century of the Seattle Buddhist Church* (Seattle: Seattle Buddhist Church, 2012), 128–129.

20. Teletype Memo from FBI Los Angeles to Director. FBI documents 100-2-29-247 (March 13, 1942) and 100-2-29-305 (March 14, 1942). My thanks to Russell Endo for sharing this document from the National Archives with me. Another priest taken in the same raid was the young Sōtō Zen priest Kenkō Yamashita, who worked as a Japanese-language teacher in 1941 (post-war he would rise to become the Bishop of the Sōtō Zen Mission of North America). He noted how the FBI waited outside of Zenshūji Temple in Los Angeles until he finished his sermon on March 13, 1942 before informing him that he and his wife would be taken into custody. He had been ready for his own arrest, but regarding his wife, he asked the FBI agents, "'Who will take care of our baby?' They stood and looked puzzled. Then they crossed out my wife's name, so she didn't have to go." Interview of Kenkō Yamashita (Mariko Yamashita and Paul F. Clark, Los Angeles, August 10, 1978; California State University, Fullerton, Oral History Program, Japanese American Project).

21. Nakamura, *White Road of Thorns*, 70. I adjusted the translation slightly as the original had *Yasenkanwa* instead of *Yasenkanna* for Hakuin's text.

22. Ibid., 14.

23. Ibid., 19.

24. FBI File Report No. 100-12176 on Daisho Tana. Report compiled by Special Agent Edmund D. Mason, Mar. 31, 1942. My thanks to Russell Endo for sharing this document from the National Archives at Riverside with me.

25. Daisho Tana, *Santa Fe, Lordsburg senji tekikokujin yokuryūsho nikki* [The Wartime Internment Diaries of an Enemy Alien in Santa Fe and Lordsburg], Vol. 1 (Tokyo: Sankibō Busshōrin, 1976), 111–118. The translation is mine.

26. Seytsū Takahashi, *Amerika kaikyō: Shōwa no mikkyō tōzen* [The American Buddhist Mission: The Eastward Advance of Esoteric Buddhism during the Shōwa Period] (Osaka: Tōhō Shuppan, 1990), 6–7; "Interview with Rev. Seytsū Takahashi," December 16, 1978 (California State University, Fullerton; Lawrence de Graaf Center for Oral and Public History—Japanese American History Collection, file OH 1616).

27. Fujimura, *Though I Be Crushed*, 71.

28. Ibid., 61–62.

29. Yoshiaki Fukuda, *My Six Years of Internment: An Issei's Struggle for Justice* (San Francisco: The Konko Church of San Francisco, 1990), 9. In

reality, Bishop Ishida's hearing board and examiner concurred with the decision to intern him because of his high rank in the Nichiren Buddhist order and also in light of FBI reports asserting that he had served in the Japanese Imperial Army for ten months in 1925 and was connected to various Japanese veterans' associations in the United States. "Memorandum to Chief of Review Section—Nitten Ishida (Japanese)" (146-13-2-11-215 Northern District of California). Alvin Rockwell Manuscript Collection, "Enemy Aliens" Box 1, Truman Library. My thanks to Roger Daniels for sharing this document with me.

30. Quoted in Christgau, *Enemies*, 34.

31. Ibid., 34.

32. Shinobu Matsuura, *Higan: Compassionate Vow—Selected Writings of Shinobu Matsuura* (Berkeley, CA: Matsuura Family, 1986), 64.

33. Van Valkenburg, *An Alien Place*, 47.

34. Takahashi, *Amerika kaikyō*, 8–10.

35. The five camps were the Kooskia Internment/Road Camp (Idaho), the Santa Fe Internment Camp (New Mexico), the Kenedy Internment Camp (Texas), the Seagoville Internment Camp for female internees (Texas), and the Crystal Alien Enemy Detention Facility for couples and families (Texas). See Christgau, *Enemies*, 39. Most of the female clerics rounded up in Hawai'i were transferred to continental US facilities by June 1942, and after a brief stay in California, were sent to a DOJ internment camp in Seagoville, Texas, established to house female detainees and some married couples. The Buddhist and Shinto priestesses spent much of their wartime detention at Seagoville, which had been transformed from a federal minimum-security reformatory into an internment camp. Initially the Seagoville camp was intended for families transferred from Latin America; then it was primarily for female alien detainees; and finally it served as a family camp like Crystal City, also located in Texas. Rev. Kanzan Itō of Mantokuji Temple in Maui, along with newspaper correspondent Ishiko Mori and Madame Hirao, who ran the renowned Nikko-ro in Seattle's red-light district, were exceptions in not being confined at Seagoville. They spent most of the war in the Sharp Park Center in California, which had originally served as a temporary holding and detention station to handle the overflow of detainees at the San Francisco immigration station. Kashima, *Judgment without Trial*, 107–108; Jerre Mangione, "Concentration Camps—American Style," in *Una Storia Segreta: The Secret History of Italian American Evacuation and Internment during World War II*, ed. Lawrence DiStasi (Berkeley, CA: Heyday Books, 2001), 121; Yasutarō Soga, *Life Behind Barbed Wire: The World War II Internment Memoirs of a Hawai'i Issei* (Honolulu: Japanese Cultural Center

of Hawai'i / University of Hawai'i Press, 2008), 47. In addition to the DOJ-operated camps, the Japanese were also sent to camps initially run by the US Army. These included Camp McCoy in Wisconsin, Fort Sill Internment Camp in Oklahoma, Camp Forrest in Tennessee, and the Lordsburg Internment Camp in New Mexico, which had opened in mid-June 1942 specifically to house Japanese. Camp Forest had two compounds: one for German POWs captured in North Africa and the other for Japanese and German internees.

36. For a detailed account of this incident, see Kashima, *Judgment without Trial*, 186–191; and John J. Culley, "Trouble at the Lordsburg Internment Camp," *New Mexico Historical Review* 60:3 (1985): 225–248. Private First Class Clarence A. Burleson was charged with murder, but found not guilty. Given insufficient evidence, the verdict favored his defense that he was simply following military protocol by shooting at prisoners attempting to escape—even if they were frail, elderly men barely able to walk.

37. Soga, *Life Behind Barbed Wire*, 78.

38. Yasutarō Soga noted in his diary that the nearby area in New Mexico was primarily Catholic and that, since the churches traditionally practiced burial, none of the local mortuaries were equipped to handle cremations. Since the Japanese Buddhist funerary tradition requires cremation, the "bodies had to be sent elsewhere." But one of the deceased, Mr. Isomura, had no family members to arrange for cremation and removal of remains from the camp. Instead, he was buried at the Santa Fe camp's cemetery, located about a thirty-minute walk from the camp proper. There, "three lone wooden posts, each about three feet high, [were] surrounded by pebbles. From left to right, the names of Hirota Isomura, Ayao Tahara, and Yahei Shiota (two other men who died in the early days of the incarceration) were inscribed on the posts in Japanese *romaji* [roman characters], together with their birth and death dates in English and their internee ID numbers." Ibid., 120.

39. Revs. Fujinaga, Kanda, Masuoka, Miyata, Okita, Tana, and Tamanaha. Masuyama, *Memories*, 133.

40. Tana, *Santa Fe, Lordsburg*, 316–317. The diary entry is from August 16, 1942. The translation is mine.

41. Morita, "Internment Camp Buddhism," 27.

42. Takahashi, *Amerika kaikyō*, 201.

43. Ibid., 69.

5. SANGHA BEHIND BARBED WIRE

1. Mary Nakamura, *White Road of Thorns: Journalist's Diary—Trials and Tribulations of the Japanese American Internment during World War II* (n.p.:

Xlibris, 2015), 102, 104. Hisa Aoki used the pen name Asako Yamamoto to write for the Japanese press. She had an exceptional education for a Japanese woman born in 1900, having graduated from Yamagata Women's Secondary School, Tokyo Higher Normal School for Women, and the Education Department of Nihon University. For more on her background, see Junko Kobayashi, "'Bitter Sweet Home': Celebration of Biculturalism in Japanese Language Japanese American Literature, 1936–1952," (Ph.D. diss., University of Iowa, 2005), 4.

2. Louis Fiset, *Camp Harmony: Seattle's Japanese Americans and the Puyallup Assembly Center* (Urbana, IL: University of Illinois Press 2009), 64–65.

3. Gibun Kimura, *Why Pursue the Buddha?* (Los Angeles: The Nembutsu Press, 1976), 146–147.

4. Brian Hayashi, *Democratizing the Enemy: The Japanese American Internment* (Princeton: Princeton University Press, 2004), 91; Charles Kikuchi, *The Kikuchi Diary: Chronicle from an American Concentration Camp—The Tanforan Journals of Charles Kikuchi* (Urbana, IL: University of Illinois Press, 1973), 60–61.

5. These comments were made by the wife of the Nichiren priest, Rev. Nichikan Murakita. Nakamura, *White Road of Thorns*, 112.

6. Jane Imamura, *Kaikyo: Opening the Dharma, Memoirs of a Buddhist Priest's Wife in America* (Honolulu: Buddhist Study Center Press, 1998), 14.

7. Matthew Estes and Donald Estes, "Further and Further Away: The Relocation of San Diego's Nikkei Community, 1942," *The Journal of San Diego History* 39:1–2.

8. Nakamura, *White Road of Thorns*, 131.

9. Ibid., 139–142 with slight adjustments to the translation.

10. Ibid., 141.

11. Ibid., 144–145. Nakamura's translation is slightly altered to make clear that "the goddess of mercy," a phrase used in the original translation, referred to the bodhisattva Kannon.

12. Anne Blankenship, *Christianity, Social Justice, and Japanese American Incarceration during World War II* (Chapel Hill, NC: University of North Carolina Press, 2016), 51.

13. Jacobus Ten Broek, Edward Barnhart, and Floyd Matson, *Prejudice, War and the Constitution: Causes and Consequences of the Evacuation of the Japanese Americans in World War II* (Berkeley: University of California Press, 1958), 127.

14. Fiset, *Camp Harmony*, 129.

15. WCCA Operations Manual, section 25, 18. In the WCCA Tanforan center, for example, manager Frank E. Davis issued an information bulletin stating: "Under no circumstances will any meeting of the Center Council or

any other organized meeting be held wherein the Japanese language is used, except where it is absolutely necessary to interpret Center regulations and other administrative matters. Japanese will not be spoken in connection with religious services or activities except where the use of English prevents the congregation from comprehending the services. The proposed use of Japanese in religious services will be permitted only with the prior approval of the Center Manager." Frank E. Davis, Center Manager, Tanforan Assembly Center, "Information Bulletin No. 20: The Use of the Printed Japanese Language and Japanese Speech," July 3, 1942, University of California, Berkeley (Bancroft Library, Reel 14, Folder B3.04). Although the date of the ban varies in primary sources, it appears that the suppression of Japanese printed materials other than dictionaries and Christian worship materials occurred in July. On July 18, in a discussion of the Puyallup experience, the *Minidoka Interlude* notes: "Japanese prints banned. Bibles and hymnals approved." Minoru Masuda, *Letters from the 442nd: The World War II Correspondence of a Japanese American Medic* (Seattle: University of Washington Press, 2008), 6. An earlier date of July 8, however, is cited by John Howard, *Concentration Camps on the Home Front: Japanese Americans in the House of Jim Crow* (Chicago: University of Chicago Press, 2008), 163. It is important to note that these restrictions on Japanese-language materials in the WCCA centers were eased in the WRA camps.

16. Greg Robinson, *A Tragedy of Democracy: Japanese Confinement in North America* (New York: Columbia University Press, 2009), 131.

17. Nakamura, *White Road of Thorns*, 136–137. These materials were reviewed by Korean members of the WCCA's Interior Security Branch, who could read Japanese, to determine if the writings might implicate an individual as a security risk. Hayashi, *Democratizing the Enemy*, 93.

18. This report was compiled by Tamie Tsuchiyama, a graduate student at UC Berkeley, as part of the university's JERS (Japanese American Evacuation and Relocation Study) project initiated in 1942 by the sociologist Dorothy Swaine Thomas.

19. Quoted in Lane Hirabayashi, *The Politics of Fieldwork: Research in an American Concentration Camp* (Tucson, AZ: University of Arizona Press, 1999), 26; also see David Yoo, *Growing Up Nisei: Race, Generation, and Culture Among Japanese Americans of California, 1924–49* (Urbana, IL: University of Illinois Press, 2000), 101.

20. Arthur A. Hansen interview of Rev. Kenji Kikuchi, August 26, 1981. Historical and Cultural Foundation of Orange County, Japanese American Council and California State University, Fullerton, Oral History Program, Japanese American Project, 60–61.

21. The three priests were Revs. Aso, Mohri, and Mukushina.

22. John Yamazaki, *Pacemaker*, October 7, 1942, 4. Quoted in Lester Suzuki, *Ministry in the Assembly and Relocation Centers in World War II* (Berkeley, CA: Yardbird Publishing, 1979), 73.

23. Daisuke Kitagawa, *Issei and Nisei: The Internment Years* (New York: Seabury Press, 1967), 67.

24. Kikuchi, *The Kikuchi Diary*, 182–183.

25. Ibid., 128.

26. Quoted in Richard Drinnon, *Keeper of Concentration Camps: Dillon S. Myer and American Racism* (Berkeley, CA: University of California Press, 1987), 68.

27. Mike Masaoka letter to Milton Eisenhower, April 6, 1942, National Archives and Records Service, Record Group 210, Commission on Wartime Relocation and Internment of Civilians 3734–3751, http://www.resisters.com /April_6_1942_WRA pdf.

28. This was the Higashi Honganji priest Rev. Masamichi Yoshikami.

29. The efforts were led by Revs. Enryō Unno and Seikaku Mizutani. Suzuki, *Ministry in the Assembly*, 79–80.

30. Senzaki refers to this letter in his address delivered in Heart Mountain titled "The Birth of the Buddha" on April 7, 1943. Senzaki / Robert Aitken Papers; University of Hawai'i Special Collections.

31. His mother-in-law was the wife of Rev. Issei Matsuura, who had been taken by the FBI. Imamura, *Kaikyo*, 15.

32. Suzuki, *Ministry in the Assembly*, 89.

33. Ibid., 90–91.

34. Anne Blankenship has noted to me that these restrictions on movement within the WCCA center were not religion-based and that Christian ministers faced the same challenges connecting to their prewar congregations.

35. Ron Magden, *Mukashi Mukashi Long Long Ago: The First Century of the Seattle Buddhist Church* (Seattle: Seattle Buddhist Church, 2012), 136.

36. Michihiro Ama, *Immigrants to the Pure Land: The Modernization, Acculturation, and Globalization of Shin Buddhism, 1898–1941* (Honolulu: University of Hawai'i Press, 2011), 77–81 and Michihiro Ama, "'First White Buddhist Priestess': A Case Study of Sunday Gladys Pratt at Tacoma Buddhist Temple," in *Buddhism Beyond Borders: New Perspectives on Buddhism in the United States*, ed. Scott Mitchell and Natalie Quli (Albany, NY: State University of New York Press, 2015).

37. Fiset, *Camp Harmony*, 105–106; Seigel, *In Good Conscience*, 260.

38. Suzuki, *Ministry in the Assembly*, 64–66.

39. Shizue Seigel, *In Good Conscience: Supporting Japanese Americans during the Internment* (San Mateo, CA: AACP Inc. and Kansha Project, 2006), 257.

40. Betsuin Jihō, "Stories from the Past: Rev. Julius A. Goldwater," *Betsuin Jihō*, March 1, 1990, 3.

41. Julius Goldwater "Draft of Speech Given at Senshin Buddhist Temple, LA" (undated): 6; BCA Archives, Hisatsune Family Papers (Rev. Julius A. Goldwater)

42. Arthur Takemoto, "Julius A. Goldwater—Subhadra (Kinsui)" (unpublished); Eiko Masuyama, Flashing Back to the Betsuin's 100 Year History, Part 13," *Los Angeles Betsuin Jiho*, July–Aug. 2002, 3.

43. Suzuki, *Ministry in the Assembly,* 96.

44. Goldwater, "Draft of Speech Given at Senshin Buddhist Temple, LA" (undated): 6. The priests from other traditions included the Shingon Buddhist Rev. Ronald Latimer and Bhikunni Dhammadena of the Theravada tradition. Suzuki, *Ministry in the Assembly,* 71–73; Interview with Ryo Munekata, conducted by Duncan Williams at Los Angeles Nishi Hongwanji Betsuin, March 21, 2004.

45. Suzuki, *Ministry in the Assembly,* 71–73.

46. Blankenship, *Christianity, Social Justice,* 64–65; Hazel K Morikawa, "Exodus: Remembered Moments," in *Triumphs of Faith: Stories of Japanese American Christians during WWII,* ed. Victor N. Okada (Los Angeles: Japanese-American Internment Project, 1998), 80.

47. Fiset, *Camp Harmony,* 134–135.

48. Blankenship, *Christianity, Social Justice,* 54.

49. Fiset, *Camp Harmony,* 103.

50. Janice D. Tanaka, *Act of Faith: The Rev. Emery Andrews Story,* documentary film (Nitto Films and Idh Ramen Productions, 2015).

51. E. Brooks Andrews, *Balancing on Barbed Wire* (Vancouver, Canada: VPGI Enterprises, 2015), 43, 99–100.

52. According to Kashima, the WRA eventually assumed control of approximately 120,000 persons, almost all of whom were of Japanese ancestry, and 118,803 of them (including those who may have originally been arrested into one of the Army or DOJ camps) ended up in one or another of the WRA camps. See Tetsuden Kashima, *Judgment without Trial: Japanese American Imprisonment during World War II* (Seattle: University of Washington Press, 2003), 136.

53. Koji Ariyoshi, *From Kona to Yenan: The Political Memoir of Koji Ariyoshi* (Honolulu: University of Hawai'i Press, 2000), 54.

54. Senzaki, *Eloquent Silence,* 105.

55. Nyogen Senzaki, "Temple Dedication Verse for the Wyoming Zendo, December 20, 1942," reproduced in Senzaki, *Eloquent Silence*, 12–13.

56. *Zazen no hiraki no toki* [The Time to Begin Zen Meditation], (Poston Bukkyo Jiin [Poston Buddhist Temple] Fall 1942). Author's collection.

57. War Relocation Authority, *The Relocation Program: A Guidebook for the Residents of Relocation Centers* (Washington, DC: War Relocation Authority, 1943), 13.

58. My thanks to Patricia Biggs for pointing out this arrangement at Manzanar.

59. E. M. Rowalt (WRA Acting Director) to Rev. S. Kowta, November 20, 1942 (Hawn Collection, University of Hawai'i, RG 210–97)

60. John Provinse to Mark Dawber, November 25, 1942 (Hawn Collection, University of Hawai'i, RG 210-97)

61. Franklin D. Roosevelt, "Four Freedoms speech," Annual Message to Congress on the State of the Union. United States Capitol, Washington, DC, January 6, 1941.

62. Michael Masatsugu, *Reorienting the Pure Land: Japanese Americans, the Beats, and the Making of American Buddhism, 1941–1966* (PhD diss., University of California, Irvine, 2004)..

63. US Congress, House, *Report and Minority Views of the Special Committee on Un-American Activities in Japanese War Relocation Centers*, House Report 717, Seventy-Eighth Congress, First Session, September 30, 1943, 21.

64. Howard, *Concentration Camps on the Home Front*, 151. The statistics on religious attendance are from the "Weekly Report, Week Ending Noon January 23, 1943, Jerome Relocation Center," microfilm, Japanese American Evacuation and Resettlement Records, Bancroft Library, UC Berkeley, part II, section 5, reel 138.

65. Howard, *Concentration Camps on the Home Front*, 165.

66. Ibid., 168.

67. Masatsugu, *Reorienting the Pure Land*, 52.

68. The policy forbidding State Shinto is outlined in the WRA publication *A Story of Human Conservation*, US Department of the Interior, War Relocation Authority (Washington, DC: Government Printing Office, 1946); quoted in Jacobus ten Broek, Edward N. Barnhart, and Floyd W. Matson, *Prejudice, War and the Constitution: Causes and Consequences of the Evacuation of the Japanese Americans in World War II* (Berkeley, University of California Press, 1954), 132. In another Q&A-style booklet, WRA Washington's "Questions and Answers for Governing Administration and Policy of the Segregation Center," the following appears: Q13: Will there be freedom of religion? A: Yes. However, since State Shinto is not recognized by the Japanese Government as being a religion there shall be no official sanction of State Shinto practices on

American soil." In UCLA's Special Collections, Manzanar War Relocation Records Box 27; Folder (WRA Segregation Handbook).

69. Robert F. Spencer, "Religious Life in the Gila Community," Japanese American Evacuation and Resettlement Study, November 2, 1942, 1. Available at UC Berkeley, Bancroft Library, MSS 67 / 14c, folder K8.51, https://oac.cdlib .org/ark:/28722/bk0013c9559/?brand=oac4&layout=metadata.

70. War Relocation Authority, *The Relocation Program: A Guidebook for the Residents of Relocation* Centers (Washington, DC: War Relocation Authority, 1943), 13.

71. Magden, *Mukashi Mukashi,* 142.

72. Donald R. Tuck, *Buddhist Churches of America, Jodo Shinshu* (Lewiston, NY: Edwin Mellen Press, 1987), 19.

73. See comments by his son, Akira Hata, in Masuyama, *Memories,* 150.

74. Robert F. Spencer, "Religious Life in the Gila Community," 10.

75. Masuyama, *Memories,* 15. The priests from various sects included: Revs. Enshō Ashikaga (Higashi Honganji), Chikara Aso (Nishi Hongwanji), Reichi Mohri (Nishi Hongwanji), Kankai Izuhara (Higashi Honganji), Gyomay [Gyōmei] Kubose (Higashi Honganji), Zaishin Mukushina (Jōdo), Nichikan Murakita (Nichiren), Tatsuya Tsuruyama (Nishi Hongwanji), and Masamichi Yoshikami (Higashi Honganji).

76. For more on this altar, see Eiko Masuyama, *Memories: The Buddhist Church Experience in the Camps, 1942–1945,* 2nd rev. ed. (Los Angeles: Nishi Honganji Betsuin, 2007), 17–19; Togo Nishiura, "Buddhist Altars and Poetry Created during 1942–1945 Relocation of Japanese Americans: Meeting Religious Needs of Internees, part 2," 4–6; http://www.discovernikkei.org/en /journal/2015/2/5/buddhist-altars-and-poetry-2/. Another notable altar was Mineo Matoba's *butsudan,* crafted during his time in the Santa Fe DOJ camp from six pieces of wood so skillfully that no nails were required. He managed to send this altar to his wife in the WRA Gila River camp. And in the Rohwer camp, Shintarō Ōnishi "hollowed out a log destined for the firewood pile to create a recess for the butsudan altar, attached hinged door, and used the bark to suggest a textured roof." Delphine Hirasuna, *The Art of Gaman: Arts and Crafts from the Japanese American Internment Camps, 1942–1946* (Berkeley, CA: Ten Speed Press, 2005), 105.

6. REINVENTING AMERICAN BUDDHISM

1. This translation from Chapter 2 of the Lotus Sutra is from Bukkyō Dendō Kyōkai, ed. *The Lotus Sutra (Taishō Volume 9, Number 262): Translated from the Chinese of Kumārajiva by Tsugunari Kubo and Akira Yuyama* (Berkeley, CA: Numata Center for Buddhist Translation and Research, 2007), 31.

2. Misao Yumibe, "Why Buddhism?" *Denson [Arkansas] Buddhist Bulletin*, April 9, 1944.

3. Eiko Masuyama, *Memories: The Buddhist Church Experience in the Camps, 1942–1945*, 2nd rev. ed. (Los Angeles: Nishi Honganji Betsuin, 2007), 105.

4. Ibid., 51. The classes for the children were divided into four groups: Class A (6 years and under), Class B (7–9 years), Class C (10–12 years), and Class D (13–15 years).

5. Kerry Yo Nakagawa, *Through a Diamond: 100 Years of Japanese American Baseball* (San Francisco: Rudi Publishing, 2000), 79, 94.

6. Ibid., 44–45.

7. The Miss Bussei contest was first adopted at the 1940 California Young Buddhists' League (CYBL) conference in conjunction with "Buddhist Day," held August 10–11, 1940, at the Golden Gate International Exposition (World's Fair) on Treasure Island.

8. Poston YBA, *Gassho: All Units Forum*, September 4, 1943) [Duncan Williams Collection.

9. They were advised by five Buddhist priests: the Sōtō Zen priests Dōjun Ochi and Daitō Suzuki, the Higashi Honganji's Noboru Matsumoto, and Nishi Hongwanji's Newton Ishiura and Kanmo Imamura.

10. The song was originally composed by YBA member Ayako Noguchi of Visalia, California, and sung at the end of the 1940 California Young Buddhists' League (CYBL) conference. For more on the camp conference at Gila River, see Gila River YBA, *Unity through Gassho: First Semi-Annual YBA Conference*, June 20, 1943.) [Duncan Williams Collection]

11. Poston YBA, *Gassho: All Units Forum*, September 4, 1943.) [Duncan Williams Collection]

12. Masuyama, *Memories*, 149.

13. For more on the history of Buddhist song culture, see Keiko Wells, "Shin Buddhist Song Lyrics Sung in the United States: Their History and Expressed Buddhist Images (1) 1898–1939," *Tokyo daigaku Amerika taiheiyō kenkyū* 2 (2002): 75–99 and Keiko Wells, "Shin Buddhist Song Lyrics Sung in the United States: Their History and Expressed Buddhist Images (2) 1936–2001," *Tokyo daigaku Amerika taiheiyō kenkyū* 3 (2003): 41–64.

14. Scholars such as Keiko Wells and Michihiro Ama note, for instance, that the pairing of Buddhist songs (*bukkyō shōka*, later called *bukkyō sanka*) with western music went hand in hand with the Japanese government's promotion of music education for elementary schoolchildren. Buddhist leaders Chikai Iwai, Seiran Ōuchi, Haya Akegarasu, and others encouraged the singing of Buddhist songs to western organ music, and composers like Seijin Nomura and Kōsaku Yamada worked on arranging Buddhist verses to

western music. These western-Buddhist hybrid songs *(sanbutsuka)* were sung at Buddhist-run educational institutions in Japan from as early as 1903.

Just as children embraced such songs, Buddhist Women's Associations in Japan promoted them as a way to show how Buddhism was also participating in a more westernized Japan. See Michihiro Ama, *Immigrants to the Pure Land: The Modernization, Acculturation, and Globalization of Shin Buddhism, 1898–1941* (Honolulu: University of Hawai'i Press, 2011), 67–68; Wells, "Shin Buddhist Song," 76–78; and Keiko Wells, "The Role of Buddhist Song Culture in International Acculturation," in *Issei Buddhism in the Americas: The Pioneers of the Japanese-American Buddhist Diaspora,* ed. Duncan Williams and Tomoe Moriya (Urbana-Champaign, IL: University of Illinois Press, 2010), 95–96.

The first edition of the *Seiten* [Sacred Texts] in 1912 contained 148 pages of Japanese chanting text and twenty-six songs to be accompanied by Western music. While the printing in Japan of new editions of the *Shinshū seiten* continued in the subsequent decades with further additions, it was the 1917 publication in Honolulu of *Raisan* [Praise] that revealed the role of local Hawai'i-based Japanese lyricists in the composition of new Buddhist songs, reflecting local culture, including the singing of children-oriented Japanese songs for Buddhist Sunday schools. Jane Imamura, *Kaikyo: Opening the Dharma, Memoirs of a Buddhist Priest's Wife in America* (Honolulu: Buddhist Study Center Press, 1998), 112. Kimi Hisatsune and other nisei composers of Buddhist hymns created songs like "Buddha Loves You," mimicking the Christian hymn "Jesus Loves Me," but with an emphasis on major theological differences such as the Buddha loving all sentient beings (including nonhumans like birds).

In time, American Buddhist musical forms moved away both from Christian-centric hymn composition (indeed, by the late 1930s, the term *gatha* began replacing "hymns") and from simply republishing songs from Japan. In 1924, the first English-language service book, *The Buddhist Vade Mecum*, was compiled by Rev. Ernest Hunt of the Honpa Hongwanji Mission in Honolulu. Beyond the language translation, the key shift was Hunt's insistence that a Buddhist service book should avoid "unduly emphasizing sect" and not mimic Christian service books, with their sections on ceremonial orders of service and hymn singing by the congregation (in contrast to traditional Buddhist rituals featuring chanting by the priests). See Wells, "The Role of Buddhist Song," 41, 77, 88, 99–100.

15. It was alternatively titled *Buddhist Gathas and Ceremonies.*

16. Buddhist ceremonies covered in the *Vade Mecum* included an order of service for the Buddha birthday and marriage and funeral services. The text

324 NOTES TO PAGES 129–130

also included "Buddhist hymns" (*sanbutsuka*)—forty-seven of them written by Dorothy Hunt and another fifty-one of them written by another white convert Buddhist, A. Raymond Zorn—that could be sung like Christian hymns with choirs and organ music. Hunt's *Vade Mecum* (especially Dorothy Hunt's compositions featuring phrases such as "Buddha's soldier's true" and "Love shall be our weapon" and A. R. Zorn's "Loyal Soldiers" with its lyrics "We are Buddha's loyal soldiers, Marching 'neath His banner true") tended toward a more Christian-oriented Buddhist music. Appropriating imagery from the converted Buddhists' former religion, it cast the Buddha as "Lord" or Christlike and evoked the Christian imagery of going into spiritual battle for and with one's Lord. The Christian influence can also be attributed to another key lyricist, R. R. Bode, who served as the organist for St. Andrews Cathedral before becoming the first director of the Hongwanji choir. For more on the *Vade Mecum* and the hybrid nature of these texts, see George J. Tanabe, "Glorious Gathas: Americanization and Japanization in Honganji Hymns," in *Engaged Pure Land Buddhism: Challenges Facing Jōdō Shinshū in the Contemporary World,* Kenneth Tanaka and Eisho Nasu (Berkeley, CA: WisdomOcean Publications, 1994), 222–223; and Wells, "Shin Buddhist Song."

17. Julius Goldwater "Draft of Speech Given at Senshin Buddhist Temple, LA" (undated), 7–8; BCA Archives, Hisatsune Family Papers (Rev. Julius A. Goldwater).

18. Ibid., 8–9.

19. Eiko Masuyama, Flashing Back to the Betsuin's 100 Year History, Part 13," *Los Angeles Betsuin Jiho* (July–August 2002): 3.

20. The journalists were YBA members Roy Kawamoto and Ayako Noguchi. John Howard, *Concentration Camps on the Home Front: Japanese Americans in the House of Jim Crow* (Chicago: University of Chicago Press, 2008), 164.

21. See *Poston Daisan Bukkyō Kaihō* 3 (April 1943), 1; *Poston Daisan Bukkyō Kaihō* 22 (October 1944), 1.

22. On the struggles within Protestant denominations to come together under a single "federation," see Anne Blankenship, *Christianity, Social Justice, and Japanese American Incarceration during World War II* (Chapel Hill, NC: University of North Carolina Press, 2016), 110–122; and Beth Hessel, *"Let the Conscience of Christian America Speak": Religion and Empire in the Incarceration of Japanese Americans, 1941–1945* (Ph.D. diss., Texas Christian University, 2015), 172–183.

23. In terms of sectarian conflict in the prewar period, the most extreme tensions resulted in lawsuits. See Michihiro Ama, "The Legal Dimensions of the Formation of Shin Buddhist Temples in Los Angeles," in *Issei Buddhism*

in the Americas: The Pioneers of the Japanese-American Buddhist Diaspora,
ed. Duncan Williams and Tomoe Moriya (Urbana-Champaign, IL: University of Illinois Press, 2010), 65–86.

24. Masuyama, *Memories,* 127.

25. Ibid.,105.

26. Kōno Kawashima, *Kōyasan beikoku betsuin gojushūnenshi: Koyasan Buddhist Temple, 1912–1962* (Los Angeles: Kōyasan Beikoku Betsuin, 1962), 176–179.

27. The three Nichiren Buddhist priests were Jitei Ishihara, Yōhaku Arakawa, and Chikyō Kurahashi. Shokai Kanai, "Salt Lake Nichiren Buddhist Temple," in *Japanese Americans in Utah,* ed. Ted Nagata (Salt Lake City, UT: JA Centennial Committee, 1996), 190.

28. I borrow the term "parallel congregations" from the work of sociologist Paul Numrich who, in his study of Thai and Sinhalese Buddhist temples in Los Angeles and Chicago, finds that those temples housed two distinct groups under one roof—namely, ethnic Buddhist immigrants and their children from Thailand and Sri Lanka as one group, and primarily white-convert Buddhists practicing *vipassana* meditation as the other. Paul David Numrich, *Old Wisdom in the New World: Americanization in Two Immigrant Theravada Buddhist Temples* (Knoxville, TN: University of Tennessee Press, 1996).

29. War Relocation Authority Community Analysis Section's Report No. 9 "Buddhism in the United States" (May 15, 1944), 5. Oregon State University, Special Collections and Archives Research Center, MSS WRA, series 1, box 1, folder 9.

30. Art Takemoto recalls that at Poston Camp I, they used "Namu Shakamuni Butsu," not "Namu Butsu" as some others had recalled. Masuyama, *Memories,* 200. The nisei Shingon priest Ōogube noted that the new Buddhist "church" was "just a shack and there was nothing that gave a solemn atmosphere. However, when the Sunday school opened and *gathas* were sung with many small children in the makeshift church, tears streamed down their cheeks." The Poston I United Buddhist Church was encouraged by a WRA camp administration eager to consolidate the Buddhists, and established in response to a petition submitted by a multidenominational group of Buddhist priests including Rev. Ryōshō Sogabe (Shingon), Rev. Gyōsei Nagafuji (Nishi Hongwanji), Rev. Jitei Ishihara (Nichiren), and Rev. Chikyō Kurahashi (Nichiren). In Poston I, the Nishi Hongwanji YBA leader and future nisei priest Art Takemoto noted that the spirit of cooperation was enhanced by some of the personalities involved, including the members of the United Buddhist Church administrative office. He recalled that the "camp temple office had one girl from Koyasan and one from Nishi

Hongwanji and they got along well." Kawashima, *Kōyasan beikoku,* 176–179, 182 and Masuyama, *Memories,* 209.

31. Bunyū Fujimura, *Though I Be Crushed: The Wartime Experiences of a Buddhist Minister* (Los Angeles: The Nembutsu Press, 1995), 95–96.

32. Earlier, in September 1943, when Rev. Bunyū Fujimura was permitted a brief parole visit to Poston II to see his family, he took the opportunity to found a new Buddhist magazine called *Jikō.* The inaugural issue emphasized the importance of his sect's members chanting the traditional "Namu Amida Butsu" *(nembutsu),* especially in the difficult circumstances of the camps. He wrote: "The Nembutsu is the 'compass of the heart and mind' for those in agony and suffering because they do not know whether to turn to the right or left; whether to go forward or to return . . . with the Nembutsu, [let us] mutually console each other and continue on our way." Fujimura, *Though I Be Crushed,* 90–92.

33. Fujimura, *Though I Be Crushed,* 96–97. In Poston III, the strong sectarianism of Nishi Hongwanji was exemplified in large-scale ceremonies organized around the sect's most elaborate ritual, the Goshōki Hōonkō, the annual service memorializing the death of the founder, Shinran. Poston III's Buddhists created special issues of their camp newsletter, the *Poston Daisan Bukkyō Kaihō,* every November and December, as part of the lead-up to the Goshōki Hōonkō in January. The special services included readings about Shinran from the *Godensho,* a classic biography written by the medieval priest Kakunyo; multiple lectures about Shinran's teachings; the singing of the sect's anthem *(Shinshū shūka);* and a *gatha* specific to the ceremony called the *Ho-onko no Uta.* Zesei Kawasaki, Memo, box 172, BCA Archives Collection, Japanese American National Museum.

34. The shift to a Nishi Hongwanji sectarianism in that sector of Poston increased especially after the arrival of Rev. Ryūei Masuoka, a priest who had previously served at the Brawley Buddhist Temple in California. Under his leadership, a shift was made to chant the more traditional "Namu Amida Butsu," which energized the Nishi Hongwanji members. Attendance at the Poston I United Church soared, and meetings had to be shifted from the recreation hall to the larger mess hall. Masuyama, *Memories,* 209.

Officiating at the Poston New Year's interdenominational service were Rev. Jitei Ishihara (Nichiren), Rev. Ryōshō Sogabe (Shingon), Rev. Gyōsei Nagafuji (Shin), Rev. Ryūei Masuoka (Shin), and Rev. Chikyō Kurahashi (Nichiren). The service volume for this occasion featured an introductory essay by Rev. Gyōsei Nagafuji that read in part:

It has been roughly two and a half years since we fellow Japanese have been incarcerated here in Poston. We have had our clothes, food, and housing guaranteed. When the bell is sounded at the mess hall, we can easily walk over their morning, lunch, and dinner and don't have to worry that we will starve. Despite the seemingly stable life we have here, there is probably not a single one of us who doesn't yearn from the bottom of our hearts for freedom and the ability to pursue work / career. Without freedom, we humans are living, but with a "half-dead" life. . . . In this third New Year in this place, let us develop the best and brightest light of our hearts to take care of each other so that we can live with a mind that transcends this place.

Gyōsei Nagafuji, "Genjikyoku o koeru shinnen." *Hōrin,* January 1945, 1–3. (trans. Duncan Williams).

35. Ron Magden, *Mukashi Mukashi Long Long Ago: The First Century of the Seattle Buddhist Church* (Seattle: Seattle Buddhist Church, 2012), 144. The lack of space and furnishings led Townsend, a sympathetic Quaker, to approve and personally oversee the transportation of two boxcars loaded with pianos, folding chairs, service books, and choir robes from the Seattle Japanese Methodist Church. George Townsend, "Service with the War Relocation Authority, 1942–1946," unpublished manuscript, 18, http:// encyclopedia.densho.org/media/ddr-densho-275/ddr-densho-275-33 -mezzanine-95748afc58.pdf.

36. Historian Ron Magden describes the Play Day: "children hunted for hidden treasures and competed in cracker-eating contests. Junior and senior high students celebrated with spoon races, baseball games, and fox-trot dancing to the Harmonaires. A giant watermelon 'feed' capped the evening." Magden, *Mukashi Mukashi,* 144.

37. This is as recalled by Ta... T... y ..... 10#d8. b.. Masuyama, *Memo ries,* 05.

38. For more on the United Buddhist Church and the Hunt Buddhist Church at Minidoka, see Magden, *Mukashi Mukashi,* 144.

39. In the WRA Manzanar camp, the struggle over facilities usage and monetary donations between the Nishi Hongwanji and Sōtō Zen sects was documented by Morris E. Opler, a community analyst for the WRA. His report was even sent to WRA director Dillon Myer. Community Analysis Section, Manzanar Relocation Center, "Buddhist Sects at Manzanar," April 12, 1944, Box 28, Folder 7, RG 122, Manzanar WRA Records, Charles E. Young Special Collections, University of California, Los Angeles.

40. Lester Suzuki, *Ministry in the Assembly and Relocation Centers in World War II* (Berkeley, CA: Yardbird Publishing, 1979), 119–120.

41. Ibid., 175.

42. Taylor, *Jewel of the Desert: Japanese American Internment at Topaz* (Berkeley, CA: University of California Press, 1993), 156.

43. *Topaz Times,* November 10, 1942, 2, https://www.loc.gov/resource /sn85040302/1942-11-10/ed-1/?sp=2&r=-0.355,0.346,1.745,0.833,0

44. Masuyama, *Memories,* 81. The program also included center administrator Ralph Merritt and other white officials from the Protestant Commission for Wartime Japanese Service, among others. Suzuki, *Ministry in the Assembly,* 126-127.

45. Masuyama, *Memories,* 148.

46. Daishō Tana, *Santa Fe, Lordsburg senji tekikokujin yokuryūsho nikki* [The Wartime Internment Diaries of an Enemy Alien in Santa Fe and Lordsburg], Vol. 1 (Tokyo: Sankibō Busshōrin, 1976), 449-451. The quoted diary entry is from December 25, 1942. The translation is mine.

47. Hessel, *"Let the Conscience of Christian America Speak,"* 2.

48. Tsukasa Sugimura, *Quiet Heroes: A Century of Quakers' Love and Help for the Japanese and Japanese-Americans* (Altadena, CA: Intentional Productions, 2014), 71.

49. Herbert V. Nicholson and Margaret Wilke, *Comfort All Who Mourn: The Life Story of Herbert and Madeline Nicholson* (Fresno, CA: Bookmarks International, 1982), 95-96.

50. Suzuki, *Ministry in the Assembly,* 148.

51. Anne Blankenship, "Civil Religious Dissent: Patriotism and Resistance in a Japanese American Incarceration Camps," *Material Religion* 10:3 (2014), 282.

52. Taylor, *Jewel of the Desert,* 157.

53. Eiichiro Azuma, *Between Two Empires: Race, History, and Transnationalism in Japanese America* (Oxford: Oxford University Press, 2005), 106.

54. Jeffery F. Burton, Jeremy D. Haines, and Mary M. Farrell, *I Rei To: Archeological Investigations at the Manzanar Relocation Center Cemetery, Manzanar National Historic Site, California* Publications in Anthropology Report 79 (Tucson, Arizona: Western Archeological and Conservation Center, 2001), 6.

55. Recalled by his daughter, Shizuko Nagatomi. Masuyama, *Memories,* 33.

56. Burton, Haines, and Farrell, *I Rei To,* 6-7; Masuyama, *Memories,* 33.

57. Burton, Haines, and Farrell, *I Rei To,* 7; Masuyama, *Memories,* 33, 58.

58. Also involved at the dedication ceremony were Senkichi Shikami and Town Hall Chairman Kiyoharu Anzai. Masuyama, *Memories,* 58.

59. Masuyama, *Memories,* 35. A thousand-dancer Obon ceremony was held during the same period at the WRA Amache camp. At Poston, four

hundred dancers, taught by the well-known Japanese classical dance instructor and Buddhist priest Rev. Yoshio Iwanaga, were viewed by five thousand onlookers. For the Amache numbers, see Allen H. Eaton, *Beauty Behind Barbed Wire: The Arts of the Japanese in Our War Relocation Camps* (New York: Harper and Brothers, 1952), 123–125; and Minako Waseda, "Extraordinary Circumstances, Exceptional Practices: Music in Japanese American Concentration Camps," *Journal of Asian American Studies* 8:2 (2005), 188. (Waseda's count is probably more accurate because she relies on a contemporaneous camp newsletter). Eaton's comment on the photo is: "One evening in the summer of 1943, over one thousand dancers of Amache, most of them dressed in Japanese costume, came together after supper, and to the Oriental rhythms of flutes, drums, and singing, carried the festival far into the night." Regarding the Poston event, see *Poston Daisan Bukkyō Kaihō* 8 (September 1943), 1.

60. "Obon Festival: Significance of Obon," August 14, 1943, Reel 1, Selected Materials Relating to the Heart Mountain Relocation Center, Record Group 210: Records of the War Relocation Authority, National Archives and Records Service, General Services Administration. Many thanks to Patricia Biggs for sharing her detailed knowledge of the sequence of events surrounding Obon at Manzanar, Rev. Shinjō Nagatomi, and the construction of the Ireitō.

61. A few months prior to this festival, WRA director Dillon Myer wrote to his staff: "At some of the centers the question has arisen as to what Japanese holidays are of special importance and in particular what if any Japanese holidays should be recognized as relocation center holidays. Under present policy no Japanese holiday shall be recognized as such by declaring a holiday from work because of it." Myer continues "However, if center residents desire to observe certain festivals after working hours there is no reason why they should not do so." Dillon Myer memo to project staff, April 2, 1943 (6-6297-P1 of 6-NOBU-COS-WP), UCLA Special Collections Manzanar War Relocation Records, Box 8, Folder: WRA Community Activities. The note on Obon is part of an attached Community Analysis Report.

62. Community Analysis Report No. 4, April 2, 1943 (6-6297-P6-BU-COS-WP), UCLA Special Collections Manzanar War Relocation Records, Box 8; Folder: WRA Community Activities, 1–4.

63. The camp newsletter reports: "E. R. Fryer, acting project director, gave an opening address to the 5,000 spectators who were crowded in front of the Canal Camp Buddhist church to witness the gala *bon odori* festival. The affair was held Sunday night with 350 dancers clad in beautiful kimonos, adorning

the colorful dancing ring which was decorated by the church committee members." *Gila River Courier,* September 30, 1942. Quoted in Minako Waseda, *Japanese American Musical Culture in Southern California: Its Formation and Transformation in the 20th Century* (Ph.D. diss. UC, Santa Barbara, 2000), 158.

64. Although the 1943 Obon was a major moment for the Buddhists in Manzanar, the initial celebration of Obon had already taken place on August 16, 1942, sponsored by a newly-formed Manzanar United Buddhist Federation. At this point, several days before Rev. Nagatomi's arrival, roughly a dozen people had already died in camp. That first Obon service, presided over by Revs. Junjō Izumida (Higashi Honganji) and Benmyō Oda (Nichiren), took place on Sunday, August 16, 1942 with "afternoon festivities to start with 1:30 PM service at the grave; 2 PM service at the river bank." *Manzanar Free Press,* August 14, 1942, 1. The press article misspells Izumida's name as Kumida. My thanks to Patricia Biggs for pointing me to this article as well as for sharing her research on the number and dates of deaths in Manzanar. By the time of Rev. Nagatomi's arrival, a temporary Buddhist Board of Directors had formed, led by Revs. Junjō Izumida and Benmyō Oda, and by Nishi Hongwanji YBA leaders. This group organized the first Buddhist Sunday service at Manzanar, in June 1942, at the recreation hall located at Block 17–15, which was held in Japanese and led by Rev. Junjō Izumida. *Manzanar Free Press,* June 13, 1942, 2. The YBA leaders included Eizō Masuyama, Jack Iwata, Sangorō Mayeda, Larry Mihara, Nob Myose, Lucille Nakamura, Michi Konishi, and Tokio Inouye. See Masuyama, *Memories,* 50.

65. Ralph Merritt, "Remarks at the Obon Festival of the Buddhist Church at Manzanar," August 14, 1943. My thanks to Patricia Biggs for sharing this manuscript with me.

66. In 1946, Revs. Mayeda and Nagatomi separately returned to Manzanar's cemetery to honor the dead. A handful of religious leaders continued annual pilgrimages until they passed away. When Sue Kunitomi Embrey, Warren Furutani, and others began pilgrimages in 1969, a number of Buddhist and Christian ministers were still making their annual visits. Thanks to Patricia Biggs for this information.

67. The fact that the highest-ranking Buddhist priest of the largest of the sects in North America was not interned was possibly due to his poor health. Others—such as Rev. Yutetsu Takeda (who served the Honolulu Nishi Hongwanji Betsuin, and passed away soon after Pearl Harbor) and Rev. Itsuzō Kyōgoku (who had resigned from the Buddhist Church of Stockton three months prior to Pearl Harbor due to illness)—seem to have been left

alone for that reason. Matsukage, however, despite his frail condition, could not avoid the mass incarceration. With his wife, who was also in poor health (she passed away in Topaz on January 18, 1945), the Bishop was incarcerated with the general populace, first in the horse stables at Tanforan and then at the more permanent WRA camp at Topaz.

68. Masuyama, *Memories*, 113.

69. Tana, *Santa Fe, Lordsburg*, 336–338. The diary entry is dated August 31, 1942. The translation is mine.

70. Suzuki, *Ministry in the Assembly*, 188.

71. The aspiration was not only to have democracy within the camps, of course, but for Buddhists to become full members and participants in an American society beyond the barbed wire. Apparently, talk of Buddhism and American democracy was so frequent that one community analyst at the WRA Gila River camp, Gordon Brown, noted somewhat skeptically towards the end of the war:

> When asked what particular contribution Buddhism has for America the usual answer is "democracy." . . . Buddhism disregards race. This pat answer is clearly a response to the particular situation in which Japanese Buddhism finds itself. Many priests are still excluded from California, some are interned. They belong to an "oppressed group." Buddhism is "against discrimination." Hence, both to aid themselves and to meet a hostile world, they must concentrate upon that particular interpretation of their religious teachings.

Gordon Brown, "Final Report on the Gila River Relocation Center as of May 20, 1945," Carr Papers, Box 55, Folder 5, Japanese American Research Project Collection, University of California, Los Angeles.

72. Michael Masatsugu, forthcoming manuscript based on Masatsugu, *Reorienting the Pure Land*.

73. Ibid.

74. "Myer Pleased with YBA Plans," *Bussei Life* 1:4 (June 20, 1943), 1.

75. Masatsugu, *Reorienting the Pure Land*, 54–55.

76. Michael Masatsugu, "Reorienting the Pure Land: Buddhism and the Making of Japanese American after World War II," forthcoming publication based on prior dissertation.

77. Ibid.

78. See issue 6 of *Hōmi*; quoted in Masuyama, *Memories*, 110–112.

79. Ibid., 113.

80. Michael Masatsugu's forthcoming manuscript based on Masatsugu, *Reorienting the Pure Land*; Masuyama, *Memories*, 110–113; and Robert Spencer, *Japanese Buddhism in the United States, 1940–1946: A Study on*

Acculturation (Ph.D. diss., University of California, Berkeley, 1946), 186–187.

81. Gila River YBA, *Unity through Gassho: First Semi-Annual YBA Conference,* June 20, 1943.

7. ONWARD BUDDHIST SOLDIERS

1. "Buddhist Soldiers" (verses 1, 4; composer, Dorothy Hunt) in *A Book Containing an Order of Ceremonies for Use by Buddhists at Gatherings* (The Buddhist Brotherhood in America, 1943)

2. Michael Masatsugu, *Reorienting the Pure Land: Japanese Americans, the Beats, and the Making of American Buddhism, 1941–1966* (PhD diss., University of California, Irvine, 2004), 63.

3. The *Manzanar Free Press* notes that in addition to Rev. Nagatomi's sermon, the service consisted of the chanting of Buddhist sutras and incense offering by family members. Enlarged photos of the two men were created by the renowned photographer Toyo Miyatake and hung in the Town Hall. "Memorial Services Tomorrow Honor Two Nisei Killed in Italy," *Manzanar Free Press*, April 28, 1945, 1–2.

4. The translated version of the speech can be found in Eiko Masuyama, *Memories: The Buddhist Church Experience in the Camps, 1942–1945,* 2nd rev. ed. (Los Angeles: Nishi Honganji Betsuin, 2007), 75–77.

5. Wayne S. Kiyosaki, *Spy in Their Midst: The World War II Struggle of a Japanese-American Hero, The Story of Richard Sakakida, As Told to Wayne S. Kiyosaki* (Lanham, MD: Madison Books, 1995), 134–135.

6. Richard Sakakida, "Undercover Agent in Manila," in *American Patriots: MIS in the War Against Japan,* ed. Stanley Falk and Warren M. Tsuneishi (Vienna, VA: Japanese American Veterans Association of Washington DC, 1995), 22.

7. Kiyosaki, *Spy in Their Midst,* 31.

8. Duval A. Edwards, *Spy Catchers of the US Army in the War with Japan: The Unfinished Story of Counter Intelligence Corps* (Gig Harbor, WA: Red Apple Publishing, 1994), 17; Paul Hara, *Mission in Manila: The Sakakida Story,* documentary film (San Francisco: Military Intelligence Service and National Japanese American Historical Society for the Military Intelligence Service Fellowship Program, 1994). Despite suggestions by several sources that Sakakida was the first Hawai'i-born nisei to become a Jōdo Shinshū Buddhist minister, there were in fact, by 1941, at least five Hawai'i-born nisei who had already completed ordination and training in Japan.

9. Kiyosaki, *Spy in Their Midst,* 49.

10. The other two were Douglas Wada and Gero Iwai, both recruited for counterintelligence work prior to the war. Douglas Wada was recruited in 1937 in the district intelligence office in Honolulu to monitor radio and wireless intercepts, develop geographical data about Japan, and translate documents. Gero Iwai was recruited even earlier, in 1931, to the Army G-2, Hawaiian department, as an enlisted investigator who monitored the Japanese American community through a network of informants and conducted surveillance on the Japanese consulate. In the days after Pearl Harbor, both Wada and Gero Iwai were involved in translating materials seized from the Japanese consulate in Honolulu and from the Japanese midget submarine that had beached at Waimanalo. They also participated in the interrogation of Ensign Kazuo Sakamaki, the submarine's surviving crewman, the first Japanese prisoner taken in the war. Pierre Moulin, *American Samurais: WWII in the Pacific: Military Intelligence Service—The Best Kept Secret Weapon in WWII* (Alexandria, VA: Socrates Institute Press, 2011), 46–55.

11. Edwards, *Spy Catchers*, 18.

12. He ingratiated himself with the Japanese throughout Manila by volunteering to help them fill out legal forms in English. The forms, issued by the US High Commissioner's Office when the United States froze the assets of all Japanese citizens in the Philippines, included a section that asked aliens to list their former military service. From this work, he provided a series of reports to the G-2, delivered through a postal mail drop. Sakakida learned that nearly fifty percent of Japanese men in Manila were former reservists, and uncovered a banker and school principal who were Japanese "sleeper" agents.

13. Kiyosaki, *Spy in Their Midst*, 81.

14. Joseph D. Harrington, *Yankee Samurai: The Secret Role of Nisei in America's Pacific Victory* (Detroit: Pettigrew Enterprises, Inc., 1979), 31.

15. Kiyosaki, *Spy in Their Midst*, 87.

16. Another American serviceman and Buddhist captured by the Japanese at Corregidor was the controversial figure John David Provoo. Provoo, a San Francisco native, had converted to Buddhism prior to the war and was studying at a Buddhist monastery in Japan when the war broke out. He enlisted in the US Army and had been working as a G-2 clerk at its headquarters in Manila before his capture. He was accused by the US Army of assisting the Japanese Imperial Army during his time as a Japanese prisoner by helping to create propaganda broadcasts and even aiding the Japanese in the execution of a fellow POW. After an initial honorable discharge, he was convicted of treason—only the eighth American citizen to be so convicted

after World War II—but that conviction was later overturned. Richard Sakakida was one of the witnesses called to testify against him. In the 1960s, Provoo returned to Japan and adopted the Buddhist priestly name of Nichijo Shaka. He spent the last years of his life leading a Buddhist group on Hawai'i's Big Island. A book-length work on Provoo is forthcoming by Naoko Shibusawa, tentatively titled *Seduced by the East: The Treason Trial of John David Provoo* (under contract with the University of North Carolina Press). Provoo's own account of his prewar, wartime, and postwar experience, as told to John Oliver, can be found in John Oliver, *Nichijo: The Testimony of John Provoo* (San Bernardino, CA: self-published, 1986).

17. For more on Arthur Komori, see Lorraine Ward, Katherine Erwin, and Yoshinobu Oshiro, *Reflections of Honor: The Untold Story of a Nisei Spy* (Honolulu: Curriculum Research and Development Group, University of Hawai'i at Manoa, 2014).

18. Edwards, *Spy Catchers of the US Army,* 55.

19. Kiyosaki, *Spy in Their Midst,* 140.

20. Ibid., 29.

21. Ibid., 24.

22. Ibid., 152.

23. Ibid., 159.

24. Ibid., 155–156.

25. On the rescue mission, see Kiyosaki, *Spy in Their Midst,* 153–154; and Edwards, *Spy Catchers of the US Army,* 159–160.

26. Kiyosaki, *Spy in Their Midst,* 176.

27. Ibid., 186–187.

28. Hara, *Mission in Manila: The Sakakida Story.*

29. In fact, only one other Japanese American was held as a Japanese prisoner of war: Sgt. Frank "Foo" Fujita, a mixed-race artilleryman whose unit surrendered in March 1942 in Java. Frank Fujita, *Foo—A Japanese-American Prisoner of the Rising Sun: The Secret Prison Diary of Frank "Foo" Fujita* (Fort Worth, TX: University of North Texas Press, 1993).

30. The approximate 6,000 breaks down to some 4,500 Nisei, a handful of Korean and Chinese Americans, and roughly 1,450 Caucasian Americans who went through rigorous language training and used their Japanese to serve in the Pacific.

31. Kiyoshi Yano, "Participating in the Mainstream of American Life Amidst Drawback of Racial Prejudice and Discrimination," in *John Aiso and the M.I.S.: Japanese-American Soldiers in the Military Intelligence Service, World War II,* ed. Tad Ichinokuchi and Daniel Aiso (Los Angeles: The Military Intelligence Service Club of Southern California, 1988), 19.

32. Some scholars have estimated that roughly 20 to 25 percent of Japanese Americans were kibei. Hiroshi Kadoike, *Nihongun heishi no natta Amerikajin tachi: Bokoku to tatakatta nikkei Nisei* [Americans Who Became Japanese Soldiers: Japanese Second Generation Fought Against Mother Country] (Tokyo: Genshū shuppansha, 2010), 28. Others have lower estimates such as 15 percent. Noboru Shirai, *California nikkeijin kyōsei shūyōjo* (Tokyo: Kawaide shobo shinsha, 1981) [published in English as Noboru Shirai, *Tule Lake: An Issei Memoir* (Sacramento: Muteki Press, 2001)], 123.

33. Francis Sill Wickware, "The Japanese Language," *Life*, September 7, 1942, 58. It should be noted that a number of Koreans with Japanese language capability were eventually recruited for this effort.

34. Eloise Cunningham, daughter of a Protestant missionary who taught at Gakushuin University prior to the war, was a part of the Army's code-breaking team in Virginia. (A parallel one also existed in Hawai'i under Commander Joseph J. Rochefort.) She recalled: "We worked out of a girl's school in Northern Virginia and it was very hush-hush. We came under great stress because nobody but us knew that the Japanese code had been broken. . . . We weren't anti-Japanese but we were trying to wreck the Japanese navy. Reischauer was in the department too, as was a Rikkyo University professor and others, such as missionaries, who had contacts in Japan." Tokyo Journal, "Interview with Eloise Cunningham," *Tokyo Journal*, December 1995, 20. Edwin Reischauer was the esteemed Harvard Japanologist who was son of August Karl Reischauer and Helen Stidwell Oldfather, Presbyterian missionaries to Japan.

35. The law, also known as the Burke-Wadsworth Act, was signed into law by President Roosevelt on September 16, 1940.

36. Daniels puts the figure at 3,188. Roger Daniels, *Asian America: Chinese and Japanese in the United States since 1850* (Seattle: University of Washington Press), 249. Sterner puts the prewar Nisei draftee figure at five thousand, but this seems high. C. Douglas Sterner, *Go for Broke: The Nisei Warriors of World War II Who Conquered Germany, Japan and American Bigotry* (Clearfield, UT: American Legacy Historical Press, 2008), 13.

37. Meanwhile, the US Navy, Marines, and Army Air Corp, with a few Air Corp exceptions (like John Matsumoto, Virgil (Nishimura) Westdale, and Koichi Shibuya during the prewar draft and Ben Kuroki as a volunteer after Pearl Harbor), largely continued the practice of not accepting Japanese Americans and Asian Americans more broadly. The Navy, for instance, made exceptions for Filipinos during the 1940–1941 period, but even then, only permitted Filipinos to serve as cooks and mess stewards. James C. McNaughton, *Nisei Linguists: Japanese Americans in the Military Intelligence*

Service during World War II (Washington, DC: Department of the Army, 2007), 29. The Adjutant General's Office issued a report in March 1941 on the number of Japanese Americans in the military to explore the issue of using them for a potential Japanese language training school. About half of the 1,690 Nisei identified at the time were in the continental US and the other half in Hawaiʻi. By summer 1941, around 3,000 Nisei were in the armed forces, with 1,000 of them in the Fourth Army (in Western Defense Command under General DeWitt). McNaughton, *Nisei Linguists*, 7, 21, 23.

38. John Weckerling, "Nisei Language Experts," in *John Aiso and the M.I.S.: Japanese-American Soldiers in the Military Intelligence Service, World War II*, ed. Tad Ichinokuchi and Daniel Aiso (Los Angeles: The Military Intelligence Service Club of Southern California, 1988), 188–189.

39. Yano, "Participating in the Mainstream," 4–36 and McNaughton, *Nisei Linguists*, 10–11.

40. Weckerling "Nisei Language Experts," 191 and McNaughton, *Nisei Linguists*, 25, 28.

41. The two Caucasian students were Dempster Dirks and Victor Belousoff. There are some discrepancies in the sources about the number of students in the initial class at the Presidio. I have used the seemingly most accurate number (60 students—58 Nisei and 2 Caucasian), but other accounts have 40, 42, or 45 Nisei in the first class and a third Caucasian student, possibly George Spence. See McNaughton, *Nisei Linguists*, 37–38; Dan Nakatsu, "America's Superb Secret Weapon of World War II," in *John Aiso and the M.I.S.: Japanese-American Soldiers in the Military Intelligence Service, World War II*, ed. Tad Ichinokuchi and Daniel Aiso (Los Angeles: The Military Intelligence Service Club of Southern California, 1988), 83 and Yano, "Participating in the Mainstream," 4–36.

42. McNaughton, *Nisei Linguists*, 27–28.

43. Harrington, *Yankee Samurai*, 82.

44. McNaughton, *Nisei Linguists*, 37.

45. Ibid., 189.

46. Ibid., 192.

47. Ibid., 6–7, 21.

48. Ibid., 192.

49. Ibid., 192.

50. Quoted in David W. Swift, *First Class: Nisei Linguists in World War II—Origins of the Military Intelligence Service Language Program* (San Francisco: National Japanese American Historical Society, 2008), 222.

51. Linda Tamura, *Nisei Soldiers Break Their Silence: Coming Home to Hood River* (Seattle: University of Washington Press, 2012), 14–15, 52, 83–85.

52. Shigeo Kikuchi, *Memoirs of a Buddhist Woman Missionary* (Honolulu: The Buddhist Study Center Press, 1991), 37.

53. Quoted in McNaughton, *Nisei Linguists,* 52.

54. Harrington, *Yankee Samurai,* 40.

55. Hiroshi Kadoike convincingly calculates these figures on nisei in Japan and their service in the Imperial Army and Navy. See Kadoike, *Nihongun heishi,* 32–35. Also see Yuzuru Tachibana, *Teikoku kaigun shikan ni natta nikkei nisei* (Tokyo: Tsukiji shokan, 1994) for an in-depth study of Japanese Americans in the Japanese Imperial Navy. For a fascinating account of a Japanese American who served in the Kamikaze Corps, see Shigeo Imamura, *Kamikaze tokkōtai'in ni natta Nikkei nisei* (Tokyo: Soshisha, 2003). In English, Sakamoto details the story of the Fukuhara family with two Japanese American brothers in the Japanese Imperial Army and one in the US Army MIS; see Pamela Rotner Sakamoto, *Midnight in Broad Daylight: A Japanese American Family Caught between Two Worlds* (New York: Harper Collins, 2016).

56. Unpublished Rev. Hōyū Ōta Memoir manuscript; Jōdoshū Kokusaibu Archives, collated in 1978 by the Jōdo Buddhist headquarters in Tokyo.

57. The Oakland Buddhist Church letter is in the collection of Rev. Tetsurō Kashima and is quoted in Tetsuden Kashima, *Buddhism in America: The Social Organization of an Ethnic Religious Institution* (Westport, CT: Greenwood Press, 1977), 49–50.

58. Greg Robinson, *A Tragedy of Democracy: Japanese Confinement in North America* (New York: Columbia University Press, 2009), 215. In Canada, such inductions into the Canadian Army were generally halted for Japanese Canadians after the September 1939 declaration of war with Germany (though not yet with Japan), with the result that only twenty five volunteers managed to enlist.

59. McNaughton, *Nisei Linguists,* 47–49.

60. Harrington, *Yankee Samurai,* 26.

61. Masayo Duus, *Unlikely Liberators: The Men of the 100th and 442nd* (Honolulu: University of Hawai'i Press, 1987), 54–55; Hodson Lewis on behalf of Little Rock Chamber of Commerce, letter to [Arkansas congressman] David D. Terry, March 18, 1942, 42, G-l Decimal File, 1942–1946, 291.2 Japanese, Entry 43, Box 445, Records of the War Department General and Special Staffs, Record Group 165, National Archives at College Park, Maryland.

62. For more on the Fort Riley incident, see Linda Tamura, *Nisei Soldiers Break Their Silence: Coming Home to Hood River* (Seattle: University of Washington Press, 2012), 105–111.

63. The support came from the Chinese American Honolulu YMCA secretary Hung Wai Ching and Shigeo Yoshida, a Nisei who served as administrator in the territory's department of public instruction. For more on Ching and Yoshida and their roles in the Council for Interracial Unity, see Coffman, *How Hawai'i Changed America*, 201–206.

64. Franklin S. Odo, *No Sword to Bury: Japanese Americans in Hawai'i during World War II* (Philadelphia, PA: Temple University Press, 2004), 154, 184.

65. Ibid., 131–132.

66. Ibid., 164, 183.

67. Ibid., 101.

68. Ibid., 154, 188.

69. Ibid., 59, 90, 98.

70. Ibid., 9.

71. Hawaii Nikkei History Editorial Board, ed. *Japanese Eyes, American Heart: Personal Reflections of Hawaii's World War II Nisei Soldiers* (Honolulu: Tendai Educational Foundation, 1998).

72. Ibid.

73. Odo, *No Sword to Bury*, 31, 108–109, 113, 157, 193–194, 238. On his reflections about gratitude to his country, see Hawaii Nikkei History Editorial Board, *Japanese Eyes*.

74. Yempuku's OSS work included the guerilla campaign at Myitkyna in Burma, which earned his unit, Detachment 101, a presidential unit citation for its devastation of a Japanese unit behind enemy lines. Moulin, *American Samurais*, 120.

75. It appears that a handful of Nisei may have secretly been allowed to live in Portland, Oregon, as part of the Foreign Broadcast Intelligence Service to monitor Japanese broadcasts. Tamotsu Shibutani, *The Derelicts of Company K: A Sociological Study of Demoralization* (Berkeley, CA: University of California Press, 1978), 85; Yano, "Participating in the Mainstream," 4–36.

76. Albert Hindmarsh (professor of international law at Harvard University) was tasked with finding suitable candidates for the navy's program in December 1940. His team found only fifty-six potential candidates among college students nationwide, so he recommended that the navy outsource the work of training to leading universities, including Harvard and UC Berkeley. The Harvard program, led by Serge Elisséef, was soon abandoned in favor of the Berkeley program run by Florence Walsh, born in Japan to missionary parents. McNaughton, *Nisei Linguists*, 58–59.

77. Michihiro Ama, *Immigrants to the Pure Land: The Modernization, Acculturation, and Globalization of Shin Buddhism, 1898–1941* (Honolulu:

University of Hawai'i Press, 2011), 167; McNaughton, *Nisei Linguists,* 58–59. The Marine Corps also had a small program based at the University of Hawai'i, outside the excluded zone for Japanese Americans.

78. In April 1942, the war department lifted the ban on overseas assignments for nisei at MISLS. Those whose "loyalty is attested to by the Commanding Officer of the school after suitable investigation" were permitted to serve in the Pacific theater of combat. McNaughton, *Nisei Linguists,* 56.

79. Sterner, *Go for Broke,* 127.

80. McNaughton, *Nisei Linguists,* 71–72.

81. Ama, *Immigrants to the Pure Land,* 121.

82. Roland Kotani, *The Japanese in Hawaii: A Century of Struggle* (Honolulu: Oahu Kanyaku Imin Centennial Committee, 1985), 108; James M. McCaffrey, *Going for Broke: Japanese American Soldiers in the War Against Nazi Germany* (Norman, OK: University of Oklahoma Press, 2013), 22–23.

83. Quoted in Richard Halloran, *Sparky: Warrior, Peacemaker, Poet, Patriot* (Honolulu: Watermark Publishing, 2002), 37.

84. Dorothy Matsuo, *Boyhood to War: History and Anecdotes of the 442nd Regimental Combat Team* (Honolulu: Mutual Publishing, 1992), 53.

85. McCaffrey, *Going for Broke,* 42.

86. Duus, *Unlikely Liberators,* 24.

87. Shibutani, *The Derelicts of Company K,* 80.

88. Leighton Sumida, oral history interview, part 1 of 5, October 21, 1998, Go For Broke National Education Center, http://www.goforbroke.org/learn/archives/oral_histories_videos.php?clip=02001.

89. Thomas D. Murphy, *Ambassadors in Arms: The Story of Hawaii's 100th Battalion* (Honolulu: University of Hawai'i Press, 1954), 82.

90. Duus, *Unlikely Liberators,* 36–37.

91. Will Hoover, "World War II Split Brothers between Japan and America," *Honolulu Advertiser,* August 14, 2005, http://the.honoluluadvertiser.com/article/2005/Aug/14/ln/508140323.html.

92. Sterner, *Go for Broke,* 17.

93. Murphy, *Ambassadors in Arms,* 64–66.

94. Woo Sung Han, *Unsung Hero: The Story of Colonel Young Oak Kim* (Riverside, CA: Young Oak Kim Center for Korean American Studies, 2011), 28–30.

95. McCaffrey, *Going for Broke,* 48–50.

96. Russell K. Shoho, *From the Battlefields to the Home Front: The Kazuo Masuda Legacy* (Fullerton, CA: Nikkei Writers Guild / Japanese American Living Legacy, California State University, 2009), 14.

97. Duus, *Unlikely Liberators*, 144; Howard, *Concentration Camps on the Home Front*, 2–3; McCaffrey, *Going for Broke*, 81–82.

98. Duus, *Unlikely Liberators*, 75.

99. McCaffrey, *Going for Broke*, 99, 105–106.

100. John Howard, *Concentration Camps on the Home Front: Japanese Americans in the House of Jim Crow* (Chicago: University of Chicago Press, 2008), 146.

101. My thanks to Anne Blankenship for pointing out how George Aki facilitated Kouchi's visits to Camp Shelby.

102. Masuyama, *Memories*, 165.

103. *Sangha News* 1:2 (February 13, 1944), 1.

104. Quoted in Duus, *Unlikely Liberators*, 58.

105. Ibid., 58. The only exception was to be Captain Pershing Nakada, commander of the 232nd Engineer Company.

106. Odo, *No Sword to Bury*, 227.

107. Akita was not as committed to his faith as his devout Buddhist father. Stanley Masaharu Akita, transcript of interview, "The Hawai'i Nisei Story, Americans of Japanese Ancestry During WWII," University of Hawai'i Nisei Project, 2006. For Akita's comments on military training, see http://nisei .hawaii.edu/object/io_1158789656486.html; for his comments on military enlistment, see http://nisei.hawaii.edu/object/io_1158784803923.html.

108. Throughout March 1943, big sendoff parties were held across the Hawaiian Islands for nisei who had entered the US Army. Kerry Yo Nakagawa, *Through a Diamond: 100 Years of Japanese American Baseball* (San Francisco: Rudi Publishing, 2000), 115.

109. Kikuchi, *Memoirs of a Buddhist Woman*, 57–58.

8. LOYALTY AND THE DRAFT

1. Translated by Toshiko Sugiyama. Original found in the *Manzanar Bussei Guide* (1943), 10–11; reprinted in Masuyama, *Memories*, 44–45.

2. Greg Robinson, *By Order of the President: FDR and the Internment of Japanese Americans* (Cambridge, MA: Harvard University Press, 2001), 169–170.

3. Louis Fiset, "Thinning, Topping, and Loading: Japanese Americans and Beet Sugar in World War II," *Pacific Northwest Quarterly* 90: 3 (1999), 123–139.

4. Tetsuden Kashima, *Judgment without Trial: Japanese American Imprisonment during World War II* (Seattle: University of Washington Press, 2003), 161; and Chizuko Omori, "The Loyalty Questionnaire," in *Guilt by Association: Essays on Japanese Settlement, Internment, and Relocation in the*

Rocky Mountain West, ed. Mike Mackey (Powell, WY: Western History Publications, 2001), 277–286.

5. The Episcopalian priest Rev. Daisuke Kitagawa noted that at Tule Lake, the WRA administrations refused permission for issei meetings, a refusal that the issei could not comprehend. Daisuke Kitagawa, *Issei and Nisei: The Internment Years* (New York: Seabury Press, 1967), 117.

6. Edward H. Spicer, Asael T. Hansen, Katherine Luomala, Marvin K. Opler, *Impounded People: Japanese-Americans in the Relocation Centers,* War Relocation Authority (Tucson: University of Arizona Press, 1969), 157.

7. Morton Grodzins, *The Loyal and the Disloyal* (Chicago: University of Chicago Press, 1956), 123.

8. Ibid.

9. Noboru Shirai, *Tule Lake: An Issei Memoir* (Sacramento, CA: Muteki Press, 2001), 97.

10. "Tule Lake War Relocation Authority Camp Block 42," Suyama Project, UCLA Asian American Studies Center, October 1, 2014, http://www.suyamaproject.org/?p=88.

11. Shotaro Frank Miyamoto, *The Career of Intergroup Tensions: A Study of Collective Adjustments of Evacuees to Crises at the Tule Lake Relocation Center* (PhD diss., University of Chicago, 1950), 302–304.

12. Shirai, Tule Lake, 100.

13. Kentaro T., "The Factual Causes and Reasons Why I Refuse to Register" (JERS 67/14, R 30.25). Quoted in Richard Drinnon, *Keeper of Concentration Camps: Dillon S. Myer and American Racism* (Berkeley, CA: University of California Press, 1987), 85.

14. The quote from Choichi Nitta can be found in Eileen Sunada Sarasohn, *The Issei: Portrait of a Pioneer, An Oral History* (Palo Alto, CA: Pacific Books/Issei Oral History Project, 1983), 191.

15. The quote from can be found in Sarasohn, *The Issei,* 218; also see Michiyo Laing, et al., ed. *Issei Christians* (Sierra Mission, CA: Synod of the Pacific, United Presbyterian Church/Issei Oral History Project, 1977), 53, 58.

16. George Aki, "My 30 Months (1944–1946)," Veterans History Project, Library of Congress, American Folklife Center, 1, http://memory.loc.gov/diglib/vhp/story/loc.natlib.afc2001001.11135/pageturner?ID=pm0001001.

17. The Episcopalian priest Rev. Daisuke Kitagawa recalled performing a funeral for a young person who had passed away at the camp hospital due to tuberculosis: "Word somehow spread throughout the camp that a young Christian minister was conducting a funeral service for a Buddhist girl. Curiosity must have gotten the better of many people, for the funeral service for the lonely young woman was well attended." Tule Lake resident Ai

Miyasaki recalled people calling Rev. Kitagawa *inu,* saying, "He only does things the administration wants and does not do things for our benefit. Some threw garbage in front of him and said, 'Dogs should eat this.'" Sarasohn, *The Issei,* 209; Kitagawa, *Issei and Nisei,* 75, 121. The Presbyterian minister at Tule Lake, Rev. Isamu Nakamura, similarly feared for his safety, noting that "the Christian church in the camp argued that their [the nisei's] loyalties should be with the country of their birth in spite of the wrong committed by the government. . . . Reverend Iwasaki, formerly of San Francisco, was treated quite unfairly by those extremists who hung a bone over his table in the mess hall saying it was the only suitable food for an *inu.*" He added that "in fact I was on their [the pro-Japan faction's] list also, but fortunately people in my block gave me enough protection to keep from being attacked." Kitagawa, *Issei and Nisei,* 174.

18. Shirai notes that the Methodist Rev. Andrew Kuroda and the Salvation Army's Ichiji Matsushima were beaten, while the JACL's former national president Walter Tsukamoto was also on the hit list. Tsukamoto happened to be out of his barrack when the attackers came, but left the words "Expect a two-by-four anytime" scrawled on the wall. Shirai, *Tule Lake,* 99.

The WRA transferred Kuroda to the WRA Amache camp with his wife and two children before letting him go to Broomfield, Colorado, in the "free zone." Sumio Koga, *A Decade of Faith: The Journey of Japanese Christians in the USA (1936–1946)* (New York: Vantage Press, 2002), 67–68; "Andrew Kuroda," Dictionary of Unitarian and Universalist Biography, http://uudb .org/articles/andrewkuroda.html.

19. Quote from Shōichi Fukuda in Sarasohn, *The Issei,* 189.

20. Andrew B. Wertheimer, *Japanese American Community Libraries in America's Concentration Camps, 1942–1946* (PhD diss., University of Wisconsin, Madison, 2004), 169.

21. The Methodist minister was Rev. Tarō Gotō and the Buddhist priest was Rev. Itsuzō Kyōgoku. The administration appointed Kyōgoku as adult education committee chair, from which position he developed recreational outlets to help Japanese-speakers adjust to life in Topaz. One of his biggest successes was the creation of the largest Japanese-language library in any of the WRA camps, consisting at its peak of 4,227 donated books (including 900 books of his own). Ibid., 169–175.

22. On Sugimoto's painting of Rev. Yamazaki, see Anne Blankenship, *Christianity, Social Justice, and Japanese American Incarceration during World War II* (Chapel Hill, NC: University of North Carolina Press, 2016), 140–141; and Kristine Kim, *Henry Sugimoto: Painting an American Experience* (Berkeley, CA: Heyday Books, 2000), 86–87.

23. Interview with John Yamazaki, Summer 1974. Quoted in Lester Suzuki, *Ministry in the Assembly and Relocation Centers in World War II* (Berkeley, CA: Yardbird Publishing, 1979), 307–308.

24. John H. M. Yamazaki, letter to Bishop Charles Shriver Reifsnider, March 8, 1943. Archives of the Episcopal Church, RG 71, Box 172, File 3. Quoted in Joanna Bowen Gillespie, "Japanese-American Episcopalians during World War II: The Congregation of St. Mary's Los Angeles, 1941–1945," *Anglican and Episcopal History* 69:2, Japanese-American Episcopalians during World War II (June 2000), 135–169: 156, https://www.jstor.org/stable/42612096.

25. Suzuki, *Ministry in the Assembly*, 308.

26. Koga, *A Decade of Faith*, 67–68.

27. Kitagawa, *Issei and Nisei*, 118.

28. Mike Masaoka, "Final Report," April 22, 1944, administrative files of the Japanese American Citizens League (JACL), Japanese American National Library (San Francisco, CA), Series 14, Box 46; Masayo Duus, *Unlikely Liberators: The Men of the 100th and 442nd* (Honolulu: University of Hawai'i Press, 1987), 52–53.

29. Baptist Paul Nagano is quoted in Suzuki, *Ministry in the Assembly*, 257.

30. Kiyota had been interviewed by an FBI agent who accused him, because of his *kendō* activities, of having connections to the pro-Japanese military group, the Butoku-kai. "I would never forget my hatred of that FBI agent. I cursed the government of the United States, which had thrown me into this camp," Kiyota said. But he could not support the violence of the radical pro-Japan Kibei group, which suspected him of collaborating with camp officials. Minoru Kiyota, *Beyond Loyalty: The Story of a Kibei* (Honolulu: University of Hawai'i Press, 1997), 80–84.

31. Ibid., 191.

32. Ibid., 98.

33. Robert Asahina, *Just Americans: How Japanese Americans Won a War at Home and Abroad* (New York: Gotham Books, 2006), 51–52, 55.

34. Suzuki claimed that Minidoka had the highest percentage of volunteers for the 442nd because its residents were primarily from the Pacific Northwest, a region somewhat less virulent in its prewar anti-Japanese sentiment than California, leading to a community "more prone to get along with the general American public than the people from California." Suzuki, *Ministry in the Assembly*, 205. The spokesperson was Yoshito Fujii. Sarasohn, *The Issei*, 219.

35. Blankenship, *Christianity, Social Justice*, 149.

36. Kashima has noted, "Until registration for the army occurred, the course of the [United Buddhist] Church was fairly smooth, but at that time

twelve of the trustees of the Church requested three other board members to resign. The twelve members feared that the hostility of the three to registration would make Buddhism appear to be a pro-Japanese religion." Kashima, *Judgment without Trial*, 55.

37. "Japs Riot; Army Moves In," *Tulelake Reporter* (November 4, 1943), 1. The Tule Lake riot had multiple causes, but the October 1943 death of a nisei significantly escalated tensions. A committee of representatives from each block (the Daihyōshakai), which was dominated by followers of Rev. Shizuo Kai, tried to negotiate an arrangement for the deceased man's family. When a permit for a camp-sponsored funeral was refused and camp administrators refused to send condolences to his widow, dissension spread, and two thousand people gathered on October 23 for the Buddhist funeral. Detainees were further inflamed by learning that the widow received only $10.66 as compensation for the work-related death. The agricultural workers then went on strike to improve safety measures. A protest followed on November 1, when a crowd of four thousand encircled the camp's administration building to demand a "re-segregation" program to remove those with pro-American sentiments from Tule Lake, especially those who volunteered for the 442nd RCT. The protesters also occupied the camp's hospital, where the chief medical officer—widely known as a racist who treated camp patients with contempt—was dragged out and beaten. In response, the white camp staff called on the military police garrison to provide security. Tanks rolled in and in a few days, the Tule Lake camp was a militarized zone with effective control shifted from the WRA to the Army for the next three months. Bunyū Fujimura, *Though I Be Crushed: The Wartime Experiences of a Buddhist Minister* (Los Angeles: The Nembutsu Press, 1995), 69; Kashima, *Judgment without Trial*, 165–166; Shirai, *Tule Lake*, 115–116; and Barbara Takei, "Legalizing Detention: Segregated Japanese Americans and the Justice Department's Renunciation Program," *Journal of the Shaw Historical Library* 19 (2005), 75–105: 78.

38. Police beat "the troublemakers" so severely with clubs that all of them were hospitalized, some left unconscious. In the subsequent investigation, WRA employees Anne Lefkowitz and Gloria Waldron reported that when they went into work on November 5 they "found a broken baseball bat and a mess of blood and black hair on the floors and spattered on the walls, which they were compelled to clean up before they could go about their duties." See ACLU's report in Michi Weglyn, *Years of Infamy: The Untold Story of America's Concentration Camps* (Seattle: University of Washington Press, 1996), 212. Harry Ueno, who had been transferred to Tule Lake after the so-called Manzanar riot, recalled seeing the stockade: "I saw from a window

there is one small tent, single tent. I ask them who is there. Reverend Kai. He is from Arkansas or something. He was a negotiating committee head. So they put in single tent. [The temperature at] Tule Lake is 10 below zero during middle of winter and no stove—nothing there. They really torture him." Japanese American Historical Society, ed. *REgenerations Oral History Project: Rebuilding Japanese American Families, Communities, and Civil Rights in the Resettlement Era* (Los Angeles: Japanese American Historical Society, 2000), 500.

39. Estimates have ranged up to 450. Tamura states that the number of stockade inmates was 350. Eileen H. Tamura, *In Defense of Justice: Joseph Kurihara and the Japanese American Struggle for Equality* (Urbana, IL: University of Illinois Press, 2013), 100.

40. Kashima, *Judgment without Trial*, 167.

41. Sachiko Takita-Ishii, "Tokio Yamane: A Renunciant's Story," *Journal of the Shaw Historical Library* 19 (2005), 168.

42. Shirai, *Tule Lake*, 131–132.

43. Rev. Kenjitsu Tsuha had served the Ewa Hongwanji Mission and was arrested after Pearl Harbor, and then sent to Army internment camps before ending up at Tule Lake. Suikei Furuya, *An Internment Odyssey: Haisho Tenten* (Honolulu: Japanese Cultural Center of Hawai'i / University of Hawai'i Press, 2017), 77, 220.

44. The two leaders of the organization were Zenshirō Tachibana and Tsutomi Higashi, the nisei son of Jōdo priest Rev. Meishun Hayashi. For more on these individuals, see John J. Culley, "The Santa Fe Internment Camp and the Justice Department Program for Enemy Aliens," in *Japanese Americans: From Relocation to Redress,* ed. Roger Daniels, Sandra Taylor, and Harry Kitano (Seattle: University of Washington Press, 1991), 65. Furuya lists the son as Ichirō Hayashi. Furuya, *An Internment Odyssey*, 337

45. They were Rev. Tesshō Matsumoto (Yakima Buddhist Church) and Rev. Shingetsu Akahoshi (Gardena Buddhist Church). Akahoshi recalled how shocked he was to see the devastation in Japan when he arrived with Rev. Matsumoto, because both believed Japan had been winning the war. Interview with Shingetsu Akahoshi by Duncan Williams, Osaka, Japan, January 31, 2003.

46. Motomu Tom Akashi, "Tule Lake Segregation Center: Resegregation and Pro-Japan Movement," *Journal of the Shaw Historical Library* 19 (2005): 117–119, 134; Shirai, *Tule Lake*, 150. Shirai supported the group initially because it was led by a Buddhist priest, but soon became disillusioned with what he felt were "terrorist" tendencies by those who ousted Rev. Tsuha and who aimed to make the organization more militant.

47. The priest was Rev. Dōjun Ochi. Soga notes that the Shichisho-kai met every seventh (*shichi*) of the month under the auspices of the Buddhist and Shinto federations, but that "was just a subterfuge, and the authorities never suspected otherwise." Yasutarō Soga, *Life Behind Barbed Wire: The World War II Internment Memoirs of a Hawai'i Issei* (Honolulu: Japanese Cultural Center of Hawai'i / University of Hawai'i Press, 2008), 174.

48. Nyogen Senzaki, Speech to Heart Mountain High School, May 26, 1950, Robert Aitken Collection, University of Hawai'i at Manoa Library, Honolulu, HI.

49. Greg Robinson, *After Camp: Portraits in Midcentury Japanese American Life and Politics* (Berkeley, CA: University of California Press, 2012), 44.

50. Ibid., 45. On December 17, 1944, the US government had announced the forthcoming January lifting of the ban on those of Japanese heritage from the west coast, a day before the US Supreme Court ruling in *Ex parte Endo* found that it was not legal for the government to forcibly hold Japanese American citizens without charge in the camps.

51. For more on the college students given permission to leave camp, see Gary Okihiro, *Storied Lives: Japanese American Students and World War II* (Seattle: University of Washington Press, 1999).

52. Anne Blankenship notes, "While not all Buddhists felt discriminated against, they comprised only 15 percent of financial aid applicants in 1943." Blankenship, *Christianity, Social Justice*, 72.

53. In Minidoka, the camp's Quaker director George Townsend was known to be sympathetic to the nisei. Townsend recalled, "Many of the larger [Christian] denominations set up Relocation Committees in their efforts to get the evacuees out of the Centers. Many religious bodies, Catholic and Protestant, established direct communication with their respective constituents within the Centers and were frequent visitors to the Center. They were given every assistance by my staff." George L. Townsend, "Service with the War Relocation Authority, 1942–1946," (Densho Encyclopedia, n.d.), 29, http://encyclopedia.densho.org/media/ddr-densho-275/ddr-densho-275-33-mezzanine-95748afc58.pdf.

54. An intradepartmental Japanese American joint board was responsible for processing the loyalty registration program. It had voting members from the WRA, the War Department, the Provost Marshal General's Office, the Office of Naval Intelligence, the Army G-2 (Intelligence) Division, and, for a time, the FBI. Their initial goal was to provide recommendations "concerning the release of subject individuals from relocation centers on indefinite leave" and then to determine if an individual could be cleared to work in "plants and facilities important to the war effort"—though this second

clearance process was taken over by the Provost Marshal General's Office in October 1943. Eric L. Muller, *American Inquisition: The Hunt for Japanese American Disloyalty in World War II* (Chapel Hill, NC: The University of North Carolina Press, 2007), 67–72.

55. Ibid., 47.

56. Ibid., 48.

57. Ibid., 50.

58. They were Harry Iba and Dorothy Ito. Ibid., 61–62, 64–65.

59. Ibid., 76.

60. For more on the draft resisters, see Shirley Castelnuovo, *Soldiers of Conscience: Japanese American Military Resisters in World War Two* (Lincoln, NB: University of Nebraska Press, 2010); Mike Mackey, ed. *A Matter of Conscience: Essays on the World War II Heart Mountain Draft Resistance Movement* (Powell, WY: Western History Publications, 2002); and Eric L. Muller, *Free to Die for their Country: The Story of the Japanese American Draft Resisters in World War II* (Chicago: University of Chicago Press, 2001).

61. At Heart Mountain, Kiyoshi Okamoto, Sam Horino, and Frank Emi organized the Fair Play Committee. Okamoto and Horino were sent to Tule Lake, while Emi and sixty-three draft resisters were brought to trial. Greg Robinson, *A Tragedy of Democracy: Japanese Confinement in North America* (New York: Columbia University Press, 2009), 212–214.

62. Ron Magden, *Mukashi Mukashi Long Long Ago: The First Century of the Seattle Buddhist Church* (Seattle: Seattle Buddhist Church, 2012), 156.

63. Eric L. Muller, "The Minidoka Draft Resisters in a Federal Kangaroo Court," in *Nikkei in the Pacific Northwest: Japanese Americans and Japanese Canadians in the Twentieth Century,* ed. Louis Fiset and Gail Nomura (Seattle: University of Washington Press, 2005), 174, 178–179.

64. Mary Farrell and Jeffrey Burton, "Civil Rights and Moral Wrongs: World War II Japanese American Relocation Sites," *The SAA Archaeological Record* 4:5 (2004), 22–25: 24.

9. COMBAT IN EUROPE

1. This section on the Matsuda family and Haru's Buddhist song lyrics is drawn from research by Keiko Wells, scholar of American studies and musicology. She has noted that the melody of "War Song" is based on "Senyu" (A Fellow Soldier), composed by Hisen Mashimo. The original song was sung in elementary schools, especially in western Japan where Haru Matsuda grew up. It was banned in the 1930s as the Japanese military authorities thought it detracted from the heroics of war. Keiko Wells, "The

Role of Buddhist Song Culture in International Acculturation," in *Issei Buddhism in the Americas*, Duncan Ryuken Williams and Tomoe Moriya, eds. (Urbana, IL: University of Illinois Press, 2010), 164–186: 170–171. I have made minor adjustments to her translation of the lyrics.

2. Ibid.

3. Staff Sergeant Robert Ozaki ordered the charge. C. Douglas Sterner, *Go for Broke: The Nisei Warriors of World War II Who Conquered Germany, Japan and American Bigotry* (Clearfield, UT: American Legacy Historical Press, 2008), 9; Duus notes that this "banzai charge" was "greatly exaggerated in the press." Masayo Duus, *Unlikely Liberators: The Men of the 100th and 442nd* (Honolulu: University of Hawai'i Press, 1987), 103.

4. Sterner notes that, "the small soldiers of the 100th, dwarfed by backpacks almost as large as they were, were sometimes bent on taking 'a mountain a day.'" Sterner, *Go for Broke*, 23.

5. Ibid., 10, 27.

6. Woo Sung Han, *Unsung Hero: The Story of Colonel Young Oak Kim* (Riverside, CA: Young Oak Kim Center for Korean American Studies, 2011), 76, 81.

7. Mike Markrich, "Kiyoshi Jimmie Shiramizu, A Son's Story: Discovering a Father," 100th Infantry Battalion Veterans Education Center, http://www.100thbattalion.org/history/veterans/soldiers-killed-in-action/kiyoshi-shiramizu/.

8. Israel A. Yost, *Combat Chaplain: The Personal Story of the World War II Chaplain of the Japanese American 100th Battalion* (Honolulu: University of Hawai'i Press, 2006), 104–105.

9. Franz Steidl, *Lost Battalions: Going for Broke in the Vosges, Autumn 1944* (Novato, CA: Presidio Press, 1997), 52.

10. Deborah Dash Moore, *GI Jews: How World War II Changed a Generation* (Cambridge, MA: Belknap Press of Harvard University Press, 2004), 73.

11. Harold T. Oie, *Military Intelligence Service* (n.p., 1990), 1–10. Copy of self-published book in the University of Hawai'i, Manoa Library's Hamilton Archives and Manuscripts, D810.S7 O38 1990.

12. Go For Broke Educational Foundation, Interview with Tadashi Tojo, January 21, 2002, Tape #4, http://www.goforbroke.org/ohmsviewer/viewer.php?cachefile=2002OHO232_03_Tojo.xml. Quoted in James M. McCaffrey, *Going for Broke: Japanese American Soldiers in the War against Nazi Germany* (Norman, OK: University of Oklahoma Press, 2013), 66.

13. Yost, *Combat Chaplain*, 117.

14. Ibid., 117.

15. Ibid., 6–7.

16. Israel A. S. Yost, "Step Off the Road, and Let the Dead Pass By," Memorial Address to Club 100 veterans, Makawao Veterans Cemetery, Honolulu, September 1947. Full text in Yost, *Combat Chaplain*, 293–297.

17. Yost, *Combat Chaplain*, 168–170. His reference is to the German Lutheran pastor Martin Niemöller, imprisoned by the Nazis.

18. McCaffrey, *Going for Broke*, 166–167. Sterner reports that the Japanese Americans were halted by General Harmon of the American First Armored Division when their unit was within seven miles of Rome. "They sat along the road watching other units march triumphantly down the Highway and into the heroes welcome lavished upon them by the liberated citizens of Rome. It was one of the saddest indignities the men who had fought so hard and given so much could have suffered." Sterner, *Go for Broke*, 39.

19. Han, *Unsung Hero*, 87–88; McCaffrey, *Going for Broke*, 196.

20. By contrast, the American casualty rate was 17 percent during the battle at Tawara Atoll in the Pacific, which is regarded as one of the deadliest battles in the two-hundred-year history of the US Marine Corps. Lyle W. Dorsett, *Serving God and Country: U.S. Military Chaplains in World War II* (New York: Berkeley Caliber Books, 2012), 97.

21. In 1996, Tanouye's Distinguished Service Cross was upgraded to a Medal of Honor after a review of service records of those who served in World War II. Tanouye's family, along with the families of twenty-one other Asian Americans, received the upgraded Medal of Honor in 2000 in a ceremony presided over by President Bill Clinton.

22. For the most comprehensive study of Masuda, see Russell K. Shoho, *From the Battlefields to the Home Front: The Kazuo Masuda Legacy* (Fullerton, CA: Nikkei Writers Guild, Japanese American Living Legacy, 2009)

23. Yost, *Combat Chaplain*, 119, 134, 171–174,

24. Ibid., 8.

25. Ibid., 200.

26. Ibid., 5–6, 18, 50, 74.

27. Ibid., 209.

28. Michael Markrich, "Masao Yamada," 100th Infantry Battalion Veterans Education Center, http://www.100thbattalion.org/history/veterans/chaplains/masao-yamada/.

29. The medic was Minoru Masuda. See Minora Masuda, *Letters from the 442nd: The World War II Correspondence of a Japanese American Medic* (Seattle: University of Washington Press, 2015), 160–161.

30. Hawaii Nikkei History Editorial Board, ed., *Japanese Eyes, American Heart: Personal Reflections of Hawaii's World War II Nisei Soldiers* (Honolulu: University of Hawai'i Press, 1998).

31. Moore, *GI Jews*, 129; Robert L. Gushwa, *The Best and Worst of Times: The United States Army Chaplaincy, vol. IV, 1920–1945* (Washington, DC: Office of the Chief of Chaplains, Department of the Army, 1977), https://archive.org/details/unitedstatesarmyo4unit.

32. Moore, *GI Jews*, 10, 119–126.

33. John Hall, "Memorandum to Colonel [William P.] Scobey," February 9, 1943, National Archives and Records Administration, Record Group 107, Box 47 Folder 4, Digitized Collection of the Japanese American Veterans Association, Washington DC, http://www.javadc.org/java/docs/1943-02-09%20Ltr%20Lt%20Hall%20to%20Scobey%20re%20442nd%20RCT%20ques-tions%20Pg4_ck.pdf. My thanks to Michael Masatsugu for sharing forthcoming research related to Buddhist chaplains. I also rely on Ronit Stahl, *God, War, and Politics: The American Military Chaplaincy and the Making of a Multireligious Nation* (PhD diss., University of Michigan, 2014).

34. William P. Scobey, letter to Colonel Charles W. Pence, April 24, 1943, Record Group 107, Box 47, Folder 10, National Archives and Records Administration II, Digitized Collection of the Japanese American Veterans Association, Washington DC, http://www.javadc.org/java/docs/1943-04-24%20Ltr%20Scobey%20to%20Col%20Pence%20re%20Buddhist%20chaplain%20for%20442nd%20Pg1_ck.pdf. Scobey's recommendation to "determine the number or percentage" of Buddhists did not, however, result in a proper survey of religious affiliation being conducted.

35. Mike Masaoka, *They Call Me Moses Masaoka: An American Saga* (New York: William Morrow & Co., 1987), 135.

36. Charles S. Reifsnider, Letter to Ellis M. Zacharias, June 14, 1943, Records of the Office of the Chief of Chaplains (Record Group 247), Security Classified General Correspondence, 1941–1948, Box 1, Folder 080, National Archives and Records Administration. Quoted in Stahl, *God, War, and Politics*, 178.

37. William Scobey to William Arnold, June 7, 1943, RG 247 (1920–45), Box 60, Folder 080 (Buddhist), NARA II. Quoted in Stahl, *God, War, and Politics*, 179.

38. William Arnold, Letter to Bishop Matsukage, March 24, 1943, Record Group 247 (1920–1945), Box 60, Folder 080 (Buddhist), National Archives and Records Administration II. Quoted in Stahl, *God, War, and Politics*, 176.

39. Ibid.

40. Bussei Life, "Rev. Kumata Volunteers," *Bussei Life* [Topaz newsletter] Vol. 1 No. 2, May 15, 1943, 2–3.

41. According to a historian of the US Army Chaplain Corps, the Buddhist Mission of North America was asked to furnish a chaplain but after

considerable effort reported that it could not find a qualified candidate. Roy J. Honeywell, *Chaplains of the United States Army* (Washington, DC: Office of the Chief of Chaplains, 1958), 221.

42. This movie short should not be confused with the postwar MGM feature-length film of the same title.

43. George Okazaki, Letter to Rev. Zenkai Okayama (Deputy Bishop), March 27, 1944. Box 172, BCA Archives Collection, Japanese American National Museum.

44. Zenkai Okayama, Letter to George Okazaki, March 31, 1944. (BCA Archives, Box 172).

45. Stahl, *God, War, and Politics,* 177.

46. George Aki, "My 30 Months (1944–1946)," Veterans History Project, Library of Congress, American Folklife Center, 3, http://memory.loc.gov /diglib/vhp/story/loc.natlib.afc2001001.11135/pageturner?ID=pm0001001.

47. Milton O. Beebe, Letter to Bishop Matsukage, March 4, 1944 (Box 172, BCA Archives Collection).

48. Brian Hayashi, *Democratizing the Enemy: The Japanese American Internment* (Princeton: Princeton University Press, 2004), 187.

49. Robert Sasaki of Waialua, Hawai'i, recalled, "We had a big party and I had a *sennin-bari* to protect me. We also went to pray to Odaishi-sama to keep me safe. I was never religious but went for my parents' sake." Dorothy Matsuo, *Boyhood to War: History and Anecdotes of the 442nd Regimental Combat Team* (Honolulu: Mutual Publishing, 1992), 53.

Families in Hawai'i also visited the leader of the Seichō no Ie (a "sect Shinto" new religion known for faith healing) in large numbers after it was rumored that her rituals over the photographs of nisei soldiers prevented harm from coming to them. According to Andrew Lind, an anthropologist studying the Japanese Hawaiian community, anxious parents brought some 1,283 photographs to her. Andrew W. Lind, *Hawaii's Japanese: An Experiment in Democracy* (Princeton University Press, 1946), 208. Groups occasionally met with the Seicho-no-Ie leader at the Higashi Honganji temple (where short-use permits were granted by the military government) as all Shinto-related shrines were closed throughout the war. Yukiko Kimura, *Issei: Japanese Immigrants in Hawaii* (Honolulu: University of Hawai'i Press, 1988), 245.

50. Ron Magden, *Mukashi Mukashi Long Long Ago: The First Century of the Seattle Buddhist Church* (Seattle: Seattle Buddhist Church, 2012), 154.

51. Go For Broke Educational Foundation, Interview with Minoru Tsubota, July 27, 2002. Tape #4, http://www.goforbroke.org/learn/archives /oral_histories_videos.php?clip=29704.

52. Robert Asahina, *Just Americans: How Japanese Americans Won a War at Home and Abroad* (New York: Gotham Books, 2006), 56; Edward Yamasaki, ed. *And Then There Were Eight: The Men of I Company 442nd Regimental Combat Team* (Honolulu: 442 Veterans Club, 2003), 117.

53. Duus, *Unlikely Liberators,* 109.

54. "Buddhists Busy Making Small Scrolls," *Denson Tribune* (May 18, 1943), 3; Jane E. Dusselier, *Artifacts of Loss: Crafting Survival in Japanese American Concentration Camps* (New Brunswick, NJ: Rutgers University Press, 2008), 132.

55. Amy Nomi [Denver YBA secretary], Letter to Topaz BCA Headquarters, September 30, 1944; October 8, 1944, BCA Archives Collection, Box 172.

56. Ibid.

57. The *go-ezō* project was led by Rev. Shintatsu Sanada. *Poston Daisan Bukkyō Kaihō* [Poston Third Buddhist District Newsletter] 20 (August 1944): 1.

58. Tayoshi Munakata, "Letter from the Battlefield," *Poston Daisan Bukkyō Kaihō* [Poston Third Buddhist District Newsletter] 26 (February 1945): 1.

59. Shintatsu Sanada, Letter to [Poston YBA Executive Secretary] George Yada, February 27, 1945, Box 12-G I / Box 15, BCA Archives Collection.

60. Shigeo Kikuchi, *Memoirs of a Buddhist Woman Missionary* (Honolulu: The Buddhist Study Center Press, 1991), 64.

61. Jōin Kihara, *Arashi no nakade: Kaisen to spai yōgi* [In the Midst of a Storm: Accusations of Being a Spy at the Outbreak of the War] (Kyoto: Nagata Bunshōdo, 1985), 3. My translation here approximates the somewhat childish Japanese grammatical forms used by the soldier.

62. Ronald Oba, *The Men of Company F* (Honolulu: 442nd RCT Club of Hawaii, 2006), 77; Shoho, *From the Battlefields to the Home Front,* 67–68.

63. Bunyū Fujimura, *Though I Be Crushed: The Wartime Experiences of a Buddhist Minister* (Los Angeles: The Nembutsu Press, 1995), 97–99.

64. Shinjō Nagatomi, memorial address, Manzanar, California. This excerpt is from a full translation of the speech in Eiko Masuyama, *Memories: The Buddhist Church Experience in the Camps, 1942–1945,* 2nd rev. ed. (Los Angeles: Nishi Honganji Betsuin, 2007), 75–77.

65. Michael Masatsugu, *Reorienting the Pure Land: Japanese Americans, the Beats, and the Making of American Buddhism, 1941–1966* (PhD diss., University of California, Irvine, 2004), 64; Official California Legislative Information, "Senate Concurrent Resolution No. 41 Relative to Highways," filed September 9, 1994, http://www.leginfo.ca.gov/pub/93-94/bill/sen/sb _0001-0050/scr_41_bill_940909_chaptered.

66. Masatsugu, *Reorienting the Pure Land,* 63.

67. Publication Committee of "A History of Japanese Immigrants in Hawaii," *Hawaii Nihonjin Iminshi* [A History of Japanese Immigration in Hawaii] (Honolulu: United Japanese Society of Hawaii, 1964), 362.

68. This was the recollection of Edwin (Bud) Nakasone of Wahiawa, Hawaiʻi, who was drafted and served late in the war in the military intelligence service. See Edwin M. Nakasone, *Japanese American Veterans of Minnesota* (White Bear Lake, MN: J-Press Publishing, 2002), 93–97.

69. Letter from Hatsuno Mihara to Brigadier General Donald J. Meyers, March 23, 1944, National Archives and Records Administration, Record Group 338, Military Government of Hawaii, Research and Historical Section, Box 182.

70. D. H. Tokunaga, "Request for Permission to Conduct Buddhist Services," Memorandum to Ezra Crane [Captain, Infantry, Intelligence Officer], April 3, 1944. National Archives and Records Administration, Record Group 338, Military Government of Hawaii, Research and Historical Section, Box 181.

71. Letter from Colonel R. C. Morrison to Office of the Representative of the Military Governor, Maui District, April 24, 1944. National Archives and Records Administration, Record Group 338, Military Government of Hawaii, Research and Historical Section, Box 182.

72. The nisei killed in action was Tadashi Kojima.

73. Quoted in John R. K. Clark, *Guardian of the Sea: Jizo in Hawaiʻi* (Honolulu: University of Hawaiʻi Press, 2007), 139. The original notebooks containing handwritten details on the deceased nisei soldiers can be found in the Bishop M. Tottori Papers, Archives & Manuscripts Department, University of Hawaiʻi at Manoa Library. Copies of the notebooks can be found at the Smithsonian Institution, Liliha Shingonji Mission in Honolulu, and the Japanese Cultural Center of Hawaiʻi. The entries note each soldier killed in action chronologically. For example, after Sgt. Shigeo Takata on September 29, 1943, the following four entries are Pvt. Himeo Hiratani (November 4, 1943), Pvt. Takumi Fukunaga (November 5, 1943), Pvt. Kaoru Moriwaki, who was posthumously given the Buddhist name Ken-sei-in Shaku Yūmon Shinji (November 1, 1943), and Pvt. Yoshisada Kuraoka (November 29, 1943).

74. Sadako Tottori Kaneko, interviewed by author, January 15, 2018 (in Liliha Shingonji, Honolulu). This memorial tablet *(ihai)* is still housed at the Liliha Shingonji Mission. For more on the *ihai* and the *toba* memorial tablets, see Jitsunin Kawanishi, "Mune ga hareru: Senjika no Hawaii jijō," [Something to Take Pride In: The Wartime Circumstances in Hawaiʻi] *Kōyasan Jihō* [Mount Kōya Bulletin] 3373 (2016): 59–61.

75. The request came from the family of the 442nd's Sgt. James Tetsuo Higashi, who had been killed in action in Italy on July 12, 1944.

76. Kikuchi, *Memoirs of a Buddhist Woman Missionary*, 65.

77. The full poem can be found in Eiko Masuyama, *Memories: The Buddhist Church Experience in the Camps, 1942–1945*, 2nd rev. ed. (Los Angeles: Nishi Honganji Betsuin, 2007), 183.

78. Japanese American women's service in the US military came primarily through their volunteering for the Women's Army Corps (WAC). Brenda Moore, *Serving Our Country: Japanese American Women in the Military during World War II* (New Brunswick, NJ: Rutgers University Press, 2003).

79. This incident is detailed in Kimura, *Why Pursue the Buddha?* (Los Angeles: The Nembutsu Press, 1976), 136–141. It was first published in the April 1953 issue of the Japanese-language *Budesto Magajin* (*Buddhist Magazine*), which in turn relied on an article written by Jitsuo Matsubara's fellow unit member, Corporal Toshio Nakano for a since defunct Los Angeles-based English weekly newspaper, Crossroads. I have relied on Kimura's account here.

80. For more on the "B for Buddhism" campaign and efforts for military cemeteries to recognize Buddhist symbols, see Masatsugu, *Reorienting the Pure Land*, 88–94.

81. Los Angeles Times, "Tribute Paid to Nisei at Hero's Last Rites," *Los Angeles Times*, May 2, 1948, 3.

10. THE RESETTLEMENT

1. Nyogen Senzaki's "Fellow Students," August 5, 1945, Zen Studies Society, *Like a Dream, Like a Fantasy: The Zen Teachings and Translations of Nyogen Senzaki* (Somerville, MA: Wisdom Publications, 2005), 53. Copyright © 2005 by Zen Studies Society. Reprinted by arrangement with The Permissions Company, Inc., on behalf of Wisdom Publications, Inc., wisdompubs.org. Note the time zone difference: the Emperor's announcement was broadcast just after noon on August 15, 1945, when it was still August 14 in the United States.

2. Nyogen Senzaki, *Eloquent Silence: Nyogen Senzaki's Gateless Gate and Other Previously Unpublished Teachings and Letters* (Somerville, MA: Wisdom Publications, 2008), 15. This poem was written on October 29, 1945.

3. Senzaki, *Eloquent Silence*, 13–15.

4. Senzaki, *Like a Dream, Like a Fantasy*, 197.

5. John Howard, *Concentration Camps on the Home Front: Japanese Americans in the House of Jim Crow* (Chicago: University of Chicago Press, 2008), 166.

6. Leonard J. Arrington, *The Price of Prejudice: The Japanese-American Relocation Center in Utah During World War II* (Logan, UT: Utah State University Press, 1962), 54.

7. Naomi Hirahara and Heather Lindquist, *Life After Manzanar* (Berkeley, CA: Heyday Books, 2018), 5–12.

8. Greg Robinson, *By Order of the President: FDR and the Internment of Japanese Americans* (Cambridge, MA: Harvard University Press, 2001), 250.

9. Aimee Semple McPherson to Governor Earl Warren, Congressman John B. Costello, and Congressman Norris K. Poulson, telegram, June 8, 1943, personal papers of Aimee Semple McPherson, Heritage Department, International Church of the Foursquare Gospel, Los Angeles, CA. McPherson's missive was shared with and quoted by the *Los Angeles Times*. "Aimee Protests Return of Japs," *Los Angeles Times*, June 9, 1943, 7. In turn, news accounts were briefly quoted in the camp newspaper. "LA Evangelist Protests Release," *Granada Pioneer* (Amache, Colorado), June 16, 1943, 3. My thanks to Greg Robinson for pointing out that McPherson died in September 1944, well before the return of the Japanese American community to the west coast.

10. Earl Warren, speaking at a press conference in Sacramento, California, June 11, 1943. Quoted in "Warren Hits Proposal," *The Bakersfield Californian*, June 11, 1943, 1. Quoted in turn by *Granada Pioneer* (Amache, Colorado), June 16, 1943, 3.

11. Stuart Whitehouse, "Kent-Auburn District Calls Meet; Others Pleased at Return," *Seattle Star*, December 18, 1944, 1, http://depts.washington.edu /civilr/after_internment.htm.

12. Lambert Schuyler, *The Japs Must Not Come Back! A Practical Approach to the Racial Problem* (Winslow, WA: Heron House, 1944), 6–8, Japanese American Evacuation and Resettlement Records, Bancroft Library, UC Berkeley, https://oac.cdlib.org/ark:/13030/kt4489r763/?brand=oac4. Quoted in Kevin Allen Leonard, "'Is That What We Fought For?' Japanese Americans and Racism in California: The Impact of World War II," *Western Historical Quarterly* 21:4 (November 1990), 463–482: 467.

13. Alexander Yamato, "Restoring Family and Community in the Santa Clara Valley: Japanese American Resettlement," in Japanese American Historical Society, ed., *REgenerations Oral History Project: Rebuilding Japanese American Families, Communities, and Civil Rights in the Resettlement Era*, Volume 4 (Los Angeles: Japanese American Historical Society, 2000), xxx–xxxi.

14. "San Benito County Board of Supervisors Resolution," April 1, 1943. Reproduced in Sandy Lydon, *The Japanese in the Monterey Bay Region: A Brief History* (Capitola, CA: Capitola Book Company, 1997), 115.

15. Ralph G. Martin, "Legion Post Arouses Ire of 7th's GIs," *Stars and Stripes*, January 5, 1945, 2. For discussion, see Linda Tamura, *The Hood River Issei: An Oral History of Japanese Settlers in Oregon's Hood River Valley* (Urbana, IL: University of Illinois Press, 1993), 216–219.

16. Tamura, *The Hood River Issei*, 235.

17. Ibid., 221.

18. Robinson, *By Order of the President*, 224–227.

19. Douglas Dye, *The Soul of the City: The Work of the Seattle Council of Churches during WWII* (PhD diss., Washington State University, 1997), 130.

20. *Ex parte Mitsuye Endo*, 323 US 283 (1944); *Korematsu v. United States*, 323 US 214 (1944). See Robinson, *By Order of the President*, 230.

21. Seattle Buddhist Church, ed., *Seattle Betsuin 1954* (Seattle: Seattle Buddhist Church, 1955), 8.

22. Robert Y. Fuchigami, *Amache: An American Concentration Camp in Colorado, August 27, 1942 to October 15, 1945* (private publication, 2000). For more on the All Centers Conference, see Lane Hirabayashi, "Re-Reading the Archives: Intersections of Ethnography, Biography, and Autobiography in Japanese American Evacuation and Resettlement," *Peace & Change* 23:2 (1998), 175–178.

23. James Sakoda, "The 'Residue': The Unresettled Minodokans, 1943–1945," in *Views from Within: The Japanese American Evacuation and Resettlement Study*, ed. Yuji Ichioka (Los Angeles: UCLA Asian American Studies Center, 1989), 247–284: 258.

24. Mrs. Cecil Itano, quoted in Carey McWilliams, *Prejudice: Japanese Americans: Symbol of Racial Intolerance* (Boston: Little, Brown, 1944), 217. See also Richard Cahan and Michael Williams, *Un-American: The Incarceration of Japanese Americans during World War II—Images by Dorothea Lange, Ansel Adams, and Other Government Photographers* (Chicago: CityFiles Press, 2016), 149.

25. Memo to John J. McCloy, Assistant Secretary of War, "Relocation of Japanese-Americans on West Coast," June 6, 1945, http://www.javadc.org /java/docs/1945-06-06%20Permits%20to%20enter,%20olive%20in%20 WDC,%20Memo%20to%20Mcloy,%20Relocation-Incidents%20Pg17_ck.pdf.

26. The *Pacific Citizen*, the JACL's weekly newspaper, noted over forty incidents of violence and intimidation in the first six months of 1945. See Leonard, "'Is That What We Fought For?,'" 468.

27. Statement by Secretary Harold L. Ickes, April 4, 1945, quoted in *Pacific Citizen*, April 28, 1945, 1.

28. Gila News-Courier, "Girl Discloses Threats During California Visit," Gila News-Courier Vol. IV, No. 40 (May 19, 1945), 1. The incident was also

noted by the WRA. Allan Markley, "Special Field Report," undated memorandum to Dillon S. Myer, http://digitalassets.lib.berkeley.edu/jarda/ucb/text/cubanc6714_b275to1_0079.pdf.

29. David Reyes, "Night Visitors Brought Halt to Family's Hopes," *Los Angeles Times* [Orange County edition], Feburary 17, 1992, 1.

30. "General Stilwell Pins DSC on Sister of Nisei Hero in Ceremony at Masuda Ranch," *Pacific Citizen*, December 15, 1945, 2. The struggle for inclusion continued three years later when Masuda's body was returned from Europe on an Army transport plane to Orange County Airport. The Masuda family wished to lay the body to rest at nearby Westminster Memorial Park cemetery, but was told "that 'restrictive covenants' barred burial of persons not of Caucasian ancestry" in the main portion of the cemetery and that someone of Japanese ancestry would need to be placed "in a plot where there are no trees or lawn." This was protested by the JACL and, after informing General Mark Clark of the Fifth Army, the Masudas were able to bury Kazuo Masuda in the formerly restricted zone with full military honors on December 9, 1948. Russell K. Shoho, *From the Battlefields to the Home Front: The Kazuo Masuda Legacy* (Fullerton, CA: Nikkei Writers Guild, Japanese American Living Legacy, 2009), 42–43, 46–48.

31. In a speech on August 10, 1988, Reagan recalled his words from that day: "Blood that has soaked into the sands of a beach is all of one color. America stands unique in the world: the only country not founded on race but on a way, an ideal. Not in spite of but because of our polyglot background, we have had all the strength in the world. That is the American way." http://www.presidency.ucsb.edu/ws/?pid=36240.

32. Shinobu Matsuura, *Higan: Compassionate Vow—Selected Writings of Shinobu Matsuura* (Berkeley, CA: Matsuura Family, 1986), 68.

33. Ibid.

34. Ibid., 69.

35. Ibid.

36. Takashi Tsujita and Karen Nolan, *Omo i de: Memories of Vacaville's Lost Japanese Community* (Vacaville, CA: Vacaville Museum, 2001), 125.

37. Yamato, "Restoring Family," xxxi.

38. Ibid.

39. Ibid., xxxii.

40. Robinson, *After Camp*, 60, 63.

41. Japanese American Historical Society, *REgenerations*, Vol. 2, 72; Hazel Morikawa, "Exodus: Remembered Moments," in *Triumphs of Faith: Stories of Japanese American Christians during WWII*, ed. Victor N. Okada (Los Angeles: Japanese-American Internment Project, 1998), 80.

42. Tsukasa Sugimura, *The Development of the Oriental Missionary Society Japanese Holiness Church of America: 1920–1950* (Masters thesis, Fuller Theological Seminary, 1992), 97, http://encyclopedia.densho.org /Evergreen%20Hostel/.

43. Japanese American Historical Society, *Regenerations,* Vol. 2, 72.

44. Shizue Seigel, *In Good Conscience: Supporting Japanese-Americans During the Internment Seigel* (San Mateo, CA: Asian American Curriculum Project, 2006), 260.

45. Seigel, *In Good Conscience,* 257. Mr. S. Kishima was instrumental in the opening of the Gardena Buddhist Church's hostel. See also Buddhist Churches of America, ed. *Buddhist Churches of America: A Legacy of the First 100 Years* (San Francisco: Buddhist Churches of America, 1998), 224.

46. On the openness of Senshin to people of all faiths, Art Takemoto stated, "We had Hanamatsuri [Buddha's Birthday ceremony]. But people were free to do what they wanted . . . . if they wished to gather, then fine. The reason that we did that was, even as we called it the Buddhist Hostel, it wasn't restricted to just Buddhists. We had the Methodist group hostel just down the road. But even those people used to come, because we had an area where people could socialize and gather, so it was not restricted to just the Buddhists. It was open to all. The Methodists on the other hand, the idea of having social activities was sort of frowned on. They were rather more—what you might call-more religiously-oriented. Whereas the Buddhists were rather . . . social-minded." Japanese American Historical Society, *REgenerations,* Vol. 2, 409.

47. Jane Imamura, *Kaikyo: Opening the Dharma, Memoirs of a Buddhist Priest's Wife in America* (Honolulu: Buddhist Study Center Press, 1998), 22.

48. Elaine Woo, "Obituaries: Rev. Julius Goldwater; Convert to Buddhism Aided WWII Internees," *Los Angeles Times,* June 23, 2001.

49. Masao Kodani, "Senshin Buddhist Temple History," in *Beyond: Faith: The Role of the Church and Temple in the Japanese American Community,* ed. Mayumi Kodani (Los Angeles: Nikkei Interfaith Fellowship / Japanese American Cultural & Community Center, 2005), 58; Betsuin Jihō, "Stories from the Past: Rev. Julius A. Goldwater," *Betsuin Jihō* (March 1, 1990), 3.

50. Julius A. Goldwater, "Draft of Speech Given at Senshin Buddhist Temple, LA," (undated), 10; BCA Archives, Hisatsune Family Papers.

51. Imamura, *Kaikyo,* 23.

52. This was the Kobayashi family. Ansho Mas Uchima and Minoru Shinmoto, ed. *Seinan: Southwest Los Angeles—Stories and Experiences from Residents of Japanese Ancestry* (Fullerton, CA: Nikkei Writers Guild Division

of the Japanese American Living Legacy, California State University, Fullerton, 2010), 23–24.

53. Ibid.

54. Japanese American Historical Society, *REgenerations*, Vol. 2, 405.

55. Richard K. Payne, "Hiding in Plain Sight: The Invisibility of the Shingon Mission to the United States," in *Buddhist Missionaries in the Era of Globalization*, ed. Linda Learman (Honolulu: University of Hawai'i Press, 2005), 108. Payne notes that other temples in the same situation sought relief in the courts, but lost. In the case of Kōyasan Temple, the group were finally able to repay this debt in 1957 when they were awarded funds from the Wartime Evacuation Compensation Bill.

56. Audrie Girdner and Anne Loftis, *The Great Betrayal: The Evacuation of the Japanese-Americans During World War II* (New York: Macmillan, 1969), 411.

57. "Flare Thrown at Hostel in Watsonville," *Pacific Citizen* Vol. 21, No. 13, September 29, 1945, 1

58. "Anti-Niseis Try to Burn S.F. Hotel," *Los Angeles Daily News*, September 20, 1945, 8.

59. The Guadalupe Buddhist Mission was cared for by Mr. and Mrs. W. J. Fisk despite Mr. Fisk's being fired from his job at Puritan Ice Co. purportedly due to his support for the temple. The Bakersfield Buddhist Temple was guarded by Ms. Emma Buckmaster, a local elementary school teacher, who retrieved requested items stored at the temple and sent them on to camps. Prewar supporters of the temple's sports program, Mr. and Mrs. Cos Lousalot, watched over the Oakland Buddhist Church. Buddhist Churches of America, *Buddhist Churches of America*, 186, 227, 262.

60. Buddhist Churches of America, *Buddhist Churches of America*, 186; Japanese American Historical Society, *REgenerations*, Vol. 2, 180; Los Angeles Nichiren Buddhist Temple, *90th Anniversary*, 39.

61. F. W. Kadletz (F.W. Kadletz & Co., Real Estate Brokers) to Frank Kuwahara, letter, September 12, 1942, Zenshuji Sōtō Mission Archives.

62. Los Angeles Department of Building and Safety to WRA Poston (Colorado River) Director Wade Head, letter, October 29, 1945, Zenshuji Sōtō Mission Archives.

63. Ibid. The letter about the temple reads in part: "a two-story Type IIIA structure housing approximately 35 Japanese on the second floor. The first floor is operated under a hotel permit from the Health Department. It is now occupied by colored people."

64. Studies on Japanese American and black neighborhood interactions include Hillary Jenks, "Bronzeville, Little Tokyo, and the Unstable Geography

of Race in Post-World War II Los Angeles," *Southern California Quarterly* 93:2 (2011), 201–235; Lon Kurashige, *Japanese American Celebration and Conflict: A History of Ethnic Identity and Festival in Los Angeles, 1934–1990* (Berkeley: University of California Press, 2002); Scott Kurashige, *The Shifting Grounds of Race: Blacks and Japanese Americans in the Making of Multiethnic Los Angeles* (Princeton: Princeton University Press, 2008); and Kariann Yokota, *From Little Tokyo to Bronzeville and Back: Ethnic Communities in Transition* (Masters thesis, UCLA, 1996).

65. Jenks, "Bronzeville," 208, 216.

66. Beyond the economic factors of the neighborhood, historian Hillary Jenks notes: "Bronzeville ceased to exist less from disputes between African and Japanese Americans than as a result of racist spatial practices by local government." She refers to a massive dislocation of African Americans caused by the building of a new city police headquarters in the district in 1950. Indeed, in the main, Japanese Americans and African Americans as two groups with a history of race-based dislocations found ways to live together for several years of what Jenks has called "Little Bronze Tokyo." Ibid., 201, 220.

67. "Hongwanji: Baptist or Buddhist?" *Los Angeles Daily News*, January 4, 1945, 5.

68. Michihiro Ama, "A Jewish Buddhist Priest: The Curious Case of Julius A. Goldwater and the Hompa Hongwanji Buddhist Temple in 1930–1940s Los Angeles," *Southern California Quarterly* 100, no. 3 (Fall 2018), 297–323, DOI: 10.1525/scq.2018.100.3.297.

69. Buddhist Churches of America, ed. *Buddhist Churches of America, Vol. 1: 75 Year History, 1899–1974* (Chicago: Nobart Inc., 1974), 191–192, 203.

70. Ibid., 195.

71. Ibid., 205.

72. San Diego Buddhist Temple, ed. *Kansha in Gassho: Fiftieth Anniversary, San Diego Buddhist Temple, 1926–1976* (San Diego, CA: San Diego Buddhist Temple, 1976), 26.

73. Masami Honda, interviewed by Duncan Williams, San Diego, 2004.

74. San Diego Buddhist Temple, *Kansha in Gassho*, 26.

75. Margaret Miki, "Mother and Her Temple," *Social Process in Hawaii* 12 (1948), 18–22: 19.

76. Ibid.

77. Ibid.

78. The antipathy towards reopening Shinto shrines was much stronger. A coalition of white and Japanese American Christian leaders, including Rev. Takie Okumura and Dr. E. Tanner Brown of the Episcopal Mission, mobi-

lized some of the 442nd veterans to call for a permanent ban of the religion on the islands of Hawai'i. For more on the anti-Shinto campaign, including against Tenrikyō facilities, in media outlets like the *Honolulu Advertiser* see Maeda, *Hawaii no jinjashi*, 38–39; and Noriko Shimada, "Wartime Dissolution and Revival of the Japanese Language Schools in Hawaii: Persistence of Ethnic Culture," *Journal of Asian American Studies* 1:2 (1998), 198. Kimura has also noted that some "shrines were disposed of by the Foreign Fund Control or were in such disarray that they were never reopened even after the return of the priests from the internment camps on the US continent. In a rare case, the Konpira Shrine, which had been confiscated by the US government during the war under the pretext that it had been functioning as an agent of the Japanese government, was secured by its board of trustees after a lawsuit was filed with the assistance of a prominent Haole lawyer that definitively proved it was simply a local religious organization without any function as an agent of the government of Japan. See Yukiko Kimura, *Issei: Japanese Immigrants in Hawaii* (Honolulu: University of Hawaii Press, 1992), 384.

79. Similar pressure was brought to bear on Japanese language schools. The 166 schools at the beginning of the war were whittled down to just 47 by July 1944. Although there was no direct attempt to confiscate the property, assimilationist nisei Christians pressured officials not only to ban assembling at the Japanese language schools, but to permanently close them. With the Buddhist leadership in internment camps, even the large Hongwanji Mission felt compelled to amend its charter to cease sponsoring language schools, though strong opposition from individual temple members prevented their outright dissolution through sale or donation of the facilities to other entities. Takaichi Miyamoto, a close political supporter of Honolulu mayor John Wilson and a member of the Territorial Democratic Committee, openly opposed the closing down of any language schools. Immediately following the end of the war, Miyamoto negotiated with Mayor Wilson to reopen the Japanese language schools: first, the Hongwanji-affiliated Palama Gakuen and Fort Gakuen in 1947, followed by other Buddhist-affiliated language schools in Aiea, Pearl City, and Kakaako. See Shimada, "Wartime Dissolution," 128–138.

80. Yoshiko Tatsuguchi and Lois A. Suzuki, *Shinshu Kyokai Mission of Hawaii, 1914–1984: A Legacy of Seventy Years* (Honolulu: Shinshu Kyokai Mission of Hawaii, 1985), 60–64.

81. Quoted in Louise H. Hunter, *Buddhism in Hawaii: Buddhism in Hawaii: Its Impact on a Yankee Community* (Honolulu: University of Hawai'i Press, 1971), 198.

82. Ibid., 199.

83. Shigeo Kikuchi, *Memoirs of a Buddhist Woman Missionary in Hawaii* (Honolulu: The Buddhist Study Center Press, 1991), 70.

84. Frank Nagao conducted most of the negotiations. Kiyoshi Matsukama, "A Minister Survives World War II in Hilo: Reverend Zenyu Aoki," in *Hilo Hongwanji: Recalling Our Past: A Collection of Oral Histories,* ed. Nobuko Fukuda, Midori Kondo, Motoe Tada, and Lillie Tsuchiya (Honolulu: Honpa Hongwanji Hilo Betsuin, 1997), 33; and Frank Katsuichi Nagao, "Hilo Hongwanji Survives World War II," in *Hilo Hongwanji: Recalling Our Past, A Collection of Oral Histories,* ed. Nobuko Fukuda, Midori Kondo, Motoe Tada, and Lillie Tsuchiya (Honolulu: Honpa Hongwanji Hilo Betsuin, 1997), 35–36.

85. Rita Goldman, *Every Grain of Rice: Portraits of Maui's Japanese Community* (Virginia Beach, VA: Donning Company, 2003), 98.

86. Seikaku Takesono, interview, March 11, 1982, Japanese Internment and Relocation Files: The Hawaii Experience, Hamilton Library, University of Hawai'i at Manoa (HWN-240, transcript 437), Addendum 6.

87. The former Bishop of the Honpa Hongwanji Mission, Rev. Gikyō Kuchiba, believed the announcements about Japan's defeat were simply American propaganda. A fellow internee recalled that Kuchiba "was among those who had misjudged the political situation" and had advocated for the interned Japanese to move to the South Pacific, not comprehending that Japan had lost her territories there. Yasutarō Soga, *Life Behind Barbed Wire: The World War II Internment Memoirs of a Hawai'i Issei* (Honolulu: Japanese Cultural Center of Hawai'i / University of Hawai'i Press, 2008), 204.

One internee in Santa Fe, Suikei Furuya, noted that the top three proponents of the *katta-gumi* were two Buddhist priests, Rev. Enryō Shigefuji and Rev. Gisei Maeda, and a Christian minister, Rev. Ikugorō Nagamatsu. Suikei Furuya, *An Internment Odyssey: Haisho Tenten* (Honolulu: Japanese Cultural Center of Hawai'i / University of Hawai'i Press, 2017), 253.

88. Takesono added that he himself was among the majority of internees when it came to hoping, at least initially, that Japan would defeat the country that had imprisoned them without cause: "When I was arrested I think 99 percent of those interned thought that they would be at a disadvantage if Japan lost the war. Truthfully speaking, we wanted Japan to win the war. We wanted to see America lose. That kind of thinking was shared by the majority. As conditions worsened for Japan and the tables were finally turned, many reconsidered returning to Japan. Until then, they were thinking of returning to a victorious Japan. I even felt that way. I had expectations of

returning to Japan with my family." Seikaku Takesono, interview, Addendum 8.

89. Soga, *Life Behind Barbed Wire*, 220.

90. Andrew William Lind, *Hawaii's Japanese: An Experiment in Democracy* (Princeton: Princeton University Press, 1946), 212–215.

91. Indeed, in March 1946, Rev. Yamazaki was indicted on charges that he made pronouncements of a "disloyal nature and reasonably calculated to cause a breach of the peace." In the court case that followed—*Territory v. Yamazaki*—Rev. Yamazaki's public statements, the transcript of an interrogation with military intelligence officials, and letters he wrote to several kibei still interned in the Honouliuli camp were used as evidence that he had violated Section 11190 of the Revised Laws of Hawaii, commonly known as the "Disloyalty Act." Even when out on bail, Yamazaki made public statements in his priestly robes about his views, which he said resulted from enduring four years of internment. In a speech to a gathering of like-minded people, he said: "The newspapers say that the United States won the war, but speaking from my spiritual faith, I believe Japan won. I will be convinced that Japan has been defeated only if I am told so by a Japanese government official or a blood relative." Some of those who attended the gathering went out of curiosity or entertainment, but others were seeking a message that could stabilize their disrupted lives. The roughly one thousand people who were active in this movement included issei who had been pro-Japanese during the war but silenced by social pressure on the islands, and some kibei. The disloyalty case was dismissed in May 1947 by Judge Matthewman, who held that the law was unconstitutional in respect to restrictions on free speech at a time when the war was over and no special war powers could be afforded to target someone like Rev. Yamazaki. With the trial over, both the priest and his followers faded from public view. See *Territory of Hawaii v. Jisho Yamazaki*—Treason / Disturbing the Peace Charge—Violation of Sec. 11190 RLH / 45 (Circuit Court, First Judicial Circuit, Territory of Hawai'i) [CR No. 18393 / 18502]; "Six Disloyalty Counts Against Japanese Priest: Waipahu Man Charged with Advising Japan Won War," *Honolulu Advertiser* (March 2, 1946), 4; and "Indicted Japanese Urges Followers to Yamato Spirit," *Honolulu Advertiser* (March 4, 1946), 1, 5. Although Yamazaki was the most well-known of the *katta-gumi* in Hawai'i, an ex-Holiness Church minister was also highly involved in this movement. Ssee Kimura, *Issei*, 363. Another religious sect drawn by this phenomenon was Seichō-no-Ie (a so-called sect Shinto movement). Seicho-no-Ie leaders claimed to have had psychic visions of Japanese planes coming back to attack Honolulu and the Japanese naval

fleet coming into the harbor, and spread rumors that President Truman was in Japan apologizing to the Emperor for using the atomic bomb. Kimura, *Issei*, 246; Dennis M. Ogawa, *Kodomo no tame ni (For the Sake of the Children): The Japanese American Experience in Hawaii* (Honolulu: University of Hawai'i Press, 1978), 319.

92. Kimura, *Issei*, 248.

93. Walter S. Kadota, quoted in Hunter, *Buddhism in Hawaii*, 200. For more on groups like the Dōshikai, Hisshōkai, and others, see Kimura, *Issei*, 244–245, 249–250 and Lind, *Hawaii's Japanese*, 212–215.

94. Anonymous Issei Buddhist priest quoted in Lind, *Hawaii's Japanese*, 217

95. Already, a number of families had been repatriated during the war as a part of the civilian prisoner exchange program between the United States and the Axis nations. There had been plans for several exchanges with Japan, but only two were conducted. After the second exchange ship, the Americans balked when the Japanese government put conditions on future exchanges based on improvements in the treatment of Japanese nationals held in American camps. On the first exchange, the Swedish cruise ship *M.S. Gripsholm*, chartered by the United States, left on June 18, 1942, with over a thousand people. It stopped in Rio de Janeiro to pick up 417 more passengers, and eventually met up with Japan's *Asama Maru* in the port of Lourenco Marques, on the east coast of Africa, for the exchange of civilians and prisoners of war. The first exchange focused on Japanese diplomatic officials and their families and other high-value individuals such as influential businessmen. Buddhist priests and their families were on the second exchange, again on the *Gripsholm*, which left Jersey City on September 2, 1943, to meet the Japanese ship *Teia Maru* in Mormugao, India. A little over half of those on the second trip were Japanese from Latin America countries whose governments forcibly rounded them up on behalf of the United States. P. Scott Corbett, *Quiet Passages: The Exchange of Civilians between the United States and Japan During the Second World War* (Kent, OH: Kent State University Press, 1987), 97.

96. The establishment of the large "family camp" at Crystal City was a major development for those yearning to reunite. The first to arrive in December 1942 were thirty-five German families who had agreed to be repatriated to Germany in exchange for Americans stuck in Europe. Initially, because the Japanese were concerned that the camp might be restricted to German internee families, they formed a Family Reunification Committee. This committee, made up of four Buddhist and Shinto priests, petitioned for Japanese to be allowed into this program so that split families could be

reunited and repatriated to Japan. Further, when it was initially announced that the program would define "family" narrowly as only the interned individual, their spouse, and any dependent children, two other religious leaders joined a petition to US Secretary of State Cordell Hull to include extended family members such as grandparents and unmarried adult children. At its peak in December 1944, the camp consisted of 3,374 individuals, including 2,371 Japanese, 997 Germans, and 6 Italians.

Especially for American-born nisei, the idea of starting a new life in Japan, a country with which many had minimal familiarity, was a daunting prospect. Many made that choice, however, rather than have their families split up. In the Crystal City camp, a large Japanese-language school was established specifically for the purpose of helping nisei learn the language and social mores of Japan so that they could integrate into their parents' homeland upon arrival. One of the main instructors was Rev. Kenkō Yamashita, who had served the Los Angeles Zenshūji Sōtō Zen Mission prior to the war. After his arrest following Pearl Harbor, and internment at the DOJ camp at Santa Fe and Army camp at Lordsburg, Yamashita was reunited with his wife and children in Crystal City. The school's 1,360 children relied on a textbook edited by the Jōdo Buddhist priest Rev. Hōyū Ōta (formerly of the Laupahoehoe Jodo Mission on the Big Island) and those in the primary grades were taught by his wife, who had made the trip to Crystal City from Hawai'i to reunite with her husband. Stephen Fox, *America's Invisible Gulag: A Biography of German American Internment and Exclusion in World War II* (New York: Peter Lang, 2000), 150–151; Yoshiaki Fukuda, *My Six Years of Internment: An Issei's Struggle for Justice* (San Francisco: The Konko Church of San Francisco, 1990), 54; Joy Nozaki Gee, *Crystal City Internment Camp 50th Anniversary Reunion Album* (Monterey, CA, 50th Anniversary Reunion Album Publications Committee, 1993), 113; Arnold Krammer, *Undue Process: The Untold Story of America's German Alien Internees* (Lanham, MD: Rowman & Littlefield, 1997), 109–110; Karen Lea Riley, *Schools Behind Barbed Wire: A History of Schooling in the United States Department of Justice Internment Camp at Crystal City, Texas, during World War II* (PhD diss., University of Texas, Austin, 1996); Hōyū Ōta memoir manuscript (Tokyo Jōdōshū Kokusaibu Archives, 1978).

97. In Canada, the aggressive push by the Canadian government to remove as many Japanese and Japanese Canadians as possible from the Pacific coast meant that roughly half of the community was set to "return" to Japan. Roughly 4,000 people ended up in Japan out of the 10,813 people originally slated to go there (42 percent of whom were Japanese nationals). Roger Daniels, "The Decisions to Relocate the North American Japanese:

Another Look," in *Asian Americans and the Law, Volume 3: The Mass Internment of Japanese Americans and the Quest for Legal Redress,* ed. Charles McClain (Hamden, CT: Garland Publishing, 1994), 6–7.

98. Just days before their deportation was to begin in November 1945, Collins filed suits on behalf of nearly one thousand nisei, halting the process. Through a series of mitigation hearings and further attempts to restore their citizenship, Collins's efforts resulted in roughly five thousand nisei remaining in the United States, though they were required to undergo a legal process spanning several decades to restore their American citizenship. John Christgau, "Collins versus the World: The Fight to Restore Citizenship to Japanese American Renunciants of World War II," *Pacific Historical Review* 54:1 (February 1985), 1–31; Donald E. Collins, *Native American Aliens: Disloyalty and Renunciation of Citizenship by Japanese Americans during World War II* (Westport, CT: Greenwood Press, 1985); Charles Wollenberg, *Rebel Lawyer: Wayne Collins and the Defense of Japanese American Rights* (Berkeley, CA: Heyday Books, 2018).

99. Buddhist temples in North America also participated in the rebuilding of war-torn Japan. The Toronto Buddhist Church, for example, sent salted salmon from Canada for food relief programs. And the Shinshu Kyōkai Mission in Honolulu was a major contributor to the postwar relief efforts, donating 325 of the first 1,000 boxes of clothing and other relief materials shipped to Japan from Honolulu after the war. Kōnosuke Nishikihama, handwritten notes in Japanese, 1967 (Toronto Buddhist Church Archives) and Tatsuguchi and Suzuki, *Shinshu Kyokai*, 81.

100. Douglas MacArthur, speech at the January 1955 convention of the Los Angeles Episcopalian Diocese, noted in *The Living Church: A Weekly Record of the News, the Work, and the Thought of the Episcopalian Church* (February 13, 1955): 21.

101. "Thousand Missionaries Seen Needed to Win Japs," *Washington Post,* January 11, 1947, 13. For evidence that MacArthur continued his call for "a thousand missionaries," see "Methodists Vote Funds to Carry 'Advance' Work, *Los Angeles Times*, June 23, 1949, Part III, 18.

102. Ray A. Moore, *Soldier of God: MacArthur's Attempt to Christianize Japan* (Haworth, NJ: MerwinAsia, 2011), 60.

103. "Gen. MacArthur Has Praise for Bible League," *Suburbanite Economist* (Chicago), June 14, 1950. The article directly quotes a letter sent by MacArthur to the American Home Bible League to express appreciation of its evangelism.

104. From a report dated January 21, 1949 in Supreme Commander for the Allied Powers Records, National Archives, Civil Information and Education, Box 5922. Cited in Moore, *Soldier of God*, 63.

105. Benjamin Dorman, *Celebrity Gods: New Religions, Media, and Authority in Occupied Japan* (Honolulu: University of Hawai'i Press, 2012), 92–93.

106. Masafumi Okazaki, "Chrysanthemum and Christianity: Education and Religion in Occupied Japan, 1945–1952," *Pacific Historical Review* 79:3 (2010), 393–417; Jolyon Thomas, "Religious Policies During the Allied Occupation of Japan, 1945–1952," *Religion Compass* 8 / 9 (2014), 275–286.

107. Bunyū Fujimura, *Though I Be Crushed: The Wartime Experiences of a Buddhist Minister* (Los Angeles: The Nembutsu Press, 1995), 100.

108. Charles F. Ernst, "Voice from Administration," *Bussei Life*, May 15, 1943; Japanese American Evacuation and Resettlement Study, Bancroft Library, University of California, Berkeley.

109. Ron Magden, *Mukashi Mukashi Long Long Ago: The First Century of the Seattle Buddhist Church* (Seattle: Seattle Buddhist Church, 2012), 150.

110. Dorothy Thomas, *The Salvage: Japanese American Evacuation and Resettlement* (Berkeley: University of California Press, 1952), 128, 125.

111. Robinson, *After Camp*, 45.

112. Ben Tsutomu Chikaraishi, interviewed by interviewed by Mary Doi, March 4, 1998, Chicago, Illinois. Japanese American National Museum, *REgenerations Oral History Project: Rebuilding Japanese American Families, Communities, and Civil Rights in the Resettlement Era. Chicago Region: Volume I*, 94.

113. Art Takemoto, interviewed by James Gatewood, May 19, 1998, Los Angeles, California, in Japanese American National Museum, *REgenerations Oral History Project: Rebuilding Japanese American Families, Communities, and Civil Rights in the Resettlement Era, Los Angeles Region: Volume II*, 398

114. This is the recollection of one of the YBA members in attendance. Ben Tsutomu Chikaraishi, 95.

115. Alice Murata, "Taking Root: Japanese Americans in Chicago," in *REgenerations Oral History Project: Rebuilding Japanese American Families, Communities, and Civil Rights in the Resettlement Era, Volume 1*, ed. Japanese American Historical Society (Los Angeles: Japanese American Historical Society, 2000), xxxvii.

116. Ernest Takahashi, "Proposed Plan for Nisei Integration in the City of Chicago," 2. Japanese American Evacuation and Resettlement Study, Bancroft Library, University of California, Berkeley, MSS 67 / 14 c, folder T1.849.

117. Tamotsu Shibutani, "The Initial Phases of the Buddhist Youth Movement in Chicago," October, 1944, Japanese American Evacuation and Resettlement Study, Bancroft Library, University of California, Berkeley, 23.

118. Michael Masatsugu kindly shared this with me from his forthcoming book manuscript.

119. Ibid.

120. Once they had found a site, Art Takemoto worked with the new BCA headquarters to distribute the new address of the temple. He sent "500, 700, 900 postcards every week" to the growing number of Buddhists leaving the various camps for a new home, writing: "Welcome to Chicago. If there is anything we can do for you, come and see us." Buddhist Churches of America Ministerial Association (Topaz, Utah) Serial #6 "The Information of the Chicago Young Buddhist Association," November 18, 1944, BCA Archives, Japanese American National Museum. With greater numbers of Buddhists arriving in Chicago that year, the temple moved to a larger space on the North Side with the assistance of Homer A. Jack, who was the Unitarian executive secretary of the Chicago Council Against Racial and Religious Discrimination, and other sympathizers. Jack secured a place for the temple at Uptown Players for a time; later, Wallace Oliver Heistad, well known for his work helping Jews escape Nazi Germany, brokered a space at the Olivet Institute for the Buddhists. The Midwest Buddhist Temple would be based at that location until a three-story building was purchased in 1948. Ben Tsutomu Chikaraishi, 98. Chikaraishi also recalled about Heistad that he was "the most wonderful fellow you could ever know. He was very accommodating. He rented the place to us for $40 a month. We had all our activities there. When we bought our own building and left, we had a bill of $2,000. He was under pressure by the board and he told the board, 'I know these people. They're going to pay it eventually when they can. And if they don't, I'll pay it myself with my own money.' So that's how he was. . . . It took us two years, but we paid all our debts."

121. The BCA organization warned in its newsletters: "We would like to make clear the organization headed by Rev. Kubose has no direct relation with the movement of Rev. Kono. Chicago Y.B.A. headed by Rev. Kono is affiliated with the Buddhist Churches of America." But this independent temple would eventually attract issei who moved to city as well as nisei, who assembled in the Ashoka Society, a subgroup named after the famous Indian king who supported Buddhism. Buddhist Churches of America Ministerial Association (Topaz, Utah) Serial #6 "The Information of the Chicago Young Buddhist Association," November 18, 1844, BCA Archives, Japanese American National Museum. Also see Japanese American Historical Society, *REgenerations,* Vol.1, 290.

122. "Religion: N.Y. Buddhists' Temple Is a Brownstone House," *PM's Weekly* (New York), October 18, 1940, 60. The New York Buddhist Church had been founded just before the war in 1938 by Rev. Hōzen Seki and grew

during the war. Like most issei Buddhist priests, Rev. Seki was interned during the war in a series of camps—Fort Meade, the hard labor road camp in Kooskia, Idaho, and the DOJ's Santa Fe camp—so his nisei wife managed the temple, which served resettlers and also many Japanese American Buddhist soldiers headed to the European front. The New York Buddhist Church coordinated with Chicago's Midwest Buddhist Church after its founding, with activities such as a joint Buddhist service for those training at Fort Snelling. Buddhist Churches of America Ministerial Association (Topaz, Utah) Serial #6 "The Information of the Chicago Young Buddhist Association," November 18, 1844, BCA Archives, Japanese American National Museum. The Buddhist Society of America, later renamed the First Zen Institute of America, was founded in 1931 by Sōkei-an with the support of influential white supporters. Janica Anderson and Steven Zahavi Schwartz, *Zen Odyssey: The Story of Sokei-an, Ruth Fuller Sasaki, and the Birth of Zen in America* (Boston: Wisdom Publications, 2018), 100–183. In New York City, Mayor Fiorello La Guardia took a public stance opposing any Japanese Americans coming to the city. But while it had fewer than two thousand Japanese Americans in mid-1942, that number nearly doubled by the end of the war. Robinson, *After Camp*, 56–57.

EPILOGUE

1. Guṇabhadra is the purported translator of the *Laṅkāvatāra Sūtra* from Sanskrit into Chinese; see Elizabeth Morrison, *The Power of Patriarchs: Qisong and Lineage in Chinese Buddhism* (Leiden: E.J. Brill, 2010), 58–59. The translation is by J. C. Cleary, *Zen Dawn: Early Zen Texts from Tun Huang* (Boston: Shambhala Publications, 1986)

For the section on Bill Higgins and Les and Nora Bovee, I have relied on the work of Dakota Russell, the museum manager of the Heart Mountain Interpretive Center. In May 2017, he kindly shared with me his unpublished research. It informs a great deal of the Wyoming portion of the Heart Mountain stones story.

2. Among those who received the stones as gifts from the Bovees was Richard Drinnon, a Bucknell University professor and author of *Keepers of Concentration Camps,* and the Japanese American filmmaker Emiko Omori. Thirteen stones were given to Professor Tetsuden Kashima of the University of Washington after Drinnon's passing, during the process of disposing of his personal property. My thanks to Kashima for his recounting of this history. Omori had gifted her six stones to the museum right before the Bovees and the Higashi Honganji priest Noriaki Ito had identified the stones as most likely a part of a Buddhist text.

3. Most instructive on the research by Professors Mori and Minowa are their two Japanese-language publications. Sōdō Mori and Kenryō Minowa, "Zenbei nikkei hakubutsukan shozō no 'Ichiji-isseki-kyō': Heart Mountain kyōsei shūyōjo bochi ato kara no shutsudohin," [The One Character, One Stone Sutra at the Japanese American National Museum: An Item That Emerged from the WRA Heart Mountain Camp's Cemetery] *Nihon bukkyō sōgō kenkyū* [Comprehensive Studies of Japanese Buddhism] 4 (2006), 97–128; and Sōdō Mori and Kenryō Minowa, "Shinkō zenbei nikkei hakubutsukan shozō no 'Ichiji-isseki-kyō': Heart Mountain kyōsei shūyōjo bochi ato kara no shutsudohin," [The One Character, One Stone Sutra at the Japanese American National Museum—An Update: An Item That Emerged from the WRA Heart Mountain Camp's Cemetery] *Bukkyō bunka gakkai kiyō* [Journal of the Research Society of Buddhism and Cultural Heritage] 17 (2008), 1–46.

4. Mori and Minowa, "Shinkō zenbei," 18–19.

5. Of the 656 stones gifted to the museum, 631 stones were legible.

6. This would be the version consisting of twenty-eight chapters in eight volumes, translated into Chinese by Kumārajīva in 406 CE. In collaboration with a team at Taishō University, Minowa discovered that the manuscript version of the *Lotus Sutra* that most closely matches the stones is the version used in the Nichiren Hokkeshū sub-lineage of the Shōretsuha or Honmon, a key piece of evidence supporting the idea of Rev. Murakita's involvement with this scripture copying and burial since he belonged to this sub-lineage of Nichiren Buddhism. Mori and Minowa, "Shinkō zenbei," 26.

7. Mori and Minowa, "Zenbei Nikkei." The 2006 article in *Nihon bukkyō sōgō kenkyū* was updated in 2008. The revised research finding was published in the *Bukkyō bunka gakkai kiyō.* Mori and Minowa, "Shinkō zenbei."

8. Some of his personal information can be found in his 1942 Form WRA 26 Individual Record, in the 1945 Final Accountability Roster Records, and in records kept in Japan at the Nichiren sect headquarters. Mori and Minowa, "Shinkō zenbei," 33–39. My thanks to Russell Endo for sharing Murakita's enemy alien file (Record Group 60 at the National Archives), including his enemy alien questionnaire and parole hearing board report. These documents show that he was arrested on March 13, 1942 and taken to the Los Angeles County Jail and transferred the next day to the Tuna Canyon Detention Station. Surprisingly, he was paroled after his enemy alien hearing on May 2, 1942 (and likely rejoined his wife in the WCCA Santa Anita Assembly Center on July 15, 1942). He then proceeded to the WRA Heart Mountain camp before repatriating to Japan with his wife on the *Gripsholm* in 1943.

9. For historical context on sutra copying in ancient Japan, see Bryan D. Lowe, *Ritualized Writing: Buddhist Practice and Scriptural Cultures in Ancient Japan* (Honolulu: University of Hawai'i Press, 2017).

10. Lowe's translation of this *Lotus Sutra* passage can be found in Ibid, 4.

11. Mori and Minowa, "Shinkō zenbei," 33.

12. Murakita was likely to have been aware of the "One Character per Stone Lotus Sutra Tower," built in Seattle in 1931. It was established by members of the Nichiren sect in the Pacific Northwest on the burial spot of a stone scripture featuring a portion of the Lotus Sutra. Sodo Mori, "The Legacy of Heart Mountain," *Interreligious Insight* 9:1 (July 2011). Made available on *Discover Nikkei*, http://www.discovernikkei.org/en/journal/2014/3/5/legacy-of-heart-mountain-1/. The practice of copying sutra text onto stone, including the practice of inscribing a single character onto each stone, known as "one stone, one character" (*isseki ichijikyō*) gained popularity in the late medieval and early modern periods in Japan. Hallie O'Neal, *Word Embodied: The Jeweled Pagoda Mandalas in Japanese Buddhist Art* (Cambridge, MA: Harvard University Asia Center, 2018), 161–162.

13. For English-language research on these sutra burials in medieval Japan, see Heather Blair, *Real and Imagined: The Peak of Gold in Heian Japan* (Cambridge, MA: Harvard University Asia Center, 2015), 81–84, 160–189; Toshiyuki Miyake, "Sutra Mounds," in *Arts of the Lotus Sutra*, ed. Bunsaku Kurata and Yoshirō Tamura (Tokyo: Kōsei, 1987), 171–174; and D. Max Moerman, "The Death of the Dharma: Buddhist Sutra Burials in Early Medieval Japan," in *The Death of Sacred Texts: Ritual Disposal and Renovation of Texts in World Religions*, ed. Kristina Myrvold (London: Routledge, 2010), 71–89.

14. Moerman has noted that, "In Japan, enshrined sutras were buried in the ground as part of a complex ritual strategy to forestall the decline of the Buddhist teachings and preserve the Dharma for a future age." Moerman, "The Death of the Dharma," 71.

15. Nyogen Senzaki's April 8, 1945 poem "Land of Liberty!" Copyright © 2005, Zen Studies Society, *Like a Dream, Like a Fantasy: The Zen Teachings and Translations of Nyogen Senzaki* (Somerville, MA: Wisdom Publications, 2005), 21–22. Reprinted by arrangement with The Permissions Company, Inc., on behalf of Wisdom Publications, Inc., wisdompubs.org.

INDEX

African American community, 63, 237, 239–240, 250, 252

Aiso, John, 163

Aki, George, 112, 180, 189, 208, 212

Akita, Stanley Masaharu, 181

Akiyama, Mickey Makio, 213

Amache. *See* Granada War Relocation Center

America as Christian nation, 2–3, 23–26. *See also* Americanization and Christianization

America as land of religious freedom, 2–3, 21–22, 26–27, 106, 258

American Buddhist organizations: Buddhist Brotherhood of America, 127, 129; Buddhist Society of America, 252–253. *See also* Buddhist Churches of America

American Friends Service Committee (AFSC), 74, 75, 108, 138, 236, 251

Americanization, 26–29; conversion to Christianity, 26, 106; and free practice of religion, 26; Buddhism as barrier to, 27–28, 105, 116–117, 210–211; and English, 29, 104–105, 161, 244; recreational activities,

105, 116, 124; American holidays, 136–139; post-war campaigns, 244

Americanization and Christianization, 24–29, 106, 116, 210–211, 227, 244, 251

Anti-Japanese popular sentiment, 55–57, 67, 70–71, 75, 229–230, 234; "yellow peril," 21–23; among other Asian Americans, 63–65; American Civil Liberties Union (ACLU), 76; at Camp Robinson, Arkansas, 169–170; local organizations, 229–230, 233

Aoki, Hisa, 78, 81–82, 89–90, 97, 100–101, 103, 316

Aoki, Tokunnon, 78, 89–90

Arson of temples, 45–46, 232, 235, 241–242, 244

Baptist Christianity, 58, 74, 131; Kichitarō Yamamoto, 73; Terminal Island Church, 73; Virginia Swanson, 73–74; Seattle First Baptist Church, 75–76; Harold Jensen, 75–76, 307; Emery Andrews, 111–112; Providence Baptist Association, 240–241; Jitsuo Morikawa, 305n93

Bendetsen, Karl R., 69–71, 76

unrest, 193–196; camp adminis-
tration, 194–196; closure of, 228,
246. *See also* Tule Lake War
Relocation Center
Tule Lake War Relocation Center
(WRA), 124, 136, 138, 228. *See also*
Tule Lake Segregation Center
Tuna Canyon Detention Center
(DOJ), 78, 89–91
Turlock Assembly Center (WCCA),
77, 98–100

University of California, Berkeley,
Japanese American Evacuation
and Relocation Study (JERS), 104,
118–119, 249
US Army, policy, 21, 42, 76, 175, 184,
197; pre-war surveillance and
arrest lists, 35; seizure of Buddhist
and Shinto properties, 45–46;
treatment of Japanese American
troops, 169–170; discrimination
against Buddhists, 177, 208,
210–211; chaplains in, 189, 203,
208–211; recognition of Buddhism, 201–204, 224–225
US Army Counter Intelligence
Corps, 34, 40–41, 152
US Army Intelligence, 27, 29, 36,
43, 161, 164; in Philippines,
153–155, 157; surveillance of
VVV, 171. *See also* Military
Intelligence Service
US Army Intelligence Japanese
language school. *See* Military
Intelligence Service Language
School
US federal government, 42, 68–70,
232–233; War Department, 20, 32,
43, 69, 220; Immigration Act of

1924, 25; Treasury Department,
36, 67; Alien Registration Act of
1940, 37; Trading with the Enemy
Act (1942), 67; House Un-
American Activities Committee
(HUAC), 70, 116; Congressional
hearings, 74–75. *See also* Executive Order 9066; Roosevelt,
Franklin D.
US Navy Japanese Language
program, 174
USO (United Service Organization),
services for 100th Battalion,
179–180; YBA cooperation, 180;
leasing of temple, 242
US Occupation forces, anti-
Buddhist sentiment, 247–248

Vandalism of Buddhist temples, 13,
59, 81, 231–232, 235, 238–239,
241–242, 244; by US military,
45–46, 244–245
Violence against Japanese Americans, 59, 64, 229, 232–233, 235, 237;
Vacaville, CA, 59, 66, 235
VVV (Triple V), 171–175, 181

War Relocation Authority (WRA)
administration, 108–109, 115–117,
145, 187; Americanization efforts,
106, 116; and religion, 114–118,
129–130, 133, 135, 197–198, 248–249;
and Buddhist holidays, 141–144;
Americanization of Buddhist
organizations, 145–148; loyalty
assessment and leave clearance,
184–189, 194, 196–198; closing of
camps, 228, 235–237; resistance to
formation of Buddhist temple,
Chicago, 250–251